MARION BUTLER
AND AMERICAN POPULISM

MARION BUTLER

AND AMERICAN POPULISM

James L. Hunt

THE UNIVERSITY OF NORTH CAROLINA PRESS

CHAPEL HILL AND LONDON

Designed by April Leidig-Higgins
Set in New Baskerville by Copperline Book Services
Manufactured in the United States of America

The paper in this book meets the guidelines for per-
manence and durability of the Committee on Production
Guidelines for Book Longevity of the Council on
Library Resources.

Library of Congress Cataloging-in-Publication Data
Hunt, James L. (James Logan), 1959–
Marion Butler and American Populism / James L. Hunt.
p. cm. Includes bibliographical references and index.
ISBN 0-8078-2770-3 (cloth: alk. paper)
1. Butler, Marion, 1863–1938. 2. Legislators—United
States—Biography. 3. United States. Congress.
Senate—Biography. 4. Politicians—North Carolina—
Biography. 5. Populism—North Carolina—History.
6. North Carolina—Politics and government—
1865–1950. I. Title.
E748.B8894 H86   2003
328.73'092—dc21   2002011994

cloth   07 06 05 04 03   5 4 3 2 1

For Ruth

CONTENTS

ILLUSTRATIONS

ACKNOWLEDGMENTS

I USED TO THINK that giving thanks in a book did no more than state the obvious; of course more people than simply the author were involved. With age, however, I see that there is more than mere ceremony to recognizing one's debts. It affirms the community of work and debate that is the basis of all scholarly endeavor.

In my excessive number of years of living with Marion Butler (I starting off thinking that a thirty-two-year-old United States senator was an old guy), I have benefited from the help, encouragement, and example of many persons. Among the most important were Dorothy Brannon, Allan Bogue, Joe Claxton, Edward Coffman, Dan Driesbach, Linda Edwards, Morton Horwitz, John Orth, and Ken Tyndall. Colleagues in the business and law schools at Mercer University have provided a stimulating and unique vantage from which to write history. A special friend in this project has been John Cooper of the University of Wisconsin. John not only suffered through an exceedingly long thesis but also continued to provide encouragement as I passed through ten years of law school and law practice before returning to university life. I am most grateful for his support.

Many people contributed to the research. Most of the work was done at the University of North Carolina libraries, including the North Carolina Collection and the Southern Historical Collection. Staff there, particularly Dick Shrader, as well as staff in the manuscripts sections in the libraries at Duke University and East Carolina University, ably pointed to the sources that provided the basis for what I have written. In the early stages of the project, the late Claude Moore provided a grand tour of Sampson County and introduced me to relatives of Marion Butler.

The book first began heading toward the University of North Carolina Press when Lewis Bateman contacted me in 1985. Long afterward, I received helpful comments on the manuscript from several anonymous readers for the Press. Although my natural reaction was to disagree with many of the comments, I realized that even I could be mistaken, and I am grateful for the critical insights. Chuck Grench, Pam Upton, Nancy Raynor, and others at the Press made putting together the final version an enjoyable experience that has substantially improved the product.

Some of the factors that produced this book are due less to individuals than to other life forces, and they are worth a moment. Although I now live in Georgia, I consider myself a North Carolinian. Many of the places familiar to Marion Butler have also been part of my life. My ancestors immigrated to North and South Carolina in the eighteenth century. They were small farmers who, for the most part, left the land in the late nineteenth century and moved to piedmont towns to find work in the mills and factories. I went to high school in Greenville, North Carolina, not far from Butler's Sampson County, and attended college in Chapel Hill, at Butler's university. I practiced law for almost five years in downtown Raleigh, where Butler also practiced, Josephus Daniels spewed forth the dogma of white supremacy, and Populists held their great conventions and where a statue of Charles Aycock still stands on the capitol square. Since 1995 I have been teaching at Mercer University, the college of two well-known Populists, Tom Watson and Milton Park, neither of whom liked Butler very much. As a result, the historical images described in this book have deep personal meaning and are not merely someone else's past.

I have approached Butler's life from the perspective of both a historian and a lawyer. I became interested in legal history while in graduate school, and attended law school and clerked for a federal appeals court judge while writing my dissertation. I practiced law and am teaching law in a business school and a law school. Law study and practice deeply affected my understanding of Populism, a cause that at its political core was an attempt to alter law through political action. It is probably impossible to summarize the general effects of legal training and practice, given that they vary enormously, but for me they mean greater attention to the vast foundation of common law, usually ignored in political history, as well as the processes and procedures of creating and enforcing rules by government. Many of the important political figures mentioned in this book were lawyers, including Populists Frank Doster of Kansas, Harry Skinner of North Carolina, and Tom Watson of Georgia. Butler was admitted to the bar while in the Senate, and even before he became a lawyer he was always oriented toward organizations, processes, and specific rules as means of achieving reform. Although I do not spend much time with Butler's legal career, my interest in the legal aspects of Populism and the relation between law and politics generally inform every page of this biography.

Finally, I owe an unpayable debt to my family. My older sister, Del Helton (a loyal Chapel Hillian); my mother, Mary Anne Hunt; my late father, Billy Lee Hunt; and my in-laws, Roy and Patsy Setzer, have helped teach me what is most important. So have David and Naomi Hunt, two of the most inspiring children in Macon, Georgia. Ruth Hunt, my wife, deserves the greatest credit for whatever I have accomplished. This book is dedicated to her because she has shown more patience and tolerance than Marion Butler would have dreamed possible.

MARION BUTLER
AND AMERICAN POPULISM

INTRODUCTION

THIS IS A BIOGRAPHY of Marion Butler, a North Carolina native who made his greatest mark in the 1890s as a leader in the Southern Farmers' Alliance and the Populist Party and as the only southern Populist ever to serve in the United States Senate. Butler's life is worth the historian's interest not simply because he held high office in the Alliance, the Populist Party, and in Congress. More broadly, his story illustrates crucial issues in the movement to expand the regulatory role of American government between 1880 and the 1930s. While a member of the Alliance in the late 1880s and early 1890s, Butler underwent a transformative education that convinced him the federal government should own or abolish monopolies, especially those which concerned transportation and money. At the same time, he understood this action as necessary to create equal economic opportunity for individuals, but not equal economic results. Like most other reformers of his generation, he had faith in the market, private property, and the idea that representative democracy was the best way to protect the interests of the masses. Butler learned this reform doctrine before he was thirty years old and retained it until his death at seventy-five in 1938. He was the most prominent Populist to apply it to the issues of the 1890s, the Progressive Era, the 1920s, and the New Deal.

For the historian and biographer the most important dimension to Butler's life was his endurance in trying to convert his economic ideas into law through politics. Butler's, and Populism's, greatest struggle was not to create a pro-producer ideology that would promote some forms of government regulation and ownership while at the same time sustaining the competitive market. The real challenge, one that Butler spent the fifty years between 1888 and 1938 trying to meet, was the political success of that ideology. That task involved the enormously complex project of building local, state, and national organizations that would attract followers, conduct elections, send believers to state and national legislatures, and enact and carry out Populist laws. This political project turned out to be Populism's greatest failure, and

Butler's life, perhaps more than that of any other person, illustrates this part
of the Populist story.

These two themes—Butler's education as a reformer and his long and
losing efforts for political success—are the experiences around which this
biography is built. In addition, my argument that Butler absorbed Alliance
doctrine and promoted it at all levels of political competition as well as in
the Senate and in the Republican Party after 1900 is intended to cause some
rethinking about Butler, about Alliance and Populist ideas, about Populist
politics, and about the relationship between Populism and what followed.

When I started this project almost twenty years ago, there was relatively little detailed information about Butler. With some notable exceptions, practically all that had been written about him was negative, sketchy, or merely
descriptive. No one had published a full biography. More specifically, no
one had considered all the key evidence: the newspapers he edited between
1888 and 1913; his votes, committee actions, and speeches as a North Carolina and United States legislator; or his personal papers through 1938. Most
of what was written about Butler focused on the few months in the summer
and fall of 1896 when he led the Populist Party in that year's presidential
election.[1]

Moreover, in the early 1980s there was a pervasive interpretation of Populist ideology and politics, and Butler's relation to it, that had first arisen with
C. Vann Woodward's 1938 biography of the Georgia Populist Tom Watson.
Because of Populism's demand for more federal government regulation,
the Alliance's use of agricultural cooperatives, and Populism's occasional rejection of the harsher attributes of political white supremacy, Populism had
come to stand for a number of causes, including southern liberalism, democracy, or even opposition to industrial capitalism. This made Populism
useful as an object of study, especially to historians trained in the 1960s.
Practically all the published histories of the Alliance and Populism in the
1960–80 period sympathized with Populism. Moreover, historians gave
greatest attention to Populism's ideological and social characteristics. Less
emphasized were its legal aims and political qualities.

One aspect of this interpretation was that those historians who seemed to
have the most influence severely criticized Marion Butler. The prevailing
view was fully articulated by Lawrence Goodwyn, who wrote in 1976 that
"Marion Butler believed in free silver, tariff protection, white supremacy,
and good government. Fundamental Alliance-greenback concepts of permanent national party realignment were . . . foreign to his thinking." Thus,
Goodwyn surmised that Butler's thoughts were "unrelated" to the broad

program of reform embodied in the 1892 Omaha Platform of the People's Party and that as a result Butler was not a "real" Populist. Goodwyn also concluded that the whole of North Carolina Populism was not "genuine."[2]

Years earlier, C. Vann Woodward offered a similar thesis. Woodward stigmatized Butler as a "practical politician" and condemned him as someone allegedly "mistrusted" by elements of the Populist Party because of his endorsement of a political strategy that involved cooperation, or "fusion," between the People's Party and other parties. Woodward also emphasized Butler's support for free silver, implying that Butler was unaware of, ignorant of, or opposed to other proposals of the People's Party. These thoughts appeared in Woodward's biography of Tom Watson and were repeated in his study of the South after Reconstruction.[3]

Several works published before the early 1980s, particularly Robert F. Durden's analysis of the Populist Party in the 1896 election, portrayed Butler differently.[4] Yet, when I began my research, it seemed that the task had already been framed by the preceding generation of Populist historians, who either agreed with Woodward or Goodwyn or relied on the same kinds of sources those men used. In particular, there was a deep-rooted assumption that Populist ideology and politics were largely defined by a clear distinction between Populists who allegedly supported the whole of Alliance-Populist reform and opposed cooperation with the older political parties and those who allegedly did not believe in all Populist reforms and supported cooperation. The former were approvingly described as genuine Populists, while the latter, including Butler, were dismissed as shallow opportunists.

This biography presents evidence against this position, using Butler's life. When I began doing research, it seemed odd, if Goodwyn and Woodward were right about Butler's lack of "genuine" Populism, that Butler became a lecturer and president in his local Alliance as soon as it appeared in his county, state president of the Alliance at age twenty-eight, and then national Alliance president. The widespread lack of information among Populist historians about Butler's Alliance experience was demonstrated by Robert Mc-Math, who in 1993 described him in the early 1890s as a "youthful lawyer." McMath, the leading expert on the Southern Alliance, knew that the Alliance barred attorneys from membership, yet he followed the Woodward-Goodwyn paradigm and described Butler as an attorney. He was not. Ironically, in the early 1890s Butler made his living as a professional Allianceman, first as president of the North Carolina Alliance and later as vice president and president of the national Alliance. Similarly, Bruce Palmer, an outstanding historian of Populism, recently published a sketch of Harry Tracy that

referred to the "Democrat Marion Butler" running for the U.S. Senate in
1900. Actually, in 1900 Butler had not been a Democrat for eight years and
was chairman of the national Populist Party.[5]

Further, according to Goodwyn, Butler was not really a Populist. Yet not
only did Butler lead the Alliance, including its cooperative dimension, in his
home county, but he also served in the United States Senate as a Populist for
six years, attended practically every major Populist convention, wrote every
North Carolina party platform, contributed to national party platforms, published a Populist newspaper, knew every major Populist leader throughout
the United States, and regularly read Populist newspapers from across the
nation. It seemed incredible that a man who had held more and higher
offices that any other Populist in the history of the movement could have
missed what a 1970s historian described as the purpose and meaning of his
political party.

Yet, as with McMath and Palmer, an underlying difficulty is at the factual
level. One telling example was Goodwyn's claim that although Butler did
not have real Populist beliefs in the 1890s, he experienced some kind of conversion in 1901, but only after having been exposed to a "genuine" Texas
Populist, Harry Tracy, during the 1900 election. The conclusion is based on
legislation and speeches Butler made in the Senate supporting the creation
of federally controlled irredeemable currency, which Goodwyn claims took
place in early 1901, when Butler's Senate term was nearing its end and he
was a lame duck. Actually, Goodwyn placed these events in the wrong year, as
Butler promoted irredeemable currency at the beginning of 1900, not 1901.
He was up for reelection and would endorse Populist cooperation with other
political parties during the 1900 election, including with the Democratic presidential nominee, William Jennings Bryan. Goodwyn also wrongly assumed
that Tracy taught Butler real Populism. Actually, Butler convinced Tracy to
support political cooperation and William Jennings Bryan in 1900. Other
factual problems involve omissions. In his seven-hundred-page study of American Populism, in which he excoriates cooperation with other parties and ar-
gues Texas was the center of real Populism, Goodwyn does not mention that
Texas Populists agreed in 1896 to vote for William McKinley, the nation's
foremost conservative politician, in exchange for having Texas Republicans
support Populist state candidates.[6]

The writings of the late C. Vann Woodward contain similar errors. Woodward was a sympathetic biographer of Tom Watson, the Georgia Populist.
He portrayed Watson as a true Populist, a man who believed in all Populist
reforms and who sought purity in Populist politics by avoiding cooperation

agreements with other parties. Unfortunately, Woodward did not describe how Watson favored a watering down of the Populist platform in 1895, in anticipation of the 1896 elections. Watson was anxious to attract persons who "are not coming to us as long as they can be made to suspect that we aim at revolution, or radical interference with vested rights." He advocated a retreat to the Alliance's Ocala Platform, which favored regulation, not ownership, of railroads as a means of achieving a "strong yet conservative" political position. He also suggested that the party "drop the subtreasury. . . . [L]et us [also] deliver our land plank from the suspicion of socialism." Woodward also neglected to mention that Watson supported Butler for chairman of the national Populist Party in 1896 and that late in the 1896 election he considered trading his Populist vice presidential electors with the Democratic candidate Arthur Sewall for a seat in the House of Representatives. Woodward persuaded readers that Watson opposed cooperation, when in fact Watson was a key member of and an enthusiastic supporter of the cooperation ticket of 1896 that included Watson and William Jennings Bryan. After his nomination he gave as his reasons for supporting the ticket the same reasons Butler and other Bryan supporters did. He became angry only after the implementation of cooperation did not turn out as he had hoped.[7]

As for Butler, with whom Watson feuded after July 1896, Woodward tried to diminish his standing as a Populist by emphasizing his support for free silver, particularly through a statement Butler made at an 1895 silver meeting in which he said he "loved the cause better than his party." Although this was supposed to mean that Butler did not support all Populist reforms, Woodward neglected to mention that in the speech Butler also said he was "a thorough Populist and believe[d] in every plank in the Omaha platform. I believe in government ownership of railroads and the telegraph." He urged the delegates to support all Populist reforms, including "complete government issue and control" of the money supply. This was the "cause" of which Butler spoke; the Populist Party was a means to that larger end.[8]

The point of these remarks is not to lay unreasonable blame on historians' mistakes. Mistakes are inevitable; a healthy exposure to Samuel Johnson's writing about scholarship makes that clear enough. Instead, I suggest that the dominant approach to important aspects of Populist politics and Butler has been shaped by fundamental factual errors. Most important, the older view posits a direct and even logical correlation between belief in certain reform principles and a particular kind of political strategy, when there was neither such logic nor such a correlation in practice. As just one example, why would the Populists' aversion to extreme party partisanship not suggest that cooperation with other parties was a political strategy more consistent with the policies of Populism than some other strategy? This biography of Butler is one among many possible means of asking such questions and replacing one view of Populism with another view that recognizes the much greater complexity of the Populist effort to win control of government at the local, state, and national levels. It is a view that emphasizes broad agreement on core Populist principles while describing enormous disagreement about political strategy and attempting to explain that disagreement without suggesting that one side was "better" or more "genuine" than the other. Indeed, it is an error to assume there were only two Populist political strategies or that Populists acted consistently among the various choices. Similarly, it is an error to assume that any particular strategy, whether Butler's or someone else's, was without both advantages and costs.

Marion Butler is particularly useful to these questions because he supported both Populist principles and, over a fifty-year period, a variety of vehicles to advance them politically: the Democratic Party, the Populist Party, the Populist Party and the Democratic Party, the Populist Party and the Republican Party, the Republican Party, and the Republican Party and the Progressive Party of 1912. Moreover, he supported cooperation among parties and solitary action by a party. What emerges from his life is a picture of Populist politics much richer than the simplistic view of silver versus irredeemable currency or fusionist versus midroader. In fact, I have tried to avoid the word "fusion" in the biography, because in the 1890s "fusion" was most often a pejorative term used by its opponents, whether Populists, Democrats, or Republicans. "Fusion" also wrongly suggested a merger of parties, when merger was the opposite of what cooperation meant for Butler and others. I have also tried to present a balanced version of Butler's life. The few previous published biographies of Populists, including Woodward's *Tom Watson*, Martin Ridge's *Ignatius Donnelly*, Stuart Noblin's *Leonidas La Fayette Polk*, Peter Argersinger's *Populism and Politics* on William Peffer, and Michael Brodhead's *Persevering Populist* about Frank Doster, while excellent examples of scholarship, are all friendly to their subjects. This seems natural given the scholarly investment required.

My own feelings toward Butler, however, have become increasingly ambivalent, despite the effort to correct previous inaccurate criticisms of him. He was a thoughtful politician, certainly as much so as any of his southern contemporaries. He was courageous and persistent, suffering ostracism, death threats, economic pressure, and retirement from political office at the age of thirty-seven because of his support for Populism and black suffrage. On the other hand, it is difficult at the current stage of American history to become too excited about his Populist ideas; most now seem irrelevant or wrong. Having the government own the national transportation network, set the volume of money in circulation, and operate as a huge bank in order to make beneficial loans to farmers seem alternately naïve and ordinary as a way of transforming the economy. Such changes could not have produced the Promised Land for middling farmers or others. Moreover, an argument can be made that Populist political goals, measured in terms of self-interest, differed only in degree from the favors sought by the industrial and transportation monopolists they detested. Farmers' desire to cartelize agriculture suggests Populism's political and economic rhetoric was often hollow. Then there is Butler and other southern Populists' commitment to white supremacy, the ugly bedrock of southern politics.

Similarly, some historians have made much of the democratic rhetoric of Populism without asking whether Populist actions were democratic or distinct from the practices of other parties. Obviously "democracy" has a range of meanings. Suffrage is one measure, and Populism, particularly southern Populism, was not notable for its interest in expanding and protecting suffrage rights except for white males. Another measure of democracy is the internal structure of political organizations. Members of American political parties have ordinarily delegated considerable power to leaders, and so did Populists. Here again Butler is instructive, because he was so clearly a dominant, even bullying, individual force, particularly in North Carolina. Yet the rank and file looked to him and others to print newspapers, raise money, get splattered with rotten eggs, make speeches, and organize meetings to advance Populist goals. They continued to delegate power to Butler and others, often the same men, year after year, apparently voluntarily and not stupidly. What kind of "democracy" does this represent? Butler's aggressive leadership cannot easily be exorcised from Populism and contrasted with the movement's alleged "democratic" purpose without a more precise definition of that purpose; he was a duly elected Populist leader. Criticisms of Butler within the party usually derived from persons who disagreed with his strategies, not because he exercised power within the Populist Party. They wanted his power, not "democracy." Would he have been a more effective Populist if he had been a weaker leader? The problem of defining, or sentimentalizing, Populist democracy has been further confused by a simplistic dichotomy between the (good, honest, more radical) rank and file and the (bad, untrustworthy, more conservative) leader, although, again, Populists consistently, and particularly in the South, looked to and followed strong leadership. Further, as this biography shows, when they did not, it often was not to the benefit of or because of Populist economic principles.

As for personal characteristics, Butler was a dynamic individual with an enormous capacity and energy to motivate and mobilize people in an organization. He was president of his county Alliance at twenty-five, a United States senator at thirty-one, and chairman of a national political party at thirty-three. He was physically attractive and well spoken, someone who would attract attention in a group. He had religious faith and could be generous. Yet his motivations, like those of most interesting people, were complex and by no means always admirable. He was ambitious, which sometimes translated into arrogance, manipulation, deception, hostility to opponents, and revenge, especially as he aged and his political hopes vanished. While sincerely committed to Populist reform, for example, he also accepted an investment in his newspaper from tobacco magnate Benjamin Duke. In the Senate, he insulted other senators as conspirators against national interest. After Populism, he tried to become a millionaire by collecting repudiated southern Reconstruction bonds, sought money to run a sham campaign for Tom Watson in 1904, and in the 1920s discussed "business" with Secretary of the Interior Albert Fall. In his later years he carried out pointless battles with Republican rivals. Ultimately, at least to me, Butler is not a "likable" figure. Whether that is a useful or desirable criteria for evaluating a political leader, including a Populist, is left to the reader.

Some additional thoughts are in order. Much writing about Populism has suffered from efforts by historians to choose sides in factional wars that have been over for more than one hundred years. I do not believe that the political strategies chosen by the party made any difference in the long run to Populist political failure. I know, Butler knew, and as far as I can tell other Populists who supported cooperation with other parties knew that their strategy had real costs. But the record is clear that so did a strategy that did not include cooperation, a difficult point for some historians to grasp. There is also the fantastically silly idea in recent historical writing about Populism that a person changes his ideology (or betrays it) if he supports a political candidate who does not agree with every single principle the person may hold. Ironically, this antidemocratic premise can lead only to total disengagement; every voter knows it is wrong. For the political historian, it is better to try to understand and describe the options and the complexity of the process of achieving political and economic change than to endorse one option over another from a safe distance. Plenty in Populism and in Butler's career helps to do that.[9]

Finally, because of the limited ideological relevance of Populism, as well as Butler's sometimes less-than-admirable personal characteristics, Butler, as well as Populism itself, is most interesting and useful because of his strategic politics. As a result, the more important part of his story is Butler's reaction to the difficulty of leading a political movement that sought to limit the power of large private corporations by expanding the power of government. The Populist task was nothing less than replacing cultural, social, local, and sectional issues with a politics focused exclusively on economic reform. In considering this, it would be a mistake to conclude that Butler changed his core reform views much after 1892 because of any motivation to hold office. Perhaps this was a weakness, particularly when it meant mouthing variations on the Alliance's subtreasury idea in response to the Great Depression. What did change was how his reform ideas were given political expression. Because of opposition to Populist principles, the only alternative to accommodating change, especially after 1900, was retirement from politics, which Butler never considered. His obsessive involvement in party politics might be considered Butler's real and most destructive ambition, because the last time he ran for office was almost thirty-eight years before his death. He would have loved nothing more than majority support for the Populist Party's Omaha Platform, which would have satisfied both his ideological interests as well as his organizational hopes; yet something close to this never existed in North Carolina or at the national level. The reasons are complex. Butler's views confronted an enormous range of barriers, including localism, the nature of state-level politics, presidential politics, racism, opposition to federal power, intraparty factionalism, bribery, intimidation, violence, the strengths and weaknesses of individual leaders, the reactions of Republicans and Democrats, the need to develop a favorable media for the Populist message, and many others. These issues have the greatest relevance to those of us living one hundred years after Populism because they concern the enduring question of the meaning of representative government in the United States, including the ability of the party system to reflect public will. My hope is that this biography can serve to clarify the connection between politics and reform that was Populism's most important and most difficult task.

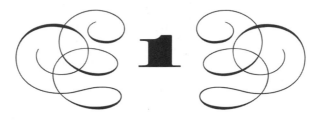

A FOUNDATION FOR LEADERSHIP

DRIVEN BY THE PROMISE of a political debate, anxious farmers hurried down the rough roads to Clinton. They knew the day's performance would be anything but ordinary. Zebulon Vance, a Democrat, Civil War governor, and outspoken critic of Reconstruction was one of the speakers. His opponent was Thomas Settle, a prewar Democrat turned Republican. Having won the nominations of their parties for governor, the men conducted a monumental canvass across North Carolina. The election occurred in 1876, a decisive crossroads in the state's political history. Although Democrats had regained control of the state legislature in 1870, Republicans still retained the governorship. The debates gave Democrats an excellent opportunity to make the evils of Reconstruction their principal appeal. Vance demanded that Settle admit he approved of the postwar amendments to the U.S. Constitution, which held out the hope of equal rights for freedpersons. Vance also wondered if Settle supported the federal Civil Rights Act of 1875, which required equal public accommodations among the races.[1] Vance's and Settle's visit to Clinton was worth remembering, as the two leaders ably advanced their ideas on the compelling issues of the day. Even the most seasoned political veteran could not help but be impressed. One novice spectator who was to have a much greater impact on politics in Clinton than either Vance or Settle was a thirteen-year-old named Marion Butler. Butler and his father had traveled the ten miles from their rural home in the western part of the county, and the effort was well spent. The debate made a greater impression on Marion than any other experience of his childhood.[2]

SAMPSON COUNTY WAS Butler's home for his first eighteen years. Almost the size of Rhode Island, it spread mostly north and south across the alternately level and gently rolling land of southeastern North Carolina. Forests of loblolly and longleaf pine, oak, and sweet gum dominated the landscape, but several generations of settlement meant there were wide expanses of cleared land as well. Dark swamps, tributaries of the Cape Fear River, covered thousands of acres. With a mild climate and fertile soil, the region was well suited to agricultural pursuits. Hogs, corn, and sweet potatoes won early acceptance as staples, and growers also produced rice and cotton. Most of the population were of English, Scots-Irish, and African descent, with Europeans always forming a majority.[3]

Sampson lacked anything resembling a city. Although Clinton served as the county seat as early as 1784, livestock frequented the town's boulevards into the twentieth century. In 1860 it could not claim two hundred residents. Adding to the bucolic splendor were meager transportation facilities, even by depressed North Carolina standards. No railroads entered Clinton until well after the Civil War. A road connected Clinton with Fayetteville, thirty-five miles west, and another extended to Wilmington, about sixty miles to the southeast. During the nineteenth century this isolation limited the county's cultural institutions. One early attempt, in the 1850s, to establish a weekly newspaper failed. In 1860 the county reported thirty-seven public "common schools," with about 1,620 students, but most children went without formal instruction. Some of the larger planters accumulated personal libraries, and others subscribed to Raleigh or Wilmington newspapers, but no agencies distributed secular reading material. Instead, Baptist and Methodist churches represented the most consistent source of intellectual stimulation.[4]

Before and after the Civil War, Sampson's social structure resembled that of other southern coastal plain communities. At its apex, a handful of elite planter families owned thousands of acres of prime farmland and several hundred slaves. The planter group, largely Democrats by the 1830s, provided much of the local political leadership. Most whites, however, particularly in the western reaches of the county, grew food crops and raised livestock for personal needs. They typically owned tracts ranging from one hundred to three hundred acres. Slaves constituted a third class. They cleared virgin stands of pine, built the county's roads, and constructed many of its buildings. They labored in field and home. After the Civil War some of them purchased land. However, most remained as workers on white-owned farms, usually as tenants. These three types—large landowning whites, lesser white farmers, and primarily landless rural blacks—characterized Sampson's population into the twentieth century.[5]

MARION BUTLER ALWAYS took pride in having been born into this community on 20 May 1863, the anniversary of North Carolina's alleged 1775 Mecklenburg Declaration of Independence. Marion became the second child and first son of Wiley and Romelia Butler. His paternal ancestors had lived in Sampson County for several generations. A great-grandfather, James Butler Sr., settled in what later became western Sampson County around 1760. The area was raw frontier as late as 1740. Thousands of hopefuls, most of them Scots-Irish, migrated to the former Tuscarora hunting grounds and established a British colony in the wilderness. James Senior got some of the land, and he and his wife raised eight children on it. Although this pioneer's life seems to have been otherwise uneventful, he apparently performed some service against the British in the American Revolution.[6]

Marion Butler's grandfather, James Butler Jr., was born about 1782 and like his father became a middling farmer with a large household. After James's marriage to Naomi Smith, around 1810, the couple had nine children. They raised crops typical of the region: corn, sweet potatoes, hogs, and cattle. Although James Junior never attained great wealth, all his children learned to read and write. He had amassed about one thousand dollars in property by 1850, including three hundred acres. This worth reflected the average for western Sampson, and James was not a slaveholder.[7]

Wiley Butler was born into this solidly yeoman clan in 1816. He grew up on the family farm but by the 1840s had become an overseer on the nearby John Underwood plantation. One of the largest farms in western Sampson, it spread over thirty-six hundred acres and included about fifty slaves. Wiley lived with Underwood's family and helped manage the production of hogs, cattle, corn, sweet potatoes, and rice. Apparently, however, he was not interested in spending his life as an overseer, and during the 1850s he began to purchase land. Ready to begin a family, he had married Romelia Ferrell by 1860.[8]

Romelia Ferrell was born in 1839, the daughter of Anderson Ferrell and Mary Dixon Ferrell. Her father owned a farm in what was then eastern Orange County, near the present city of Durham. Her mother, a native of Wilmington who had been raised by wealthy grandparents, married Ferrell about 1830. Anderson Ferrell's untimely death, the result of a drowning in the mid-1850s, prompted Mary's quick return to eastern North Carolina.

Yeoman success: the birthplace of Marion Butler.
(Courtesy of the North Carolina Division of Archives and History)

She settled in Clinton in 1855, where she remained until her death almost forty years later. Despite the untimely demise of her father, Romelia grew up in relatively genteel circumstances. She received some formal education and became a devout Episcopalian.[9]

After their marriage, Wiley and Romelia Butler settled into a small frame house in the western Sampson community of Huntley. The farmstead was a busy place. In 1860 Wiley owned almost two hundred acres, a horse, four cows, an ox, and twenty-seven hogs. He planted corn, sweet potatoes, peas, and beans. He and Romelia made wine from local fruit and butter from their cows' milk. By southern standards, Wiley even rose above his ancestors by acquiring three slaves. Romelia gave birth to eight children between 1861 and 1879, including four daughters, Florence, Cornelia, Romelia, and Mittie, and four sons, Marion, George, Henry, and Lester.[10] The Civil War seems to have caused relatively little disruption to the Butlers. Military operations and railroads avoided Huntley, and Wiley, in his late forties, did not leave home. In fact, the 1860s were years of economic gain. Wiley supplemented his farm income with a turpentine still, a small manufactory fed by rosin from longleaf pines. Altogether, his sale of over fifteen hundred dollars' worth of products in 1869 represented one of the largest incomes in western Sampson.[11]

During the 1870s and early 1880s Wiley further increased his wealth. Taking advantage of the freeing of slaves and the growing commercialization of agriculture, he became a rural merchant. By 1877 he had increased his real property holdings to almost three hundred acres, property valued for taxes at over $2,200. Although not an immense sum, it was notable in the depressed business climate of western Sampson, where most individual holdings were worth about $100. In 1882, Wiley claimed about $100 in cash, about $1,000 in debts owed to him, and an additional $500 worth of goods that were probably inventory. He was the second wealthiest person in Honeycutts Township. Although Wiley's income fell below that of several planters in eastern Sampson, by the middle 1880s he was among the more prosperous men in the county.[12]

As a result of Wiley's efforts, Marion grew up in a comparatively comfortable atmosphere. Another important factor in the boy's life was that both his parents placed a high value on Christianity and education. Little is known of the character of Wiley Butler except that he was taciturn, a teetotaler, and a Baptist. His most significant position of community activity was as clerk in the local Baptist church, a sign that he was trusted with money. Romelia Butler remained an Episcopalian despite the lack of an organized congregation nearer than Clinton. Denominational differences, however, did not interfere with the passing of Christian learning on to the Butler children. Romelia also helped establish a well-run school. Public education in Sampson largely ceased to exist in the late 1860s and early 1870s. In 1869 the county spent less than three thousand dollars to maintain fifty-six schools. In 1874, with Romelia among the leaders, a group of Huntley citizens built Salem High School, which opened in January 1875 with Isham Royal as its first principal.[13]

Salem provided Marion Butler with his first real school experience. He enrolled at the opening session and stayed there until his graduation in 1881. Salem attracted boys and girls from all over the county. It consisted of a crude, one-room frame structure and an adjacent Masonic Hall, used by music classes. At least one sentimental observer considered it a place where rural youth had "real opportunities for self development." Students received instruction in languages, mathematics, English, and history. Girls learned domestic and social skills, while boys practiced oratory.[14]

Unfortunately, information about Butler's life during his first eighteen years is scant. There are no extant letters from him or from family members to him, nor are there recorded Butler's memories, fond or otherwise, of the farm, his parents, friends, or relatives. Butler was never one to reflect much about his past. Nonetheless, the indirect evidence shows both typical and atypical forces at work. As for the typical, like most North Carolinians he grew up on a farm, and nothing suggests that he traveled out of Sampson County. He witnessed the prevailing varieties of eastern North Carolina labor, including the exploitation of landless blacks and whites. He imbibed the dogma of the Democratic Party. He was raised in a Protestant church. He grew up in a crowded house in which his mother was responsible for the education of the children. Less typically, Butler's parents were important members of the community. Modest wealth, based on farming and merchandising, set his family apart. Perhaps these circumstances, together with the emphasis on uplift through education and religious faith, helped stimulate a few special traits. An early observer, for instance, remarked that young Marion had a "zeal for work." He also displayed a seriousness that appeared as aloofness or, less politely, snobbishness. Unusually handsome, with glossy black hair, the broad-shouldered young man stood over six feet tall by the time he was eighteen. He already possessed an arresting voice that commanded attention.[15]

BUTLER'S POTENTIAL appeared most clearly in his enrollment, in 1881, at the University of North Carolina. At that time the school was still suffering from the economic dislocations of the Civil War and Reconstruction. Before 1860 it had been one of largest colleges in the nation, but postwar political disputes in state government led it to close in 1870. For the remainder of the nineteenth century its financial circumstances remained precarious. At matriculation Butler chose the course that led to a bachelor of arts degree. This meant his first two years focused on Greek, Latin, mathematics, French, English, and chemistry, while the junior and senior years emphasized chemistry, botany, geology, literature, astronomy, and physiology. Generally, Butler was an average student at Chapel Hill, with grades usually ranging in the seventies and eighties. Nonetheless, he showed ability in some areas, earning a 95 in Rhetoric and a 96 and 97 in business law courses taught by President Battle. The latter were designed to instruct "such legal principles, civil and criminal, as every businessman ought to know."[16]

Despite the recitation method of instruction, which required long hours in the classroom, Butler's performance outside class revealed more about his interests and abilities. Library records suggest that he was an avid reader. He studied articles in many leading journals, but the *North American Review* seems to have been his favorite. Books borrowed from the library reflected an in-

terest in politics, history, and current affairs. He perused George Bancroft's
History of the United States; works by Thomas Babington Macaulay, Edward
Gibbon, and Montesquieu; and histories of North Carolina. He consulted
collections of exceptional oratory, including Daniel Webster's speeches. He
apparently read political economy texts, including a study of socialism.[17]

Butler also belonged to the Dialectic Society, a literary organization. The
two university literary societies formed the center of student life outside of
coursework. The faculty even required each student to join one or the other.
Officially, the university wanted them to regulate conduct while giving students a forum in which to develop skills relevant to public life. The societies
always gave political skill preeminence. Formal debates focused on current
topics, and students arranged the society halls as miniature parliaments.
They soon learned that power derived from coalition building, and in the
struggle for recognition they mastered electioneering, oratory, and legislative maneuver.[18]

Butler joined the Dialectic Society on 16 September 1881 and quickly
achieved success. During his sophomore year he won election as secretary
and junior debater. As a senior, society members chose him to be their commencement orator and president. Such honors could not be accomplished
by quiet politeness. The factions necessary to elect officers often derived
from residence hall groups, and the hall faction's foremost function was to
develop and maintain bloc voting. In this polity, student leaders generated
bloc voting by pressuring peers to vote for the faction's candidates. Occasionally, they used physical harassment against those who challenged an expected allegiance. Further borrowing from their elders, partisanship could
include "treating" potential political friends with alcohol before an election.
Dialectic Society factionalism reached a destructive peak in 1884, when disappointed office seekers threatened secession. By 1885 various forces had
smoothed over the difficulties, but recurrent turmoil spurred the rise of vol-
untary social fraternities.[19]

Butler thrived in these upheavals. Indeed, the greatest divisions among
society members arose during the very time he was president. The substance
of his leadership, however, was less dramatic. In short, the fun was in gaining office, and Butler lacked much real purpose after achieving power. Although complimented by his colleagues as "elaborate and entertaining," his
presidential address was long-winded and inconsequential. It suggested that
"order" should be the guiding principle of the Dialectic Society and of society generally: "Disorder makes a society [lose] respect for itself." He spent

great efforts in scolding uncooperative members who insisted on exiting meetings before they were adjourned.[20]

Yet election success allowed Butler to give speeches of greater interest. These remarks display his earliest ideas about current affairs, particularly race and the need for economic and social change. First, in three speeches given in 1883 and 1884, he articulated a catalogue of racist assumptions. During one debate he argued that whites lacked any responsibility to educate former slaves. The black man was "destitute of genius, without glory, unprogressive, sensual, and stolid." He seemed better off in bondage. At least then he was "protected, well fed, and well clothed." Further, during the Civil War, many slaves "turned traitor" and committed "foul outrages upon their mistresses." These "demons" forfeited a right to public education supported by whites.[21]

In contrast, Butler portrayed white society, particularly white southern society, as a great achievement. He traced the accomplishment to "Nordic" unity. Germans, after all, were "our ancestors," and civilization was the product of "Northern Tribes." Especially telling was his assumption that "white civilization" was triumphant because of its commitment to "progress." As a result, his use of the term "unprogressive" when describing blacks was probably chosen with care. Butler argued that civilization demanded a devotion to "material, intellectual, moral, and industrial progress." To achieve this, "education is the biggest possibility of all and on it hangs the hopes of humanity."[22]

Even more revealing of his undergraduate mind was Butler's senior oration, which he delivered at commencement on 4 June 1885. Titled "The Heroes and Conquests of Invention," its opening theme was that historians had failed to identify the "true heroes in the cause of humanity." Instead of military leaders and royalty, "patient inventors, the great captains of industry, [and] the promoters of peace" deserve the most gratitude. It followed that the connection between textiles and progress surpassed the relationship between victory in battle and national glory. Manufactures made England and New England wealthy, and it was now the South's task to duplicate the opportunity. The region needed only to "make extra-ordinary efforts to secure immigration" and make "the most liberal concessions to capital." Soon, the world would be the South's marketplace, and "the false antagonism between labor and capital will be silenced, and these twin giants of industry will stand together in holy union."[23]

At twenty-two, Butler had drunk rather deeply at the New South well. Like other devotees of that economic religion, popular among southern town boosters and journalists, he assumed industry and capital would increase the region's wealth and there could be no losers in the process. Further, mass education fueled change. Only blacks would remain behind; they lacked the ability to contribute to modern progress. Butler's racism and his glorification of education and industrialization reflected common opinion in the 1880s, but the forcefulness with which he articulated the ideas is striking, particularly considering that he was a farm boy who had never been out of North Carolina. He understood that industrial development was a future goal, not a present reality. He perceived tension between capital and labor. He had begun to consider the relationship between education, politics, and the economy.

Butler's college experience pointed toward a public career. Despite the classical curriculum, his years in Chapel Hill successfully introduced him to contemporary political and economic ideas. In the Dialectic Society, moreover, he gained experience in the world of politics and showed an early ability in organization and oratory. Nonetheless, Butler seemed to make few enduring friendships. Although Joseph Caldwell, editor of the *Charlotte Observer*, later claimed Butler was "rather an off ox in his class," with "no chums," who "surrounded himself with profundity, silence, and mystery,"[24] actually Butler was just an unusually serious young man. At Chapel Hill, organizational goals linked his acquaintances, particularly in the Dialectic Society. It is much easier to imagine him scheming with fellow Dialectic members in his South Building room over an election than going out on a midnight frolic.

Largely because of his political interests, it was predictable that, sometime during his last years in college, he decided to become a lawyer. About half of the bachelor of arts recipients in his twenty-five-man class became attorneys. In 1885, North Carolina placed few barriers before hopeful lawyers: there were no formal educational requirements and only a perfunctory oral examination required before receiving a license to practice. As a result, legal education consisted of little more than a brief apprenticeship with a practicing attorney or enrollment for a short period in a law school. After graduation, Butler planned to remain in Chapel Hill, enroll in the university's eight-week summer law school course, and then stand for his license in the fall.[25]

IN A STROKE OF fate that changed Marion's life, on 20 April 1885, Wiley Butler died of "chronic inflammation fever." His oldest son would not be able to prepare for the bar examination or begin the lean years of practice that afflicted new lawyers; he was needed at home. Four of his brothers and sisters still lived there, and Wiley's will promised support for the children to age twenty-one or marriage. In addition, Marion had no financial assets. Nonetheless, on his return to Sampson County he decided that a career in small farming and merchandising, such as his father's, was not for him. Seeking to fulfill some of the ideals he preached at Chapel Hill, he threw himself into the cause of education, in particular the success of Salem High School.[26]

Butler became Salem's principal in the summer of 1885. He immediately used his college organizing skills in a campaign to attract students by advertising Salem in the Clinton *Caucasian* and *Fayetteville Observer* newspapers. The ads described the school as conveniently located about eleven miles from Clinton and twenty-four miles from Fayetteville. Undeterred that this established its isolation, the enthusiastic young educator boasted that "the instruction and discipline" at Salem were "as thorough and complete as can be found in any academy or High School." The school possessed a "well equipped literary department," a "first-class, fine tone piano," a set of encyclopedias, an unabridged dictionary, and a map of Sampson County, prepared by the principal. There was even a "Philotechnic Literary Society" for older boys.[27]

The promotional efforts worked. In 1886, Salem enrolled 74 scholars and employed three teachers. The next year, there were 101 students and five teachers. Salem's progress appeared most prominently at its graduations. In 1888, over a thousand supporters had lunch on the grounds and heard declamations from the Philotechnic Society. Amid fields of cotton and corn, student debaters considered whether "the internal revenue system should be repealed." Butler's broader community interests were also apparent, including his relationship with Sampson County Democrats. Daniel G. Fowle, elected governor that fall, gave the graduation speech, and F. R. Cooper Sr., editor of the Clinton *Caucasian*, presented a medal for best orator. The *Fayetteville Observer* congratulated "Professor" Butler and remarked that Salem was "one of the best and most progressive schools in eastern North Carolina."[28]

Butler also acted for schools beyond Sampson County. In the middle and late 1880s he was a member of the North Carolina Teachers' Assembly. The group brought teachers together during the summer to listen to lectures and discuss educational issues. It met at the coastal resort of Morehead City, where it attracted the state's younger educators, particularly those, such as Butler, who saw education as a moral crusade. The organization became a

Rural life.
(Courtesy of the North Carolina Division of Archives and History)

political lobby for better schools and improved teacher training. Butler engaged in some artful and revealing politics at the assembly's 1887 convention. From the group's beginning there was tension between public and private school teachers. Although Butler ran his own school, he allied himself
with expanded public education. The public school teachers' most important goal was to establish a state normal school for women. A leader in this
movement was Edwin A. Alderman, superintendent of the Goldsboro city
schools. According to the later recollection of E. P. Moses, Butler rose at the
assembly, "smashed a slate . . . fixed up by a little coterie of private school
teachers, nominated . . . Prof. E. A. Alderman for President of the Assembly,
put the motion [himself], and had the satisfaction of seeing [his] motion
adopted by a very large majority." This action put the support of the assembly behind the normal school.[29]

Forced by his father's death to return to Sampson County, Butler succeeded at several challenges. First, he improved an educational enterprise
in an area that lacked a long tradition of organized schooling largely because
he possessed an enormous ability and energy to exude confidence and motivate others. A second and larger accomplishment was that although relega-
tion to Huntley might have led to obscurity, it actually became the foundation for a national public career. By the time he was twenty-five, Butler had

demonstrated an interest in public issues and, more important, a capacity for translating ideas into action in an unlikely place. Perhaps this drive was related to his devotion to economic change through industrialization or his belief that greater government responsibility, most clearly in education, was essential. But it was a friendly fate that sent him back to a rural community. This distinguished him from other important Tar Heels of his generation, the generation that came of age after Reconstruction. Walter Hines Page, Josephus Daniels, Charles B. Aycock, and Edwin A. Alderman are perhaps his best-known contemporaries. Like Butler, these men believed they had a special mission to rebuild the state and that industrialization and education presented direct paths to a desirable future. Yet they abandoned rural or small-town homes on reaching adulthood. In contrast, farm problems impacted Butler in ways that bypassed the others, dramatically affecting his life's perspective. Altogether, Butler at twenty-five appears as a bundle of potential. He was handsome, eager to participate in and even control organizations, and comfortable with public speaking and public life. He had little time for frivolity, including friendships—male or female—or family matters not connected to some public cause. Equally important, he was curious and smart about power, including what could be done with it. He was already sensitive to the relationship between economic structure and politics, at least to the extent of realizing the connection between industry and wealth. The only real question about his future was the direction and consequence of his abilities, not whether he had the capacity to make an impact.

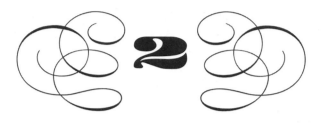

AN ALLIANCE EDUCATION

WHILE MARION BUTLER established himself as a popular educator, some southern farmers began a political revolt. Declining crop prices, scarce money, high interest rates, lack of affordable credit, high transportation costs, and expensive manufactured goods protected by tariffs appeared as tangible symptoms of an unjust economy. More broadly, these farmers feared that the rural way of life, so revered in Jeffersonian rhetoric, was no longer preeminent. Yet neither economic depression nor a perceived decline in rural importance produced the agrarian movement of the 1880s. More important was a political confidence that something could be done to make things better. For southerners, the primary vehicle of hope was the National Farmers' Alliance and Industrial Union. Under the leadership of Charles W. Macune of Texas, it promoted cooperative marketing of agricultural products, encouraged scientific farming, and demanded legislation reducing the power of corporations, especially railroads and national banks. The Texas Alliance was an all-white secret union that restricted membership to farmers, workers, country doctors, and teachers. Lawyers and merchants, representatives of urban and corporate greed, could not join. The order arranged itself in a hierarchical manner, with a local "sub-Alliance" composed of ten to fifty members as the basic unit. Above the sub-Alliances were county Alliances, state Alliances, and national Alliance organizations.[1]

By the mid-1880s many North Carolina farmers, especially small and middling landowners, were complaining about declining prices for land, cotton, and tobacco, expensive credit, and high transportation and marketing costs. They feared losing their land for taxes or debts, growing increasingly resentful of the booming prosperity of North Carolina manufacturers, especially in the tobacco industry. They felt threatened by urbanization, as the promise of excitement and economic opportunities lured youth from the countryside. From the outset, some of their anger was directed at the state legislature, which appeared wholly unsympathetic to their problems.[2]

The deeper causes of distress in North Carolina and the South were complex. First, staples, especially cotton and tobacco, declined in profitability. After 1870, cotton prices slid to under ten cents a pound, a value that persisted for the rest of the century. At the same time, productivity per acre did not increase dramatically, meaning increases in cotton acreage could not produce prosperity. Second, the price problem partly resulted from weak demand, but it also took place during a period when the federal government carried out a policy of deflation by relying on increasingly scarce national bank notes and a limited gold supply to provide the money needs of the economy. Critics of this policy assumed an increased money supply would solve the crop price decline. A third cause was the status of white and black rural labor and the related question of agricultural finance. North Carolina farmers divided into diverse classes, from large landowning planters to landowners holding less than 250 acres, to landless laborers or sharecroppers. Tenants and sharecroppers made up more than a third of North Carolina's rural labor. The task of financing agriculture, particularly for lesser landowners and the landless, was adversely affected by the collapse of antebellum banking, the increase in commercial farming, and the failure of the Reconstruction Congress to redistribute southern land to freed slaves. Ultimately, the system's limitations elevated the rural merchant, often also a landlord, to the center of regional finance. Thousands of stores opened, many of which charged interest rates in excess of 50 percent on commodity advancements. This debt, in turn, was secured by liens on the debtor's crop. The borrower aimed to pay up at the end of the year, despite depressed prices. Altogether, increased reliance on cotton and other staples, declines in staple prices, the federal policy of deflation, the rise of tenancy, and the merchant system of financing transformed southern land from a source of wealth to one of economic stagnation and poverty.[3]

Another cause of dissatisfaction was the rapid development of the southern railroad network after 1865. In theory, more railroads should have meant cheaper transport to market for farmers. Yet the railroad business became a chaotic combination of fierce competition and monopoly, incessant lobbying to obtain special favors, including low taxes, and generous treatment for some shippers and discrimination against others. The quasi-public legal and political status of the railroads, plus a reasonable sense among farmers that freight rates were unfairly excessive — they did not fall as was expected —

generated anger and frustration. Federal efforts to address the complaints, such as the Interstate Commerce Act of 1887, did not make an appreciable difference.[4]

These troubles led many North Carolina farmers, particularly among the small and middling landowners, to organize under the leadership of Leonidas La Fayette Polk. Polk, a former Confederate and a Democrat, did not challenge the increasing reliance of farmers on cash crops such as cotton. Indeed, he embraced profit, believing that production methods, credit, transportation, and marketing practices could be reformed. To these ends, Polk urged the creation of an agricultural college, asked for a federal bureau of agriculture, and supported a statewide stock law that would restrict roaming livestock to fenced-in areas. By the mid-1880s, the stock law debate had been going on for years, and Polk linked a prohibition against free-ranging livestock to progressive husbandry. Many landless farmers, fearing the loss of free grazing rights, disagreed. Yet such conflict did not seriously threaten Polk's leadership. Initially Polk formed Farmers' Clubs, which tried to teach the latest scientific techniques as well as to foster rural fellowship. The Farmers' Clubs led, in early 1887, to the North Carolina Farmers' Association, which promoted self-help and farmer influence in the legislature. As for the latter, the association supported better roads and a statute voiding contracts purporting to secure debts with growing crops, the crop lien.[5]

Polk's efforts laid the groundwork, but the arrival of the Texas Farmers' Alliance achieved a more complete mobilization. The Tar Heel Alliance began in the spring of 1887, when the first sub-Alliance appeared in Robeson County. By October there was a state organization, with Syndenham B. Alexander as its president, Polk as secretary, and Elias Carr, president of the Farmers' Association, as chairman of the executive committee. The Alliance attracted large and small landowning farmers, tenant farmers, rural doctors, and teachers. It often included women, but excluded blacks, atheists, lawyers, and merchants.[6]

Sampson County was a logical place for Alliance success. Commercial agriculture was expanding, as production of cotton, the county's leading cash crop, increased more than 500 percent between 1860 and 1890. Yet cotton prices fell from eleven cents a pound in 1879 to less than nine cents a pound in 1887. Moreover, tenancy was the condition of just over one-third of Sampson farmers in 1890. Growers could expect little help from elected officials. Democratic Clinton attorneys dominated local politics, and they had no intention of tampering with the economic and political status quo, which protected existing credit, transportation, and marketing arrangements.[7]

L. L. Polk: original leader of the North Carolina Alliance.
(Courtesy of the North Carolina Division of Archives and History)

Alliance organizers first appeared in the county in January 1888. Over a
ten-week period, five men set up sub-Alliances from Newton Grove to
Goshen—almost twenty altogether. They posted announcements that they
would be at a church or school, described the order to those who showed
up, and then formed a sub-Alliance. Sampson farmers joined the Alliance
primarily because it promised a cooperative scheme of buying goods. The
Alliance planned to purchase material, such as fertilizer, and then sell it to

members at low prices, thereby avoiding the high prices and credit of local merchants. According to an organizer, "Farmers in Sampson are becoming deeply interested in the Farmers' Alliance. They are beginning to see and realize the truth that money is being saved to the farmers by the Alliance."[8]

IN MARCH 1888, John Owen organized a sub-Alliance at Salem school. Butler gave permission for Owen to use the school and also became an Alliance-man himself. In fact, just days after the Salem meeting, on 21 March 1888, a county-level Alliance appeared in Clinton, with "Prof. Maxion [*sic*] Butler" as its first president. Butler's reasons for joining the Alliance had nothing to do with economic radicalism. As already suggested, he was a pro-education, pro–New South, white supremacy Democrat. Moreover, although he had grown up on a farm and ran a school for rural children, farming was not his vocation. As the son of a merchant and as a hopeful attorney, Butler was connected to classes expressly excluded from Alliance membership. Yet he lived in an agricultural community. The Alliance apparently offered a unique chance to combine his interest in economic "progress" with a passion for organization and leadership. Given Butler's interest in public affairs and his community, it is difficult to imagine Butler not joining an organization supported by most of his neighbors. He was already a Mason and a member of the Sampson County Agricultural Society; the Teachers' Assembly; the Knights of Honor, a social and charitable group; and the Democratic Party.[9]

His election to the Alliance county presidency derived from similar causes. Although only twenty-four years old, Butler had already demonstrated a great willingness and ability to take charge of any group. Lacking a dependent family and a full-time, year-round job, he certainly had the time and inclination to take on such tasks. But the Alliance clearly offered a different opportunity. By early March 1888, almost three years after graduation from Chapel Hill, Butler had decided to retire from full-time teaching. He became coeditor, then sole editor, of the only county newspaper, the Clinton *Caucasian.* He was not elected Alliance president until after it was known that he planned to assume editorial duties. Butler borrowed funds for the publishing venture, perhaps as much as a thousand dollars, which he used to purchase a stake in the newspaper. Financial maneuvering was essential, because he lacked much property of his own; indeed, his taxable assets were limited to a horse. Like many other rural weeklies of the era, the *Caucasian* had a circulation of about one thousand. F. R. Cooper had established it in 1882 and had chosen the distinctive racial title.[10]

By the summer of 1888, Sampson County had become a bastion of Alliance power. The Alliance's principal activity was bulk buying of material for farmers and cash discount sales of the goods to members. The Alliance also emphasized rural "economy." This meant crop diversification and staying out of debt, which was endorsed by one Sampson farmer because it was "better for us to live the lives of ground hogs for two years than to be eaten up by the canker worm known as the mortgage." Both the buying program and education in farm economics were discussed at a variety of regular meetings and social gatherings, complete with the substantial rituals of a fraternal organization. The Salem sub-Alliance had eleven officers, including doorkeepers, a sergeant at arms, secretaries, lecturers, and various other titled persons, when the group's total membership was only forty. From the beginning, women attended meetings and won approval for being "strong in the faith."[11]

The Alliance quickly became the dominant force in Butler's life. He published its news in the *Caucasian*. He attended get-togethers of all kinds and presided over the county organization's quarterly meetings. These meetings featured discussions on the efforts of the sub-Alliance and county business agents, who were responsible for making bulk purchases. Sampson farmers seemed pleased with his work. One reference to the "county President, Prof. M. Butler," praised him for his "excellent ability," which was "really adapted to control an immense body of brethren." The Alliance reelected him president in July 1888.[12]

From the beginning, however, Butler's job required more than supporting cooperatives and ensuring parliamentary order. Sampson Alliance members knew the cooperative buying program challenged the merchant-dominated crop lien system, under which merchants sold goods on credit and obtained a lien on crops. As a result, they faced social and economic ostracism, particularly from an element "composed mostly of lawyers and merchants." Some explained this, vaguely, as a logical consequence of the Alliance determination "to put an end to monopolistic oppression and monetary and landed aristocracy." Butler, however, believed that caution, not unnecessary conflict, was advisable. As editor of a newspaper that was the mouthpiece of the local Democracy as well as the county Alliance, he was in a position to smooth growing tension, and he welcomed the opportunity.[13]

The dispute between the Alliance and merchants in Clinton reflected the political dilemma of the Alliance. Although the organization was officially nonpartisan and dedicated to self-help, it always had political goals. The Alliance never "turned to politics," because politics was part of its raison d'être from the beginning. Moreover, Alliancemen tended to be Democrats. Democrats made up the state leadership and, like Butler, published almost all the Alliance newspapers. Yet the concerns of the Alliance differed from those of the attorneys and other townsmen who dominated the inner circles of the Democratic Party. Specifically, by 1890 the Alliance wanted convict leasing to corporations stopped and prisoners put to work on public roads. It supported simplification of the rules of civil litigation, including an increase in the jurisdiction of nonlawyer justices of the peace. This had important implications for the legal enforcement of debt. Evidencing a desire to curb railroad rates and limit railroad political power, the Alliance wanted a ban on free passes to public officials and a railroad commission to achieve rate regulation and equitable taxation of railroad property. All these things, which seem tame compared with later demands, required the passage of legislation by the North Carolina General Assembly, not just resolutions in local, secret meetings. In contrast, the creed of conservative North Carolina Democracy maintained that railroads and manufacturers should pay low taxes and not be subject to regulations on labor or rates. This faction had no interest in developing imaginative policies to benefit middling or small farmers; it also had the supreme political advantage of not requiring new and sweeping legislation. As the Alliance learned, in lawmaking it is almost always easier to do nothing.[14]

These conflicting ideals first clashed in the state elections of 1888. In Sampson County, because of their overwhelming strength, Alliancemen seized the reigns of Democracy, suggesting that the Alliance could transform Democratic policy throughout the state. Butler eagerly grasped this opportunity to merge Alliance ideas and Democratic organization. It was the kind of political tactic—linking Alliance ideals with formal party organization—he would spend most of the next fifty years trying to execute. Delegates elected him chairman of the county Democratic convention and instructed its candidate for state senator, Edwin W. Kerr, to support an Alliance railroad commission bill in the next legislature. Kerr, a Clinton attorney, typified the ruling clique. He was not used to taking orders and objected to the railroad commission. Nonetheless, Butler and his fellow Alliancemen elected Kerr to the senate and expected him to support a commission.[15]

Between 1888 and the summer of 1892 Butler, like most rural southerners, assumed Alliance reform could be advanced within a Democratic context. This belief is not surprising. It would have been much more surprising for Butler and others to throw off the chains of Democracy easily and quickly, particularly given the early success of the Alliance in their party. Even be-

yond the issue of political strategy was the question of whether the aims of
the Alliance and the Democracy were contradictory. This possibility also
does not seem to have occurred to Butler and other North Carolina Alliancemen for some time after 1888. In fact, it is clear that they were not necessarily contradictory. Butler's reform ideology, for example, reflected a
faith in the harmony of the Alliance and New South development, the latter
of which had long-standing support among Democrats. He consistently promoted both strands of reform, including government regulation of business, better public education, agricultural cooperatives, private property,
capital development, and industry. He viewed the Alliance and the Democratic Party as harmonious means for increasing collective and individual
wealth. In editorials he urged entrepreneurs to "commence small establish-
ments" that could "gradually swell themselves with their growing profits." He
extended a welcome to capitalists willing to build a cotton mill in Clinton.
The town's "busy, hustling population, reveling in thrift and prosperity,"
would make ideal employees. Clinton offered "constant and rapid improvements. . . . Everybody [is] busy and [there are] new buildings going up in
every direction." Butler proclaimed Georgia's Henry W. Grady, a leading ex-
ponent of New South ideas, the greatest southerner of the postwar era. As
for agriculture, Butler declared "cotton is a failure" that should be replaced
by "fruit growing and stock raising." Putting this idea into action, he served
on a committee to organize truck farming and to market produce coopera-
tively, which culminated in the formation of the state Truckers and Fruit
Growers' Association. He supported the state cooperative Alliance Business
Agency, which intended to sell farmers goods at reduced prices, and in 1888
he endorsed a nationwide Alliance protest against jute manufacturers, who
had formed a trust and raised the price of jute bagging for cotton.[16]

The program of the Democratic Party was easily joined to these reforms.
Butler's earliest editorials praised the administrations of Governor Daniel
Fowle and President Grover Cleveland. On the other hand, the protective
tariff, a Republican principle, was an unconstitutional subsidy to northern
industry hurtful to the southern farmer. White supremacy, of course, was the
crucial reason to vote for Democrats. A true southern patriot, he desired
government "managed by white men only." The so-called Lodge Force Bill,
a congressional effort to protect black voting through federal supervision of
elections, appeared to southerners as a cruel effort to resurrect the injustice
of Reconstruction. Yet Butler was already willing to point out when individual Democrats violated the "true" principles of his party, which he linked to
the Alliance. This was the rub. What was "true" Democracy in North Car-

olina and the nation? When, in early 1889, Edwin Kerr helped defeat the proposed railroad commission bill in the state legislature, Butler criticized him. More broadly, the *Caucasian* complained that the entire Democratic General Assembly "disobeyed the order of the people."[17]

FOR BUTLER, 1890 marked a decisive turning point. He embarked on a political career, sparked by developments far from Sampson County. As Samuel Johnson once remarked, an individual's motivations for taking action are always mixed. Certainly this applies to Butler. There can be little doubt that he wanted recognition and power and that running for local office was understood as a stepping-stone to bigger things. His ambitions before 1890 are apparent enough. On the other hand, months of attending and leading Alliance meetings and of reading and editing Alliance papers had a deep effect on his thoughts; these educational forces proved more transforming than the classical program of study at the University of North Carolina. At heart Butler was always a reformer, genuinely attracted to new ideas about political economy, especially if those ideas struck at monopoly and reaction. At this time, perhaps the most important external factor was the 1889 Alliance national convention. In St. Louis the Alliance wrote its first platform expressing a unitary set of national political demands. The platform defined Alliance reforms as relating to land, transportation, and finance and proposed a major shift in federal power. Regarding land, Alliancemen wanted prohibition of foreign ownership and asked that lands given to corporations, particularly railroads, be returned to the federal government. The Alliance remedy for unjust transportation was federal ownership of railroads. Financial change, however, was most important. The Alliance wanted federal control of the money supply, which meant the abolition of national banks, paper money "issued in sufficient volume to do the business of the country on a cash system," and the free coinage of silver. Although not included in the official demands, a committee also proposed that the federal government establish a system of warehouses, known as subtreasuries, empowered to issue loans to farmers of up to 80 percent of the value of their crop stored in the warehouse. The loans would provide credit, allow farmers to sell crops when prices were highest, and inject millions of dollars into the economy at periods when rural areas were starved for cash. The reforms drew on decades of producer-oriented thought in a range of organizations and were not unique to the Alliance. Yet because of their clear, succinct articulation, they had the effect of a bombshell at the grass roots, including for Butler.[18]

The demands immediately affected North Carolina politics because many Alliancemen responded by demanding the election of federal legislators who would endorse the Alliance proposals. U.S. Senator Zebulon Vance was up for reelection in 1891, and the struggle initially focused on him. A campaign, spearheaded during 1890 by L. L. Polk, targeted Vance's unwillingness to support the subtreasury. In the end, the dispute ended with an uneasy peace, as Vance agreed to a compromise and Polk remained a Democrat. Efforts to select Alliance supporters for the House of Representatives had more success. Alliancemen won nominations in five of the state's nine districts, and five Alliance Democrats won. The activity in the federal arena also affected state issues. In its conventions of 1889 and 1890, the state Alliance demanded a railroad commission, fair taxation of railroads, an increase in funds for public schools, a criminal penalty for interest charges in excess of the state limit, and a law exempting mortgaged land from property taxes. It actively sought legislators pledged to advance these concerns in Democratic Party nominating conventions. The Alliance exerted a powerful influence in those conventions and in the ensuing elections.[19]

Butler's actions during this political transformation are best understood by considering his reaction to the 1889 St. Louis demands, the platforms of the state Alliance, and his view of their relation to the Democratic Party. During 1890 Butler reevaluated his earlier reform ideology, which was rooted in a hybrid of Alliance and New South ideas, and developed an Alliance-based theory of political economy. The result of the Alliance's educational process was that he publicly supported all the St. Louis proposals. He endorsed the subtreasury idea, describing it as a measure "born of necessity." He believed the government's obligation was too limited under the plan and more warehouses than it contemplated should be built. He endorsed free silver coinage and favored the abolition of national banks and national bank notes. He questioned the prevailing system of privately financed agriculture. As for state reforms, he concluded the government must regulate private property used for a public purpose; the necessity of a railroad commission followed. Similarly, convict leasing to private corporations and the donation of railroad passes to public officials constituted private intrusions on public rights. Altogether, Butler's evolving vision of political economy accepted a greater role for the state and federal government, with the ultimate purpose of destroying monopoly and establishing a "fair" market for producers.[20]

Butler's gradual acceptance and synthesis of Alliance ideas reflected the enormous educative power of the Alliance. Although he was a college graduate surprisingly familiar with contemporary ideas about politics and the economy, Butler absorbed the Alliance message eagerly, apparently not seriously questioning whether it was the best way of resolving the problems of his neighbors. His early activities in the Alliance became a logical extension of his interest in education. In the Alliance, he accepted the roles of both learner and teacher. Not only did he attend Alliance meetings and read Alliance literature, but he also took on the key educator roles within the Alliance structure, lecturer and editor. He did this well before he began any personal political activity. Moreover, he eventually became a teacher at all levels of the Alliance hierarchy—local, state, and national. Because of his later political success, Butler should be viewed as one of the outstanding students and teachers of the Alliance movement, a model reflection of the Alliance's ability to inform and persuade through mass instruction. The Alliance also fulfilled the hopes Butler placed on education as an undergraduate and as a young schoolmaster. Seeing politics as an educational venture naturally followed.[21]

Perhaps this process was not so difficult because Butler's new understanding did not need to displace some of his existing views. The Alliance platform affirmed private property and inequalities in its ownership. It did not challenge the desirability of industrialization, the benefits of individual economic initiative, and racist discrimination. Indeed, the money, land, and transportation planks indicated that the Alliance supported rural capitalism by making it cheaper for owners to ship farm goods and finance cash crops. Presumably, if mistakenly, Alliancemen believed this would be enough to increase profits to crop producers. Also important was that African Americans, excluded from the Alliance, were not given an equal role in the reformed economy. While the Alliance challenged Butler's thoughts about the role of government, initially it offered little basis for changing his racial views or the political implications of his racism. As a result, in 1890 Butler easily maintained his earlier commitment to reform through Democracy because the party was already correct on many issues and could easily be shaped to meet changing needs. Identifying himself as "first, last, and all the time a Democrat," Butler concluded that "the constitution of the Alliance is in entire harmony with the principles of the Democratic party."[22]

This perspective produced a predictable response to a leading controversy of 1890, the flap between Polk and Vance over the subtreasury. Butler chose to support Senator Vance. In the *Caucasian* he informed Polk that

"[Polk] could not be who he is without the Alliance," a statement that indicated Butler believed most Alliancemen preferred Vance to Polk. Vance was a "champion," whose decision to introduce, but not support, the subtreasury bill was "identical with the [Alliance] demands." The differences between Polk and Butler resulted primarily from Butler's limited political experience. Butler, who was more than twenty-five years younger than Polk, saw the political purpose of the Alliance as the dominant policy-proposing body within Democracy. Although Polk remained fearful of Republicans, his political maturity, independence from local politics, and freedom from ambition within the Democratic Party allowed him to see the Alliance as a national political movement in its own right. Butler, on the other hand, saw only the continued ease of uniting the Alliance and the party in Sampson County. At the 1890 Third District Democratic congressional nominating convention, for example, he presided, and Alliance influence, as in 1888, controlled. Allianceman Benjamin F. Grady became the nominee, and several other Alliance members, including Butler, received token votes. The convention's "Democratic" demands resembled the St. Louis Alliance platform: free coinage of silver, a federal income tax, an end to speculation in agricultural futures, prohibition of alien ownership of land, the subtreasury, and abolition of the national banks.[23]

The political demise of Edwin W. Kerr, the county's state senator, also confirmed Butler's faith in the merger of the Alliance and the Democracy. Unlike Vance, Kerr still tied his political future to the railroads and the merchants, and in 1890 he commenced a reelection campaign by challenging anyone to debate him over the railroad commission. Butler eagerly accepted, thereby entering the state senate race. He diligently compiled rate information and studied the reports of other states' railroad commissions. On the stump, he used this data to argue that the railroads discriminated against sections within North Carolina and among different types of shippers and that they charged exorbitant rates. By the time the county Democratic convention met, Butler's nomination was assured. Moreover, the county's Democratic-Alliance platform endorsed free coinage of silver, federally issued paper money, abolition of national banks, prohibition of alien ownership of land and speculation in agricultural futures, and a state railroad commission.[24]

Kerr and his allies did not take the loss gracefully. They bolted and chose an independent candidate, John A. Beaman, a Clinton merchant. The ensuing campaign was anticlimactic. Beaman symbolized the lawyer-merchant cabal, lacked newspaper support, and failed to conduct an active canvass.

An opportunistic Republican endorsement did not appreciably aid his cause. It even permitted the *Caucasian* to emphasize the connection between genuine Democracy, the Democracy represented by Butler, and the Alliance. In November, Butler won the election handily. He did worst in the "urban" Clinton precincts, and he did not seek and did not get African American votes.[25]

THE VICTORY WAS a part of widespread Alliance success in North Carolina. Of the 170 men elected to the assembly, approximately 110 were Alliance members. Still, real results depended on the enactment of Alliance proposals; clearly, Alliance affiliation alone could not accomplish anything. Butler, the youngest of the state's fifty senators, was more than willing to provide some of the necessary leadership required to turn ideas into law. He checked into Raleigh's Yarborough House hotel two days before the opening of the 1891 session. The next day, when Alliance representatives formed a legislative caucus, they chose him to preside over their meetings. From this moment forward Butler would occupy center stage in Alliance-based politics.[26]

The first order of business was to elect a United States senator. L. L. Polk, although not a member of the assembly, renewed his campaign to make Vance's election contingent on active support for the subtreasury. However, most Alliance Democrats, including Butler, had already been instructed by local party conventions to vote for Vance. As a result, the issue was whether the Alliance could make Vance's election contingent on resolutions acceptable to both Vance and the Alliance. The Alliance caucus devised a resolution that would tell "our Senator and Representatives in Congress to vote for and use all honorable means to secure the financial reforms adopted by the Ocala convention of the Farmers' Alliance." The Ocala convention, held just weeks earlier, had produced a document that largely reiterated the 1889 St. Louis demands. Butler introduced this resolution in the senate but was unable to obtain a vote on the senate floor. Vance's supporters knew Vance was not wholly in agreement with such an instruction. Eventually, the stronger Alliance demand withered under the pressures of party loyalty. An Allianceman introduced another resolution that bound Vance only "to secure the objects of financial reform as contemplated in the platform by the Ocala meeting." Because "objects" could be reduced to more money volume, which Vance favored, it passed easily. In the senate the vote was 46 to 0, with Butler voting for it.[27]

The legislature then turned to a bill to establish a railroad commission.

Again Butler's leadership was crucial. He proposed a joint drafting committee, and this committee of five senators and nine representatives, including Butler, composed a bill, held a hearing, and published a committee report. At the hearing, Fabius Busbee, a Raleigh railroad attorney, suggested that the commission would be an unconstitutional denial of his clients' due process rights. After the hearing, debate escalated, with Butler often at the center of controversy. He tried to have the railroad commissioners' salaries set at twenty-five hundred dollars a year, but this amount was considered excessive. He successfully opposed efforts to require the commission to contain at least one member of the minority political party and to make the commission elective. Most significant, disagreement on whether the commission would be required to consider construction costs when setting rates produced a spat between Butler and fellow Allianceman J. S. Bell. Bell supported the provision, but Butler characterized it in the *Caucasian* as nit-picking that benefited railroads. Bell called Butler a demagogue, and Butler replied that Bell "would make a good pair" with Edwin Kerr, "who had delighted to call me a demagogue, and [to] apply the same epithet to all who favored a commission."[28]

Butler applauded the bill that eventually passed. It established a three-person commission with authority to regulate freight and passenger rates. It empowered the commission to reevaluate railroad property for taxes. Butler understood that not only did the commission promise to solve the problem of unfair rates and taxation but that it actually altered the structure of state government. The commission received extensive powers formerly reserved to constitutional branches and was designed to serve as both a legislature in setting rates and a "quasi court" in resolving disputes between railroads and shippers.[29]

Butler's reform work did not end with the commission. He also introduced a bill to study "the organization and regulation of private corporations." Although it failed, he wanted a law that would abate the crush of private incorporations. He objected to the tendency of legislators to enact permanent corporate charters with special privileges. Similarly, he sought to repeal a law giving railroads the power of eminent domain. His general aim was not to stifle the form of business known as the corporation. In fact, he would make it more attractive by eliminating special favors for some and regulating private property for public benefit.[30] The Alliance also wanted changes in legal procedure, and Butler introduced bills intended to speed up trials and pay state attorneys salaries, rather than fees for individual cases. He advanced the Alliance proposal of increasing the jurisdiction of justices of the peace and thus facilitating more informal decision making. He introduced a bill to regulate the fees of law enforcement officials in the claim and delivery of debtors' personal property, an important issue for debtor farmers. Altogether, Butler's legal reforms sought to reduce the costs and formalities of litigation.[31]

In addition, Butler supported increased funding for public education. Farmers agreed about the need for better common schools, and the 1891 legislature raised taxes for them. On the other hand, Alliance members disagreed about higher education. Despite the Alliance's official endorsement of a state normal and industrial school for women, many opposed paying taxes for it. The *Trinity College Country Life* argued that, as far as college graduates were concerned, the state already had "an over-production of these thin-faced gentry with high-sounding titles." Butler, on the other hand, repeating arguments he had made for several years, believed women especially needed higher education in order to become competent schoolteachers, to become financially independent while single, and so as not to "raise ignorant children." Yet an instruction from his tax-weary constituents required him not to vote for the bill. Undeterred, he helped publish an address supporting the school and asked his supporters to reverse their instruction. When this failed, he abstained on the normal school vote. Even without his ballot the legislature created a college for white women at Greensboro.[32]

The assembly achieved about as much as the Alliance could have hoped. It began the process of railroad regulation and increased funding for basic education. There were, however, notable disappointments. An attempt to diminish the power of the monopolistic American Tobacco Company lost, as did efforts to reduce the legal rate of interest for some contracts, limit agricultural liens, tax incomes, provide free school textbooks, and establish the secret ballot.[33] Yet for the Alliance these were fringe issues. Its platforms never intended to challenge the state's expanding market economy or dramatically shift the distribution of wealth among either whites or blacks. The organization wanted a clearer exercise of public authority over some types of businesses, such as carriers and lenders, to remedy marketing and financial inequities. Equally important, it was already clear that the Alliance's most important goals required federal action. Politically, it was no longer enough to control the state legislature.

Butler emerged from the assembly with a new and growing reputation. Leading newspapers singled him out for commendation. Naturally, not all the developing reputation was positive. Senator J. S. Bell's criticisms ex-

posed his tendency to assume others' bad motives, to seek to dominate political strategy, and to attack persons who got in his way. Whether these are
demerits or merits for a leader depends on one's perspective. At any rate,
they seem to have been consistent with his behavior as far back as his student days at Chapel Hill and therefore were rooted in traits independent of
political affiliation or ideology. As a public figure Butler was almost always
supremely self-confident, demanding, and interested in subordinating others to his leadership. Yet his record as schoolmaster, editor, lecturer, Alliance
president, and state legislator produced concrete results in organization, education, and law. Even if self-gratification was, as with most human beings,
a compelling motive for action, Butler acted diligently and successfully for
the Alliance. Politically, his leadership began to signal conservative Democrats, to whom he remained a minor figure, that he might be less Democrat
than Allianceman. A new force in North Carolina politics—young, motivated, and brandishing the cause of producerism—was on the scene.

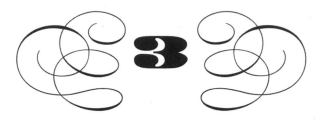

THE CRISIS OF ALLIANCE POLITICS

WHILE BUTLER EMERGED as a leader in North Carolina, some Alliance members moved toward independent politics. In 1890 in Kansas and the Dakotas, they broke ranks with the two older parties and endorsed "People's" candidates. In addition, at the December 1890 Alliance meeting in Ocala, Florida, plans were made for a mass convention of reform groups, to be held in February 1892. The convention's purpose was to prepare reformers for the coming election. Some Alliance members, however, were less patient. In May 1891, a meeting in Cincinnati established a separate national organization, the People's Party.[1]

Separatism was neither inevitable nor universally approved. Opposition derived from state and regional political traditions and was complicated by the federal nature of the union and presidential politics. For example, midwestern Republicans appeared more eager to break old party ties than were their southern Democratic counterparts, especially for state elections. This was more a result of third-party traditions in the region, such as the Union Labor Party, and the absence of whites' fear of black voting and officeholding than any greater commitment to Alliance principles. In contrast, during 1891 former national Alliance president Charles Macune, a Texan, hoped to keep Alliancemen within the Democratic Party, and the current national president, L. L. Polk, sent a letter to the Cincinnati convention advising caution in forming a third party. Still, even some southerners began to question the amount of reform possible within Democracy. Former president Grover Cleveland, who was intensely unpopular among southern Alliancemen because of his financial conservatism, was the Democracy's likely presidential candidate for 1892.[2] The distinction between a national third party and separate state third parties, especially for southerners, was crucial. A new national party could choose a presidential candidate and unite Republicans and Democrats in congressional elections under the Alliance platform. A state party lacked equally clear legislative goals and promised to inject race into southern elections.

In North Carolina, the Alliance caused sharp factionalism in Democratic politics. Conservatives' negative reaction to Alliance influence was a principal source of tension. Samuel A'Court Ashe, editor of the popular Raleigh *News and Observer,* wrote that government should interfere with the individual citizen as little as possible. Because of the incongruence of this principle with Alliance reform, in state politics it was in the interest of Ashe and others to label Polk and his followers as supporters of a state-level third party in 1891, although they were not. Alliancemen also disagreed among themselves. One faction, probably the largest, believed they should control the Democratic Party. This was the position of much of the state's leadership, including Butler and Polk. Another large group included men willing to compromise Alliance goals for the sake of keeping the Democracy in power. A common theme among these agrarians was fear of black rule. A very small group wanted independent action. The lack of interest in this option resulted from the perceived success of the Alliance within Democracy.[3]

AT THE END OF HIS senate term Butler believed the Alliance would dominate his party in both North Carolina and the nation. He therefore felt no one had any need to leave the Democratic Party. Essential to this perspective was the assumption that President Grover Cleveland's opposition to an expanded money supply, including the free coinage of silver, would doom his renomination. As a result, Butler complained when the new third party was formed in Cincinnati: "Is it not economy and politic to use," he asked, "the machinery already in existence to do our bidding for justice and good government?" It was only a matter of time, after all, before Democrats in the South and West could overthrow the eastern wing of the party and install Alliance principles.[4]

The intraparty fight revealed Butler's increasing synthesis of Alliance reform principles. The starting point for Butler's perspective was the Alliance's Ocala Platform. He supported all its proposals, and more important, his discussions revealed a new grasp of their interrelationships. During 1891 Butler portrayed the overarching goal of Alliance politics not merely as a series of specific laws but also as public control of the "instruments of commerce," the most important of which was money. Free coinage of silver would not suffice, nor would a onetime increase in circulated dollars "be of great benefit," except "as a means of temporary relief." Instead, Congress should abolish national banks, allow the free coinage of silver, create sub-treasuries, and increase the amount of money in circulation to fifty dollars per person. All this should be done to benefit "wealth producers," who were broadly defined as persons engaged in agriculture, manufacturing, and mining.[5]

In July 1891, Sampson's Alliancemen elected Butler to the state Alliance convention in Morehead City. The order faced two key problems. First, its ability to aid farmers through economic self-help programs, in particular the cooperative agencies, was becoming doubtful. Second, disagreement over its political relationship to the Democratic Party was producing a crisis that threatened to shatter the four-year-old organization. The state leadership, especially the president, Elias Carr, although committed to Alliance reform, rejected a challenge to Alliance opponents in the Democracy. Because Carr was retiring, the convention posed the question of whether new leadership would alter the order's political future.[6]

On 12 August, Butler became the state Alliance's third president. Although the evidence is limited, there clearly was contention over who would be Carr's replacement. Thomas B. Long wrote Polk that he would not support anyone "who is not your friend." Perhaps Butler's triumph represented a compromise between those Alliancemen who, like Polk, were increasingly dissatisfied with Democracy and those loyal to the party. Butler, after all, made his reputation as an Alliance editor and legislator willing to work as a Democrat. Moreover, his reform credentials and leadership skills were obvious enough. He had risen quickly through the ranks from local president, lecturer, and editor to state senator. He spoke well to groups and knew how to run an organization. He supported all the demands of the national and state Alliance and the cooperatives. In addition, Butler clearly sought the job; as with other leadership positions, he desired both the benefits and the burdens of leadership. It may also have mattered that Butler's youth had allowed him to avoid entanglements in previous statewide disputes. As a result, most of the state's Democratic newspapers said little about the convention, other than to reassure themselves that conservatism prevailed. The *Progressive Farmer* stated that Polk had nothing to do with the elections.[7]

From the beginning, Butler enjoyed being Alliance president. One of the more important of his responsibilities was lecturing. He traveled throughout the eastern part of the state, expounding the Alliance program. Occasionally, he appeared with prominent reformers, including U.S. Senator William

A. Peffer of Kansas and James B. Weaver, an Iowan who became the People's Party's first presidential candidate in 1892. The experience broadened his influence and helped his growing reputation for convincing oratory. Also important was administrative work. Butler appointed congressional district lecturers and confronted a decline in membership, which began in late 1891. The reasons for the decline were complex. Political disagreements played a role, and worsening economic conditions meant that dues were difficult to pay. In response, Butler developed plans for an Alliance Cooperative Relief Association, which would provide up to two hundred dollars for members' agricultural losses. When the program was implemented, however, undercapitalization and overwhelming demand crippled it.[8]

As North Carolina's president, Butler began to participate in the national reform movement. He attended the November 1891 Alliance meeting held in Indianapolis, where delegates rededicated themselves to the Ocala demands. Although a newcomer, Butler was chairman of a committee from the cotton states that tried to develop a means "to regulate the quantity, consumption, and marketing time and price" of cotton. He also attended the Conference of Industrial Organizations, a meeting of reform groups in St. Louis in February 1892. The conference reflected increasing sentiment for a national third party. Butler did not play an important role at St. Louis, perhaps because of his opposition to the third party. Nonetheless, he was on the 120-member platform committee. Back home, Tar Heel Alliancemen were "impressed with the solemn conviction that the enactment [of the platform] into law, and the faithful enforcement of law, will bring relief to our distressed industrial people."[9]

In fact, the St. Louis platform was a crucial component in Butler's evolving Alliance education, which was now reaching maturity. By early 1892, his comprehension of the manner in which the Alliance's reform demands were inextricably linked, along with how they articulated a broad critique of the American political economy, formed the foundation for beliefs that would last the rest of his life. His Alliance perspective found its clearest expression in a series of speeches he gave in late 1891 and early 1892. The substance of the speeches was particularly important because Butler was not an orator who played primarily to his listeners' emotions. As one Allianceman noted, he was "a cool, deliberate speaker," who emphasized the logic of reform. Contemporaries stressed his ability "to marshal his facts and arrange his arguments."[10]

Based on three years of Alliance teaching, Butler believed the current era had witnessed a betrayal of American ideals. The original principles of Amer-

ican government, embodied in the Constitution, represented the grandest
political plan ever contemplated. Butler looked to legal principles to define
needed reform. The source of the present problem was that Article I, Section 8, of the Constitution, which gives Congress power to regulate interstate commerce, created broad obligations that were ignored. Butler believed
these obligations included exclusive federal authority over the "instruments
of commerce"—land, transportation, and money. He argued that an expansive reading of "commerce" was necessary because since the Civil War there
had occurred "the greatest social, industrial and political evolution the
world has ever seen." This change produced the evils that caused rural depression, including centralized private power and a corruption of public
power for monopolistic ends. The remedies were apparent. The Constitution required the federal government to own the railroads. The government
should also own and operate the "transmission of intelligence," meaning
telegraphs and telephones. Regarding money, he demanded abolition of national banks and proposed subtreasuries to provide financial relief. The
Constitution also required public control of the money supply and a just
and flexible volume in circulation.[11]

Butler's analysis did not cite industrialization, commercial agriculture, or
urbanization as the causes of rural depression. Instead, government inaction and monopolistic greed by a few were to blame. Moreover, his intended
beneficiaries were "wealth producers," a massive group that included anyone responsible for the creation of material wealth. Butler's inclusive definition of producers prevented him from promoting a class struggle between
workers and owners over property rights. Instead, he believed the goal was
harmonious coexistence, absent monopolists, with each individual retaining "an honest reward" for labor. Altogether, Butler's political economy supported enormous growth in the regulatory functions of government in
banking and transportation, but little else. Maldistribution of wealth, unless
it involved monopolies, was not a major concern. With the important exception of protecting the needs of rural producers, there was no sweeping cultural critique in Butler's reform message, particularly on issues of race or
gender. Further, although in theory his ideas would enhance democracy for
producers, it left unanswered the daunting question of what democracy
should mean among producers. Because producers made up the great mass
of Americans, this was a gaping hole in Butler's and the Alliance's political
theory. It would never be fully resolved.[12]

IN EARLY 1892 Butler concluded that the appropriate political expression of these ideas was for the Alliance to control the North Carolina Democratic Party. He believed the Alliance was strong enough to elect candidates at all levels and could compose a Democratic platform in harmony with the February 1892 St. Louis document. He encouraged Alliancemen to elect friendly delegates to the Democratic state convention, and he called a special meeting of sub-Alliance representatives to be held the day before the 18 May Democratic convention.[13] Butler's ambition was novel. In 1888 and 1890, Alliancemen either lacked power to exert controlling influence or they focused on local legislative races.

Reactions to Butler's plan revealed deep division over Alliance politics. First, Polk's *Progressive Farmer*, which for some months had been leaning toward a national third party, agreed with Butler as to state matters. It announced that "our complaints are mostly national, hence we can afford to divorce state and national politics," and it encouraged Alliancemen to turn out for the Democratic primaries: "We will get as much reform as through a new party, and not run the risk of losing all chances." Further, "we cannot risk negro supremacy here. We must do the best we can." Polk privately stated that he hoped the "Butler programme may be carried out successfully." Others also approved. A Sampson County Allianceman argued that "Bro. Butler is doing big work. He stands uncompromisingly on the St. Louis demands." H. H. Boyce of the reformist *Arena* in Philadelphia was certain that Butler would have the state Democratic convention "absolutely under his control." The Alliance's *Washington National Economist* considered the state "wise, able, and conservative" and implicitly approved the distinction between state and national politics.[14]

On the other hand, there were rumblings for a state third party. Among the most vocal representatives of this group was Abbot L. Swinson, who later became an ardent supporter of political cooperation with Republicans. Swinson, editor of the *Goldsboro Agricultural Bee*, argued that the old parties represented capital, not people. He criticized Butler for attempting to merge the Alliance with the Democracy. According to James W. Edwards, an Allianceman, Swinson had asked Butler to form a third party, but Butler had refused. Edwards, however, considered Swinson "a crank" who "thinks he is the smartest man in Wayne County." Swinson eventually called a meeting to organize a local third party only days before the state Democratic convention in May. A few other local units of the new party appeared during the late spring.[15]

A more substantial Alliance faction rejected both a third party and Butler's stand. Some of these men objected to the drift of national Alliance thinking, particularly the more radical declaration in the St. Louis platform for government ownership, not simply regulation, of railroads. Elias Carr, former Alliance president, and J. Bryan Grimes, a Pitt County planter, represented this group. Their correspondence reveals a greater concern for the threat of Republicanism, including a high tariff, than do the comments of Butler or Polk. The *Progressive Farmer* revealed they had some following when it unconvincingly denied reports that sub-Alliances voted for resolutions criticizing Butler's strategy.[16]

Democratic opponents of the Alliance further complicated Butler's plan. These men considered the St. Louis platform "the most diabolical fabrication that ever emanated from the brain of men posing as [statesmen]." They understood the threat Butler posed and poured forth a torrent of abuse usually reserved for Republicans and African Americans. The *Wilmington Messenger* advised, "Butler and his gang should be turned out faster than they got in." The *Daily State Chronicle*, under the editorship of Thomas Jernigan, declared, "Butler, Polk, and other Third Party men plan to disrupt the Democratic party." Jernigan considered the possibility that the St. Louis platform could be "grafted" to a state Democratic document as "absolutely ridiculous."[17]

The struggle climaxed on 17 May, the day of Butler's Alliance meeting, and on 18 May, when the state Democratic convention met. Over eighty delegates appeared for the Alliance caucus. Butler presided; Polk also attended. In this great moment of political choice, Alliancemen irreparably divided over strategy. John J. Laughinghouse of Pitt County led a group opposed to Butler's plan, while other delegates demanded Democratic support for the St. Louis proposals. Some of the latter threatened to abandon Democracy if the St. Louis platform was not approved. Butler managed to get the convention to approve the St. Louis demands, but little else could be agreed on. Delegates failed to identify a preferred nominee for governor, although Butler urged them to nominate an Alliance candidate.[18]

At the Democratic convention an uneasy compromise prevailed. The three principal tasks confronting delegates were the selection of a nominee for governor, drafting the state platform, and the instruction of at-large delegates to the party's national convention. In the governor's race, attention focused on George Sanderlin, an Allianceman who supported the St. Louis platform; Julian S. Carr, a Durham industrialist; Thomas M. Holt, the current governor and a textile manufacturer; and Elias Carr, the former president of the Alliance. Although the extremes of right and left, Holt and

Sanderlin, led in the early balloting, neither mustered a majority. Elias Carr, the Allianceman who rejected the St. Louis platform, became the compromise candidate. The party's platform reflected this middling course. Less radical than the St. Louis document, it nonetheless echoed Alliance demands for free coinage of silver, abolition of national banks, and an end to speculation in agricultural futures and foreign ownership of land. Compromise also prevailed in the instruction of national delegates—there was not any.[19]

Butler recognized that his ambitious plan had failed, and he complained that the platform was "not specific enough." Yet he and others expressed general satisfaction with the result. He enthusiastically endorsed Carr's candidacy, considering it evidence of Alliance influence. Suggesting that he took a long-term view of political strategy, he consoled himself that it was a fundamental tenet of reform politics that "action should always be taken on [the] line on which the largest group of reformers are united." Similarly, the *Progressive Farmer* described the Democratic convention as a "signal triumph of the cause of reform over the political 'machine,'" and both Polk and his newspaper endorsed Carr. James Lloyd's *Tarboro Farmers' Advocate* cheered Carr and declared, "While the platform is not what is desired, yet it should be satisfactory to all."[20]

But defeat was deeper than these hopeful Alliancemen believed. Regular Democrats viewed the convention quite differently, emphasizing the triumph of old values. The *Charlotte Daily Observer* declared the Carr nomination to be "a distinct victory over the extreme element represented by Polk and Butler." As a result, the convention did not end the tension between the Alliance and the Democracy, nor did it unify the Alliance or vanquish anti-Alliance Democrats.[21]

BECAUSE OF THESE unsettled issues of control and the looming factor of presidential politics, Butler's efforts to turn North Carolina Democracy over to the Alliance collapsed during June and July. First, in the weeks following the convention many Alliancemen who supported Butler's plan decided that only a new party could advance their cause, at least for federal elections. On 18 May, 150 persons met in Raleigh and selected delegates to the People's Party's national convention. Nonetheless, at this meeting the long-standing distinction between state and national politics prevailed, as it adjourned before making it clear whether there would be a state ticket. On 23 May, an organizational meeting of a state Populist Party convened in Charlotte. Although it planned county organizing conventions and congressional nominating conventions for June, it also did not announce whether state and local candidates would be selected.[22]

Of equal importance was Polk's shift toward the third party. During the first half of May he continued to support Alliance Democracy in North Carolina but abandoned the national Democratic Party. Butler's relationship with Polk worsened because Butler remained committed to national and state Democracy. He even put pressure on Polk to stop his newspaper's endorsement of national Populism. As a result, on 31 May Polk withdrew the *Progressive Farmer* as the state Alliance organ. He then directed its policy to full encouragement, national and state, for Populism. Polk, however, did not have to face the consequences of his bold move. Within days, on 11 June, he died in Washington. The "what-ifs" created by these facts are legion; Polk, for example, was a likely candidate for president as a Populist. What is sometimes lost in the analysis of Polk's career, however, is that he encouraged support for reform within Democracy from the founding of the Alliance in North Carolina in 1887 until less than two weeks before his death in June 1892. Given Polk's broad ambitions for Alliance reform, his actions confirm the enormous political tensions that affected Alliance members.[23]

Despite Polk's death, the North Carolina Populist Party moved forward. By the end of June, fifty-six of the state's ninety-six counties were organized, and several congressional districts had nominated Populist candidates. In early July a North Carolina delegation participated in the Populist national convention in Omaha, Nebraska. It witnessed the nomination of James B. Weaver for president, Butler's former speaking partner, and the ratification of a platform that endorsed traditional Alliance demands for financial reform, government ownership of railroads, and prohibition of foreign ownership of land. Yet there were still lingering doubts about a state Populist ticket. The Martin County Populist convention, for example, endorsed the state Democratic platform but retained the right to remove the names of Democratic candidates from its ballot who opposed the St. Louis demands. Not until mid-July did the new party call for county nominating conventions and schedule a state convention for 16 August.[24]

North Carolina Populism began without any contribution from Butler. The twenty-nine-year-old Alliance president initially did everything he could to defeat the third party, both national and state. He still maintained that the best opportunity for reform was with Democracy and that a state Populist ticket "would be greatly to be regretted, and should be prevented if possible." Despite his recent exposure to the national Alliance, he retained a local focus. His narrow perspective appeared in an early July letter to Elias Carr, in which he claimed that the state ticket was "a hundred times more important to us that the national [Democratic] ticket." He visited some of the new Populists in an attempt to convince them to return to Democracy and even persuaded the Alliance executive committee to "loan" him money for his anti-Populist travels.[25]

Much like Polk several weeks earlier, however, Butler's new distinction between national and state politics allowed him to move gradually toward a break with his party, starting at the national level. His reaction to the Cleveland candidacy proved decisive. In early June he wrote Carr that the selection of Cleveland would "narrow" even a good party platform. He kept "some hopes" that delegates understood the opposition to Cleveland and would "not blindly and willfully doom the party to defeat." When Cleveland won the nomination he complained, "The Democrats do not usually waste their time in chasing rainbows, [and] are not accustomed to cripple themselves when starting in a race, as they are now doing." On 9 July he wrote Alliance leader Syndenham Alexander that the state Democratic Party should recognize the right of Democrats to vote against Cleveland and for James B. Weaver. In mid-July the *Wilmington Messenger* reported that Butler supported Weaver.[26]

Yet he remained a Democrat for purposes of state politics through July. He believed the third party could not win and that by not winning it would allow anti-Alliance elements, namely Republicans, to come into power. Thus, in early and mid-July, he tried to inject race into the campaign in a way that had never characterized his newspaper. In mid-1892, Butler was ideologically uncomfortable about challenging the need for white political solidarity. He maintained the same racist views about the abilities and rights of blacks as he had articulated in college. As a result, his newspaper announced that "Anglo-Saxon rule and good government" were "paramount." He published Sambo jokes and vitriolic correspondence demanding a "white man's government." This, of course, was the same expedient reform and racism theme struck by the *Progressive Farmer* in May. However, in contrast to Polk, for Butler leaving the Democratic Party meant giving up a local power he had cultivated since the late 1880s. Butler could look back on the past four years and fairly conclude that he had helped change the Democracy. No other North Carolina Allianceman who later became a Populist had so much political influence to lose by joining the third party. Populism presented Butler with the option of abandoning his own county organization.[27]

Between the middle of July and the first week in August, Butler's political

strategy reached a crisis point. The triggering event was the Third Congressional District nominating convention, held in Clinton on 20 July. In choosing the district's presidential elector, a fight developed over Alliance Democrats' reaction to the Chicago convention, which had nominated Cleveland.
Alliance forces, led by Butler and Cyrus Thompson, a Jacksonville physician,
refused to endorse the national platform and walked out when a motion to
elect a Cleveland elector was made. Reassembling separately, with resolutions introduced by Butler, they pledged to support the Weaver elector who
would be chosen at an upcoming Populist convention. Once word got out
that Butler rejected Cleveland, the Democratic press read him out of the
party. Furnifold Simmons, the party chairman, directed upcoming conventions for state offices to ban opponents of Cleveland. The order silenced the
voices of a large number of Alliancemen who opposed Cleveland and ended
the short history of Alliance Democracy.[28]

Within days Butler left the Democratic Party. Democratic journalist Josephus Daniels, who recorded his memories over forty years later, wrote that
Butler, in early August, told him there was going to be a Populist nominating convention in Clinton, and that he intended to prevent the men from
making "damn fools" of themselves. According to Daniels, on 6 August a
group of Populists on their way to the meeting stopped by the *Caucasian*
office and invited Butler to join them. Daniels reported Butler told them
that the Alliance had won great success in Democracy, would control the
next legislature, and would elect Carr, a reform governor. The Alliancemen
replied they could win on their own and "were tired of having a row in every
primary and convention." Apparently, Butler was convinced. When Sampson
County's Populist convention was called to order later that day, he became
its leader.[29]

Daniels, Butler's bitter political enemy for more than forty years by the
time he wrote this account, used the story to argue that Butler's shift to Populism was based on political expediency and not on any sincere sympathy
for reform. Daniels correctly pointed out that Butler did not make his decision to leave Democracy until his local power base was about to evaporate.
The point is revealing about Butler's political strategy and ambitions, suggesting his dependence on the continuing support of Sampson's farmers.
Yet the conclusion lacks meaningful context. Daniels's account did not mention that Butler had already stumped the state for every item on the St.
Louis platform and articulated a comprehensive understanding of the inter-
relation between Alliance goals. Daniels did not note that Butler had already endorsed Weaver, the Populist presidential candidate, or that three

months earlier Butler had tried to have the state Democratic Party run by the Alliance under a platform that called for government ownership of railroads and government money. Daniels also failed to mention the Simmons order and the personal abuse heaped on Butler by Democrats. Further, Daniels did not consider the reforms for which Butler was responsible as a legislator. He did not evaluate Butler's view that the third party would be a political failure, the only apparent difference between Butler and the Alliancemen who persuaded him to become a Populist.

As a result, Daniels's account is misleading. It suggests that Butler's journey to Populism consisted of a short walk on a hot summer day across the main square of Clinton. Instead, it involved an intense education between 1888 and 1892. By early August 1892, Butler was already supporting Weaver and Alliance control of the state Democracy. His shift to Populism is comparable with the path taken by L. L. Polk. Like Polk, Butler moved in stepwise fashion from Democratic reformer to supporter of national and state Populism. Indeed, Butler's acceptance of Populism is more remarkable than Polk's, given that Butler had limited exposure to the national movement, lacked Polk's age and political experience, and lived in a coastal plain county where white racism drove politics.

The question of Butler's broader motivation, even more so than the decision to join the Alliance in 1888, is important. By August 1892, Butler certainly believed in and supported the Alliance-Populist program. Speeches, editorials, and action in the state legislature and in the Alliance make that clear. This suggests the real question that dogged Butler in the summer of 1892, through the 1890s, and beyond: Through what political means could those ideals become law? Butler preferred the Democratic Party initially because he understood that in North Carolina both the Democratic and Republican Parties were strong and that a new party would have great difficulty drawing voters, particularly in the east. The chances for success with a new party were slim. Further, state politics were deeply affected by racial alignments, and Populism was neither willing nor able to challenge those alignments. When he joined the Populists, Butler saw reform as being for whites only. The future cooperation with black Republicans would have seemed impossible. Butler's decision to join the Populist Party was immediately motivated by the perception that his political career among white farmers in Sampson County would be over if he did not leave the Democracy. Certainly this shows a sense of self-preservation, and it would not be the last time the rank and file, misguided or not, would push him in a particular direction. Yet it is ironic that Butler's willingness to follow his neighbors was portrayed by Daniels as expedience. Perhaps, in Daniels's view, Butler would have been more "principled" if he had told his neighbors to go to hell and had stayed a Democrat, despite his support for the Alliance. This was the kind of choice Daniels made, after all. At its root, Butler's decision was a function of his political ambitions, his faith in Alliance principles, and his willingness to follow his supporters. It is difficult to make sense of his choice without accounting for all these factors.

In the years before he became a Populist, Butler's understanding of economic justice underwent dramatic change. His earliest editorials boosted Clinton, awaited the New South revolution, and advocated diversified agriculture and cooperatives. By 1892 he had confronted the county seat politicians and become a prominent legislator and editor. Underlying these experiences was an education that trumped his years in Chapel Hill; it included immersion in reform literature and contact with rural leaders. This persuaded him that "wealth producers" deserved new federal laws mandated by the Constitution. Joining the Populist Party was one consequence of this education, but Butler's experience revealed that faith in Alliance ideology was only one among many causes in the complex decision to support or reject third-party politics.

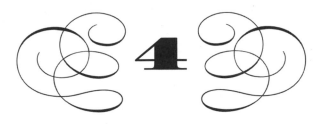

THE BEGINNING OF POPULIST POLITICS

BUTLER'S DECISION to join the Populists came at a pivotal moment in Alliance history. Within hours of becoming the leader of Sampson's Populists, he boarded a train for the annual Alliance convention in Greensboro. The meeting reflected the merger of what was left of the Alliance and the third party. One newspaper estimated that 90 of the 104 delegates were Populists. Despite the recentness of his departure from Democracy, Butler helped lead the unification of the Alliance and the People's Party. In a presidential address he blamed political tensions in the Alliance on "the monopoly corporations and the money power," which meant the "people must now submit like slaves or take political action for themselves." Their needs were "crystalized in the St. Louis platform—in land, transportation and finance, the three great cardinal principles of the Second Declaration of American Independence." Butler also offered an apology for his recent political maneuvering. The Alliance effort to control the state Democratic convention was a "mistake," and the withdrawal of the *Progressive Farmer* as the state organ was a "misunderstanding," for the paper had been "ever . . . true to the people" and "the most powerful agency of this Order in furthering its plans and executing its purposes."[1]

The delegates tried to conduct routine business but were hurt by a massive membership decline, which had accelerated since late 1891. The organization failed to admit its causes or devise effective solutions. Instead of political and ideological turmoil and the ineffectiveness of Alliance programs, Secretary-Treasurer W. S. Barnes blamed poor crops, low prices, and high interest rates alone, which meant farmers could not pay dues. The members also learned about the $455 "loan" provided Butler by the Alliance executive committee, which he used to promote Alliance-Democratic unity in the

spring. The convention resolved to cancel the note and indicated that Butler satisfactorily justified "the secret work." It also reelected him president.
As for the order's future, there was strong interest in maintaining self-help
efforts, particularly the State Business Agency and the Cooperative Relief
Fund. The Business Agency, with a capital of almost $35,000, was the most
financially secure Alliance agency in the nation. Nonetheless, for Butler the
emphasis had shifted to legislation. This meant the Alliance should become
a political device through which people could be educated to the rationale
of Populism.[2]

THE FOCUS ON POLITICS reappeared at the first Populist state nominating
convention, held just days later, on 16 August. Despite his relatively late conversion, Butler emerged as the party's dominant force, repeating a pattern
of organizational influence that could be traced from the Dialectic Society
to the Teachers' Assembly, the Sampson County and state Alliances, and the
1891 General Assembly. Delegates chose him chairman of the convention,
chairman of the platform committee, and presidential elector-at-large, a
critical position that required speaking across the state for Populist candidates. Actually, there was little competition for quality leaders, as the party
lacked experienced and capable spokesmen. Perhaps the most revealing
blunder in this regard was the nomination of Wyatt Patrick Exum for governor. Exum, a physician-farmer from Wayne County, was generally unknown
in Alliance or political circles. Even the Populist press did not know what to
make of him, describing him simply as a man who "has never been in politics." Omitted was any evidence of a serious commitment to the demands of
the party, his short temper, and his tendency to violence. Other selections
proved embarrassing. Thomas B. Long, candidate for auditor, resigned from
the race after it was claimed that he took funds from the North Carolina
Railroad. R. A. Cobb, the candidate for lieutenant governor, was accused
of stealing hogs. William A. Guthrie, candidate for associate justice of the
supreme court, was a corporation lawyer from Durham and a relative of the
industrialist Julian Carr; he had switched political parties twice in the past
five years. The Populist candidates, able or not, ran on the national Omaha
Platform and on state planks demanding full taxation of railroad property,
support for the railroad commission, a fair vote count, a 6 percent limit on
contract interest rates, and "encouragement" to education, agriculture, and
manufacturing.[3]

Despite problems with some of the nominees, the party managed a spirited effort. The small but determined group of reform newspapers was especially remarkable. In addition to the *Progressive Farmer* and the *Caucasian*, the *Henderson Vance Farmer*, the *Tarboro Farmers' Advocate*, the *Whitakers Rattler*, the *Hickory Mercury*, the *Salisbury Carolina Watchman*, and the *Marshville Our Home*, among others, spearheaded the crusade. Unfortunately for the agrarians, the papers were underfinanced weeklies, and most appeared in editions of less than two thousand. Democratic boycotts exacerbated the poverty of the Populist press. Democrats pressured readers to cancel subscriptions and persuaded merchants to drop advertising. Despite handicaps, however, the Populist press championed the party's message. The *Vance Farmer* argued for subtreasuries, while the *Rattler* denounced sectionalism, printed the Omaha Platform, stressed government ownership of railroads, and argued that Populist legislation would revive the golden days of Andrew Jackson.[4]

In his *Caucasian*, Butler spent most of the campaign attacking Democrats, apparently because he thought political choice, not ideology, presented the most difficult decision for voters. Much of the criticism addressed election practices: Butler was "in favor of white supremacy, but [was] not in favor of cheating and fraud in order to get it." He denounced the Democratic "rowdies" and "town roughs" he often faced, which included rotten egg throwers in Wilson. Butler perceived similarly foul motives in the sudden establishment of a competing weekly in Clinton, the *Sampson Democrat*. He complained that it caused him to lose "about all of [his] advertising" and that he was "pressed for money and had . . . difficulty making both ends meet." In early October a suspicious fire swept through the center of Clinton, destroying the *Caucasian* office and press. Reportedly, the fire began in the adjacent Alliance store. Butler lacked insurance, and only by using James Lloyd's *Farmers' Advocate* press was he able to publish during the rest of the campaign.[5]

Another persistent theme of the *Caucasian* was that Populism was the home of true Democrats. This would become a common line of contention throughout the 1890s. Butler argued that his old party repudiated its Jeffersonian heritage and now supported plutocracy. For the most part, this appeal assumed the People's Party should be composed of white former Democrats. This allowed Butler to attempt an escape from black voters by pointing out what all whites knew: Democrats relied on bribed and coerced blacks to win elections. Similarly, he stressed that Republicans were not becoming Populists, at least in eastern North Carolina, where the vast majority of Republicans were black. Nonetheless, Populism generated greater ambivalence in Butler's version of white supremacy. An African American minister told him after a speech that his words had just won 150 black votes for Pop-

ulism. Butler saw African Americans at the state convention and was aware
that some Populists nominated blacks for local offices. The liberation from
the Democrats' hypocritical "white supremacy," the persistence of Butler's
own racism, and the undeniable fact that at least some black voters were attracted to Populist reform initiated an ambiguous relationship between
African Americans, Butler, and third-party politics in North Carolina, one
that remained intensely complex in 1892.[6]

The Populists also made dozens of speeches. Their orators included some
of national stature, such as presidential candidate Weaver and Mary Elizabeth Lease of Kansas. Butler, however, was the Populists' leading orator. In
September he spoke in twenty-seven places in twenty-seven days, traveling
from Whiteville to Waynesville. During October and early November he
spoke in thirty more towns. Often he appeared with other North Carolina
Populists, usually Wyatt Exum or attorney Harry Skinner of Greenville;
he also debated Democrats Charles B. Aycock and Robert B. Glenn. Butler's
speeches reflected the emotions of the campaign. Reports describe sweating
orators, surging, noisy crowds, crudely formed platforms, angry hecklers,
and crowded courthouse squares. When Butler returned to Clinton, for example, a band of mounted Populists and Populist musicians provided him
with a special carriage. Less friendly receptions happened more often. Democrats in Lincolnton jeered. In Windsor, Democrats prepared giant, insulting canvasses with quotations from old issues of the *Caucasian*. White women
once offered Aycock a bouquet of flowers, but Butler received nothing.[7]

His oratorical style remained as controlled as it had been on the Alliance
circuit in 1891. According to the *Progressive Farmer*, he "took hold of his audience [with] words of truth and sledgehammer logic and facts, never using
a joke nor stopping for pent up applause." Populists praised him for this
strategy, which produced calm amid the fierce personal attacks of Aycock
and Glenn, considering his efforts a "cool, deliberate and intelligent mode
of warfare." The substance of Butler's remarks reflected his broad vision of
the reform movement. His speeches were also more forthright than much
of the material in the *Caucasian*, perhaps suggesting the urgency of personal
appeals. He reaffirmed that "laborers and men in all honest callings" did
not enjoy just rewards and that only sweeping legal reform would effect
change. This meant a federal income tax, abolition of national banks, the
creation of subtreasuries, the issue of all money directly by the federal government, and government ownership of railroads. Holding up a copy of the
party's program, Butler shouted that for real relief "you have to go to the
Omaha platform to find it." The gesture pointed the way to the abolition of

monopolies in transportation and finance and relief for the farmer. In contrast, Butler portrayed Glenn's and Aycock's emphasis on the need for a lower tariff, the threat of the "Force Bill" and excessive Union war pensions, and Weaver's purported Civil War record as demonstrating the emptiness of the Democratic campaign. Further, Democratic efforts to manipulate white racial prejudice were a dishonest attempt to scare the voter. He repeated this last point for years, even decades, without much success.[8]

Butler's leadership became even more important because of Exum's incompetence. In late August, just two weeks after his nomination, it was reported that Exum was found guilty in the Goldsboro Mayor's Court of using obscene language in a post office. Rumors also arose that he had previously been indicted for threatening a man's life. Exum made his worst mistake in late October, when during a debate he called Aycock a liar and refused to apologize. Following the confrontation, Butler, Aycock, and Exum left for Goldsboro, with a planned stop at Exum's home. After arriving at the farm, Butler asked Exum to apologize. He demurred, and another exchange of hostilities ensued. This time Aycock called Exum a liar and a scoundrel. Exum responded by pulling out a "big knife," leaping at Aycock, and cutting the future governor's head and arm. Butler jumped into the fray and separated the two men. The Democratic press had little difficulty using the incident to suggest Exum's unfitness for high office.[9]

Populist politics never occurred in a vacuum, and the reaction of North Carolina's Republicans to the Populist uprising further complicated Butler's plans. The Grand Old Party (GOP) was a significant if burdened force. During the 1880s, it consistently won over 40 percent of the statewide vote. Yet Democratic control of the General Assembly produced gerrymandered legislative and congressional districts, legislative control of local government, and an election law that facilitated Democratic irregularities in vote counting and registration. Moreover, internal disputes over federal patronage and tension over strategy between black and white Republicans threatened success. Predictably, the formation of the Populist Party elated Republicans. Disagreement arose, however, over whether to nominate a full Republican slate or to support the Populists' state candidates. The debate demonstrated the organizational opportunities presented by the Populist uprising as well as the weight of history. Arguments for and against Republican candidates peaked during June and July, the same time Butler struggled over the choice between Democracy and Populism. J. C. L. Harris's *Raleigh Signal* maintained that Republican support for Populists was the best plan and that corrupt blacks and federal officeholders controlled the faction that supported a separate ticket. The agitation against a separate ticket failed on 7 September, when Republicans met and nominated a full slate of candidates.[10]

The Democrats, having selected their candidates in May, presented a well-organized force when compared with the Populists and Republicans. Chairman Furnifold Simmons expertly coordinated the distribution of literature, the registration of voters, and the appearance of Democratic speakers. The party's campaign themes evidenced a course that would be followed for the rest of Butler's life. They downplayed economics and focused on the impending threat of black Republican rule. Republicans and Populists allegedly forged a statewide "fusion" agreement, "fusion" being a pejorative term that implied an unholy alliance of blacks and turncoat whites. Supposedly, the union supported "social equality" and desegregated public schools. Although grossly overstated, Democrats correctly perceived a real friendliness between rank-and-file Populists and Republicans. Some of this friendliness, especially in the piedmont, can be traced to opposition politics dating back to Reconstruction. Without the formal approval of their state organizations, a small number of local Populists and Republicans even carried out agreements to support each other's legislative and congressional candidates. Ultimately, however, hypocrisy characterized the Democratic racial position. As Butler knew, Democrats needed as many black votes as possible to carry the election. In November, more blacks were counted as Democratic than Republican or Populist.[11]

Another common Democratic tactic was libelous attacks against the integrity of Populist leaders. Presidential candidate Weaver appeared as a dastardly criminal, guilty of Civil War atrocities. Harry Skinner became a fond target of eastern papers, which only months before portrayed him as talented and patriotic. S. Otho Wilson, a prominent Raleigh Populist, allegedly led a violent secret Populist political order, Gideon's Band. Wilson, Butler, and the *Progressive Farmer* denied the organization existed. Democrats accused Butler of almost every sin imaginable. He was a gambler, a drunkard, and had stolen over one thousand dollars in Alliance funds. He was even "caught in the commission of a crime that is condemned and despised by honorable men the world over" while in college. The *Clinton Sampson Democrat*, without tongue in cheek, reported rumors that Butler and Exum sold the Populist Party to the Republicans for fifty thousand dollars. Democrats labeled him a deceiver, a traitor, and a "morally insignificant specimen of humanity." The *Charlotte Daily Observer* helped to popularize a nickname when it announced, "MaryAnn Butler is a 'bad egg.'"[12]

On election day, Democrats won a sweeping victory. They captured the

state's electoral votes for Cleveland, all the state-level offices, 8 of 9 congressional districts, and 139 of the 170 seats in the General Assembly. Populists
elected three state senators and eleven house members, while Republicans
elected Thomas Settle to Congress and put a mere seventeen men in the
state assembly. The Populist vote, about 17 percent of the total for state
officers, was extremely disappointing. Only three counties, Nash, Chatham,
and Butler's Sampson, managed a Populist plurality. Another seventeen
counties counted at least 25 percent of their votes for Populists, but virtually
all these were in the east. Overall, the performance in the piedmont and
mountain sections, where whites composed a greater majority, was particularly distressing. Urban support was virtually nonexistent—Populists drew
almost exclusively from rural Democratic ranks, and the few Republicans
who voted for Populists tended to be in counties where local cooperation
was arranged.[13]

Reaction to the results was as heated as the campaign itself. Democrats
announced that the election marked the political death of the People's
Party and Butler; they even conducted a mock burial of the defeated Populist leader. Populists and Republicans responded by dismissing the result as
fraudulent. In fact, Democrats had employed bribery, intimidation, false
counts, and the denial of ballots to registered voters. Butler claimed that
Simmons had used "corporation money" to purchase black votes. There was
deep and lasting effect among Populists to this experience. Democratic tactics, particularly because practiced against formerly loyal members of the
party, left a permanent mark of disgust and distrust. The fraud seemed to
motivate continued opposition as much as the need for economic reform.
In turn, this helped drive a shift in campaign strategy for 1894 that would
make vote fraud, not Alliance reform, the leading issue in state politics.[14]

The result deeply troubled Butler, but it also suggested an opportunity.
He was impatient by nature and expected something more from a campaign
than party leadership. In his relatively short public life, he had never before
lost so completely. Even the failure to capture the state Democratic Party
earlier in the year was not comparable. His career so far suggested that he
believed the end of politics was getting power and that Alliance-Populist
proposals would be meaningless unless they could be enacted into law.
Moreover, the election seemed to confirm his earlier view that Populists did
not comprise a plurality in any region of the state. Butler had further assumed that few Republicans, white or black, would become Populists, another conclusion supported by the election. This meant future recruits had
to be white Democrats, particularly in the east and the piedmont. At the

same time, the bitterness of the recent campaign made it improbable that Butler would return to the Democracy. Tossed into this complex bag of considerations was the fact that Democrats won by only a plurality, not a majority. This suggested Populists now held the balance of power, but it did not answer how or whether that power might be exercised.[15]

ANOTHER IMPORTANT consideration for Butler was that by November 1892 the Alliance was not providing a basis for Populist growth. Just one week after the election he traveled to Memphis for the annual meeting of the national Farmers' Alliance, held in a hall of the Young Men's Hebrew Association. Division prevailed, primarily along sectional and political lines. Especially important was disagreement over the order's next president. Midwestern Populists favored South Dakotan H. L. Loucks, while southern Democrats supported Charles Macune. Macune had earned the wrath of Populist Alliancemen by supporting the third party for some of 1892 but then returning to Democracy just before the election; Loucks won the presidency. Macune, claiming a Populist conspiracy against the "real" reform movement, then severed his Alliance connections. In contrast, as a southern Populist and former Democrat, Butler turned good relations with the Macune faction and the midwesterners into election as national vice president. He helped his candidacy with a speech in which he argued against sectionalism and for Populist politics. The delegates adopted a platform reaffirming support for a subtreasury, government ownership of railroads, an income tax, free coinage of silver, and an increased volume of currency.[16]

The meeting provided Butler's first success at a national level—he was only twenty-nine—but a crisis in the state Alliance shifted his attention back to North Carolina, where he was still president of the state organization. In early 1893 triumphant Democrats mounted a determined attack on the Alliance. As Butler predicted, the failure of the third party ensured that the new General Assembly, unlike in 1891, owed little to the Alliance. When given the opportunity, Democrats were more than willing to use the legislature as a pawn in the party's interest. In 1893 the state House of Representatives retaliated by passing a bill to repeal the Alliance charter. The ostensible justification was an alleged inequity in member liabilities for Business Agency debts, yet Democrats really believed agency funds were used in the Populist campaign and that the charter allowed the agency's money to serve as a "nest egg for Marion Butler's next campaign." Butler and other Alliancemen denied the allegations and presented amendments to the charter that would remove any doubt as to the personal liability of agency shareholders. Legislators rejected the amendments and passed a law that limited officers' salaries, allowed Alliancemen to withdraw their investments from the agency fund, and made ultra vires use of agency funds illegal. Ironically, the assembly acted to restore Democratic power by amending a private company's charter; the Democrats had not made a habit of punishing other companies, such as railroad corporations, because of political activities. Equally ironic, Butler had used Alliance funds before August 1892 to benefit the Democratic Party.[17]

During the summer of 1893 Butler's second term as state Alliance president ended. The organization was in dire straights. Dues paid declined dramatically from almost nineteen hundred dollars in the first quarter of 1892, before the rise of Populism, to about eleven hundred dollars in the first quarter of 1893. In the first quarter of 1894 less than seven hundred dollars was collected. Despite this, Butler displayed continuing faith. In a lengthy opening address at the August 1893 annual meeting, he cited the need for "cooperation and organization" among agricultural and industrial workers. He described the continuing purposes of the Alliance as "social and moral development," "intellectual development," and "cooperation in business efforts and industrial pursuits." He contrasted the farmers' failure to cooperate with urban businesses and professionals, which used unity to achieve favorable relationships with government. After the meeting the *Progressive Farmer* evaluated Butler's two years as president. It remarked that his administration was "an agreeable disappointment to thousands of his friends all over the state" but that his "splendid executive ability, brilliant leadership, pure unselfishness, untiring energy, and pluck . . . won the constant admiration of friends and demoralized all opposition." The paper cited mistakes, including Butler's hesitation to support a state third party, but it explained them as errors of the "head" rather than the "heart." It blamed decline not on Butler but on "the work of outsiders and a few traitors within."[18]

The newspaper captured the essence of Butler's experience. It recognized he supported and acted for all aspects of the Alliance program and was a preeminent example of the educational power of the Alliance. If there was cause for criticism, it was related to politics. Even on this point, however, the *Progressive Farmer* concluded that his actions did not harm the Alliance. His turn away from Democracy, regardless of whether it had occurred in late May 1892, like Polk's, or early August, did not change the order's fate, as the Alliance was ideologically and politically divided before and after those months. On the other hand, the *Progressive Farmer* did not ponder whether

Butler's doubts about the viability of a state Populist ticket were confirmed by the problems of the third party during the election: a weak press, the race issue, bribery and fraud by Democrats, the poor quality of Populist candidates, the continuing independence of most Republicans, the fragile quality of party organization, and the conservative legislature produced by Populist defeat. The harsh lesson was that it was unlikely the Alliance and the Populist Party would ever be the sole vehicles through which Alliance goals could become law.

THE END OF BUTLER's Alliance presidency redirected his attention to the future of the People's Party. Immediately after the 1892 election, Butler developed a political strategy he believed would respond appropriately to the election results. First, as for national politics, he concluded that Populists should offer a new political message to white Democrats by emphasizing financial reform, particularly the free coinage of silver. This was based on his assumption that white Democrats made up the only likely source for Populist growth. As the nation slipped into depression in 1893 and as President Cleveland feared increased economic woes if the de facto gold standard was not maintained, inflation via silver gained adherents, especially among Democrats. Because of popular assumptions about the need for money backed by metal, however, the bimetallic option was more palatable than Populist demands for government paper money issued so as to ensure a circulation of fifty dollars per capita. But there was no disagreement that genuine bimetallism would increase the money supply. Butler's interest in the political uses of silver appeared in his decision to speak at the Bimetallic League convention in February 1893. The brief address focused on the negative effect of a gold standard on cotton producers. He labeled free silver as the "burning question" in the South and traced growers' current distress to the "shrinking volume of currency." Consistent with the Populist platform, he boosted free coinage as a first step toward increasing the money in circulation.[19]

The catalyst for full agitation of the silver issue was congressional debate over repeal of the Sherman Silver Purchase Act. The 1890 law required the government to increase its silver purchases to 54 million ounces per year and provided that payment for the silver would be with legal tender notes redeemable in silver or gold. In practice, however, government redemption of the notes was in gold, and thus the act effectively diminished the gold in government reserves. Supporters of the gold standard feared that if government gold reserves dropped to zero, government debts would have to be redeemed in silver, destroying the gold standard and creating economic chaos. As a result, the Cleveland administration believed that by ending the required purchases, the government's gold reserves and gold money could be saved. In July 1893, Cleveland called Congress into special session to repeal the Sherman Act. The president did the silver movement a great favor. Spurred by a worsening national economy, a cry went up from farmers in the West and the South, who assumed Cleveland's policy guaranteed more declines in crop prices. Nonetheless, Democratic and Republican supporters of gold repealed the Sherman law.[20]

Butler's political attraction to silver—and it was always primarily a political and not an economic attraction—increased during the fight over the Sherman Act. In July 1893 he described the Sherman Act as "all that stands between us and the power and greed of the few shylocks who own and control the gold supply of the world." Delay would be fatal: "If we can't check and defeat the dark and bold schemes to enslave the wealth producers of America now, pray when can we?" When the repeal bill passed, he made vigorous attempts to attract silver Democrats, including Charles Aycock and Zebulon Vance, to his party. On the other hand, he portrayed Democrats friendly to Cleveland, such as U.S. Senator Matthew W. Ransom and Josephus Daniels, as evidence of the reactionary quality of the Democratic Party.[21]

Butler's use of silver was a political decision. He still believed that only public control of the money supply and an increase in the volume of money commensurate with economic growth, not simply free silver, would facilitate genuine relief. Only the government, not private national banks, had the right to issue money. He supported any form of public money, including "silver coinage and legal tender notes," that would raise the circulating medium to the Alliance-Populist standard of fifty dollars per person, a huge increase. Thus, the People's Party favored "the government issuing its own notes," "without the intervention of banking corporations, state or national." Money was simply the "representative of values, a medium of exchange, a mere convenience—a sign representing value or property." Because silver was old Alliance doctrine and had been rejected by both old parties but was more popular than Populism's fifty-dollar standard, as a political device it could expand the Populist electorate by drawing white Democrats.[22]

Silver, of course, was primarily an issue for congressional and presidential elections. During 1893, Butler chose another cause for North Carolina Populists: the fairness of the state's voting and local government laws. The voting statute used so effectively in the 1892 campaign gave Democrats virtually unrestricted control over registration and vote counting. As for local government, state law required the election of key local officials by the Democratic General Assembly. This appointment system vitiated local government by insuring Democratic officeholding even in Republican counties. Unlike silver, Butler's focus on voting and local government extended his party's reform agenda outside traditional Alliance-Populist boundaries, although it corresponded to the Populist ideal of increased democracy with a small *d*. Indeed, given its implicit assault on a political system directed to maintaining white supremacy, the attack on voting regulations in North Carolina was arguably the most daring thrust against existing political structures in the history of American Populism. Yet it derived not from some hazy or sentimental liking for "democracy" but from the political needs of a young politician who was struggling with the costs of leaving Democracy. As a result, political ambition and election strategy made Butler more accepting of interracial politics. He henceforth argued that "what is good for a white laborer in the South and West is equally good for a colored laborer," not just because this made economic sense but also because it had become a political imperative. Butler believed in white supremacy and assumed that the People's Party was a white man's party. But he also believed it was a party whose economic ideas would need the support of both whites and blacks to prevail.[23]

Butler's first year as a Populist demonstrated the enormous barriers to third-party politics. Nonetheless, he consistently defended Alliance and Populist principles. In speeches, in his newspaper, and at Alliance and Populist meetings, the persistent effects of Butler's Alliance education were clear. Yet translating these beliefs into law through politics proved infinitely more complicated than personal conversion. Butler's original base of support, the Alliance, collapsed under the pressures of competing political, personal, and reform visions. From the beginning, the North Carolina Populist Party lacked potential for significant growth primarily because of factors beyond its control, including the continuing strength of Republicanism among African Americans; the existence of a moderate reform wing of Democracy that successfully exploited white racism; the fact that key Populist demands required federal, not state, legislation; the regional differences in North Carolina politics; and Democratic control over local government and voting procedures. As a political leader who wanted both Populism and his own career to rise, Butler's response to the challenges posed by defeat in 1892 was not surprising. It seemed stupid, from his perspective, not to respond in any way to the defeat and simply run the same kind of campaign over again. He attempted to increase the standing of the Populist Party and its reforms by focusing on issues such as silver and voting rights that were arguably consistent with Populism and could also provide a realistic basis for Populist growth. Butler did not accept public life in order to lead a "movement culture," to make friends, or to make a social statement. He became a Populist to have a hand in the control of government. By 1893, Butler's lifelong search for the political means to obtain power through Populism was under way.

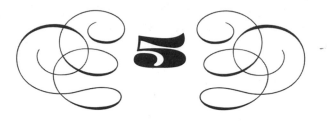

A POLITICAL REVOLUTION

IN 1893, Butler advanced his new North Carolina issues by deciding that Populists and Republicans, although maintaining separate organizations, should become allies to promote fair elections and local government. Political coalitions were not a plan unique to Butler or North Carolina. The history of Populism shows that every state Populist Party depended on coalition or acquiescence by one of the older parties for statewide success. Even in the stronger Populist states, including Kansas and Texas, elections in 1890 and 1892 revealed a critical inability to win a three-way race. Butler's decision demonstrated how far he had come from his Republican-baiting days. Unlike when he was a Democrat, it now mattered that Democrats could perpetuate their power by fraud if the voting and local government laws were not changed. Populists could not hope to change these laws on their own. Further, the rewards for success could be substantial. Butler knew the 1895 General Assembly would elect a United States senator for the seat held by Matthew Ransom, and he might claim that seat if Democrats could be defeated.

From Butler's perspective, achieving the coalition proved surprisingly easy. The *Fayetteville Observer* reported that in November 1892 Butler met with Republicans John James Mott, J. C. L. Harris, and Daniel L. Russell Jr. to discuss the possibility of Republican inaction or cooperation. The Republican connections became more developed after his discussions with Thomas Settle III and Richmond Pearson in 1893. From the beginning, Butler offered Populist support for Republican candidates in exchange for Republican endorsement of Populist candidates. Although winning elections was the short-term aim, the long-term strategy was to draw permanently from

Democracy persons disgusted with that party's policies. He urged Settle and Pearson to stress fair elections as the rallying point.[1]

Initially, the relationship between Butler, Settle, and Pearson was kept from the Populist and GOP rank and file. Secrecy would put Democrats off guard; it was also useful for quelling potential dissent among Republicans and Populists. Yet it had costs. Butler's promise to Pearson that Pearson would not have Populist opposition if he ran for Congress was made without consulting the Populists in Pearson's district. As late as August 1893, the *Progressive Farmer* doubted the validity of the "rumor" that Populists and Republicans would cooperate. This indicated the lack of an agreed direction. Further, when Butler's ally Congressman Thomas Settle supported President Cleveland's effort to repeal the Sherman Act, Butler expressed surprise to Settle, particularly in "view of coming events in North Carolina." Nonetheless, he promised to keep the *Caucasian* quiet about Settle's position.[2]

CENTRAL TO BUTLER'S coalition plan was an ambitious expansion of the *Caucasian*. After the election he purchased the *Tarboro Farmers' Advocate*, along with its subscription list, and established a new office in Goldsboro. On 2 February 1893, he issued the first edition of the Goldsboro *Caucasian*. Butler chose Goldsboro because of its strategic location at the junction of North Carolina's most important east-west and north-south rail lines. He soon claimed his paper was "read by more people than any other in the state." He dropped the "Pure Democracy and White Supremacy" slogan that had been on the paper's masthead, and labeled the *Caucasian* "Independent in Politics" and "Devoted to the interests of the wealth producers of North Carolina." Growth also required a more professional staff. J. E. Spence, formerly of the *Moncure Alliance Echo*, and W. G. Hollowell were hired to perform editing, sales, and production tasks, while Butler's first female employee, Hettie Whitehurst, became the bookkeeper.[3]

Financing the expansion was difficult. Subscriptions, at one dollar a year, provided some money, as did advertisements. Butler also attempted to raise capital of ten thousand dollars by incorporating the Caucasian Publishing Company. After allotting himself a controlling interest in the company, he appealed to all opponents of the Democratic Party to buy the remaining shares. He wrote Settle that he planned to "make the *Caucasian* a great southern weekly, and to establish it on a basis that will make it not only a powerful but also a permanent force in the South and in North Carolina." A persistent penury indicates that not much investment was forthcoming. Moreover, the residents of Wayne County met Butler's new enterprise with intense hostility. The *Goldsboro Headlight* welcomed him by announcing that it was "a shame and disgrace to count such a fellow as one of our citizens."[4]

In 1893 Butler made a decision of more lasting importance than moving the *Caucasian* to Goldsboro. On 31 August he married Florence Faison of Sampson County. Butler had known her for at least two years. During that time, although Alliance and Populist responsibilities often kept him away from home, frequent letters sustained the relationship. Faison possessed a keen intellect and a deep interest in public affairs. When Butler seemed to doubt that he had made the right decision by joining the Populists, she encouraged him to persist. Their honeymoon included a visit to an unusual mecca of romance, the United States Capitol. Butler conceded that Faison was a much better politician than he, and for the next forty-five years she was his closest political adviser. A descendant of Sampson's planter elite, Faison was an unlikely Populist. Her grandfather, William Faison, had possessed several thousand acres and more than two hundred slaves, making him the largest landowner and slaveholder in Sampson County. In 1857, Edward L. Faison Sr., Florence's father, inherited over thirteen hundred acres of the portion of the family estate called Mount Pleasant in eastern Sampson County. This land passed into her and Butler's hands following the demise of Populism, after her father's and brother's deaths.[5]

DURING 1893 AND 1894 Butler spent much time working for the state and national Alliances. In North Carolina, he was a frequent speaker at sub-Alliance meetings and was chairman of the state executive committee. Continuing decline pressed hard on the faithful. Annual dues receipts had fallen from over eleven thousand dollars in 1889–90 to about three thousand dollars in 1893–94. At that time, desperate plans for a revival were introduced at the annual convention. One proposal supported buying and selling exchange cooperatives. Although an exchange opened in Raleigh, business was not good, and by August 1895, cooperative marketing included only small amounts of produce. Delegates discussed a "Labor Exchange," which would have provided work for the unemployed; Butler supported it, but nothing came of the idea. The order also created the North Carolina Farmers' State Alliance Manufacturing Company. Unfortunately, it required five thousand dollars of nonexistent capital. Butler also worked for the national Alliance. In February 1894 he attended the National Alliance Supreme Council in Topeka, Kansas, and gave a speech urging farmers not to abandon the Alliance. The delegates adopted a platform that copied the St. Louis program of 1892. They also elected Butler national president. His election was the result of several factors: the organization was dominated by Populists; North Carolina was the leading Alliance state; and as vice president, Butler was already the likely successor.[6]

The prospects for rejuvenating the national organization were not good. Since L. L. Polk's death, the Alliance had stood for rural cooperation, the St. Louis platform, and the Populist Party. These policies did not produce growth or even maintain the status quo. Yet Butler persevered. He arranged to have the 1895 national convention in Raleigh, hoping that the beginning of a Polk monument, for which he had raised over seven hundred dollars, might inspire delegates. He also made plans, which failed, for a national Alliance exchange, a fertilizer bulk purchase contract, and a relief program. He met with Alliance allies, including J. R. Sovereign of the Knights of Labor, in an effort to unite reformers. He appeared before the U.S. Senate Committee on Post Offices and Post Roads on behalf of the organization, where he argued in favor of a government-owned telegraph system. He told the senators that all natural monopolies, including railroads, should be publicly owned.[7]

IN CONTRAST TO THE Alliance, politics in 1894 offered considerable hope. The off-year election scheduled for November allowed voters to focus on local candidates and issues. The potential distraction from state-level and especially presidential politics, as the 1892 contest showed, was enormous. Another reason for Populist hope was the successful effort to unify Republicans and Populists. In early 1894 Butler, as chairman of his party's executive committee, intensified correspondence with Richmond Pearson and Thomas Settle and encouraged other Republicans, including H. L. Grant of Goldsboro, J. C. L. Harris, and Daniel L. Russell Jr., to adopt cooperation. He wrote Pearson that "ballot reform should be made the rallying cry," adding that after a new election law was achieved "we can consult as to other measures and methods of reform." As party chairman, Butler delayed local Populist nominations so that cooperation plans could be solidified.[8]

Despite his early efforts at secrecy, cooperation never had much to fear from the rank and file. Populist support for coalition was widespread, and disagreement tended to focus on details. Further, given the legacy of biracial politics from Reconstruction, there was at least some precedent for joining together blacks and whites opposed to Democracy. In May 1894, Pearson publicly announced Butler's promise to support his congressional candidacy. Populists in Pearson's district criticized Butler and extracted a promise that he would refrain from interfering in local matters, but they agreed to support Pearson. Butler told Pearson that their anger was justified; he added that he would appreciate Pearson's letting him speak to Populists about strategy. There was no serious opposition in the Populist press to cooperation with Republicans, which was widely considered a possibility even among Populists not aware of Butler's activities. In fact, relations between local Populists and Republicans were so friendly that they endorsed cooperation on General Assembly candidates without prompting from Butler or the state organization. Given their common experiences with Democratic fraud in 1892, Populists and Republicans naturally agreed about the need for election law reform.[9]

Another good omen for success was President Cleveland's unsuccessful effort to stabilize a worsening economy. When the Sherman Silver Purchase Act failed to stop the drain on the national gold reserve, Cleveland proposed to issue federal bonds to increase the gold in the treasury. Butler used Cleveland's troubles as part of his continuing attempt to bring wavering Democrats to Populism. He accused the president of being in a corrupt bargain with gold, Wall Street, and national banks. Similarly, Cleveland's dispatch of federal troops to crush striking railroad employees at Pullman, Illinois, prompted Butler to describe the president as a "tool of corporate interest, a traitor, and a drunkard if reports are true." Some of this appeal was successful. J. J. Long, of the Alliance executive committee, and William H. Kitchin received grand welcomes when they left the Democratic Party and joined the Populists.[10]

The Populist campaign got under way in earnest in June 1894, when the party executive committee formally called for delegates to the state convention. The committee adopted Butler's broadened appeal to white Democrats, urging anyone in favor of free silver, a further increase in legal tender beyond free silver, an income tax, election reform, effective antitrust laws, and economical government to participate in the Populist conventions. The criteria highlighted the state-level issue of election reform, and the committee selected Butler to write the party platform. In late July, Butler met with Republicans H. L. Grant, Robert M. Douglas, J. J. Mott, J. C. L. Harris, and O. H. Dockery, who favored cooperation. Three prominent African American Republicans also conferred: A. R. Middleton, James H. Young, and

Henry P. Cheatham. By this time secrecy was less a consideration than the need to mobilize Populist and Republican forces.[11]

The second North Carolina Populist convention met on 1 August, and Butler ran the affair without dissent. A committee on the platform was appointed, with Butler and Harry Skinner as its most prominent members. After it ratified his draft, Butler read the document to the delegates. The platform combined traditional Populist-Alliance concerns with what Butler considered the key issues of the election. It endorsed the "principles of the People's party, both state and national." It demanded the abolition of national banks, the substitution of "legal tender Treasury notes" for private national bank notes, and the free coinage of silver. All money of every form should be legal tender, money should be issued in sufficient volume to put the country on a cash basis, and volume should be increased according to business needs. The platform advocated corporate and personal income taxes, direct election of senators, an end to speculation in "agricultural and mechanical productions," and strong immigration restriction. Populists expressed sympathy with industrial labor, but they criticized strikes and urged "the wise use of the ballot" to solve "the grave conditions that confronts [sic] our social progress." Most important, the party demanded a new election law and an end to legislative appointment of county commissioners and justices of the peace. It even made a direct appeal to black voters, supporting four-month school terms "for both races" and stating that "every man white or black must have free access to the ballot box." This did not mean that Butler or the Populists had abandoned white supremacy, but it did show that certain concessions were in order.[12]

The platform demonstrated the key components of Butler's political strategy. North Carolina Populism now stood for rearranging local government and voting rights as well as new methods of banking and transportation, the latter of which could be addressed only by Congress. The platform, with its implication of some black political rights, was more radical than anything ever proposed by the Alliance or the Populist Party in or before 1892. The party supported both increased political democracy at the local level and federal regulation in the interests of producers. In 1894, North Carolina Populism also contemplated greater economic justice by strengthening the market, competition, and private property so that "every man shall prosper according to his labor and his merits." Populists wanted more government intervention in the economy, but not so much as to interfere with their own property rights. They wanted industrial development, but not of a venal and monopolistic variety, and commercial agriculture, as long as the system increased opportunities for producer profits. Populism meant expanded black rights, as long as those rights could be exercised within the context of white control. The mixture of reform and tradition was an amazing political accomplishment, undertaken only two years after the collapse of Alliance Democracy.[13]

The delegates chose candidates for the few state offices at issue. They endorsed two Republicans, William T. Faircloth and David M. Furches, and two Democrats, Walter Clark and Henry G. Connor, for the supreme court. They picked Allianceman William H. Worth for state treasurer. It would be difficult to imagine a less philosophically coherent group. Faircloth was a conservative Republican, while Clark approved of many Alliance reforms. Worth was the Populist business agent of the state Alliance, whereas Connor was a Wilson attorney whose primary occupation was executor of the estate of a national bank president. The nominees for the high court reflected several factors. First, few lawyers became Populists. Second, despite Butler's appeal to judicial nonpartisanship, the ticket was a ploy to draw recruits from both old parties to the Populists. Third, the nomination of two Republicans demonstrated Populist good faith toward cooperation. Finally, the nominations and the emphasis on nonpartisanship attacked the current Democratic court, particularly a recent election law decision.[14]

Butler's strategy and the convention put Democrats on the defensive. Turmoil over national issues contributed to the challenge, as Cleveland's policies irritated many party members and generated dangerous divisions. In a convention dramatically different from the one in which the Alliance attempted control in 1892, Democrats wrote a short platform that simultaneously demanded free silver and praised Cleveland. They ignored Populist proposals for new voting laws and longer school terms. The party nominated four incumbent justices, James E. Shepherd, Armistead Burwell, James C. McRae, and Walter Clark, for the supreme court. Shepherd, Burwell, and McRae represented extreme conservatism; Shepherd considered the Reconstruction-era abandonment of common law pleading as dangerously radical. The party chairmanship fell to a young James H. Pou, who lacked the political skills and gall of his predecessor, Furnifold Simmons.[15]

In contrast, Republicans developed an energetic new strategy. To be sure, not all of them wanted a relationship with Populists. The *Union Republican* shuddered at agrarian economics and proposed coalition with "manufacturers, [and] the businessmen of the state." Most Republicans, however, regarded the independent policy of 1892 as a regrettable failure. H. L. Grant,

Settle, and Pearson, among others, lined up cooperation delegates for the Republican convention by drawing on the strongest bonds between white and black Populists and Republicans—a bitter hatred of Democrats and the belief that Democratic thievery could be stopped with a new election law. At the convention, under the leadership of Grant, the state ticket chosen by the Populists won approval. Equally important, the Republican platform demanded a new election law and a new county government law, just as Populists had hoped. A cooperationist, Alfred Holton, became state chairman.[16]

After the conventions, Populists did not perceive unity with Republicans as a contested issue. The Populist press unanimously agreed on the perfidy of the Democratic Party, and not a single paper opposed cooperation. The *Progressive Farmer* congratulated North Carolina Republicans on their sincere efforts to depose the state's "Wall Street Democracy" and informed its readers that many rank-and-file Republicans would become Populists. Butler's newspaper portrayed helpful Republicans as men of "good character" pledged to carry out election law reform. Further, Republicans drafted a platform that was the "best ever put forth by that party." Even the racial aspects of the coalition received positive attention. There was favorable discussion of the Populist plank endorsing four-month schools for both races; Butler stated it was intended to help rural blacks.[17]

Despite the potential for overwhelming complexity, cooperation was easily consummated at the local level, where the rank and file selected congressional and state assembly candidates. Populists and Republicans tended to agree about the aims and means of the campaign and organized cooperation in a variety of ways. They selected candidates jointly, or delegates met separately and nominated partial party tickets, leaving the remainder of the slots for the other party to fill. Local parties also ratified the other party's choices or, in districts where Democrats were a decided minority, chose a buffer candidate to ensure success. Butler met and corresponded with Populists to make sure cooperation proceeded smoothly and to guarantee a just representation of Populists. The most significant problem during the campaign involved one of the "nonpartisan" nominees for the supreme court. Democrat Henry G. Connor, embarrassed by his choice, declined to be included on the ticket, citing business responsibilities. Republicans hoped Connor's exit would allow them to pick one of their own as a replacement, but Butler asked a Raleigh attorney, Walter A. Montgomery, who was sympathetic to the farmers movement and who had been a Democrat, to replace Connor. Republicans agreed to put Montgomery on the ticket.[18]

In addition to supervising the details of cooperation, Butler directed other features of the campaign. As early as January 1894, he formed People's Party clubs. He planned one to three clubs in each township, intending to use them to appeal to white Democrats. Unlike the Alliance, the clubs were not secret, did not require dues, and could include citizens of all occupations. Not surprisingly, most units appeared where the Populist Party was already strongest. Butler also took on the enormous task of ensuring fair elections by asking local Populists to become judges of election. The existing law required Democratic officials to appoint judges from minority parties, and Butler sought reliable men to fill the positions.[19]

His campaign activities extended to the stump. Because of his duties as campaign coordinator, however, he made far fewer speeches than in 1892. Nonetheless, the appearances drew large crowds. Butler's speeches reflected the logical, legalistic approach that had characterized his oratory since 1890. They also contained the same comprehensive reform vision. Early in the campaign he usually appeared at Alliance functions, such as a 12 July address at Elizabethtown. There, in a grove by the Cape Fear River, he complained that farmers had produced great wealth but that this wealth was in the hands of monopolists, who had taken it by means of "legalized stealing." The only remedy was to pass laws that would make the "stealing" illegal. For three hours Butler catalogued those laws. Most important, they would require railroads to be publicly owned and money to be taken out of the control of corporations and monopolies.[20]

Different themes appeared in a debate with Furnifold Simmons at a rural store, where Butler directed his remarks to Democratic failings. As in 1892, Butler focused on attracting members of his old party. According to the Populist, Democrats in Washington failed to achieve tariff or currency reform. Indeed, they had done nothing but help monopolists and "shylocks." Butler perceived his old party's obsession with the tariff as part of a conspiracy by Democrats, Republicans, and "the money powers and the railroad monopolies" to confuse the public. He argued that the contraction of currency was a more serious source of economic decline and stated that he would rather "pay the tariff under the [Republican] McKinley bill than . . . pay the tariff under the Democratic [tariff] on a single gold standard." Regarding the income tax, he claimed that the law passed in 1894 as part of the Democratic tariff was a "fraud," a "sham," a "humbug," and a "cowardly makeshift." It was not graduated, as the Populists demanded; it would raise only a fraction of the needed revenue; and it "was passed for campaign purposes to fool you and is so drawn that it will prove a failure." Butler also attacked the state election law. In 1892, he claimed, Simmons used the law to encourage vote stealing, false registration, the appointment of incompetent election judges, and ballot box stuffing. Butler justified cooperation as an attempt to defeat fraudulent elections.[21]

The Democratic campaign responded in kind. Among the more outspoken journals was a resurrected *News and Observer*, recently reorganized after being purchased by Josephus Daniels. Daniels's paper attacked Populist support for "fiat money," arguing that the use of "gold and silver, and state bank notes properly secured," would allow recovery. Similarly, the *Clinton Sampson Democrat* opined that "the socialistic tendencies of populism on the one hand and its reckless extravagance on the other should cause our people to think seriously." The Clinton newspaper warned of the Populist threat to capital and published a letter by a purported "laboring man" that urged workers to vote for Democrats because Democrats employed them and Populists were poor. The *Fayetteville Observer* distinguished the irresponsible Populist demand for government-issued legal tender notes with free silver, a safe Democratic reform. Another tactic was to claim that the alleged omission of government ownership of railroads and the subtreasury from the state Populist platform was evidence that Populists abandoned their principles. It was true that the subtreasury and railroad demands were not specifically mentioned in the 1894 platform, but they never had been. As in 1892, express approval of the national platform by the state platform implicitly endorsed those reforms. Butler responded that he did not think that the federal subtreasury or ownership of railroads would be decisive political issues in the state election. Nonetheless, he reaffirmed his support for the proposals and offered to meet any Democrat "at any time or place and discuss these great questions."[22]

Democrats also mustered blistering personal attacks. They accused Butler of having no principles except personal gain. He was inconsistent, unreliable, and a crypto-Republican. The *Charlotte Daily Observer* considered him "nearer to being an absolute boss tha[n] any man North Carolina has . . . known." His handsome physical appearance and careful grooming habits led to the claim that he kept his followers in line by "billowy hair and . . . [a] buoyant brow." Democrats dismissed Butler's appeals to blacks with the comment that "he has no friendship or use for them other than a spasmodic desire to get their votes." The *News and Observer* added that he ought to change the name of his paper so as to persuade "the colored man that he is his friend."[23]

As in 1892, the Democratic strategy also included intimidation and corruption. To counter Butler's plan for Populist presence at the polls, Chairman Pou wanted at least twenty-five Democrats to guard each voting place. He advised challenges to Populists and Republicans suspected of illegal registration. William B. Rodman, party chairman in the First Congressional District, mailed hundreds of dollars to local party workers for the purpose of purchasing the votes of blacks in eastern counties. One Democrat surmised that "the biggest pile of money" would ensure black support; another reported, "Two negroes have volunteered to carry their township for the democratic nominees for $25.00." Many varieties of fraud, including improper challenges to voters, took place.[24]

Despite illegal Democratic efforts, on 6 November Republicans and Populists swept Democrats from control of the state legislature. Populists alone composed a plurality in the next General Assembly, which suggested the spectacular effect of the Populists' placing themselves on cooperation tickets. Populist W. H. Worth won election as state treasurer, and seven coalition congressmen, including three Populists, were sent to Washington. Moreover, because of the recent death of Senator Vance and the end of Senator Ransom's term, the legislature had the unusual opportunity to select two new U.S. senators. Butler's judicial strategy was also successful. Faircloth, Furches, Clark, and Montgomery formed a cooperationist majority on the state supreme court.[25]

Although the contest emphasized state matters, an interview given by Butler to the *News and Observer* just after the victory showed he was now prepared to return to federal goals. He used the interview to promote the subtreasury and government ownership of railroads, stating that "money should be issued and credit based upon products." The real need was for government control of currency and a flexible, not a metal-based, money supply. Both financial and transportation reforms were supported by the principle that "great interests must be controlled either by the government or by corporations, and where the corporations are monopolies per se they should be put in the hands of the government."[26]

MOTIVATED BY THE stunning triumph, in December Butler announced plans to move the *Caucasian* to Raleigh. He hoped it would issue a daily edition. He had great faith in the power of newspapers and regretted the Democratic monopoly of the daily press. His new paper would "be a People's party paper, and . . . strike from the shoulder on People's party principles." Butler, with Florence and their baby daughter, had just arrived in the capital when the first Raleigh edition of the *Caucasian* appeared on 27 December 1894. He hired Baylus Cade as associate editor and Robert C. Rivers as foreman of its press. He also retained a Goldsboro edition under W. G. Hollowell and continued the Clinton edition under E. M. Peterson. This newspaper "empire" suggested his optimism in Populism's and his own future.[27]

Butler could not hope to finance these operations from subscriptions or advertising. The Raleigh market was crowded; others already published six weeklies and dailies in the town of ten thousand. Butler received about two thousand dollars a year as president of the national Alliance, and his anticipation of five thousand dollars a year in salary as a U.S. senator provided means for subsidy. He reached for more support by incorporating the new Caucasian Publishing Company and turning to Republicans and recently elected Populists for help. Early stock subscribers included Populists William A. Guthrie, Congressman William F. Strowd, Alonzo Shuford, W. H. Worth, and Republican J. C. L. Harris. Another investor was Benjamin N. Duke of the Durham tobacco clan. The Dukes were Republicans, attracted to that party by its high tariff stand and conservative financial program. Yet during 1894 Duke supported Populist candidates, including the congressional campaign of William F. Strowd of Chapel Hill. Just after the election he sent five hundred dollars to Settle, to be given to Butler. By the end of the year Duke wanted to purchase one thousand dollars' worth of stock in the *Caucasian.* The meaning of Duke's support would become clear during the upcoming legislature. At the time, it was common practice for North Carolina politicians or editors from all three parties to appeal to Duke and his money. In June 1894, for example, Josephus Daniels asked Duke for his opinion "of the best method of enlarging the circulating medium."[28]

The end of the campaign provided an opportunity for Populists to evaluate the election and Butler's role in it. Populists overwhelmingly favored the result and Butler's leadership. There is not a single extant Populist paper that took the editorial view that coalition was wrong, that it was a betrayal of principle, or that it threatened the enactment of demands as stated in the party's national platform. An individual exception was Populist George E. Boggs of Waynesville, who was not so pleased. Boggs published a statement in which he claimed that with more education and without Republican cooperation the state could have had a Populist majority by 1896.[29]

Ironically, Boggs's complaint showed why cooperation politics became a permanent part of North Carolina Populism. Although Boggs argued that Populism would grow without cooperation, he failed to address the critical question of which voters would turn to Populism based on education about its principles. Mountain whites? African Americans? Textile millworkers?

Rural yeomen in the piedmont? Democratic former Alliancemen? Cooperation, at least, provided a concrete, if flawed and costly, answer as to how the Populist minority could exert influence and use that influence at all levels of state politics. It offered a way to reach out to eastern and piedmont Democrats disgusted with Cleveland's pro-gold policy as well as to African Americans and Republicans who wanted election reform. Boggs's proposal ignored the past six years' evidence that even Alliancemen, much less other Democrats and Republicans, were not likely to be attracted to Populism for its creed alone. There were simply too many other dimensions to politics, including established party and personal strengths and local loyalties that had no direct relation to the federal issues of money or railroads. Moreover, Populism had many limiting features, such as its lack of special attention to the economic problems of African Americans, industrial labor, and urban voters. Most important, while correctly seeing that cooperation raised problems, unlike most North Carolina Populists Boggs failed to acknowledge that voters operated within a political structure which required success at the local level. Cooperation was attractive because it offered a mechanism for success in that arena. As a result, throughout the 1890s local Populists, not Butler and the state Populist organization, would be the foremost advocates of Republican cooperation. Only a Democratic paper praised Boggs's analysis, whereas the *Progressive Farmer* disagreed and defended Butler.

During 1894 Butler battled for political power and won. There were no dramatic changes in his understanding of the goals of Populist reform. Indeed, at this time he reached the pinnacle of national Alliance leadership and continued to advance the goals of that order. The challenge after 1892 was to develop a means of giving his reform ideas political meaning in the towns and counties of North Carolina. He concluded that in the short run this meant using Republican votes to overthrow the Democratic regime. The victory instantly had broader implications. It convinced Butler that another type of cooperation, this time on federal financial reform, could start the entire nation down the road to a Populist era. The result would revolutionize the national party system, advance Butler's career to the highest levels of the federal government, and change both the Congress and the presidency. In late 1894 all things seemed possible.

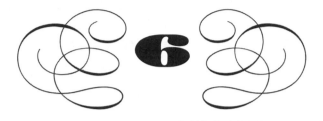

SILVER AND THE SENATE

FOR THE FIRST TIME since Reconstruction, Democrats in 1895 did not write North Carolina's laws. During its three-month session, the legislature increased the property tax for schools and reduced the legal rate of interest on oral contracts to 6 percent per year, but its most significant accomplishments were an election law and the reorganization of local government. To a large extent Butler's future political strategy depended on favorable election laws, and the assembly crafted a statute that contrasted sharply with the antidemocratic, anti–third-party laws that were gaining favor in other states. At least for Butler, it had become part of Populism's charge to upset that trend. Under the new election law, registrars and judges of election could be qualified only after recommendation by a state party chairman and appointment by a clerk of court, who was elected at the county level. The legislation strictly penalized bribery and coercion and made it more difficult to challenge voters on election day, destroy or disqualify ballots, or distort vote totals by a fraudulent count. A section for illiterate voters allowed different colored or specially marked ballots for each party. The law provided for strong ballot boxes and the counting of ballots in candidates' presence.[1]

Local government was also reordered. Under the existing county government system, the General Assembly appointed justices of the peace, the initial layer of the judicial hierarchy. The justices, in turn, selected the county commissioners, the men who had authority to direct county affairs. This ensured that justices and commissioners would be Democratic and white even in Republican and black majority counties. The new statute, however, provided for the election of justices at the township level, the smallest unit of government. In addition, county voters won the power to elect the three county commissioners. Nonetheless, the law allowed up to two additional commissioners to be appointed by a superior court judge, elected on a statewide basis, if five electors petitioned that the "business of the county" would be "improperly managed" and two hundred voters approved the petitions, at least one hundred of whom owned real property. To make the antiblack implications of this compromise of local government clear, the two new commissioners could not belong to the party that held a majority on the commission.[2]

The legislature also elected two new U.S. senators. The coalition parties agreed that each of them would choose one senator, with Populists getting the six-year position and the GOP getting the two years remaining in Vance's term. Butler easily won the unanimous approval of Populists for Ransom's old seat. Republicans, however, were divided. The traditional rule was to have one eastern senator and one from the west, so the choice had to be a westerner. Butler tried to convince the assembly to nominate someone in favor of free silver, and he approved of the eventual choice, Jeter C. Pritchard of mountainous Madison County. He also seems to have promised the Republicans a full six-year term in the next election, at least if cooperation was renewed in 1896. Butler presented his credentials to Vice President Adlai Stevenson in February 1895, but the Senate did not go into session until late in the year.[3]

Populists reacted favorably to the assembly. The *Progressive Farmer* announced, "As a whole it was the best legislature that has assembled since the war." It particularly commended the new local government and election laws. Populists also congratulated themselves on Butler's elevation to the Senate. The *Wadesboro Plow Boy* reported that after Butler's nomination, "speaker after speaker arose to second the same. Not a dissenting vote or whisper could be heard. Never was there a nomination of any man for any place more unanimous." Its editor promised that "standing boldly and firmly upon the great and undying principles of Populism," Butler "will hold aloft the people's banner and defend the right and condemn the wrong."[4]

The new senator made a substantial contribution to the assembly's work. Although not a member, he appeared on the floors of both houses, buttonholed legislators, and directed strategy during caucuses. He worked with other nonlegislators, including Daniel L. Russell Jr. and Harry Skinner, to prepare proposed laws. By achieving a productive body of reform, he hoped to increase political support for Populism. Yet, as in the preceding campaign, he assumed the deliberations should appeal to "the cautious and hesitating class," meaning primarily white Democrats. Caution manifested itself in several contexts. First, Butler fought against pressure from some Baptists,

Marion Butler, about the time of his election to the U.S. Senate.
(Courtesy of the North Carolina Division of Archives and History)

Methodists, and Populists to eliminate state funding for the university in
Chapel Hill. Denominational leaders worried about the future of their colleges, and more important, many Populists resented the privilege symbolized by the university. As in 1891, Butler strongly supported public higher
education, and the university received its regular appropriation.[5]

Butler's efforts to advance a "cautious" reform image reached its most dramatic application in a series of maneuvers connected to Benjamin N. Duke.

Duke, a Republican, was friendly toward Populists for the time-honored reason that he wanted a genial relationship between his business interests and those in power. Butler and the new Populist state treasurer, W. H. Worth, along with Populists in the legislature, were willing to help. As already noted, Duke made useful donations to the cooperation campaign and invested in Butler's Raleigh newspaper. By January, installments in Duke's one-thousand-dollar *Caucasian* stock purchase began flowing to Worth, who acted as both state treasurer and bookkeeper for the Caucasian Publishing Company. Worth's bond as state treasurer was largely paid for by Duke.[6]

After the legislature got under way, Duke exerted some influence. His lobbyist, James E. Stagg, pressured legislators not to pass any labor bills, such as those which might limit hours or child labor. Although such bills had not been contemplated by the Populist platform, none were passed. Duke also wanted no new taxes. The evidence that Butler helped Duke on this issue is uncertain. The legislature did not raise tax rates on banks, which the Dukes owned. On the other hand, it enacted a graduated tax on the capital stock of corporations besides banks, railroads, and insurance companies. It is doubtful this bill could have passed without Butler's knowledge or support. Duke also opposed a new antitrust law, and here Butler's role is clearest. Duke opposed a bill, the substance of which is uncertain, introduced by Senator J. E. McCaskey of Martin County. He thought it made any partnership or corporation illegal and would "utterly destroy business." In fact, Duke believed the motivation for the bill was not antimonopoly reform but intercorporate warfare sponsored by rival tobacco magnate R. J. Reynolds of Winston. Duke met with Butler about the problem and discussed it with Settle. Butler advised a quiet fight against the McCaskey bill, which never came to a vote.[7]

Perhaps surprisingly, Populists other than Butler seemed to believe there was not anything unsound about at least some of Duke's proposals. Worth, the former state Alliance business agent, praised Duke's ideas on taxes. He wrote Duke, "We need more practical businessmen to shape such [tax] legislation." Similarly, Butler could not have opposed the McCaskey proposal without help from Populist legislators. The Agriculture Committee determined the fate of McCaskey's bill. There, long-time Alliancemen and Populists unfavorably reported it. The committee chairman, Populist James M. Mewborne, was the current president of the state Alliance.[8]

Race challenged Butler's efforts at moderation. Although the local government bill contained "protections" against too much black power, the legislature appointed a black doorkeeper and passed a resolution honoring Frederick Douglass at his death. Democrats condemned giving any black, including a legislative doorkeeper, authority over a white, but their complaints prompted Butler to respond that the black man "is entitled to the dignities and honors of citizenship whenever his intelligence and character qualify him for them, and the white man is entitled to them upon no other ground." Moreover, "to make the negroe's [sic] real or supposed inferiority an argument for denying him the honest fruits of his achievement is to do him a great wrong." These statements did not repudiate Butler's deeper racism, but they signaled the important ways in which cooperation changed the racial possibilities of Populism. Although the *Caucasian* only vaguely supported the Douglass resolution, it vigorously repudiated Democrats' violent criticisms of Douglass.[9]

As part of the effort to use the legislature to attract converts, Butler strategically used his newspaper during the session. Weekly circulation expanded to more than fifteen thousand, and after 6 January, the *Caucasian*, with Raleigh, Goldsboro, and Clinton editions, was supplemented by the *Raleigh Daily Caucasian*. The only daily Populist paper ever published in the South, Butler claimed it circulated to more than three thousand homes. For financial reasons, however, this expanded newspaper operation lasted only a few months. When Benjamin Duke wrote Worth that he would be glad to pay for his stock whenever the paper needed the money, he was quickly informed, "We need the money *now*." The *Caucasian's* board of directors suspended the daily at the end of the legislative session, and on 28 March, Butler consolidated the Goldsboro and Raleigh editions into one Raleigh publication. Anticipating his imminent move to Washington, Butler then chose Hal W. Ayer, former secretary of the North Carolina Agricultural Society and reporter for the *News and Observer*, as its managing editor.[10]

DURING THE ASSEMBLY the Supreme Council of the national Alliance met in Raleigh. As its president, Butler opened the meeting and delivered a welcoming address. Curiously, but perhaps symbolic of the order's stagnation, he gave essentially the same speech he delivered at the state Alliance meeting in 1893 and at the Topeka convention in 1894. He stressed the importance of rural cooperation in business and renewed his plea for laws that would alter the financial system. Although the *Caucasian* and the *Progressive Farmer* described the convention with enthusiasm, the organization clung morbidly to its former glory. The meeting climaxed with the laying of a monument cornerstone at L. L. Polk's grave. In the memorializing of their departed leader, at least, the delegates found justification for their presence.[11]

The meeting signaled the beginning of the end of Butler's Alliance career. Because of his new responsibilities as senator, he did not seek reelection as president, although he took a position on the five-man executive committee. In the following months the national Alliance slid toward disintegration. By early 1896 it retained only a few thousand members, most of whom lived in North Carolina. Its annual meeting, held in February 1896 in Washington, was a small gathering of diehards. The Alliance's platform that year included new requests for the initiative and referendum and postal savings banks, but currency and railroad reform continued to be mainstays. Although the record is unclear, Butler probably attended the meeting. He was not, however, reelected to the executive committee. A final gathering, held in Washington in February 1897, was the last gasp. When the North Carolina Alliance failed to pay its dues later that year, the national Alliance organization evaporated.[12]

North Carolina's Alliance persisted, eking out a weak existence until 1941, but Butler's participation in it as an officer ended in August 1895. He owed the Alliance a great deal. Its doctrines formed the basis of lifelong political ideals. Its arrival in Sampson County in 1888 transformed his views about farmer organization, the relationship between government and the economy, as well as the political means to achieve reform. The prominence he achieved as an Alliance official boosted him to political success. Yet, by 1895 the organization had become too feeble to aid the political movement based on its principles. Despite Butler's efforts, since late 1892 it had been made irrelevant by the failure of its cooperative efforts, the formation of the People's Party, splintering over political strategy, and increasing political turmoil over federal financial policy in each of the three major political parties. Politics, not a "nonpartisan" fraternal organization, now directed the farmers' fate.[13]

BUTLER'S NATIONAL POLITICAL presence intensified after his election to the Senate. Now aggressively implementing the strategy he adopted after 1892, he sought to create a coalition based on financial reform, particularly the free coinage of silver. By early 1895 political and economic events had propelled silver to the forefront. President Cleveland's efforts to maintain the gold standard failed to lift the nation out of a worsening depression.

Moreover, neither the repeal of the Sherman Act nor a series of gold bond issues in 1894 rescued the sagging federal gold reserve. Large segments of the public, searching for a solution to the depression, seized on silver as the remedy for the nation's woes. Many Americans, agreeing with a basic principle of Populism, concluded that only an increase in the money supply could restore prosperity. Politically, silver pitted creditors against debtors, inflationists against deflationists, Wall Street against the producer. Legally, the silver remedy was a federal statute providing for the unlimited, or free, coinage of silver in which the weight ratio of a silver dollar to a gold dollar would be 16 to 1. The price of silver had declined so rapidly by 1896, to about sixty-nine cents an ounce, that "free" silver would actually mean a ratio of 30 silver to 1 gold dollar, a massive difference.[14]

Although largely composed of farmers in the South and the West and western silver mining interests, the silver movement attracted diverse followers. It claimed supporters among Populists, Republicans, and Democrats. Yet the political fate of silver, much like that of Alliance proposals, was shaped by the fact that initially silver sentiment did not dominate either the Republican or the Democratic Party. As a result, silver supporters came to widely differing conclusions about a proper political strategy. Some hoped to prevail within the Republican or Democratic Party. Others endorsed the Populists, who had advocated free coinage as part of their financial program since 1892. Still others, led by the American Bimetallic League, formed a separate silver party in 1895.[15]

The manner in which Butler understood and portrayed the crusade for silver became an important part of American Populism. Most important, he believed silver served only as a convenient political rallying point and that it was economically distinct from the demands of Populism. In January 1895 he stated, "The storm center of politics is the financial question, and the free coinage of silver furnishes a tangible issue." Although the public was, as yet, only focused on silver, "what they really want is a change involving the entire overthrow of the present financial policy." The *Caucasian* explained: "Free silver is wanted merely [as] an entering wedge." It proposed that "what was really needed was not free coinage of silver but an issue of fiat money." After all, "if the government can convert fifty cents into a dollar [by coining silver] why can it not as well convert nothing into a dollar?" Since 1891 Butler had held that monetary reform demanded absolute government control of money volume and that volume should be increased and maintained by the government based on economic needs; the rise of silver as a political issue did not alter that view.[16]

As for political strategy, Butler argued that Populists had an obligation to fight for changes, such as silver, "that are not only the most important, but also the most timely, [those which will] draw from the old parties the greatest number of voters whose interests are identical, or nearly akin, to those who already compose the People's party." It was folly, he thought, to "advance certain issues into the larger realm of political persuasion until the people are ready for [them]." Moreover, a party that advocated "with equal force all things that are right and all reforms that should be made" could "never win a victory itself." It was therefore the duty of Populists "to so manage their cards, as to compel a realignment upon the lines [that is, financial reform] they themselves have laid down." Butler believed that campaigns are largely symbolic and that voters are most concerned with what a candidate broadly represents.[17]

As a result, he never thought silver should or would become a substitute for Populism. In his first Sampson County speech after election to the Senate, he stated that he believed "in every plank of the People's party platform, and that sooner or later these demands must be carried into effect by the government." He was "not in favor of sacrificing a single principle of the People's party." He "entirely disagree[d]" with any attempt to drop the government ownership of railroads plank from the platform. Butler so "ardently believe[d]" in the Omaha Platform that he vowed "the Populists must not stop [political agitation] until they get the entire platform enacted into law."[18]

Butler's implicit criticism of Populists who wished to dilute the platform was in response to the possibility that political considerations, including silver, could affect the long-term economic goals of the party. In 1895 there were some Populists who, responding to electoral defeat, wanted to change the Populist program in order to build up the party. Yet even this path was not necessarily the same as dumping all Populism's historic goals. One such Populist was Georgia's Tom Watson, whose congressional service had made him something of a national figure. During the fall of 1895, Watson was ready to return to the less radical prescriptions of the Alliance's 1890 platform. He urged Populists to drop the subtreasury idea, because Democrats and Republicans "are not coming to us as long as they can be made to suspect that we aim at revolution, or radical interference with vested rights." His suggestion would "put our party in such a strong yet conservative position that the millions of honest voters who want reform, but fear revolution, can join us." Watson's politics, if not his proposal, echoed what Butler had been saying about the necessity of party growth. Both men believed in Pop-

ulism. Both men knew that to win, there must be more Populist voters. Both
men knew from hard personal experience that there were few additional
Omaha Platform voters, particularly in the South, and thus some mechanism had to be found to attract newcomers.[19]

In 1895, a favored way of uniting various free silver groups was to hold
nonpartisan meetings. One such silver convention was held in Memphis in
June 1895. Sponsored by the Central Bimetallic League, it attracted more
than two thousand delegates, most of whom were southern Democrats. Butler spearheaded North Carolina's participation at Memphis. In naming delegates to the convention, the state Populist executive committee repeated
Butler's statements about the relationship between silver and Populism. It
praised free silver but, responding to concerns about dilution of essential
principles, noted it did "not surrender any of the other principles of the
People's party as expressed in the Omaha platform." It encouraged the convention to support all Populist demands. Once in Memphis, Butler gave a
dramatic speech in which he stated that he "loved the cause better than his
party and was willing to unite with any party to promote it." This reflected
his political faith in reform and cooperation. Yet he also said that he was "a
thorough Populist and believe[d] in every plank in the Omaha platform. I
believe in the government ownership of railroads and the telegraph." He
urged the delegates to become full-fledged Populists. Resolution of the
financial crisis, according to Butler, depended on the abolition of national
banks, an income tax, silver, and, most important, "government issue and
control" of money in addition to free silver. The official report of the North
Carolina Populist delegation denounced opposition "to the financial relief
proposed in the Omaha platform," and a *Progressive Farmer* reporter found
the delegates "enthusiastic in their unqualified devotion to the People's
party cause and the Omaha platform."[20]

Immediately after the Memphis meeting Butler began to implement a silver political strategy in North Carolina. The goal was to shift dramatically
the posture of his party away from the arrangements of 1892 and 1894. Although a majority of Democrats supported silver, the bitterness that had
arisen between Populists and Democrats since 1892 meant that cooperation
with Democrats would be difficult. In Butler's mind, however, Populism had
nothing to lose under his silver plan: either supporters of silver would unite
or the Democratic rank and file would reject the gold stance of their leaders
and become Populists. At first, the evidence pointed toward the latter. As
late as April 1895, even Josephus Daniels's *News and Observer* praised Grover
Cleveland's fight for "sound money" and endorsed a gold man, Hoke Smith

of Georgia, for president. As a result, much more was involved in Butler's co-operative plan than silver. For southerners, the issue was squarely presented: Could silver drive Democrats from their party and fundamentally realign the party structure?[21]

Butler and a few silver Democrats and Republicans agreed to cosponsor a nonpartisan rally in Raleigh in September 1895. Unfortunately for these men, the convention failed to demonstrate that silver could unite members of different political parties; it also confirmed that Democrats were not yet committed to silver candidates. Of the 270 delegates, about 240 were Populists. Yet differences among the delegates suggest why Butler believed the Democratic leadership would continue to hedge on silver and Populists could reap the benefits among the rank and file. The few Democrats present refused to support a resolution that bound participants to vote for silver candidates for federal office. On the other hand, the Populist majority, led by Butler, rejected a Democratic resolution that purported to limit demands for financial reform to free silver.[22]

In the months after his election to the Senate, Butler advanced the essential attributes of his silver strategy. The strategy did not involve a repudiation of the Omaha Platform. It also had little to do with cooperation between parties. Instead, it aimed to create a new political force under Populist leadership. Butler believed the silver issue would unite silver men and discredit the Democratic Party. In his view, both were essential for long-term Populist, not simply silver, success in the South. When national Democrats failed to endorse a strong silver candidate, Populists could appear as the principled reformers, and the Democratic Party in the South would collapse. Butler's plan assumed rank-and-file Democrats were willing to break party ties for silver and that neither old party would select a genuine silver candidate for president in 1896.

IN NOVEMBER 1895, Butler arrived in Washington for his first session in the Senate. The Senate met in the north wing of the Capitol, in a chamber completed just prior to the Civil War. Its prestige attracted many of the nation's leading politicians, including Henry Cabot Lodge, John Sherman, Benjamin Tillman, William Allison, and Nelson Aldrich. Of course, Butler, the lone southern Populist, could not claim any national stature. At thirty-two, he was the youngest member of the Senate. He was the second youngest, after Henry Clay, in the Senate's history. From the beginning, however, his brash style showed he was not intimidated by the Senate as institution or by its more well known members. His youth and record of success seemed to convince him that he represented the dominant wave of the future. He arrived believing that hard work and the nation's indignation would allow Populism to prevail.[23]

The record of Populists in Congress did not provide much basis for optimism. Although they began arriving in Washington soon after the 1890 elections, Populists had always been a small group. In the Fifty-second Congress, elected in 1890, two senators and nine representatives could be considered Populist or supportive of Populism. Of these eleven, six were from Kansas, while the others, including Georgia's Tom Watson, either joined the People's Party after their election or identified themselves as independents. The Fifty-third Congress, elected after the formation of the national People's Party in 1892, contained three Populist senators and ten representatives. Of these, eight hailed either from Kansas or Nebraska; there were no southerners. Following the 1894 elections, largely because of defeat in Kansas, only nine described themselves as full-fledged Populists. For the first time, however, there was significant southern Populist representation, including Butler in the Senate.[24]

Butler's two Populist Senate colleagues, William V. Allen and William A. Peffer, were midwesterners. Allen, an early supporter of the Alliance, came to the Senate from Nebraska in 1893 because of a Democratic and Populist coalition. By 1895 he was known for his opposition to Cleveland's financial policies. Kansas Populists chose William Peffer, a former Republican, to represent them in 1891. Peffer edited the pro-Alliance *Kansas Farmer* and like Butler had hesitated to join the third party, believing that reform could be achieved through an established party. Because he was not reelected after 1896, Peffer's service with Butler lasted less than two years.[25]

When Congress convened in December 1895, the initial question was which party would organize the Senate. Although Republicans possessed a plurality, the three Populists, along with Silver-Independents James H. Kyle of Nebraska and William Stewart and John P. Jones of Nevada, held the balance of power. Consistent with its owner's national political strategy, Butler's newspaper argued for organization based on support for silver. In late November, Butler, Allen, Stewart, and Peffer issued an invitation to fifty-two other supposedly silver senators to organize the upper body on that issue. Not surprisingly, considering that this was an affront to party regularity, they ignored the invitation. During the ensuing organization vote, Populists abstained, producing a Republican triumph. According to Allen and Butler, the abstention embarrassed silver Democrats. It also demonstrated that Populists were a distinct political force.[26]

Financial reform dominated Butler's first months in the Senate. Precipitating his activity was President Cleveland's desire for a new bond issue. In December, Butler offered an unsuccessful resolution that would have forced the treasury secretary to redeem greenbacks with silver. On 3 January 1896, he introduced another bill to prohibit federal bond issues without prior congressional approval. Members of both old parties, particularly Democrat David Hill of New York and Republican John Sherman of Ohio, delayed this measure for months. Although the bond bill eventually passed in the Senate, it failed in the House.[27]

Butler took to the floor on behalf of his proposals on numerous occasions. The most complete statement of his purpose took place on 29 May 1896. Much of the presentation portrayed the allegedly conspiratorial nature of currency contraction. Butler displayed a letter that he described as an instruction from the nation's bankers and bondholders, indicating their intention to control the presidential nominations of the two older parties. He surmised that they planned to nominate William McKinley as the Republican candidate. He also guessed that they would "ignore the Democrats, allowing free silver men to control their convention." But this was only because the conspirators knew a Democratic declaration for silver would be shallow and that the party would not nominate a real silver man. True silver Democrats, according to Butler, would see the ruse and advance their financial principles by allying "with all other silver forces in America regardless of party name." Of course, only the People's Party stood against the "money power."[28]

Prodded by amused Republican senators to be more specific about the conspiracy, Butler identified the persons responsible for the gold standard as the same "class of capitalists" who had hoarded gold and demanded excessive interest rates on bonds during the Civil War. He also described the alleged fraud of federal statute revisers in the 1870s who inserted a clause in the federal code which limited silver as legal tender to transactions of less than five dollars. He offered a Populist answer to the conspiracy, a government-controlled currency sensitive to national growth. Instead of delegating the power over money volume to private banks, which as lenders adored appreciating dollars, the government should regulate money volume according to increases in population and business.[29]

Butler attacked gold in other ways. He introduced a bill that would have made the silver Mexican dollar and the Japanese silver yen legal tender, as well as one that would have prohibited mortgages and contracts payable only in gold. He proclaimed that under a People's Party president, the mints would be "thrown open to the free and unlimited coinage of silver." Contraction would cease, and the president would "urge Congress to increase the circulating medium as fast as population and business increase." A Populist chief executive would also advise "the abolishment of national banks, and have all money issued direct by the government." These pleas fell on disdaining ears. The boastful claim that Populists would soon inaugurate their own president drew derisive laughter.[30]

Butler introduced additional legislation with Populist roots. It included two constitutional amendments. One sought a federal income tax, but no action was taken on it. The second would allow Congress to override a presidential veto with a bare majority. He argued the veto was a relic of monarchy, but the Senate Judiciary Committee buried his resolution. After his appointment to the Post-Office Committee, Butler introduced a bill to provide postal telegraph or telephone service at post offices. The Populist platform demanded government ownership of telegraphs and telephones, and Butler believed that private telegraph service was too slow and too costly and was dominated by the Western Union monopoly. In addition, because "government is simply an agent of the people to do for all of the people what can be better done by a public agent than by each private individual in his own behalf," the same principle of government ownership applied to railroads. The postal bill failed to achieve a floor vote.[31]

Butler also supported rural free delivery (RFD). In later years he disputed with others, including Tom Watson, about who could claim the title of "Father of Rural Free Delivery." Actually, more than a dozen men had legitimate claims to RFD's paternity. Butler's assertion rested on his amendment to the postal appropriation bill in his first session. Although previous Congresses provided small sums for experimentation, the Cleveland administration claimed that none was large enough for an experiment, and the funds remained unspent. Butler's amendment appropriated another fifty thousand dollars, which was added to the existing money. The first RFD trial resulted. The amendment barely passed in the Senate, by a vote of 27-25, with all three Populists voting for it.[32]

Butler's first months in Washington can be evaluated in several ways. One measuring stick is success as a legislative leader. On that score, Butler managed to get his antibond bill and RFD amendment approved. On the other hand, he failed to achieve positive gain on more central Populist issues, such as government telephones, telegraphs, and railroads and the income tax. Of course, other lawmakers and a president who disagreed with practically everything the Populists stood for vastly outnumbered Butler and his allies. This ideological isolation became a defining characteristic of Butler's Senate career. Perhaps his ability to articulate the principles of the Omaha Platform on the Senate floor, especially as they pertained to government control of currency and ownership of natural monopolies, was the most success possible.

On the other hand, it is the duty of the minority to attempt to persuade others. Although a coalition builder in party politics, in the Senate Butler took a very different approach. Butler believed he needed more support from voters, yet he assumed Populists would soon dominate the opposition in Congress. He usually addressed his colleagues as he might harangue a group of hecklers. He insulted other senators as a matter of course, accusing them of diabolical crimes against the nation. The best example of his confrontational style occurred near the end of the session, when, exasperated by the intentional delays of the gold men, he complained the Senate had accomplished nothing since December. A "sham battle" for election advantage stifled every request for useful legislation. Yet even Peffer felt obliged to interrupt, telling Butler that because of the late hour, "we are all getting hungry. I know I am."[33]

Butler's opponents exploited the problem. Republican William Chandler of New Hampshire denounced his "undignified and unbecoming threats." Chandler, in the polite idiom of the Senate, referred to him as "my violent friend from North Carolina." Senator David Hill, a man well accomplished at witty repartee, proved especially capable of defending himself from Butler's blows. In one exchange Hill delivered effective, if irrelevant, blasts, ably turning a discussion of administration policy into an analysis of Butler's departure from the Democracy and the complexity of North Carolina politics. Although most of the Senate chuckled, Butler managed little more than an angry repetition of the conspiracy theme.[34]

If he failed to achieve popularity in Washington, the style and substance of his performance won nothing but praise from Populists. Referring to one of his nastier speeches, the *Progressive Farmer* reported, "If old party tricksters ever did get a scorching, they got it then." The *Warren Plains People's Paper* announced that Butler was "goading the animals in the Senate with his sharp, stinging sarcasm[;] the whole outfit from Tammany Tiger Hill and old Hyena Sherman to the little administration jackals and White House cuckoos are snarling and snapping at his heels." The *Caucasian, Progressive Farmer,* and *Wadesboro Plow Boy* detailed Butler's presidential veto, antibond, pro-silver, and RFD efforts. The *Dallas Southern Mercury*, the voice of Texas Populism, praised Butler's antibond bill.[35]

BETWEEN JANUARY 1895 and June 1896 Butler emerged as a national reform leader. Although still in his early thirties, he arranged his election to the Senate and once there managed to become a powerful spokesman for Populism. He presented the framework of the Omaha Platform at the highest level of government. He chose to articulate this doctrine in a manner that emphasized his opponents' greed and corruption. This probably confirmed many senators' stereotype of the demagogic appeal of Populism. Yet Butler viewed himself as a hardworking representative of the oppressed, as someone who needed to be angry. Equally important, he was not satisfied with holding a seat in the Senate. He did not seek higher office but immediately after his election began campaigning for Populist success in a presidential election more than a year away. He conquered local and state politics; he now wanted to make the nation resemble Sampson County. The coming election provided an opportunity to unite political strategy with his faith in the correctness of Populist principles. Butler's work placed him at the forefront of Populists who believed that a realignment of parties was imminent. He believed that both old parties would fail to recognize the yearnings for change and voters would reject those parties, especially in the South. He wanted the highest political success for Populism, and he was about to get his chance.

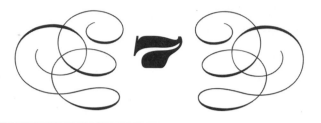

PREPARING FOR A NEW ORDER

BUTLER'S NATIONAL political strategy dramatically affected his leadership
of North Carolina Populism. Because Republicans were virtually certain to
nominate a gold man for president, cooperation with Tar Heel Republicans,
unlike in 1894, contradicted his plan for unity among silver forces. This produced conflict and uncertainty among rank-and-file Populists, who were primarily and quite naturally concerned about political survival at the county
level. Some hoped that state and national issues could be separated and that
cooperation with the GOP would continue. Another possibility was for Populists to run their own candidates. Butler attempted to avoid both cooperation with Republicans and an independent People's Party campaign. In
early 1896 he thought a coalition ticket for state candidates and presidential
electors, distinct from the Populist Party and based on support for silver, was
the best tactic. He stated that this ticket "would put us in the position of cooperating for a great and fundamental principle and [also] avoid being successfully charged with cooperating for spoils." The resolutions passed at
Raleigh's Populist-dominated silver convention in 1895 could serve as the
basis of a coalition. Most important among these was the pledge to support
a silver man for president, regardless of his party.[1]

The plan had several weaknesses. First, it relied on the assumption that
Democrats would not choose a sincere supporter of silver for president. Second, it did not establish how state candidates would be chosen. Finally, Butler's ideas ignored the ease with which Republican cooperation had been
generated at the local level two years earlier. Many Populists did not approve
of suddenly breaking ties with white and black Republicans. For Butler, this
negative reaction was ominous, for previously his strategic plans had be-

come policy without significant dissent. Obviously, all did not share his national focus. Many Populists leveled criticisms, not so much at the idea of a silver coalition, which most endorsed, but about the uncertainty regarding a state ticket and local candidates. The sharpest criticism came from persons who wanted cooperation with Republicans on the ground that the greatest threat to Populism was renewed tyranny by Tar Heel Democracy.[2]

By the spring of 1896 the party was slowly pulling itself apart on the point. There was mounting pressure for continued Republican cooperation, particularly for local offices and the legislature. At an informal meeting of Anson County Populists in April, the men gathered in the *Plow Boy* pressroom agreed with Butler about an independent silver presidential electoral ticket, but they wanted cooperation with Republicans on state and local candidates. Giving up existing ties to advance federal legislation seemed unduly risky. Letters to the *Progressive Farmer* also maintained that continuing friendships at the township level made cooperation with Republicans most logical. The disagreements did not relate to Populism's ultimate economic goals. J. Z. Green, who favored Republican cooperation and presided at the Anson County meeting, believed that "the position of Senator Butler and the rank and file of the Populists of this State is . . . [that] [t]hey would like to see all of the principles of the Omaha Platform crystallized into law." Although silver alone could "not afford the needed relief, . . . it would be a step in the right direction." Butler's newspaper reiterated that it "would be delighted to cooperate on the Omaha Platform in full. But if we can't do that, then we want to cooperate on some principle in that platform."[3]

Butler tried to resolve the differences in his favor at an April 1896 Populist executive committee meeting. He proposed that Populists should not support "goldbug" candidates, which meant there would not be an agreement with Republicans unless silver was the basis of cooperation. Even then, as part of the price of an agreement, the GOP would have to help elect a Populist governor and eliminate U.S. Senator Jeter Pritchard, who now appeared to support gold. Finally, any consideration of cooperation should wait until after the national presidential campaign was under way. Butler's proposal triumphed, but only barely. Although Republicans had already proposed a joint ticket, offering Populists the positions of lieutenant governor, secretary of state, treasurer, and superintendent of public instruction, as well as renewed congressional and legislative cooperation, the executive committee rejected their offer by a 9-to-8 vote. Harry Skinner, who now emerged as Butler's principal contender for party leadership, and Cyrus Thompson, the physician-Allianceman from Onslow County, led the minority. They believed the coalition should be renewed if Republicans gave Populists the governorship.[4]

The executive committee's actions reflected complex divisions among the rank and file. Those who supported Butler's plan included Populists who believed the party might prevail on its own, because of its overall merits or because of the new emphasis on silver. As one Populist reported, the black vote might validate this conclusion: "The colored people are split all to pieces and 4 to 1 say they will vote for silver, and they say they will go into the P.P. convention[,] that they are dun [*sic*] with the old Rep. Party." Yet Butler's plan was also supported by antiblack, anti-Republican Populists, some of whom joined the party after 1893. The rationale of the pro-Republican Populists was equally diverse. One group believed cooperation would prevent total Republican victory and thereby help silver and preserve the fair operation of the election law. It feared black rule in the East and a repeat of Reconstruction. Others thought GOP cooperation would advance reform because reactionary Democrats were the primary threat to Populism. Each position, including Butler's, assumed the electoral weakness of the Populist Party, particularly the inability of Populists to control the General Assembly.[5]

Butler's new plan immediately affected the Republican and Democratic Parties. Once friendly Republicans portrayed him as autocratic, bosslike, and a "Benedict Arnold." They made it clear that they could never consent to the free silver ultimatum and focused their attention on local Populists, hoping that success there would undermine the new strategy. Some Democrats, on the other hand, applauded his opposition to Republicans. Many even hoped the friends of silver could be united, preferably under the Democratic banner. In addition to challenging Democratic conservatives, these men faced the difficulty of uniting rank-and-file Populists and Democrats, who harbored animosities dating to the Alliance insurgency.[6]

ALONG WITH HIS activities in North Carolina and in the Senate, during early 1896 Butler emerged as a leader in the national Populist Party. He viewed the task of the national organization as twofold. First, the party needed new adherents. Unfortunately, the political appeal of the key Omaha Platform demands, particularly irredeemable currency and government ownership of railroads, remained limited, whereas silver, a subsidiary Populist issue, had gained support. The party had no prospect of victory in southern states where it should have had at least some appeal: Virginia, Tennessee, South Carolina, Mississippi, and Florida. Further north, the party lacked any realistic hope of triumph in vast areas of the Old Northwest: Minnesota, Wisconsin, Illinois, and Indiana. Given the anti-Populist orientation of the heavily populated Northeast, it was difficult to imagine how Populists could expect to elect a Congress or a president under such conditions. Worse, election failures in 1894 of even the leading Populist Parties, in Texas, Georgia, and Kansas, confirmed the problem. As a consequence, Butler advanced his belief that growth required a new party posture, one that would allow Populism to benefit from support for silver. Second, Populists had to accept the responsibility of organizing this larger group.

Another prominent southern Populist understood the reasons for Butler's plan to increase the size of the party. Georgia's Tom Watson wrote him, "So far as I can see, we are in complete accord." On the selection of a new national chairman, which would occur at the party's nominating convention, Watson said that the man should have "nerve enough to rule with a rod of iron those hot-headed recalcitrants who want to load us down with extreme isms. Sen. [William V.] Allen could do it; you could do it; [James B.] Weaver can't; nor can [H. L.] Loucks or Sen. [William A.] Peffer." Watson also told Butler that his greatest fear was a distortion of Populism from the Left, not from a dilution of its basic principles. The recent Georgia Populist convention "adopted the most conservative platform the party has ever put forth." He further advised, "Those of us who favor this moderate and conservative course should begin to educate public sentiment on that line, in our papers, to the end that the extremists shall not control the next national convention."[7]

The party's leadership formally addressed Populist presidential campaign strategy at the national committee meeting in January 1896. Butler hoped to accomplish two goals there, both of which derived from his silver coalition plan. First, he wanted the party to declare its intent to unite forces under the banner of financial reform. Second, because he doubted Democrats would support silver, he wanted to delay the Populist national convention until after the nominating conventions of the two older parties. Butler's views prevailed. Along with James Weaver and Ignatius Donnelly, he helped write the resolutions adopted by the committee, which stated that it did not "desire to change in any particular the principles of the People's party." Yet to end the "disgraceful conditions that now oppress the people," the party proposed an alliance between Populists and persons in favor of financial reform "who are not yet ready to become members of our organization" and who would hold a convention at the same time and place as the Populist convention. The goal was a unified slate of presidential electors. Equally important, the Populist convention would be held just after the Democratic convention.[8]

Immediately following the meeting Butler helped promote the Populist Party's coalition strategy at the National Silver Conference in Washington. The delegates planned a silver convention to be held simultaneously with the Populist convention in July. In a speech, Butler declared that the delegates were setting in motion the great revolution that he envisioned. He used the silver forum to promote the entire program of the Populist Party. He praised the Omaha Platform as a "broad, manly, and defiant protest against every form of organized monopoly and oppression": "I believed in that platform [in 1892] and I believe in it now. I believe that every plank in it must be enacted into law before we can have a return to true republican government." Yet, Populists "have learned a great deal about the tactics and methods which is [sic] absolutely essential to . . . successfully contend against the common enemy." Presently, "a majority of voters . . . are opposed to the policy of both old parties." "Unfortunately," a "majority of the voters . . . are not ready to accept the entire platform of the People's party." Thus, those who oppose the money power should "join hands on what we do agree on."[9]

As summer and the national conventions moved closer, Butler reiterated his belief that Republicans would nominate a gold man for president, presumably William McKinley. Next, Democrats would choose a "straddling" silver supporter or someone who did not want immediate free coinage. The failures of the older parties would then produce "a grand convention of patriots in St. Louis" in July, at the Populist convention. The late-July convention allowed for "a movement so large and so formidable by the time the two old-party conventions are held that the rank and file of the two parties will endorse it if their leaders do not." To assure victory for monetary reform, Butler maintained that genuine silver supporters, including Democrats, would convene with Populists to select a joint ticket. Populists, as the only unified party within the reform coalition, would have a good chance to pick one of their own for the presidency.[10]

Butler's final major public statement before the nominating conventions was "Why the South Wants Free Coinage of Silver," an article in the *Arena*, a reform journal. He stressed that to ensure a fair distribution of goods, the volume of money must be increased "exactly in proportion to the increase of population and business." Further, all money should be "coined or issued by the government," and "every dollar [should] stand on its own bottom — every dollar to be a dollar without being redeemed in another dollar." If "the full and free coinage of [silver and gold] should not make enough money to keep pace with increasing population and business, then the South wants more legal tender dollars made of something else furnished by the government (not by banks), and such additional money to be real dollars, everyone to stand on its own bottom and not to be redeemed in other dollars." More broadly, financial reform meant that "every citizen would have equal opportunities." Although "some would grow rich and some would remain poor, . . . in each case it would be the man's own fault and not the fault of the government." In terms of political economy, Butler simply repeated in the article what he had been arguing for several years: the federal government should take responsibility for creating a more flexible money supply, the federal government should oppose monopoly, and federal action would effect an equal economic opportunity to acquire wealth. Politically, the article evidenced Butler's pattern of using silver politics to promote Populism.[11]

THE SUMMER OF 1896 represented one of the most important seasons of Butler's life. During those months his activities had an impact on the entire nation. His rise had been spectacular. Only four years earlier he was an embattled Democratic Allianceman in Sampson County, hoping that his party would not nominate Grover Cleveland for president. Ironically, by 1896 not only had Cleveland's nomination proved of considerable benefit, but now Butler believed and hoped that his old party would nominate someone like Cleveland.

By the time Republicans met in St. Louis, William McKinley's nomination was assured. McKinley, a former congressman and the governor of Ohio, became well known in the 1880s as an ardent ally of a high tariff. Although formerly a friend of expanded silver coinage, in 1896 he agreed to go along with the GOP platform's official endorsement of the "existing gold standard." Yet even Republicans could not avoid the silver movement. Westerners, men largely from silver-producing and agricultural states, threatened to leave the party if the convention declared for gold. Their most distinguished leader, Senator Henry M. Teller of Colorado, tried to defeat the gold plank. When his proposal failed, Teller and others walked out.[12]

The Republican convention encouraged Butler's hopes for a national ticket that could unite Populists and silver supporters. Teller's bolt, in particular, set a good precedent for disappointed Democrats. It also suggested that the Coloradoan might be an ideal presidential candidate. Butler agreed with national Populist Party chairman Herman Taubeneck of Illinois that Teller should be considered because he could maintain the Populist reform initiative and avoid partisan friction. Taubeneck told Butler, "We must compel the democrats to take Senator Teller or hold them responsible for a division of the silver forces in the coming campaign." By late June the *Caucasian* was promoting Teller's candidacy.[13]

In the three weeks between McKinley's nomination and the national Democratic convention, Butler continued to believe that Democrats would not nominate a legitimate silver candidate and that the only way they could do so would be to choose a "nonpartisan" figure such as Teller. The *Caucasian* confidently announced that there was no danger Democrats would really declare for free silver. Any purported silver candidate would be nominated "with the help, connivance, and permission of the eastern gold men." Further, in a preconvention speech, Butler criticized Democrats severely, warning that a free silver pledge that came out of the Democratic convention would be abandoned.[14]

Butler's silver strategy got its first real challenge in North Carolina. Holding its nominating convention on 14 May, the GOP renewed its earlier attempts to divorce state and national issues and obtain a state cooperation agreement with Populists. The party nominated Daniel L. Russell Jr., a three-hundred-pound bullnecked cooperationist from Wilmington, for governor. Russell offered a study in contrasts. A scalawag during Reconstruction, he served briefly, in the 1870s, as the South's only Greenback Party congressman. In 1896 he was a free silver Republican and increasingly friendly to the antirailroad, trust-busting rhetoric of Populism. Yet he was unpopular among much of the party's black leadership, endorsed a protective tariff, and remained loyal to McKinley. His party invited cooperation by nominating candidates to only one-half of the state ticket, providing the Populists with an opportunity to fill the remaining slots.[15]

The state Democracy met on 25 June. Dramatically, the party shifted away from the reactionary policy of 1894 and endorsed free silver and a federal income tax. It criticized monopolies, national banks, and trusts. Some Democrats even favored cooperation with Populists. In fact, Butler urged these men to avoid nominating a full ticket, pending the presumed union of national silver forces. Yet this faction lacked sufficient power for such a rebellion, and the convention filled every available position with a Democrat.[16]

The result was that an enormously difficult situation confronted North Carolina's Populists. Republicans, with their McKinley/Greenbacker candidate, begged them to cooperate, guaranteeing them important state-level

positions. On the other hand, Democrats came out squarely for silver, something that seemed unlikely with Cleveland in the White House and the disastrous Raleigh silver convention fresh in everyone's memory. There was
even a possibility of formal Democratic cooperation. Although time was running out, Populists disagreed about what to do. Whether silver coalition,
agreement with Democracy, agreement with Republicans, or none of the
above could claim the allegiance of the party was unclear. Butler's inability
to control the rank and file and his policy of delay pending the final national conventions exacerbated the uncertainty. Although he wanted a silver
alliance, that seemed both unlikely and certain to alienate many North Carolina Populists. In the meantime, while waiting for the national conventions, he used the older parties' interest in Populist votes as a bargaining
chip, corresponding with leaders in both.[17]

Butler's hopeful scaffolding of silver coalition politics came crashing
down at the Democratic National Convention in early July. Delegates unhesitatingly rejected Teller but made an unequivocal demand for free silver
by selecting William Jennings Bryan, a former congressman from Nebraska,
as their presidential nominee after Bryan gave a dramatic pro-silver speech.
Bryan had an impeccable reputation as a silver advocate, entirely dispelling
Butler's previous assumptions that his old party would straddle. For vice
president, however, they chose a dubious silver supporter from Maine, Arthur Sewall, a national banker.[18]

From Butler's standpoint, the Democratic convention radically changed
the calculus of the election. Instead of opening the door for a unified silver
ticket, with its roots in Populism and which Populists could lead, the Bryan
nomination placed silver leadership squarely in the Democratic Party. The
irony, of course, was that the Democrats' action was a clear by-product of
Populist ideas and Populist politics. In this sense the silver strategy had
worked too well. Worst of all, differing reactions by Populists to Bryan made
party unity unlikely. Some, especially in the Midwest, where cooperation
with Democrats had been carried out since the party's beginnings, wanted
to nominate Bryan or even accept the entire Bryan-Sewall ticket. Others, believing Bryan could not represent Populism and that Democracy was untrustworthy, opposed both Bryan and Sewall.[19]

Butler raged at the Chicago Democrats. Privately, he complained that
Bryan's nomination was selfish and threatened financial reform. The choice
aimed to cripple Populism, not advance silver. Publicly, his newspaper argued that party bosses would corrupt a Bryan administration, that the
Democracy was still "treacherous and incompetent," and that the nomina-

tion of Sewall showed this. The vice presidential nominee was a "heavy load." On the other hand, Butler generally praised Bryan. The Nebraskan represented the best Democratic choice in twenty-five years; he was "sincere, honest, earnest, and aggressive." Bryan "would have made a splendid candidate for a third party."[20]

In the short time left before the Populist national convention, Butler did not choose a single plan of action. He did not adopt the views of either the Bryan supporters or the independent ticket men. He still clung to the hope that a reform coalition based on free silver and led by Populists could be achieved. Two options appeared. Populists might nominate Bryan but choose their own vice presidential candidate. There was also the possibility, which Butler seemed to prefer in mid-July, of selecting a separate Populist ticket and later arranging joint Bryan-Populist electors in the states. Both possibilities, it was thought, could unify silver supporters and preserve independent Populism.[21]

BUTLER ARRIVED IN St. Louis, the site of the Populist convention, on 20 July. Up to this time he had maintained good relations with most Populists, including those lining up against Bryan. His correspondence with Watson has already been noted. The *Dallas Southern Mercury*, which vigorously opposed Bryan, had never criticized him. In fact, in contrast to its routine denunciations of party chairman Herman Taubeneck, one letter writer to the *Mercury* thought Butler, who actually was ineligible because of his age, would be a good vice presidential nominee. Butler also remained friendly toward Bryan. In an interview given immediately upon his arrival, he praised Bryan's "brilliancy, youth, and ability." Yet he did not endorse Bryan as a candidate. He maintained that Populists should preserve their organization and promote the "interests for which the People's party stands."[22]

After surveying conditions in St. Louis, Butler publicly proposed two alternative strategies. First, he suggested that a separate Populist ticket be named, with agreements on joint presidential electors to be worked out with Democrats. Second, he proposed that the party might maintain independence by nominating its own vice presidential candidate and then unite the reform forces by nominating Bryan for president. Delegates immediately perceived problems with Butler's ideas. Self-described "midroaders," who claimed to be independent ticket supporters but who are more accurately viewed as anti-Democrats, considered both to be unacceptable forms of cooperation. In contrast, a Bryan-Sewall supporter contended that the plans represented

The hero and the goat: Bryan and Sewall, 1896.
(Library of Congress)

a Republican effort to divide the silver vote. Nonetheless, a coalition of pro-Bryan and anti-Sewall delegates gradually developed around the second plan. As a result, on 21 July Butler was selected as the convention's temporary chairman.[23]

The convention began the next day, when about fourteen hundred delegates filled Convention Hall. In the opening address, Butler tried to appeal to common interests by denouncing both old parties. McKinley represented "aggregated capital and combined greed," and Cleveland had led the nation to the brink of bankruptcy. The recent Democratic convention attempted to steal the Populist platform and disrupt the Populist Party. After a delegate interrupted, "Why don't they steal our transportation plank?" Butler answered: "The old Democratic habit got the better of them there. They straddled that question." He then addressed the theme of Populist independence, arguing that the party must survive because Democrats could not be trusted. Of course, the difficult political issue was how best to maintain independence and advance reform. Butler saw Democratic domination and Republican money, the latter of which he associated with anti-Bryan sentiment among Populists, as twin dangers. Perhaps these remarks were ill advised, as Bryan and anti-Bryan delegates responded by openly accusing each other of being agents of the other parties. Butler ended with an appeal for unity.[24]

After Butler's address the delegates recessed until that evening. The primary activity of the night session was to be a report by the credentials committee, which would provide the first indication of the strengths of the Bryan and anti-Bryan forces. Yet when eight o'clock arrived, the hall stood in darkness. For the next forty-five minutes, confusion reigned. Fears of a conspiracy for Bryan entranced midroaders, who charged that the lights had been intentionally cut off. Historians have been unable to discern why the lights were not on, although an electrical storm is a credible explanation. At any rate, it is not clear that any faction was hurt or helped by the delay. Butler adjourned the convention until the following morning.[25]

On the second day, a crucial test came when delegates elected U.S. Senator William Allen, a Bryan proponent, to the permanent chairmanship by a vote of 758 to 564. The voting behavior of the North Carolina delegation indicated Butler's position as well as the complexity of the alignments among the delegates: It split exactly in half between Allen and James E. Campion, the anti-Bryan nominee. Most important, the vote did not represent simple opposition or endorsement of cooperation, nor did it measure silver sentiment versus support for the Omaha Platform. Instead, it primarily reflected strategic concerns linked to state politics. Butler, Hal Ayer, and James Lloyd, who supported Allen, were interested in a Bryan and Populist joint ticket and silver coalition. W. H. Kitchin, who also voted for Allen, was an outspoken racist who rejected continued cooperation with Republicans in North Carolina; he preferred Bryan and Sewall. James Ramsey of the *Progressive Farmer* and Ed Kestler, who supported Campion, distrusted Democrats. Both had supported Republican cooperation in 1894; Kestler was angry with Butler for opposing it in 1896.[26]

The impact of state politics was equally apparent the following day, when the convention voted to nominate a vice presidential candidate before choosing the presidential nominee. Among the North Carolinians, all but the most extreme anti-Bryan element initially endorsed the nomination of a candidate for president first. This vote, however, depended on a promise from midwestern Bryan men that a southern Populist would be nominated for vice president after Bryan was chosen. Because of a growing fear that the midwesterners would not carry out their promise, North Carolina's delegates, including Butler, changed their votes and unanimously approved the nomination of a vice president first. The shift united the anti-Bryan and anti-

Sewall Populists and produced a narrow victory, 738 to 637. Texas, Georgia, Mississippi, and North Carolina were the only delegations to cast unanimous votes for the vice presidential selection first. As the stronger southern Populist states, they were least likely to be comfortable with surrendering Populism's separate political identity to Democrats. Their votes also suggest tensions between the political concerns of western and southern Populists.[27]

Before the nominations the convention took up the platform. Historians have tended to ignore that it was adopted by voice vote, with only "a few cries of dissent." Both Lawrence Goodwyn and Stanley Jones viewed the platform as part of a policy contest between midroaders and Bryan men. Goodwyn maintained that, in the end, the platform was a victory for midroaders: "The tenets of the Omaha Platform were reincorporated in the new 'St. Louis Platform.'" Goodwyn is correct, because everything won in 1892 was reaffirmed in 1896. Jones, however, came to the opposite conclusion. He believed Bryan men defeated midroaders, apparently because they dominated the platform committee and the document included a special plea for free silver. Actually, the lack of disagreement about the platform suggested that anti-Bryan and Bryan men were fundamentally united about the legislative goals of Populism. Individual state political issues seemed not to affect the core ideological purpose of the national party. This was certainly true for Butler and the North Carolina delegates.[28]

At the evening session on 24 July the convention nominated Tom Watson for vice president. Watson, who was not in St. Louis, won on the first ballot. His victory could not be credited to midroaders alone; they lacked sufficient votes to elect anyone. Instead, Watson depended on the support of Populists, including Butler, who wanted both Bryan and a southern Populist vice president. Those men wielded the balance of power. Moreover, Watson's response to his nomination showed that he was acceptable to Butler and others because he agreed with them, and not the midroaders, about a Bryan-Watson ticket. Watson stated that a Bryan-Sewall nomination would threaten the existence of the third party and that a Populist vice presidential candidate could maintain party harmony, which is precisely what Butler believed. Watson noted that western Populists were committed to Bryan and that as a result a failure to nominate Bryan could dismantle the party. He concluded this should be avoided, because he believed, as Butler did, that Bryan was "a man of unblemished character and brilliant ability." Moreover, like Butler, Watson thought "there is no reason that we should not cooperate with the Democrats to the extent that we agree," that by "agreeing to cooperate" we "do not compromise on principles, stultify our record, or disband our organization." Watson, sounding a great deal like Butler, concluded that the cooperation ticket would "harmonize all factions, unite the silver forces, and at the same time prevent a possible split up of [the Populist] party."[29]

On 25 July, Bryan received the Populist presidential nomination. The delegates knew that he might oppose an endorsement that excluded Sewall, but they wanted him anyway. Two factors overcame any hesitancy. First, there was overwhelming personal sentiment in favor of the Nebraskan, even among southern Populists. Second, the Butler-Watson Populists, who held the balance of power, voted for Bryan for the practical reason of holding Bryan's supporters in the party and sealing the compromise begun with Watson's nomination. Although the anti-Bryan men offered S. F. Norton, who later supported Bryan, as Bryan's opponent, their faction suffered its greatest numerical defeat on this issue: 1,042 to 321. Only a majority of Populists from the Maine, South Carolina, Wisconsin, and Texas delegations supported Norton, and only the Texas and minuscule South Carolina party were unanimous for Norton. Because of political conditions in those states, both delegations were unusually anti-Democratic. On the other hand, Alabama, Georgia, Colorado, Kansas, and North Carolina, all states with significant Populist membership, went for Bryan. North Carolina's delegation voted 72 to 20 for Bryan; Butler was among the majority. Once again, state political needs shaped the voting. Both anti-Democratic midroaders and supporters of renewed Republican cooperation opposed Bryan.[30]

After the nominations Butler wanted to become the party's chairman, the person responsible for organizing the national canvass. Certainly this was yet another example of his incessant need to be in charge and his super self-confidence that he was the best person for the job, even when the task offered unlimited difficulties. Yet it also reflected his desire to see Populism succeed in a great cause. Delegates elected him to the position because during the convention he positioned himself squarely between the pro-Bryan westerners and the anti-Democrats. Unfortunately, the chairmanship required not only a thick skin but also something akin to a political death wish. It conferred only weak powers, meaning his authority depended on the compliance of the badly divided and often provincial state organizations. Worse, the compromise ticket ensured that large segments in the party were already disappointed, and naturally the person who supported the compromise and then became responsible for carrying it out was an easy target. Some Populists grumbled that Butler was a "traitor," pocketing the bribes of either McKinley or Bryan or, better yet, both at the same time.[31]

Butler's leadership and the behavior of the delegations in St. Louis, including the North Carolina delegation, suggested that Bryan's nomination was a political, not ideological, compromise, the purpose of which was to save the Populist organization and help elect a reform-minded president. It was not the culmination of a "silver conspiracy." The nomination of Watson, the unanimity of support for the platform, the praise of Bryan as a near Populist, not simply a silver man, and the actions of southern Populists, including Butler and Watson, who wanted both immediate financial reform and to preserve the national Populist organization and its principles, demonstrated this clearly. Certainly the strategy chosen had heavy costs, but so would have had any of the other options considered.

The convention also displayed the dramatic effect of varying state conditions on national Populist politics. Bryan's nomination drove home the fact that government ownership of railroads and irredeemable currency, the party's keystone national issues, lacked decisive political meaning in individual states, including in those where silver was popular. On the other hand, a general demand for monetary reform existed in 1896, and in St. Louis most Populists concluded that the party would be foolish to sit out the fight, especially if it could advance the party's original political goal of realignment. Perhaps more critical, four years after their party's creation, Populists still held minority status in all the states in which they operated. Populist politics required state-level success, and American politics was still driven by state-level issues. It therefore mattered that even in a presidential election Populists responded primarily to their own state conditions and that these responses also had to take into account the actions of other parties. In the West, Democrats tended to be Populist allies, while in the South, as in North Carolina, Republicans and Populists found common cause at the state level. Thus, after the convention, Bryan remained most popular among the westerners, who seemed willing to resolve all differences in favor of increasing his vote. In contrast, others, most notably Texans, concluded that abiding by the results of the convention would be destructive to their state party. Extending the North Carolina model, they eventually opted for state-level cooperation with Republicans in exchange for support for McKinley's electors. Local acts, impelled by perceptions of local political need, shaped the St. Louis convention and impeded Populist hopes for national success.[32]

Historians have noted that the St. Louis result was not wholly pleasing to anyone. Butler reflected this ambivalence. Nothing would have made him happier than a large popular groundswell for Omaha Platform Populism. Alternately, he would have been satisfied with a weak Democratic candidate for president and a true silver coalition. Either case would have made his actions as a senator, party leader in North Carolina, and national chairman of the People's Party much easier. Under the conditions that developed, however, he described the nominations as simply "the best possible thing that could be done." If either extreme faction prevailed in St. Louis, the People's Party would have split and McKinley would have been assured of victory. Political compromise, in Butler's mind, saved the larger cause of reform. Looking to the future, he believed the item of immediate overriding importance was Sewall's resignation. This could create a ticket as close as possible to the ideal he had promoted before Bryan's success at the Democratic convention.[33]

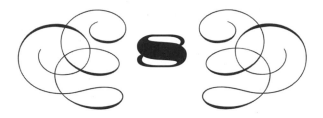

POPULIST PINNACLE

THE ST. LOUIS convention shaped Butler's strategy in North Carolina. First, cooperation with Democrats on presidential electors was in order. Second, because of Butler's silver coalition idea, there should be some kind of agreement with silver Democrats on state offices. Accordingly, after returning from St. Louis, Butler met with the new Democratic chairman, Clement Manly. Manly's executive committee tentatively supported presidential cooperation. Butler, however, responded that presidential cooperation depended on state cooperation. Of course, these were revolutionary proposals for both organizations, and the discussions produced heated debate among Democrats. The wing that still defended gold and Cleveland denounced all forms of cooperation. On the other hand, some Democrats saw a golden opportunity to jettison conservatives. E. J. Hales's *Fayetteville Observer* advocated open primaries for local offices, and Josephus Daniels initially supported national and state cooperation. For their part, Tar Heel Republicans tried to prevent silver from dictating political arrangements. They desperately fought any agreement between Democrats and Populists.[1]

Many Populists also opposed Butler's strategy, yet most wanted to renew relations with Republicans. For this group, bitterness toward Democrats trumped silver. A small number wanted to avoid cooperation altogether, perhaps the most thoughtful of which was James Ramsey of the *Progressive Farmer*. Ramsey, who had supported cooperation in 1894 and who eventually accepted it again in 1896, initially argued that Butler's decision to delay decisive action and make his appeal to silver Democrats was a serious error. Ramsey would have held an early national convention, written a strong Populist platform, and waited for the inevitable stampede to Populism by unhappy Democrats. Ramsey's comments represented the best articulation of the alternative to cooperation—Republican or Democratic. He accurately perceived the high costs of delay, uncertainty, and political maneuver. However, why Ramsey thought Democrats would respond to Omaha Platform Populism any more than free silver is unclear. Since 1892 Populism had stood for the Omaha proposals, always remaining open to new converts on that ground. For the most part, they did not appear. Ramsey's complaints, the ambitions of the emerging pro-Republicans, such as Harry Skinner, and Butler's convoluted negotiations made it painfully clear that no Populist had yet found a straightforward means to victory.[2]

Butler discounted criticism from pro-Republican Populists as well as Ramsey and planned to have his ideas approved at the Populist nominating convention. He retained a grip on party policy, although it was increasingly shaky. Incredibly, given the recent history of animosity between Populists and Democrats, on 12 August his Populist executive committee issued a broad formal offer of cooperation to Democratic chairman Manly. For the Populists, Butler wanted five of the state's eleven vice presidential electors and a Populist governor, treasurer, superintendent of public instruction, and supreme court justice. Democrats could have the remaining state officers and elect a pro-silver successor to Senator Jeter Pritchard. Leading Democrats promptly rejected the offer, at least for the time being. On 13 August, they voted against cooperation beyond presidential electors and perhaps congressional seats.[3]

At the ensuing Populist nominating convention, the key division was between Butler, who persisted with his plan to avoid Republican cooperation, and Harry Skinner, who favored an agreement with Democrats on presidential electors but wanted Republican cooperation to continue in state and local contests. The platform generated scant disagreement. The delegates affirmed their "unqualified allegiance" to the national Populist platform, the new election law, the county government law, and the 6 percent interest law. They condemned Democrats' unwillingness to enforce the state's existing antitrust laws and Governor Elias Carr's recent lease of the state-owned North Carolina Railroad to the Southern Railway Company.[4]

During the convention Butler advanced his new coalition strategy by supporting William A. Guthrie for governor. Guthrie, a Durham lawyer with close ties to Julian Carr's businesses, was an unlikely Populist. Yet Butler believed Guthrie, an early Bryan supporter, could attract silver Democrats as well as Populists and would be an ideal Democratic-Populist candidate. The Skinner faction endorsed Cyrus Thompson, anticipating a deal with Republicans in which Daniel Russell would be dropped. In the balloting, Guthrie prevailed by more than 2 to 1, suggesting both Butler's degree of control over the party as well as the significance of the opposition. Next, Butler nominated Oliver H. Dockery for lieutenant governor. He explained his choice of this recent Republican, now a Populist, by describing Dockery as one "who will cooperate with us for 'victory and free silver.'" Once again, Butler was trying to construct the broadest possible coalition. He also knew that given the Populist demand for the governorship, in a cooperation arrangement the candidate for lieutenant governor was expendable. Butler's supporters cast almost eight hundred votes for Dockery, while state senator James Mewborne, the Skinner candidate, won less than three hundred. After these victories, Butler skillfully sought to pacify the losers by endorsing Cyrus Thompson for secretary of state. When Butler's candidates also dominated the new executive committee and his editor, Hal Ayer, became the new party chairman, his triumph appeared complete.[5]

The Populist convention illustrated Butler's strategic adaptations to political change. In 1896 he first sought silver cooperation and then Democratic cooperation; when these strategies seemed to fail, he supported the nomination of a full Populist ticket that leaned toward silver supporters and included Democrat-Populists and Republican-Populists. Wonderfully orchestrated, the convention served primarily as a posturing device that left all political doors open. Cooperation with Republicans was still possible. Cooperation with Democrats was still possible. An independent Populist ticket, though least likely, was still possible. A combination of the three options at local, state, and federal levels was possible. Yet however brilliant from the standpoint of political gamesmanship, the result naturally produced uncertainty. As the *Progressive Farmer* put it, although the independent ticket nominated in Raleigh was "strong" and the platform "not bad," the election itself remained "enveloped in mystery."[6]

The response of Republicans and local Populists added another layer of complexity and showed the limits of Butler's authority. On 15 August the GOP attempted to achieve unilateral cooperation by filling the spaces previously left blank on its state ticket with the names of the Populist nominees. Because they were not willing to give up the governorship and because Dockery was unacceptable, Republicans simply retained their choices for the two top spots. This action put intense pressure on local Populists to act, even without the blessing of the state committee. By the end of August, in dozens of counties, local Populists simply ignored Butler's wishes and renewed Populist-Republican cooperation for county and legislative offices. Apparently, in the townships, Butler's high-level, nationally focused maneuvering seemed less relevant. There the issues were personal bitterness toward Democrats,

a history of cooperation, and the more tangible results of local officeholding, especially under the new county and town government law. Butler's absence contributed to this development. For much of the late summer he was
in Washington, busy with the national campaign. For the first time in the
party's history, the day-to-day leadership during an election fell to someone
else, Hal Ayer.[7]

Although aware that local cooperation undermined their efforts to avoid
the Republicans, Butler and Ayer tentatively consented to it when it did not
contradict free silver. Yet even this compromise proved impossible to enforce. First, by early September, Populists in fifty-three of the state's ninety-
six counties had already arranged cooperation with Republicans for local
and legislative offices, usually regardless of whether it advanced silver. Second, some Populist candidates, including Harry Skinner in the First Congressional District, also arranged Republican cooperation on their own regardless of silver. Both kinds of actions demonstrated a clear repudiation of
Butler's strategy at the county level by the rank and file. Making state affairs
even more complex, some Populists arranged local Democratic-Populist
cooperation.[8]

These developments and the passage of time produced a Populist executive committee meeting with Republicans on 9 and 10 September. By this
time, it was believed that some kind of resolution on candidates for congressional and statewide offices was needed. Both sides agreed to cooperate except in the races for governor and United States senator. Republicans promised to support Populists in four congressional districts and in the contests
for secretary of state, treasurer, superintendent of public instruction, and associate justice of the supreme court. In explaining the action, the Populist
committee returned to the leading rationale of 1894: Cooperation would
protect the free ballot and local self-government. It also hinted that Russell
would soon be dropped and stressed that the new congressional delegation
would be for free silver. Suggesting the real reason for the agreement, Ayer
informed Butler that, excepting himself, most of the committee wanted cooperation merely "for the purpose of beating the Democrats."[9]

Butler was neither present at the meeting nor entirely pleased with the result. Although the arrangement scuttled yet another of his hopeful strategies, it may have seemed the least bad of several bad options. Butler viewed
rule by either Republicans or Democrats alone as disastrous. Butler and
Ayer also consoled themselves that even this agreement, made less than two
months before the election, was not necessarily final. A better one might be

obtained from the Democrats. The hazy nature of the Republican state alliance appeared less than two weeks later, on 21 September, when the Populist executive committee formally agreed to a division of presidential electors with Democrats. The bargain created six Bryan-Sewall electors and five Bryan-Watson electors on a unified slate.[10]

The potential suggested by the presidential bargain finally bore fruit from Democrats as the election went into its final weeks. Thanks in large part to William Jennings Bryan, silver Democrats gained ascendancy within their party and set forth to defeat Populist-Republican cooperation. Despite his absence from North Carolina and his party's earlier agreement with Republicans, Butler encouraged a last-minute push for Democratic cooperation on state candidates. Apparently, the ballots had not yet been printed. He found an important ally in Bryan, who put pressure on Chairman Manly and Josephus Daniels to bring about an agreement. The crucial moment came in early October, when Daniels and Manly asked Ayer to make a cooperation offer. Ayer demurred, largely on the ground of Populist pride, forcing the Democrats to come up with their own plan. On 12 October, they promised Populists a nearly equal division of congressional seats and state offices. They also offered to support Guthrie for lieutenant governor or for U.S. senator, but they were not willing to jettison their candidate for governor, Cyrus Watson. Ayer hurriedly called together the Populist executive committee, which rejected the offer by a 16-2 vote. Although the proposal seemed very close to what Butler wanted, it flunked the litmus test on the governorship. Ayer defended the decision by claiming that no self-respecting Populist would vote for the conservative Cyrus Watson and that Russell's failure to come off the Republican ticket was the primary reason Populists had wanted to renegotiate cooperation in the first place. From the beginning, Butler had always placed great emphasis on the importance of a Populist governor, and the Democrats' hesitation on that point proved fatal. Nonetheless, the Democratic offer was a credit to Butler's persistence, and he regretted its failure.[11]

With alignments in place less than a month before the election, the Populist campaign tried to focus on the treachery of Democrats and the benefits of the new election law. Not surprisingly, however, this did not sit well with many, including pro-Democratic Populists, and especially the party's candidate for governor, William Guthrie. In mid-October Guthrie wrote pathetic letters to Butler, complaining of Russell's refusal to step down and of Ayer's inability to achieve cooperation with Democrats. Facing the prospect of contributing to the election of a Republican, on 27 October Guthrie abandoned Populism and asked true Populists to vote for Cyrus Watson and the other Democrats.[12]

The Guthrie fiasco, which was infinitely more embarrassing than the Exum debacle of 1892, symbolized the Populists' political dilemma. In 1896 the party lost the unity of ideology and strategy that had led it to victory in 1894. State, local, and national issues did not produce consistent political goals or allies. Butler's silver coalition plan, which may have worked to unite Populists, failed to do so because silver became too closely associated with Democracy, most Populists were unable to transcend their distrust of Democracy at the county level, and the state Democratic Party hesitated to endorse an acceptable form of cooperation. Republican cooperation in 1896 was not Butler's idea. It was the product of local Populists who feared a return to Democratic rule at the county and state levels. They, and not the state committee, entered into cooperation agreements first and without regard for the silver issue. Ironically, the triumph of localism in North Carolina bore a close resemblance to Butler's problems in the national campaign.[13]

BUTLER KNEW THAT his principal task as national chairman would be to hold together the diverse elements of the party. He believed that the compromise reached in St. Louis was the only way the party could sustain itself. He also believed that the Bryan-Watson ticket fairly represented a silver-reform coalition and could be elected. At the same time, he realized that the appeal of Populism was limited. It was nonexistent in the most populated parts of the country; perhaps it amounted to 2 million votes out of a total electorate of 13 million. This, in addition to the Electoral College, in which state political parties determined the presidential electors, required that Populists have good relations with Democratic leaders for Watson and Bryan to win. Butler never doubted that it was possible for both Bryan and Watson to be elected.[14]

Operating from Washington's Old Wormley Hotel, Chairman Butler initially focused on Arthur Sewall's elimination from the race. Southern Populists, in particular, believed that Sewall's withdrawal was imperative. W. S. Morgan of Arkansas wrote Butler that Sewall was "the one dark cloud that obscures the rays of the star of our hope." Tom Watson claimed that more pressure from westerners would force Sewall's resignation: "The Democratic managers cannot afford to keep Sewall in and if our [national] committee takes a bold position and holds it, [Democratic chairman James K.] Jones will back down." When Sewall had still not resigned by mid-August, a breach

Candidate Billy's busy day.
(Library of Congress)

began to develop between Watson and Butler on how to get rid of him. Watson believed it would be best to threaten to withhold Populist support for Bryan unless Watson was allowed to become the Democratic vice presidential nominee. This was similar to Butler's demands on North Carolina Democrats regarding state-level cooperation. Here, however, Butler made the decision that in national politics Populist leverage had greater limits and that a strong threat would play into the hands of conservative Democrats and lead to a McKinley victory. The practical effect of the Butler policy was to mandate the creation of electoral tickets with both Sewall and Watson electors.[15]

As in North Carolina, however, simply because the party leadership decreed a strategy did not mean that local Populist organizations would comply. To be sure, many state leaders began negotiating with Democrats for Bryan-Watson-Sewall slates of electors. But in two key Populist states party members went in opposite directions. Anti-Democratic Texans were unwilling to support a Bryan-Watson ticket, much less an electoral slate with Sewall. They traded Republican support for state-level Populist candidates for Populist support for McKinley. In contrast, the Kansas party arranged state-level Democratic cooperation in exchange for support for Bryan-Sewall electors, leaving out Watson. Both actions, particularly given that they derived from the two strongest state Populist organizations in the country, signaled the priority given to state political needs.[16]

In August controversy over the notification of Bryan and Watson exacerbated the Sewall issue. The problem arose when Butler decided that no formal notification of the nominations would be sent. He worried about the possible tone of Bryan's response, although he assumed that time would generate sufficient pressure on Democrats to effect full cooperation. Yet his decision produced criticism from Populists who viewed the lack of notification as an affront to party dignity. The criticisms caused Butler to agree to notify the candidates, although the notifications would not take place until September.[17]

Despite growing tension over Sewall and notification, from the beginning Butler vigorously promoted the Bryan-Watson ticket. He was "determined to see that Watson is the next Vice President of the United States" if "there is any way under heaven to accomplish it." He thought a patient posture and a calculated, broad appeal would produce a groundswell for Watson. A magnanimous stand, as opposed to self-righteous belligerence, would allow Populists to be favorably contrasted with gold supporters and insincere silver men. This behavior should convince many Bryan supporters to become Populists. Patience was important, because Butler's party was "the one that must settle questions of great concern to the people that are not present in the present campaign."[18]

The heart of this strategy, of course, was to expand support for Populism by emphasizing silver. The obvious weakness of this path was that, for most Democrats, particularly southerners, even a modest step in the direction of national reform kept them clinging to the party because they already had so many other reasons to do so. Moreover, the policy discounted Democratic desires to reach out for converts of their own by adopting some Populist proposals, which made Populism less politically distinct. On the other hand, Butler's plan harmonized with Populist political principle. It placed the getting of reform, not political organization, first. In that sense it was the opposite of the kind of practical politics for which some historians have criticized Butler. His long-term policy, which assumed new members would be attracted to Populism because of its unselfish behavior, was incredibly idealistic, not pragmatic.

Butler sought as many Watson electors as possible, including more than Populist strength fairly required. He made it clear to state committees that they should not trade Watson electors for Democratic endorsements of state candidates. The Kansas party's desertion of Watson in this way distressed him enormously. He also advised Populists at the state level to threaten separate action if arrangements were not satisfactory, but preferably only as long as it seemed necessary to avoid a defeat for Bryan. This kind of plan was implemented in North Carolina. He pressured Democratic chairman James K. Jones for better electoral arrangements. Finally, he pushed for "everything we possibly can [get] for Watson" in the states where Bryan was likely to win and Populism was strong.[19]

In September, Butler coordinated the much-awaited notification process with Senator William V. Allen; Allen wrote Bryan, while Butler drafted Watson's notice. The substance of the letters was very different. Allen's notice recognized Bryan's adherence to Democracy. Butler, by contrast, produced a ringing defense of Populism and the party's strategy. He told Watson that Populism represented the strivings of the "wealth producers" and those "engaged in legitimate business interests," while the older parties represented the "personal greed of the money changers, corporations, trusts, [and] monopolies." Populists declared first for free silver and had long protested "the surrender of the government function of issuing paper money to national, state or private banks." Only the People's Party stood for "the suppression of monopolies and for the equal protection of all citizens against the encroachment of individual and corporate power." The Democrats' choice for vice president proved they could not carry out meaningful reform. Butler explained Populist support for Bryan, "a man who stands in the broadest and truest sense for American institutions and American principles," as an achievement that put "country over party." In offering the vice presidential nomination to Watson, Butler noted that if the Democracy really wanted reform it would not have nominated Sewall and, in turn, the Populist convention would not have felt impelled to nominate its own candidate. Victory depended on "the cooperation of the silver forces of all political parties."[20]

Perhaps the most telling commentaries on Butler's letter came from those who might have been expected to criticize it. The *Dallas Southern Mercury* regarded it as representative of "the cowardly truckling policy that has characterized the whole [national committee] program." The paper rendered this verdict, however, after it received a highly distorted version distributed by the anti-Populist Associated Press. With full text in hand, the *Mercury* apologized and described Butler's effort as "a document of great force," which should be read by every Populist in Texas. Watson reportedly was pleased with the tone and content of the letter.[21]

Butler expressed similar sentiments in private campaign correspondence. He emphasized the long-term effects of the contest. He assumed that even with Bryan, "bosses" managed Democracy, and that after the election gold men would be in control. On the other hand, patriotic Populist behavior would convert honest Democrats, and by 1900, "we will naturally gather together all of the reform elements that are now supporting Mr. Bryan under our own banner . . . and it will be necessary for the plutocrats to unite upon one candidate." Butler also sent many letters to industrial workers and manufacturers. For example, he combined a friendly exchange with the socialist Eugene Debs with statements to manufacturers that silver inflation could improve their businesses. Nonetheless, he understood Populism would not appeal equally to each section of the nation. Apparently he conceded all states east and north of Ohio to McKinley, while Bryan victories in Indiana, Illinois, Michigan, Minnesota, and Iowa seemed "critical."[22]

In mid-September, Watson began a speaking tour through Texas, Kansas, Nebraska, and Colorado. Surprisingly, and in direct contrast to party policy, he denounced any Populist support for Sewall and urged southerners to respond negatively to insults to one of their own, Tom Watson. He contrasted himself with greedy party managers who effected cooperation out of a love for office. Yet he proclaimed support for the cooperation that included him and he praised William Jennings Bryan. Watson's false and inconsistent message produced an irrational reaction. Texas Populists, many of whom would vote for McKinley, cheered Bryan's running mate. Kansas Populists, upset at not being able to vote for Watson, mistakenly complained about a national chairman who was as disgusted with conditions there as they were. Butler did not approve of Watson's performance. Because he believed Sewall could not be eliminated by threats and might not resign, Watson's hostility served no purpose. Butler still believed Populists could advance only by pressing "our claim as the party that has sacrificed the most for the advancement of these principles."[23]

This was a disagreement over means, not ends. Watson's shrillness was his method of doing what he thought was best for cooperation. He believed that he could drive Sewall from the ticket and he and Bryan could be elected. The controversial portions of Watson's speeches had nothing to do with opposition to Sewall, the Omaha Platform, silver, or opposition to cooperation. Instead, they revealed disagreement over how Populists should react to Sewall's remaining on the ticket. Watson thought that support for Sewall jeopardized the party, whereas Butler believed that a failure to promote the joint electoral tickets was a greater danger. Despite the speeches, Butler viewed Watson the Populist as "brilliant" and "true as steel." He praised Watson's Lincoln, Nebraska, speech, which did not attack Sewall. He planned to publish the speeches in a Populist handbook, and he wanted to send Watson on a tour of the Old Northwest so that anticipated victories there could be credited to Watson and Populism.[24]

Butler's optimism about Watson was misplaced. On 27 September Watson chastised Butler for "insulting criticisms" of his Texas and Kansas speeches. He decided not to finish his part of the Populist handbook. He was also angry at Butler's inability to change the vice presidential conditions, but Butler was equally disappointed at Sewall and the Democratic leadership's behavior. Thus, nothing Watson said about the Democrats or Sewall was new or disagreeable to Butler. The question, as before, was what to do about the problem. Unfortunately, Watson now contended that his disappointments resulted from a sordid conspiracy. Real Populists, said the candidate, those "who want no office and hunger for no pie, . . . have been tricked, sold out, betrayed, misled." Watson opined that if only separate Bryan and Watson tickets had been created in some states, such as North Carolina and Kansas, "Mr. Sewall would have had to get out."[25]

Watson's personal attacks surprised Butler. He knew that an effort to establish a separate Bryan-Watson ticket in North Carolina would not force Sewall out. He also knew that in every other southern state, including Watson's Georgia, Bryan-Sewall electors could win even without votes for Watson. Separate tickets there would be futile, and Populists would get no credit for Bryan's success. Outside the South, "Watson or no Bryan" sentiment would simply produce a greater defection of western Populists to Sewall. Butler thought that it was "too plain for controversy that if results [are] what we are fighting for, and the future interest of the party is what we are interested in, in addition to the welfare of the country, that we could not possibly by [separate tickets] have secured anything like the results that we will secure by our present course." Unfortunately, Watson's "political judgment and his perception of the present political situation is [*sic*] badly at fault." In a 30 September response to Watson, Butler criticized Watson's claim that attacks on Sewall could bring the Maine banker down. Populists had two choices: to oppose Bryan out of revenge for ill treatment by Democrats or to help Bryan. The point, as Butler stated in a letter to Populist George Washburn, was that it "is nonsense to be talking 'middle of the road' when the one hope of defeating the common enemy is by union of forces." Further, "it is a part of our creed to place country above party and individuals," and Watson's position did neither.[26]

As the campaign moved into October, Populists faced another serious problem—a lack of funds. The Washington headquarters ran on the ludicrous sum of $150 a week, which was not enough to pay for stationery, rent, help, or postage. Most campaign workers were Washingtonians who toiled for little, "being friends of the cause." Butler helped through the ethically dubious act of obtaining five hundred thousand franked envelopes from his Senate office. He noted that few contributions amounted to more than $25, and most were under a dollar. As of mid-September he had received only $275 from the entire state of Georgia. He attempted to keep financial problems from the public gaze, always fearing the embarrassment they would produce.[27]

During the final month of the election, Watson and other anti-Democratic Populists escalated their attacks on Butler's national committee. The rationale of the criticism, however, was unchanged. Watson continued to complain that he got the short end of electoral bargains and blamed "treason," "plots," and spineless submission to "outrages." A perverse idea that now united Watson's anti-Democrats was that the best result would be a defeat of Bryan that could be blamed on Democratic intransigence. As a result, a significant number of southern Populists in Alabama, Georgia, and Texas supported McKinley.[28]

Butler, however, still believed Watson might win if Sewall could be forced to withdraw after the election or if Watson won enough votes to throw the vice presidency to Congress. By the end of October, cooperation electoral slates existed in twenty-eight of the nation's forty-five states. Butler's plan achieved greatest success in the West and the Midwest and was least successful in the South. In the latter region, hatred for Democracy by Populists

FUN FOR THE POLITICIANS, BUT ROUGH ON THE BUSINESS MAN.

The businessman's dilemma, 1896.
(Library of Congress)

ranked as the most obvious reason. Further, from the Democratic standpoint, except in a few states such as Tennessee and North Carolina, there
was no realistic threat of a McKinley victory.[29]

As the campaign neared its end, Watson's unpredictability and bitterness
engendered fears that he was on the verge of collapse and that he might re-

sign just before the election. The fears were justified. In mid-October Evan P. Howell, Democratic editor of the *Atlanta Constitution*, visited Watson. Although details of the meeting, as well as related discussions between Watson and Populist national committee members H. W. Reed and George Washburn, remain unclear, evidence suggests that Watson considered trading his vice presidential electors for a clear run for Congress. Washburn told reporters that "Mr. Watson would rather be vindicated in his own town, in his own district, in his own state and in the whole nation than be vice-president. His southern pride is aroused and the people of Georgia are rallying around him because he is a Southerner." Of course, to accept a provincial "vindication of honor" seemed to put Watson among the office-hungry politicians. At any rate, the discussions failed to remove him from the race. Once again, Butler was caught off-guard. He viewed the fact that Watson may have discussed the possibility of selling electors to Sewall's Democrats as "very inconsistent, if not absurd."[30]

The putative congressional deal was not Watson's last confrontation with the chairman. In mid-October he mailed his nomination "acceptance" letter to the executive committee. Butler hoped to use it as a centerpiece in the Populist campaign book. However, because Watson failed to affix proper postage, the letter lay undelivered in the Washington post office from around 15 October until about one week later. Butler finally had the letter by 26 October. Watson largely repeated the same complaints he had been making for weeks. The only novel content was Watson's request that Populists refrain from voting for the cooperation slates on the ground of Democratic betrayal.[31]

Partly because the letter said almost nothing new, Butler wrote Watson seeking compromise. In exchange for official publication of Watson's letter, which attacked him, he asked Watson to delete the part that advised Populists not to vote for the cooperation electors. Butler demanded to know whether "any personal or party injustice, however great, [can] justify us in being responsible, either directly or indirectly, for placing in power the stock jobbers, monopolists, trusts, the British gold ring, and all of the combined robbers of the people and the enemies of good government."[32]

Watson wasted no time in responding, and with a proper stamp. On 28 October he penned a long personal attack on Butler, which was dominated by expressions of lost honor, feelings of persecution, and misstatements of fact. Watson did not believe that his "acceptance" letter was really lost. Butler always had personal "ill will" toward him. Butler's continuing criticism was "a public affront" that degraded and "publicly humiliated" him. He thought

Democrats had not shown enough "respect" for Populists. Watson blamed Butler for not obtaining Sewall's withdrawal. Butler's only role during the election was "to act with me and for me." His arguments were "unanswerable."[33]

Despite Watson's letters, Butler promoted the Bryan-Watson ticket until the
end. In the campaign's final days he issued two public letters, one to North
Carolina Populists and one to all Populists. He told North Carolinians that
he regretted his inability to play a larger role there. He emphasized that a
McKinley victory would serve foreigners, gold, and the trusts; it would eliminate the possibility of reform legislation. Moreover, his followers should not
let "any embarrassments and disappointments about the Vice-presidency . . .
prevent us from doing our full duty as Populists." Butler's advice to all Populists was broader. Their enemies were "nonproducers," who by cunning
"have aggrandized themselves by seizing the humble accumulation of others, produced by labor." Even "black and white are now alike struggling." Cooperation with Democrats did not hurt the party, because the organization
"must ever remain the guiding force in the American republic, led by the pi-
oneers of the great army of reform."[34]

Election day, 3 November, did not bring the millennium. Bryan managed
about 500,000 fewer votes than McKinley and lost 271 to 176 in the electoral count. Despite Bryan's loss, cooperation resulted in unparalleled success for lesser Populist candidates. About twenty-five Populist representatives
and senators, the most ever, would be in Washington for the next Congress. In
western and southern states, Populists won scores of local and state offices.
The third party, with the help of Democratic and Republican allies, also prevailed in North Carolina. Bryan carried the state by 19,000 votes, and most
of the state's congressmen were Populists. Hal Ayer became state auditor,
Cyrus Thompson was elected secretary of state, and Walter Montgomery
won a full term on the supreme court. Republicans and Populists vastly outnumbered Democrats in the senate and in the house. The governor's race
represented the greatest Populist setback. Guthrie's last-minute departure
left the party without a candidate, and Populists divided their votes. As a result, Russell became the first Republican governor since the 1870s.[35]

BRYAN'S DEFEAT angered Butler. He complained of Democratic treachery
and Republican bribery. He believed that although most Americans would
benefit from Populism, voters seemed unable to support it because of irrational party attachments and hatreds. Nonetheless, he thought Populists
should continue to display the selflessness that would make them "the nu-

cleus around which the patriotic hosts must and will gather to redeem a betrayed republic." In the meantime, there would be depression and oppression, with "four more years of lockouts and strikes, [and] four more years of reduced wages and idle labor."[36]

Butler was also angry with Populists who criticized his leadership. In response to a postelection diatribe by Watson, he fumed that Watson was "so wrapped up in his vanity and narrow selfishness" that he had forgotten that the purpose of the Populist Party was to bring about reform. He accused Watson's followers of accepting Republican bribes. Watson himself, however, was more foolish than corrupt, as shown by his interest in trading his electors with Sewall for a seat in Congress. Butler also ridiculed Watson's new claim that a midroad ticket could have been successful, an idea Watson himself rejected until the very end of the campaign. In November, independent tickets overwhelmingly failed, and even Bryan had been beaten. Ultimately, Watson was both hypocritical and self-centered, a loser whose capacity for political mobilization was limited to a small part of Georgia.[37]

Other reactions to the election showed a deeper and more permanent rift than Butler appreciated. Many Kansans and other western Populists believed that a continued union of parties, not Butler's union of reformers, was desirable. In contrast, Watson and some of the Texas Populists constructed a pseudohistory of the election. A contradictory tale of villains and dark conspiracy, its political purpose was unclear. Watson, for example, denounced a wide variety of fellow Populists, including Peffer, Weaver, Allen, and Butler, as traitors. Conveniently forgetting the cooperationist stage of Watson's career, the *Dallas Southern Mercury* reasoned that the persons who prevailed at St. Louis were just "not Populists." The paper then implicitly affirmed the St. Louis result by stating that if Butler had merely demanded Sewall's withdrawal, "there is no doubt but that his demand would have been complied with and Bryan and Watson would have been elected."[38]

North Carolina Populism also revealed traits of disintegration. The feud between Butler and Skinner persisted. The main point of contention after the election was whether Populists should support Jeter Pritchard's reelection as U.S. senator. Butler had attacked Pritchard since early in 1896, and Populists did not agree to support Pritchard under the terms of cooperation. On 14 November Butler announced that Pritchard had "radically changed" his views on currency and that he favored the election of a man who held the same views Pritchard did in 1895. The Skinner wing, however, stuck by Pritchard, claiming that Populists were duty bound to reelect the Republican.[39]

The 1896 election represents the high point of Butler's political career. He tried to mold a successful national coalition based on Populism that would save the Populist organization, failing primarily because of structural impediments to reform politics. Most important, he was unable to fashion a national coalition that responded appropriately to the widely varying needs of state Populist organizations. In 1896, disagreements about presidential strategy reflected differences in the politics of individual states and regions, not ideological disputes about reform principles. The platform adopted in St. Louis, as well as the broad support for Bryan and Watson among Populists, suggests the point. Moreover, the alienation of many Populists from the campaign was not related to cooperation per se but to Democrats' perceived treachery in cooperation, as statements by Watson and the Texans established. Further, Watson, Texans, Kansans, Butler, and the Populist supporters of Bryan all supported some kind of cooperation. Different versions of cooperation, not a contest between "midroaders" and "fusionists," defined Populist politics in 1896. The primary reason was that few Populists escaped the pressing needs of state politics long enough to conceptualize a successful national political reform movement. Butler tried, but the defeat of his silver coalition suggests he did not lead a true national party. At the most, the People's Party was a coalition of state organizations bound together by Alliance ideology, each of which held minority political status in its own state.

Equally significant was the reaction of Democrats and Republicans to the third party. A successful anticooperation presidential strategy could exist only in states where both the older parties refused to respond to the third party. Of course, the People's Party did not operate in a political vacuum. State-level Republicans and Democrats reacted vigorously to the challenge with a wide range of strategies, including cooperation and absorption of Populist doctrine. In fact, the Populist Party and either the Republican or the Democratic Party in every state with a significant Populist contingent approved some form of cooperation before 1897. Butler's actions tried to accommodate these challenges, yet the deeper problem was that cooperation was traditionally driven by state, not national, needs, and state issues varied widely across the nation. By contrast, Populism wanted new federal laws, but at the national level neither silver, Bryan, cooperation, nor the Omaha Platform was able to create a unified and effective national movement. As a result, the party's future was bleak.

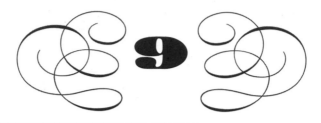

FACTIONAL POLITICS

AFTER THE ELECTION there was little time to ponder the deeper meaning of recent events. Butler was occupied with the demands of national Populist politics, the Congress, and the troublesome state of affairs in North Carolina. Conditions in North Carolina needed immediate attention, for the General Assembly convened in January, and Pritchard's Senate seat and Populist legislation were at stake. Joined by Harry Skinner, Pritchard lobbied hard for the support of Populists. As for Populist legislation, the state platform demanded making all coins of the United States equal legal tender, prohibiting contracts payable in gold, improving public education, reducing railroad rates, and adopting a law against railroad passes. Populists also disliked Governor Elias Carr's recent lease of the largely state-owned North Carolina Railroad to J. P. Morgan's Southern Railway Company.[1]

Hoping to repeat the successes of 1891 and 1895, Butler arrived in Raleigh just as the session began. His first task was to organize a Populist caucus that would ensure Pritchard's defeat. Yet Republicans met Populist legislators as they alighted from their trains. Seventy-two Republicans and ninety-eight Populists and Democrats sat in the assembly. Because Republicans united behind Pritchard, he needed the votes of only fourteen Populists to be re-elected. On 8 January Butler's efforts to achieve solidarity in the Populist caucus failed, as almost twenty men bolted. He only managed to delay a final vote for the Senate seat and hoped to split the pro-Republican faction by offering Cyrus Thompson as his nominee.[2]

The state's newspapers understood the fight involved more than just a position in the Senate. Pritchard, who voted for McKinley, could not be defended as the candidate of financial reform. Yet both the Republican press and the portion of the Populist press that endorsed Pritchard praised Skinner, denounced Butler, and argued that the caucus bolters were simply adhering to a Populist promise made in 1895. In other words, Pritchard Populists conceded that their overriding interest was not financial reform but good relations with Republicans. Democrats hoped Butler's position would end Republican-Populist cooperation. The fight was so important that corruption played a role. According to the *Progressive Farmer*, which supported Butler, Republican techniques were "the most infamous ever known in the political history of the state." One legislator who voted for Pritchard later admitted that Republican job offers enticed Populists. Skinner himself became the Republican U.S. attorney in eastern North Carolina in 1901.[3]

On 20 January enough Populists voted for Pritchard to send him back to Washington. Butler refused to forgive and forget. Furious at the Skinnerites, he even accused Tom Watson, who had endorsed Pritchard out of spite, of wanting a deal with Republicans for a congressional seat. He suspected a conspiracy led by national Republicans, including party leader Marcus Hanna of Ohio. Ultimately, Butler described the source of the defeat as "Mark Hanna and his crowd, assisted by the Southern Railway." In the week following Pritchard's election, the Populist legislative caucus, led by Butler, proclaimed that the bolters, led by the "arch traitor" Skinner, were no longer Populists. Isolated, the caucus blasted Republicans, Democrats, and Skinnerites alike.[4]

Although Butler visited Raleigh only occasionally in the weeks after the Pritchard defeat, he remained in contact with Populists in the assembly. He instructed his allies to press for items in the party's platform, such as bills to prevent discrimination against silver as legal tender, to lower telegraph and railroad rates, to abolish free railroad passes, and to make the railroad commission an elective body. Generally, Populist efforts at extending corporate regulation and advancing currency reform failed. One reason was that Pritchard Populists tended to vote more with Republicans against such measures than with the Butler Populists. As if this did not complicate matters sufficiently, there was a new factor: Governor Daniel L. Russell. The former Greenbacker displayed a keen interest in some reform issues, particularly cancellation of the lease of the North Carolina Railroad, better public education, and more effective railroad regulation. Yet Butler had opposed Russell in 1896 and during the Pritchard fight accused him of manipulating patronage in order to lure Populists. If Russell was to achieve regulatory reform, he would have to make amends with the Populist senator.[5]

That opportunity arose when a bill to annul the lease of the North Carolina Railroad to the Southern Railway came before the legislature. Butler had his Populist caucus adopt a resolution against the lease. Russell also supported annulment, and suddenly the Butler Populists found themselves following the governor's lead. Most Republicans, however, as well as most Pritchard Populists, rejected the attack, and a coalition of Republicans, Democrats, and Pritchard Populists defeated it. Butler made a special trip to Raleigh to fight for the bill; he proclaimed that the affair proved the need for government ownership of railroads.[6]

After the lease fight, Butler gave Russell a broader chance to prove himself a reformer. Initially, some Populists contended that the governor was trying to build up a personal following. Yet near the end of the legislature Russell opposed a Republican local government bill that the Butler Populists feared would mean black control in eastern North Carolina. This caused them to reevaluate Russell favorably, especially after Republicans and Pritchard Populists passed the bill over Russell's objections.[7]

ALTHOUGH DISAPPOINTED by events in North Carolina, Butler was optimistic about the effect of the 1896 election on Congress. When he returned to Washington for the first session of the Fifty-fifth Congress, the Populist caucus issued a defiant statement defending the party's actions during the recent campaign. Sounding like Butler's personal product, it announced that if Bryan had been elected, "the money questions would have been speedily settled" and "the transportation question and other vital issues presented by our platform would have at once become the storm center of political discussion, and the People's party would soon acquire second if not first place in the politics of our country."[8]

The most important legislation passed during the session was the Dingley tariff. Its high rates would satisfy even the most ardent protectionists. Populists, however, had always considered the tariff an unjust way to raise revenue. During the Dingley debate Butler applied this principle of Populist political economy and attacked the idea that either lower or higher tariffs could produce prosperity. Its inevitable failure to improve the economy would show that the "People's Party has offered the only cure for trusts, the only recipe that has ever produced prosperity—more money and no monopolies." More specifically, economic recovery depended on government ownership of railroads and a "sufficient quantity of legal-tender money to increase as population and business increases." Nonetheless, Butler believed farmers could benefit from agricultural bounties on wheat, corn, cotton, and tobacco, and he declared against free trade for manufactured goods,

Harry Skinner: Populism's Judas?
(Courtesy of the North Carolina Division of Archives and History)

because "international commercialism" was "antagonistic and fatal to the genius of our republican institutions." Populists Allen, Butler, and William Harris of Kansas, who had replaced William Peffer, abstained from voting on the Dingley bill.[9]

Much of Butler's work in the session involved the postal service. He fought the Loud Bill, which aimed to increase rates for second-class mail. He argued that because cheap second-class matter included weekly rural newspapers and reform tracts, monopolies hoped the bill would shut down the sources of radicalism. The Loud Bill failed. Butler also protested against the fees paid railroads for carrying the mail. He thought the government should own, not rent, its postal cars, claiming it paid the New York Central eighty-five hundred dollars a year to rent a car that cost thirty-five hundred dollars. The Senate rejected his proposals on railroad postal fees. Finally, he introduced a bill to establish postal savings banks, another Alliance-Populist reform. He believed the banks would both allow rural people to set aside money and produce revenue for the government. With only fifty cents needed to open an account and a limit of five hundred dollars per account, the system would transfer the national debt to working people and away from "a few large capitalists holding government bonds."[10]

Butler tried to advance Populism in other ways. He introduced a resolution promoting a federal initiative and referendum, a constitutional amendment to allow an income tax, and a bill "to prevent discrimination between various kinds of legal-tender money of the United States, and to maintain the equal debt paying and purchasing power thereof." Regarding the income tax, he remarked that although 1 percent of the population owned 70 percent of the nation's wealth, the current tax system drew from the poor to pay for the protection of the wealthy. He also wanted the government, which held their defaulted mortgages, to assert public ownership over the Union Pacific and Central Pacific Railroads. Butler and William Allen argued this "would make a fair practical test [of public ownership generally] and would kill Government ownership forever if it did not prove successful." This idea did not come to a vote. Another application of Populist principle involved immigration. Populists complained that the nation wrongly opened its "ports to the pauper and criminal classes of the world" and demanded restriction on immigration. Butler and the other Populists successfully supported an immigration bill with an English literacy test, but President Cleveland vetoed it during his last days in office.[11]

Butler's actions during the session established a pattern that would persist for the remainder of his Senate career. He opposed the proposals of the dominant Republicans and injected Populism at every opportunity and used his committee positions, such as with the Post Office, to try to promote Populist principles and legislation. Extremely active both as an instigator of legislation and as a debater, he was able to translate his understanding of Populist proposals and principles into support for or opposition to specific legislation. Yet, because of the weakness of his party in Congress, he was unable to have much of an impact on the shape of new laws.

DESPITE SETBACKS IN North Carolina and the Senate, Butler's most frustrating occupation in 1897 was as chairman of the national Populist Party. After Bryan's defeat, divisions hardened over strategy. Most important, men unhappy with more Democratic cooperation in national elections instigated an organized attack on the Butler-led national committee. Many in this group believed the first step to recovery would be a conference early in 1897. Butler, however, thought a conference would attract Populists who were "a hindrance and dead weight, if not an element that would be dangerous and troublesome." However, he agreed that the Democratic Party was trying to entice Populists and proposed a party edict denouncing that effort. He also believed "we must bring other planks of the People's party platform to the front besides this silver question; and, on account of the position taken by the Railroads in the last campaign, the railroad question is not only one of the strongest for this purpose, but one of the most timely."[12]

Of course, he had no power over Populists who were intent on calling a meeting and criticizing continued national cooperation. Paul Vandervoort, president of the National Reform Press Association and a Butler opponent, scheduled a meeting of the association in Memphis for February 1897. Besides leading the anti-Democratic Populists, Vandervoort believed Jesuits had controlled President Cleveland and had recently won over McKinley. Vandervoort's plan caused an uproar. Opposing Populist editors called for a separate meeting in Kansas City, while others sought compromise. Harry Tracy of Texas, a moderate among anti-Democrats, asked Butler to call a meeting of the national committee to coincide with the Memphis convention.[13]

Still trying to avoid a confrontation and a formal challenge to his leadership, Butler refused to call a Populist meeting for Memphis and also refused to approve the Kansas City meeting. He accepted that Vandervoort had a right to convene his organization. Nonetheless, he opposed Vandervoort's purpose, which was to overthrow the policy of the national committee. Claiming that Vandervoort was not a real Populist, Butler tried to have him

voted out as leader of the Press Association. He asked several friendly editors to go to Memphis for this purpose. Yet many responded that such an assault would fail because Vandervoort already controlled a majority of delegates. More ominous, one editor thought the bad Populist apples were largely
southerners and that the party's future was in the West. Perhaps the only
member of the national committee who wanted to go to Memphis was George
Washburn. Washburn, however, supported a broader Populist meeting because, as he told Butler, "the most that they can do is to advocate breaking
away from the democratic party and making an issue of paper money, government ownership of railroads and perhaps direct legislation and such action would be no more than you and I believe in."[14]

The Memphis and Kansas City meetings reflected both division and hope
for reconciliation. The Memphis convention denounced Democratic cooperation, but Washburn wrote Butler that he, Charles Vincent of Indiana, and
J. H. "Cyclone" Davis of Texas, who were present, hoped the party's factions
could be united. At the Kansas City meeting, delegates chose Knights of
Labor leader J. R. Sovereign to head the pro-Bryan Populist press. Sovereign
also hoped for harmony and expressed respect for the leaders at Memphis,
particularly John Parker of Kentucky and Frank Burkitt of Mississippi.[15]

After the press meetings, anti-Democrats again pressed for a convention
that would formally repudiate cooperation. Burkitt, Parker, W. S. Morgan,
Jacob Coxey, and Milton Park sent Butler a letter requesting a national committee meeting that would prepare for a convention. Once again, Butler responded that this was not a good idea. Persons "furnished with Republican
money" would try to influence Populist policy. As an alternative, Butler proposed a national committee meeting dedicated to achieving harmony to be
held in February 1898. He believed most Populists supported his position.
He even mailed a survey to committeemen from each state asking whether
there should be a national convention in 1897. Eighty-five indicated that
there should not be a meeting, nineteen supported a call, four were uncertain, and thirty-five did not respond. Butler concluded that 90 percent of
the national committee, all the elected Populists in Washington, and most
Populist newspapers opposed an immediate convention.[16]

He also campaigned to convince Populists that this policy was best. He
warned that the persons opposed to his strategy were a minority funded by
enemies of reform. Butler claimed that in 1896 Tom Watson had been an
unwitting tool of Republicans, and N. A. Dunning, Watson's friend and adviser, counseled Populists to vote for McKinley because Republicans paid
Dunning. Further, assuming that "there certainly can be no disagreement as

to our platform," delay until 1898 would create needed support from Republicans disgruntled with McKinley. In the meantime, any Populist convention would degenerate into the divisive question of cooperation versus no cooperation. Butler received considerable encouragement for his efforts. Reuben Kolb wrote him that Alabama Populists were behind him, and J. R. Sovereign, Charles Vincent, and H. W. Reed rejected a convention. In writing Milton Park of Texas, Sovereign denounced the McKinley-Populist deal in Texas in 1896 and argued that the alleged "midroaders" had placed party over principle.[17]

Butler's opponents, tired of waiting, called a conference to reorganize the party in Nashville on 4 July 1897. They conceded the party's differences were "not as to the correctness of principles embodied in the St. Louis and Omaha platforms, but as regards the policy to be henceforth pursued to advance the cause of the people in their irrepressible conflict with both the Democratic and Republican parties." Accordingly, they stacked their conference against supporters of cooperation by deciding that participation in the primaries to elect delegates could include only those "who will vote the straight Populist party ticket." This prevented debate over strategy by assuming that "true Populists" had to agree that cooperation was "absurd." The Nashville delegates endorsed the same Populist platforms adopted in 1892 and 1896 and created the National Organization Committee with Milton Park as chairman.[18]

Butler strongly condemned the meeting, arguing its participants were sore losers unable to abide by the wishes of the majority. He seemed especially upset at its second-guessing of the 1896 strategy, including the use of silver: It was "only through the silver question that we can reach the ears of such voters to impress them with the vital necessity of more legal tender money and the public operation of every natural monopoly." He also ridiculed their political strategy:

> Every one knows that if the committee had attempted this course that our party in three-fourths of the states would have rebelled against such action as an attempt to betray the party into the hands of McKinley's backers. They know that it would have split the party in twain, leaving a minority standing with the committee for such a policy. They know that over half of the rank and file of our party would have refused to vote such a ticket, if all of the leaders of the party had combined in advising it. They know that notwithstanding our party organization was more or less demoralized on account of the peculiar and unfair condi-

tions we were forced to meet, that yet the result would have been ten times more disastrous if we had pursued a different course.[19]

During 1897 Butler's policies and his opponents' response once again demonstrated the absence of a true national Populist Party. In presidential politics, there were Populists committed to Democratic cooperation; Populists, like Butler, who wanted to keep the existing Populist organization but not foreclose future political cooperation; and Populists who wanted a revamped Populist organization opposed to cooperation. No one, however, had a clear idea about how to attract needed converts. Given the slowly improving economic conditions, Butler's claim that most new Populists would have to be Republicans disappointed in McKinley suggested the party's dismal prospects. His efforts to remain leader also reflect a dogged determination to shape the party's policy that bordered on irrationality. From his earliest days as an Allianceman, Butler had always been at the center of every reform and political organization he joined. Now that he operated at the highest level, he was unwilling to surrender power, even though it would have relieved him of a great personal burden. He believed he had the best interests of the party in mind, that he had the support of most Populists, and that his actions were backed by his defense of Populist principles in Washington. Nonetheless, the desire to control seemed so ingrained in Butler's political behavior that it took on a life of its own, despite its propensity to saddle him with impossible tasks and its harm to his career.

IN MID-1897 Butler returned to North Carolina from Washington and set out to prepare his party for the 1898 elections. After the General Assembly, Populism split decisively between pro-Republicans, an element that was skeptical of more cooperation, and Butler and his followers, who were still looking for a credible reform-based alliance. Butler's growing closeness to Governor Russell affected his evolving strategy. Russell appealed a federal district court's order prohibiting interference with the lease of the North Carolina Railroad, appointed antilease men to the railroad's board of directors, and asked the railroad commission for reduced railroad rates and increased railroad taxes. In late September 1897, he removed James W. Wilson and S. Otho Wilson from the railroad commission because the Wilsons had a financial interest in a hotel that served the North Carolina Railroad. Butler consulted with Russell on all these issues and approved when Russell replaced the Wilsons with a Democrat and a Populist.[20]

Butler also mounted a new and broad campaign for state-level reform. He took over the editorial reigns of the *Caucasian* from Hal Ayer and embarked on his most extensive speaking tour since 1892. Butler's speeches detailed the treachery of organized Democracy and Republicanism, the falseness of the Skinnerites, and the dangers of trusts and railroads. A livelier *Caucasian* promoted the whole catalogue of Populist ideas. It praised public education, endorsed merit appointments to public jobs, and affirmed the Omaha Platform, stressing government ownership of railroads. The paper opposed the annexation of Hawaii and imperialism, attacked monopolies, demanded municipal ownership of public utilities, and called for enforcement of North Carolina's anti–railroad pass law and the popular election of federal judges. It promoted political cooperation, praising Bryan and Democratic senator Benjamin R. Tillman of South Carolina, because "they come nearer to the People's party platform" than did other Democrats.[21]

Although Butler's work suggested optimism, it took place in an increasingly threatening political context. During 1897, North Carolina Democrats became interested in recapturing the state by a violent coup. The biracial quality of cooperation in 1896 and Republican and Populist control of local government provided the issue. In contrast to the Populist need to discuss national issues, Democrats knew that a focus on local conditions could return them to power. A key irritant to whites was the success of cooperation in the counties, townships, and towns. There, hundreds of blacks held offices as justices of the peace, postmasters, school committeemen, and county and city officers, particularly in the eastern part of the state. Historian J. G. deRoulhac Hamilton, a contemporary, believed a crucial moment was November 1897, when the Democratic executive committee officially bemoaned control of the state by a large number of "ignorant" voters. Populists, including Butler, understood the meaning of "ignorant." Butler had already guessed that if a renewed effort at Populist cooperation with reform-minded Democrats failed in 1898, the "negro scarecrow racket" would be the Democrats' theme. He always believed, however, that this was a sham issue and that the real motivation for Democratic action was conservative economics.[22]

As a result, Butler reminded Populists that politics was a struggle between monopoly and the people and that racial appeals supported monopoly. He claimed to be "the negroe's friend and desire[d] his rights protected, as every good citizen desires," but black domination was impossible because even if blacks were a majority, which they were not, "the whites would rule on account of their superior intelligence." At a speech in Rocky Mount in November 1897, he stated that Democrats exaggerated black crimes for political advantage, especially assaults on white women. When members of the Democratic press reported that Butler claimed their party hired blacks to assault white women, he denied it: "I have declared positively and unequivocally in favor of white supremacy and Anglo-Saxon rule. I have further declared that . . . the class of citizens, if there were such, either white or black, who attempted to stir up race prejudice for the purpose of calling attention from and defeating great economic reforms that concern the welfare of [nine-tenths] of our population, [was] the worst and most dangerous element of society." The episode revealed both Butler's and the Populists' continuing unwillingness to challenge white rule. Butler always believed in white control; his great disagreement with Democrats was their leaders' cynical and hypocritical political use of white racism to deflect economic reform. His opposition to Republican cooperation in 1896 made it clear that although he did not oppose blacks taking a subordinate role in his party, a genuine biracial politics committed to equality was not an essential ingredient of Populism. Instead, his core position on race was that white race-baiting to sustain monopoly was a crime. Beyond that, he had concluded that blacks should possess basic civil rights but could not seek equality with whites. Even this concession, of course, greatly distinguished Butler from other southern political leaders. Yet it did not form the basis for an attack on the ill treatment of African Americans. Despite his efforts to bury it, race was about to reclaim its position at the center of state politics.[23]

JUST AFTER THE Rocky Mount speech, Butler returned to Washington for the second session of the Fifty-fifth Congress, which lasted through mid-1898. As before, he offered various means to advance Populism, including use of the Post Office. In support of his earlier postal savings bank bill, he gave a speech in which he argued that the government could use its deposits to construct a postal telegraph system, purchase government-owned railroad cars, pay the national debt, or avoid future bond issues. Further, postal banks would have a positive effect on citizens. They would "encourage the man to deposit his dimes instead of blowing them into dramshops and beer saloons." This "would lessen poverty and want; it would rob the almshouses of much of the work with which they are overburdened; it will educate the young into knowledge of economy and the proper use and value of money." Despite this appeal, which reflected ideas about thrift and avoidance of debt previously advocated by the Alliance, the bill failed.[24]

Butler also continued to support rural free delivery. He backed a $250,000 appropriation to allow a final evaluation of whether the system might become permanent. The Appropriations Committee, however, struck any money for RFD, claiming that the public did not really want it. Butler responded, "Nobody ever proposed [RFD] until action was first taken up by the organized farmers, the Farmers' Alliance, and the granges, and clubs, and wherever the experiment has been tried the sentiment has been unanimous in its favor." Nonetheless, the Senate defeated the appropriation by a vote of 25 to 22. House support for RFD kept the issue alive in conference, and there Butler and other senators saved the appropriation.[25]

Another familiar postal matter was the pay given railroads for transporting mail. Butler proposed to reduce the railroad appropriation from over $30 million to about $24 million. He opposed a suggestion to "investigate" rail costs, sarcastically remarking that "it sometimes surprises me that there is a Senator on the floor who would take the trouble to investigate the matter." There was "such an air, such an atmosphere, around that it would be so much better for us to let these things drift and not interfere with the vested rights of monopolies, that a man would get along more agreeably, that it would be pleasanter all around, that it would be easier for a man to get along and get reelected." He surmised that "the monopolies run Congress, and the man who protests is looked upon as an enemy to capital, and is often made to feel very lonely." The amendment to reduce the rates was easily defeated; an "investigation" was planned.[26]

Setbacks did not prevent Butler from promoting other reforms, which included three constitutional amendments. He renewed efforts for an income tax and to elect senators directly. He introduced an amendment to provide for the election of federal judges. Under the proposal, judges and Supreme Court justices would serve eight-year terms, with each associate justice of the Supreme Court elected by the citizens of a federal circuit. The chief justice would be elected by all the people. More radically, the amendment sought to extinguish federal diversity jurisdiction, admiralty jurisdiction, and jurisdiction over disputes between two states, which would devolve to state courts. All three amendments were either tabled or referred to committees, where they expired.[27]

The most important activity of the session involved war with Spain. Contrary to the suggestions of some historians, the Populist reaction to the Cuban revolution against Spain overwhelmingly favored American support for the Cubans. Both midroaders and Bryan supporters were drawn to the Cuban fight because they empathized with an oppressed people struggling for fundamental rights. Having no desire for the United States to possess new land, they viewed intervention as a humanitarian gesture. In general, they also did not fear that the war would distract from reform but thought it could even provide a vehicle to advance their views. Thus, the *Caucasian* forthrightly demanded the "absolute freedom of the Cuban people and the establishment of a Cuban Republic."[28]

On 11 April 1898, Butler introduced a joint resolution declaring that the Cuban republic should be recognized, that Spain should withdraw its troops, and that the president be "empowered, and directed to use, if necessary, the entire land and naval forces of the United States to carry these resolutions into effect." Yet a subsequent message from McKinley objected to Cuban independence and asked for authority to restore peace without recognizing the revolutionary government. Butler complained that the president's message was "in the interest of Spain and not in the interest of Cuba; [it was] a message in the interest of [Spanish] bondholders and not in the interest of liberty; a message that causes rejoicing among the bond dealers and stock gamblers in Wall Street; a message that causes every Spanish fiend and devil who has been persecuting Cuba and dishonoring our flag to build bonfires and rejoice."[29]

When the Senate voted on Cuba, Butler cast his ballots for independence. On 17 April, along with the other Populists, he voted for a declaration of war between the United States and Spain and for recognition of the revolutionary government. This passed in the Senate. The House, however, rejected independence and demanded in conference that it be dropped. The House version passed in the Senate on 19 April. Butler voted against the change, arguing that it was the result of a Spanish bondholders' scheme to establish a regime "that will do the bidding of the common financial and monopoly syndicate of looters and pillagers of that fair island."[30]

Defeat on independence signaled that there would be other disappointments. Butler introduced a resolution requiring the war to be financed by an income tax, silver certificates, and greenbacks. The administration, however, backed a bond issue, to be paid in gold. According to Butler, although Abraham Lincoln had favored greenbacks and an income tax to fund war, thirty years later the Republican Party "has become the champion of slavery for both white and black; a party that to-day is in the hands of the money lenders and the monopolists; a party that by somebody, probably one man [Marcus Hanna], was mortgaged in the last campaign to all of the allied trusts and monopolies for a mammoth campaign fund and is under contract to pay its campaign debts with legislation at the expense of every wealth

The Senate, April 1898.
(Library of Congress)

producer and every legitimate interest in the country." In contrast, Populists wanted an income tax: "No one asks that men of wealth be discriminated against. My complaint is that those who have enjoyed the bounty of the government and grown rich from the toil of others should try to shirk paying a mite of their wealth to defend the flag." Further, the income tax was not intended to destroy wealth: "The Lord did not make us equal. We say that we are all free and equal; but that is in another sense. We have different abilities and powers. Some men will create more wealth than others. We all know that. Nobody wants to take from the man who is prosperous and industrious and give to the man who is idle and trifling." As a result, Populism stood for the principle that the best course is for government "to see that competition is left unrestrained and unrestricted. . . . [Government should] preserve to every individual and to every business enterprise the opportunity to compete freely and to be protected against discrimination by law."[31]

Butler also invoked Populism to support an issue of $150 million in greenbacks for the war. He attacked Republicans and Democrats for seeking to "outvie each other in claiming to be the hard-money party, each one denying that he was in favor of fiat money." He had "heard them boast that they were in favor of a system of money that should be as large or small as the metal accidentally happened to be found in the mountains. To say that we are limited absolutely to a gold standard or a bi-metallic standard, whichever you please, dependent entirely on gold, or on silver, or both, to chance, for the money necessary to transact the business of the greatest and richest nation in the world" was an "absurdity." Instead, the nation needed "an honest yardstick to measure values, a money yardstick, that . . . is exact in length —that is, the quantity of dollars—compared with the population and business each year."[32]

Butler's proposals had no discernible impact on war revenue. Senators defeated attempts to impose a stamp tax on manufacturers' inventory, to get greenbacks issued, to enact an income tax, to enact an excise tax on revenue from interstate commerce, to prohibit banks from using war bonds as a basis for national bank notes, to impose an excise tax on yachts, to tax trusts, and to reduce the interest paid on bonds. The final vote on the war revenue bill revealed the triumph of gold.

Butler's experience in the second session of the Fifty-fifth Congress repeated an established pattern. He introduced a wide range of legislation, linked his proposals to arguments derived from the Alliance and Populism, and watched his work be ignored or defeated. Focusing on postal reform and the war, he unsuccessfully demanded government control of the money supply, an income tax, and direct election of federal senators and judges. Despite the losses, however, he continued to believe in the ultimate success of Populism. Unfortunately, as the next election approached, the prospects of the People's Party were not good.

THE NARROWING OF REFORM

THE CRISIS OF the national Populist Party continued in early 1898, propelled by more disagreement over presidential strategy. The midroad National Organization Committee renewed its demand for a joint conference with Butler's committee in an attempt to force a confrontation. Butler responded by mailing letters to Populists opposing a meeting. The midroaders met anyway, in St. Louis in January. They proposed that state Populist organizations hold referenda on whether a Populist presidential nominating convention should convene in July 1898, May 1899, or February 1900. Butler replied by issuing a statement with other Populists in Congress that asked reformers to unite. He coordinated the request with similar appeals from Senator James Jones, chairman of the Democratic Party, and Charles Towne, a leader of the Silver Republicans. Butler's message described a purported conspiracy among Cleveland Democrats and McKinley Republicans that aimed to advance gold by retiring greenbacks, issuing bonds, and increasing the power of national banks. As for politics, Butler argued that only through cooperation could the People's Party have any hope of success. Nonetheless, he would "never favor another national cooperation on the same terms as the one of 1896," which occurred only because of unpredictable events at the Democratic national convention. Instead, a different scheme could "advance our principles, strengthen the party, [and] test the sincerity of those who claim that they want to be our allies."[1]

Despite this self-destructive bickering, Butler promoted his understanding of Populist political economy. An article he published in the *Arena* in March 1898, "Trusts—the Causes That Produce Them—the Remedy," restated his support for the Omaha Platform. The three "instruments of commerce" were still money, transportation, and the transmission of intelligence, just as they had been in 1891. Money was the "lifeblood of commerce," cheap transportation was "an essential factor in business," and intelligence was the "information that controls the markets and affects vitally the business world." These instruments produced "natural monopolies," so they should be run by the government. Butler's vision of the purpose of this legislation also remained consistent with what he had been saying since the early nineties. Under Populism such instruments would be used by wealth producers without discrimination, and "then there [would be] healthy competition, with widespread industrial activity, and general prosperity and happiness." Nationalization was intended to create "equal opportunities for every individual and every independent business enterprise."[2]

It was increasingly difficult to be optimistic about the political appeal of such arguments, even among reformers. No one understood this better than two individuals who sent Butler criticisms of the article. One, a Single Taxer, concluded "that a sound monetary system and the proper control and regulation of the means of transportation" were "utter futility." Only by "taxing the land to its full rental value [is one able] to secure to the people the product of their toil and cause a just distribution of wealth." Even more negative was the response of a New York Socialist Laborite. He complained that the persons likely to benefit from Butler's proposals would be "small capitalist[s]," not workers. Government ownership, "combined with government money," would "relieve" current problems but was no real solution. Ultimately, Populism was a "reactionary palliative," hardly comparable with "the complete overthrow of capitalism which all socialists desire, and the inauguration of the cooperative commonwealth which is Industrial Democracy."[3]

In June 1898, after more than a year of delay, Butler finally decided there should a meeting of his national committee in Omaha to prepare for the November elections. Yet many national committee members did not plan to attend, and a fight over proxies ensued between the National Organization Committee and Butler's committee. Because fewer than thirty of the more than one hundred national committee members actually came to Omaha, control of about seventy-five proxies determined the meeting's result. Further, in Omaha, Butler appointed men to a credentials committee who opposed the midroaders. With the support of this committee and what appeared to be an even division among those attending, Butler held a slim majority of votes.[4]

At the meeting, Butler and moderate midroaders hammered out what came to be known as the Omaha Compromise. The agreement attempted to map out a national political strategy acceptable to most Populists. It pro-

vided that a presidential nominating convention planned by some midroaders in Cincinnati for 4 September 1898 be called off, that Butler remain as
national chairman, that his national committee not interfere with state nominations, that future official notices from the national chairman be clear and
brief, that delegates to the next national convention be chosen based on
1892 Populist vote, and that there be an early presidential nominating convention in order to avoid an 1896 variety of cooperation. Butler concluded
that the gathering succeeded because he retained the chairmanship and because the separatist element of the midroaders, including supporters of the
Cincinnati convention, appeared defeated. Similarly, moderate midroaders
concluded that the extreme pro-Democrats lost power. As a result, many
Populists mistakenly interpreted the "compromise" as a victory for their own
views.[5]

The ineffectiveness of the Omaha Compromise became immediately apparent. Some Populists, spearheaded by former Bryan supporter Wharton
Barker, rejected it entirely and formed what amounted to a second Populist
Party by going forward with plans for a presidential nominating convention
in Cincinnati. Barker blamed the moderate midroaders, whom he viewed as
excessively committed to preserving the current party organization, as well
as Butler for the party's troubles. Many midroaders opposed Barker's Cincinnati convention. The Progressive Farmer believed it was doomed to fail.
Moreover, Texans wanted a statement from Butler that he would stand by
the Omaha Compromise; if forthcoming, Barker's convention would not
get their support.[6]

The compromise and Butler's determination to retain his office caused
some of his allies to urge him to resign the chairmanship. They sensed he
now held on to the position out of personal honor to the detriment of the
party. One wrote that the job had been "his greatest political misfortune, as
well as [his] greatest personal burden and annoyance." Another concluded
that Butler faced only "defeat as national chairman and bitterness." Recent
struggles destroyed the confidence of too large a portion of the party for
him to lead unification, and he now had only "remnants of a Populist party
behind him." Supporters contrasted Butler's decline as a party leader with
his work in the Senate. Harry Tracy noted that in the latter place he had
"shown nerve, judgement, and loyalty to our principles," and Eltweed Pomeroy described his legislative achievements as "fine work."[7]

Yet, after six years of seeking and obtaining influence in the highest
reaches of the party, Butler had no intention of giving up power. If Populism
could not be revived under his leadership, he thought, it could not be re-

vived at all. In late July he wrote Milton Park, "I voted for those [Omaha] resolutions and did so in good faith. I frankly admit that I did not favor all that was in the resolutions, neither did all of the committee." In fact, "some things were rather humiliating to me." On the other hand, his committee had been mistaken about the good intentions of at least some midroaders, so Park should help him defeat the Cincinnati convention. Park responded in a friendly manner but wanted an official statement that the Omaha Compromise would prevail. In August, Butler went on a speaking tour of the West, including Texas. His speeches were well received. In Texas he delivered attacks on the Democracy and a defense of Populism. More important, he pledged adherence to the Omaha Compromise and promised to call an early national convention in 1900. Butler's speeches appear to have undermined dissent in Texas; Park now believed Butler wanted to carry out the compromise.[8]

This easing of tensions had a negative effect on the Cincinnati Populists. Other than Wharton Barker and Ignatius Donnelly, few noteworthy Populists supported the gathering. One of Butler's correspondents believed only eighty-seven people attended, while a newspaper reporter counted a mere seventy-six. With the exception of a new emphasis on the initiative and referendum, the Cincinnati Populists did not propose anything new in the way of reform. They even disagreed about strategy, particularly the desirability of nominating a presidential candidate more than two years before the election. When the men demanding nominations prevailed, those who objected bolted and denounced the others. The several dozen Populists left chose Barker and Donnelly as their presidential and vice presidential nominees.[9]

The strategic and personal battles of the past two years, slowly improving economic conditions, and vigorous demands by southern Democrats for disfranchisement of black voters did not bode well for a coordinated Populist congressional campaign in 1898. And because the Omaha Compromise required that the national committee not interfere with state nominations, state parties opted for cooperation or noncooperation depending on local conditions. Ominously, both strategies failed. The defeat of cooperation in Kansas was particularly complete, and midroaders in Georgia lost decisively. There were some relative triumphs, such as the ability of midroad Texans, in a losing effort, to retain their ground or of cooperationists in Nebraska, who elected two congressmen. On the whole, however, the party suffered crippling decline in 1898. Most serious, defections meant that Populism no longer held the balance of power in many places, a particularly devastating fact in cooperation states.[10]

THE 1898 ELECTION in North Carolina was one of the most dramatic in the state's history. Butler initially tried to achieve success by bringing together Populists and reform elements in the Democratic Party, as he had in 1896. He believed an arrangement could be based on financial reform and that Populists should call an early state convention and propose cooperation. He announced this position in March, simultaneously with the release of a statement by William Jennings Bryan encouraging unity among opponents of gold and monopoly. Butler recognized that many Democratic leaders opposed cooperation, but he appealed to the party's rank and file. Consistent with his policy since 1892, he still assumed "our only hope for recruits in the future is from this class of voters," meaning white Democrats. The need to attack the Democratic leadership while courting the rank and file naturally had a confusing effect on *Caucasian* editorials, a problem exacerbated by disagreement between Butler and Hal Ayer, the day-to-day operator of the paper. By this time, Ayer wanted another Republican agreement. He told Butler, "Nothing gathered from [the Democrats] gives me any right to think that a spirit of conciliation on the part of the Populists, can accomplish anything." Butler complained about Ayer to R. C. Rivers, his paper's business manager, but Rivers replied that they were suffering terrible personal abuse from Democrats and that many Populists, as in 1896, supported Republican-Populist cooperation.[11]

Disagreement at the *Caucasian* mirrored conditions in the party. Otho Wilson's *Raleigh Hayseeder* raised the specter of Democratic disfranchisement of poor whites, which it claimed top Democrats favored. Along with Harry Skinner, Wilson endorsed Republican cooperation. The *Pittsboro Chatham Citizen* disapproved of cooperating with Democrats, largely on the ground that Democrats would get Populist votes and then oppose Populist reforms. A March meeting of party representatives indicated that in the eastern part of the state, local organizations overwhelmingly favored cooperation with Republicans as a matter of basic survival. Especially critical of Butler's plan was the *Progressive Farmer*, which viewed it as demoralizing. For the time being, it supported an independent ticket, although, as in 1894 and 1896, it later approved cooperation with the GOP. On the other hand, J. P. Sossaman's *Charlotte People's Paper* endorsed Butler's idea if it could be "honorably" accomplished. It blasted the *Progressive Farmer* for not attacking Republicanism. J. F. Click's *Hickory Times-Mercury* also thought Butler was trying "to do the fair and reasonable thing along the line of [the party's] cardinal principles."[12]

Predictably, most of the GOP's leaders tried to disrupt Butler's plan. Their newspapers pointed to the enormous threat presented by an abandonment of cooperation, including the potential loss of black voting rights. W. L. Person, an African American, wrote Butler asking for a state constitutional amendment that would protect the voting rights of blacks and poor whites. Aware of the Populists' ambivalence on race, Person argued that an amendment would be "the salvation of the poor white man" as well as the African American. Yet one Republican who failed to promote the customary union with Populists was Governor Russell; his individual fortunes were now tied to Butler's politics more than to the goals of his own party. Russell, with Butler's help, continued his battle against high railroad rates and the lease of the North Carolina Railroad, despite opposition in the GOP. As a result of this unlikely alliance, Russell and Butler agreed to unite their supporters for the election. Critics labeled the Russell-Butler partnership a "new party," but actually it represented the kind of reform-based coalition Butler had worked for since 1894.[13]

As in 1896, North Carolina's Democrats divided into supporters and opponents of an agreement with Populists. The pro-Populist Democrats tended to be strong for Bryan. E. J. Hale, editor of the *Fayetteville Observer*, wrote Butler that cooperation could accomplish a "re-union of [former senator Zebulon B.] Vance's whites free from Ransomite control." The coalition received encouragement from Bryan himself, who wrote a public letter to Josephus Daniels stating "co-operation is both wise and necessary." Walter Clark told Butler that the letter "has had a *fine* effect. The Pierpont Morgan officials are much alarmed I learn, fearing that the Democratic state convention may pass resolutions denouncing the 99 years lease and demanding 'lower fares and freights and no free passes.' " By May, however, the trend was against an agreement. Charles B. Aycock, a rising Democratic star, proposed a straight fight. The balance of power fell to men such as William B. Rodman, a Bryan supporter who also believed the party would not grow "if in order to win we must descend into a wild scramble and trade for office." Ironically, these Democrats' rejection of cooperation gave conservatives more power than their numbers warranted, a consequence that would have long-term effects.[14]

At the Populists' convention on 17 May, Butler managed to defeat the pro-Republicans. Cyrus Thompson, now a Butler supporter, replaced Hal Ayer as party chairman. The platform approved earlier platforms and added, according to Butler's wishes, criticisms of the ninety-nine-year lease and support for an initiative and referendum and for public education. Butler also obtained a resolution approving his goal of achieving the cooperation of all who "can and do agree with the People's party on our State and national principles and policies." Because there would not be any elections for state executive offices, cooperation was necessarily limited to congressmen, judges, and state legislators. The convention established a committee to effect agreements for those offices.[15]

The days following the Populist convention were exceedingly tense: the future of North Carolina politics hung in the balance. Democrats in favor of cooperation cheered the Populist convention; Josephus Daniels described the Populists' actions as a victory for Bryan and silver, and E. J. Hale told Democrats opposed to cooperation to join the Republicans. Others, however, warned that an agreement with Populists would be a disaster. A Wilmington paper complained that the Populist position discounted what it viewed as the principal campaign issue, that "men of the Aryan stock must and shall control in North Carolina." Butler's Populists made a formal offer of cooperation, which was delivered to Democratic chairman Clement Manly. It proposed a nonpartisan judiciary, "free silver and anti-monopoly congressmen," and an "anti-monopoly" legislature. In addition, the General Assembly should oppose labor injunctions and the lease of the North Carolina Railroad, support the Populists' election and local government laws, and reduce railroad, telegraph, and telephone rates. Butler believed the offer would be accepted, but his friend James Lloyd wrote him on 26 May that it would probably be rejected because "railroad attorneys and hirelings are in control of the [Democratic] convention."[16]

Lloyd perceived conditions accurately. At their convention on 27 May, Democrats "respectfully declined" the Populist offer, with none other than Josephus Daniels reading the communication to the delegates. Daniels's actions typified his political behavior. Although he knew persons unfriendly to Bryan dominated the convention and although he was a sincere supporter of Bryan, he was not willing to lead the sort of bolt that Butler's cooperationist strategy required. Thousands of Bryan Democrats throughout the state repeated his actions. The party's platform adopted some Populist ideas, including legal tender greenbacks to finance the Spanish war, an income tax, no free railroad passes, direct election of senators, and opposition to the removal of lawsuits to federal courts by corporations. These were not insignificant developments, as they, like silver, suggested the effects of Populism outside the third party. But the planks seemed politically meaningless; the delegates also endorsed national chairman Jones's policy of uniting silver forces while repudiating the Populist offer.[17]

The Democratic rebuff left Butler's Populists floundering. Butler himself was in Washington and "surprised" by the result. Cyrus Thompson, the new state chairman, asked for advice as to the proper course, but Butler seemed to lack a definite answer, at first attempting only to direct the selection of suitable congressional candidates. But even this limited activity lacked promise. Butler's bitterness about political failure was translated into personal revenge against opponents, and Harry Skinner, running for reelection in the First District, felt the full brunt of his animosity. Butler tried, with the help of Republicans and Thompson, to unseat Skinner.[18]

By July an inexorable movement toward a Populist deal with Republicans had developed. Many Populists assumed that without the GOP the party would have no influence. And because an agreement with Democrats seemed foreclosed, the Populists had nowhere else to turn. Since 1892, rank-and-file Populists had recognized that the greatest support and the greatest benefits of cooperation existed at the local and legislative levels. As a result, local Populist organizations fashioned legislative tickets with Republicans without the approval of the state leadership, just as they had in 1896. Sensing the drift, when Republicans held their state convention in late July, they offered to cooperate. The only reason given was to retain the election law and local government. Cooperation, once animated by the rhetoric of democracy, had been reduced to avoiding angry retribution from Democrats.[19]

After the GOP convention Butler remained uncommitted. For a time he seemed content to criticize both old parties and monitor local conditions and nominations. In particular, he wanted candidates friendly to Democratic cooperation to receive Populist nominations. This, at least, might make an eventual agreement with Republicans more palatable. Nonetheless, busy in the Senate and with the affairs of the national party, he failed to discuss the possibilities publicly, which led to confusion. Rivers wrote him that "the [*Caucasian*] would be better off financially if it would be in harmony with the policy of the State Committee's programme, which is [Republican] fusion and nothing else." Ultimately, the defeat of Butler's original policy, the strength of pro-Republican sentiment in the party, the tendency of local Populists to enter into agreements on their own, the most organized Democratic campaign since 1892, and the need to develop a coordinated response brought about a meeting between Populist and Republican leaders on 1 September. They decided to preserve "majority rule by facilitating joint tickets for the legislature at the county level." Butler does not seem to have been present, and much like his response to the messy state ticket in 1896, he accepted the arrangement with mixed emotions.[20]

Masterminded by Furnifold Simmons, Butler's nemesis from 1892, the furious Democratic campaign offered persuasive cultural, economic, and political appeals to white North Carolinians. Often inconsistent and usually offered with a backdrop of violence, it was more like a military conquest than a search for votes. Democrats criticized the negative effect of Populist-Republican rule on capital and its tendency to burden business with increased taxes. Yet they also linked Populists to gold through their Alliance with Republicans. A promise to keep taxes low and improve commercial conditions generated donations, which were used to fund a massive attack on an alleged "Negro rule." As many Populists realized, the Democratic strategy was primarily a cynical effort to exploit the racism of the white majority, because it was clear that cooperation never intended or accomplished any threat to white supremacy. Although cooperation placed a significant number of blacks in public office, Democrats exaggerated this effect to advance a larger goal. The real Democratic task was to foment a hatred that would support intimidation and violence, and they assigned unrepentant Populists the unhappy role of white men who betrayed their race: "Negro supremacy means negroes in every office, mixed schools, intermarriage, [and] social equality."[21]

The most impressive characteristic of the campaign was the effective manner in which it was delivered. Simmons made racism energetic and fun. He organized picnics and barbecues with the theme that only the Democracy would stand up for whites. White Man's Unions generated solidarity, the party distributed white supremacy buttons, and a giant White Men's Mass Meeting was held in Goldsboro just prior to the election. Simmons distributed thousands of broadsides and arranged for the publication of white supremacy "supplements," or pictorial newspapers, that were included in practically every Democratic newspaper. The supplements featured outrageous cartoons depicting Republicans and Populists as hideous figures and blacks as members of an ugly, barbaric race. The emotions of the campaign were especially well expressed in the speeches of Charles Aycock. His performances were often accompanied by horseback processions, women in white dresses, and elaborate platforms covered with banners that proclaimed devotion to white supremacy. Aycock explained the campaign in a way that drew on whites' greatest fears. According to him, the state's white women demanded Democratic rule. Woman, who represented "our highest ideal of beauty both in form and spirit," was presently "in an attitude of appeal to us for protection": "I call upon you white men, Democrats, Populists, Republicans, to rally to the cause of Democracy this year and let us put an end forever to this strife, this outrage, this wrong." At its core, the white supremacy campaign consciously manipulated white assumptions about black sexuality.[22]

Yet no real disagreement existed among white men over the political or

Furnifold Simmons: Butler's political superior and successor.
(Courtesy of the North Carolina Division of Archives and History)

legal standing of women. Gender, in short, was a sham issue, even more so
than white supremacy itself. This is not to say that such whites as Aycock did
not believe in the need for white men to protect white women or did not
fear black rapists. They did. But North Carolina Populists concurred. They
did not stand for any change in the status of black or white women; neither
did white Republicans. That was the beauty of Simmons's campaign: it ex-

ploited an issue on which white men already agreed by successfully, if falsely, suggesting that the opposition did not agree. The strategy also had the advantage of not requiring any new legislation. Of course, lying about one's purpose and misrepresenting the opposition was not a new political tactic, nor was it one limited to gender, race, or the nineteenth century. In contrast, however, Populists, Republicans, and Democrats really did disagree about taxation and currency. But those were subjects on which Democrats had a tough time finding unity and achieving success, and so they did not choose to organize a campaign around those themes. Voters also disagreed about what men should be allowed to vote and whether black men would be allowed to hold offices in local government. But here the issue on which whites disagreed was not black power but black participation. Early in the campaign Democrats made a decision not to campaign on a promise of disfranchisement, both because of federal constitutional concerns and the possible reaction of poor whites. By effectively, if deceptively, transforming the campaign into complaints about alleged black power, not black participation, Democrats had an effective cause. In short, both race and gender, as used by Democrats, were wholly contrived issues; their white Populist and Republican opponents did not disagree with them about the subordinate economic and political role of either blacks or white women. Rather, these whites disagreed with Democrats about economic reform and the right of black men to participate in North Carolina politics.[23]

To carry out the Democratic plan, intimidation was widely practiced and appeared in many forms. Consistent with Aycock's message, some ostracism was sexual. As a Democratic paper explained, "Men who expect to be white men must vote the white ticket." If they did not, they might expect to become celibate, since it was woman's duty not to "recognize any but true white men." The campaign's most dramatic manifestations of intimidation were "Red Shirts," organizations of armed men, particularly in the southeastern portion of the state, that warned blacks and others to stay away from the polls. Red Shirts participated in many incidents of violence. Less flamboyant Democrats also engaged in attacks. Former Populist William H. Kitchin broke into a black official's house and threatened him with death if he did not resign. More subtle forms of intimidation included compiling lists of Populists to contact and challenging voters' qualifications.[24]

Amazingly, some Populists initially believed they could prevail by making an issue of the election's character. In one sense, this was predictable, because Populists supported the Democrats' racial message. It was the manner and method of the Democrats, as well as their failure to address economic issues, that was objectionable. According to the *Caucasian*, the Democracy had "begun a campaign of prevarication, misrepresentation and abuse that is repulsive to honorable men." A recurrent Populist theme was the hypocrisy of the white supremacy message: Democrats, through bribery and intimidation, had always relied on black votes. Populists also claimed that if Democrats came into power they would disfranchise blacks and poor whites. To these ends, the party published a handbook and placed a "supplement" in Populist newspapers. The handbook downplayed "Negro rule" by arguing that whites were morally and numerically superior. Populists had never portrayed their movement as a liberator of black people, and this election was no exception. Little attention, however, was given to the positive results of cooperation, apart from the election law.[25]

Other Populist writing focused on economic principles. This criticized Democracy for "the robbery of the people by the quiet inauguration and firm establishment of a pernicious, class-favoring financial system and by an entrenchment in power of great trusts, corporations, monopoly syndicates, etc." The answer to such perfidy appeared in 1892, at the Omaha Populist convention. Although Democrats stole portions of the Omaha Platform in 1896, Populists that year "proved true to principle without reference to party, and did everything possible to throw together the strength of all forces professing to favor the same purposes and ends." In contrast, the state Democrats' 1898 convention was "full of lawyers who were mostly the agents and employees of railroad rings, trusts, and corporations." These men did not want reform but hoped instead to "install another epoch of depression, business stagnation, and then inaugurate another orgy of bond issues, syndicate swindles and monopoly steals."[26]

Butler played a leading role in the campaign. He arranged an ambitious speaking tour. Although he received death threats and some of his engagements were canceled, including a Wilmington rally, he appeared often and before large crowds. In part, the speeches sought to harmonize the campaign with the Omaha Platform. Butler stated that government control of money, transportation, and the transmission of intelligence offered the only means to make the economy fair. In Clinton, he argued that the party's principles were the same as in 1892:

If silver was not restored by free coinage and . . . greenback money was not restored, the national banking act wiped out, and the control and direction of the other instruments of commerce were not taken from the hands of the private monopolies and returned to the control of the

people, where, under the Constitution they belonged, the price of cotton and all other products would fall lower, times would get harder, and
. . . more trusts and monopolies would spring up every day to control
every branch of industry in the country.[27]

However, he gave greater attention to the race question. In one speech he
held up a copy of the *Democratic Hand-Book*:

> I have read it through. As I read it my heart sank with pity and sorrow
> and disgust. . . . Is there anything about free silver and the dangers of
> monopolies and trusts? No. What is on [the] first page? My fellow citi-
> zens, what is their creed and doctrine today? On the first page there is
> but one thing. What is it? "Nigger." Turn to the second page; what is on
> that? "Nigger." Turn to the next page and what is on that? "Niggers and
> coons." And the next page? More niggers and more coons. And so on
> through the book to the last page; and what is on this? "Nigger, nigger,
> nigger."

Yet blacks had not demonetized silver, burned greenbacks, or organized the
monopolies that "are bleeding both white man and black man, every merchant, lawyer, doctor or farmer or laborer who works for an honest living."
Populism was a white man's party committed to white supremacy, but Democrats used race to defeat an alignment of reformers.[28]

In this manner Butler tried to point out the lie in the Democrats' claim
that the election was about white supremacy or, even less important, the
protection of white women. Tellingly, race and gender were never significant components of Butler's politics. As for race, he believed white people
were superior, that they should rule, and that they did rule. On the other
hand, he believed a Populist government would improve the economic conditions of black people and that black men had a right to vote. Race, in politics, was like the tariff. It was largely irrelevant to genuine political discourse
and was not a legitimate issue for mobilizing voters. As for gender, he had almost nothing to say. He had supported the creation of a state normal school
for white women in 1891, although his constituents forced him to abstain
from voting for it in the legislature. He had acted with women in the Teachers' Assembly in the 1880s and in the Alliance, appearing with Mary Elizabeth Lease in one series of speeches. He never believed, however, that the
Alliance or Populism dealt specifically with gender issues. For Butler, it was
one thing to support teacher training for women, which he did, and another entirely to believe women should participate in party politics, which

he did not. Generally, throughout the nineties he seemed wholly uninterested in any political discussion of policies that would either change or maintain the status of black or white women, unless it was to complain about Democrats' shameful use of the fears of white men. He always remained focused
on the need for economic legislation according to the national Populist platform, which neglected issues of race and gender. To Butler, cultural politics
were the politics of hypocritical conservatives, such as Charles Aycock, who
were unwilling to confront the greater divides of economic reform.[29]

Butler's actions became increasingly bitter and aggressive as the campaign progressed. In a widely published letter he decried Democratic intimidation tactics as "revolting and shocking." He attacked leading Democrats
for supporting the "revolutionary and plutocratic doctrine" that only those
who own property should rule. He argued that Democrats intended to pass
a disfranchisement law aimed at the poor. He maintained a detailed correspondence with Populists about local cooperation. His most dramatic excur-
sion in this area sought to avenge Harry Skinner's apostasy in 1897 by col-
laborating, on a limited scale, with Democrats Furnifold Simmons, William
B. Rodman, and Democratic First District congressional candidate J. H. Small.
Butler encouraged Populists to abandon Skinner.[30]

As the election neared it became clear that Democratic threats and violence, not their arguments, were having the greatest effect. Butler received
reports of "shaky brethren," especially from the east. Increased Democratic
pressure, which included disrupting Populist meetings, shootings, and property destruction, scared even the most loyal Populists. They feared Democrats would take ballot boxes, incite riots, commit murder, and begin a
race war. Democrats forced Populists nominated for office in New Hanover
County to withdraw in October. Throughout this turmoil Populists did not
contest the desirability of white supremacy; their party, of course, supported
white supremacy. Some Populists, including Butler, even tried to eliminate
black candidates. Butler advised a Northampton County Populist to take a
black man off the local ballot or he would not give a speech there. One eastern North Carolina Populist complained that "it is pretty hard for a white
man in this county to vote side by side with a negro or republican—one of
the toughest things that a Pop is called on to do." At the Democrats' White
Men's Mass Meeting in Goldsboro, none other than the 1896 Populist candidate for governor, William A. Guthrie, presided.[31]

Sophisticated organization and intimidation produced an overwhelming
Democratic victory. Democrats won 134 of the 170 seats in the state Senate
and House. Populists won 6. The scope of the triumph charged the victors

with a sense of unrestrained power. Some suggested that there should be a taxpaying qualification for voting and that the whipping post for criminals be reinstated. More popular, despite campaign promises to the contrary, was that the best means of permanently accomplishing Democratic hegemony was to "forever eliminate the ignorant and purchasable negro as a factor in N.C. politics." There was no better demonstration of the confidence produced by Democratic success than events in Wilmington. On the day after the election, whites there decided they would not wait until the end of the defeated mayor's and aldermen's terms to seize power. "Order" was fully restored when the self-described "progressive element," which controlled "95 per cent. of the property and paying taxes in like proportion," burned an African American newspaper office and began a shooting brawl that killed more than a dozen blacks. The "better" elements received help from the White Laborers' Union, which sought to exclude black workers as competitors.[32]

Populists reacted to the election with fury. The *Pittsboro Chatham Citizen* thought that "many a poor unsuspecting laboring man had been frightened by the hypocritical negro scare-crow to either stay at home or else vote for the railroad interests and thus fasten upon himself which neither he nor his children will likely be able to shake off in the next twenty years." The victors used "money, liquor, lying, fraud, bulldozing, ostricism [*sic*], and every meanness that can be thought of. They worked day and night. Used women; preachers, and every body[;] they brought the power of society to play. Those who owed merchants were made to keep their mouths shut, stay away or scratch." Populists also realized that it was a charade. As the *Hickory Times-Mercury* explained, "The nigger will now get a rest." The issues of race and gender would disappear as quickly as they had been raised, only to be resurrected at the next election. Butler agreed. His newspaper announced, "By intimidation and violence, which has resulted in blood-shed, and by the wholesale use of money they have succeeded in frightening or buying or keeping from the polls about thirty thousand votes." Good Bryan Democrats had "been used as tools and catspaws by [an] unscrupulous gold and monopoly ring." Moreover, the cooperation with Republicans had proved costly.[33]

In 1898 Butler witnessed a critical weakening of Populist strength. The leading reason for decline, in North Carolina and in the nation, was the increasing irrelevance of Populist reform. At the national level, midroaders and cooperationists failed to resolve their differences or develop effective issues, while in North Carolina violence and white supremacy became the dominant political forces. As a consequence, the party lost the balance of power it had achieved in 1892. Butler continued to believe that Populism could appeal to other reform elements, particularly silver Democrats. In the meantime, the process of Populist education could continue. Yet it was becoming more difficult to be optimistic, and failure produced frustration. Butler's maneuvers against Harry Skinner and his conspiratorial accusations against midroad leaders tended to increase the divisiveness his cooperation strategy needed to avoid. In addition, he had overextended himself. He tried to direct Populists in the national legislature, lead the party's national organization, and control his state's party. Defeat and disagreement inevitably produced criticism and made him a scapegoat for Populism's decline. Consecutive losses in elections had never been part of Butler's experience, but they were about to become a habit.

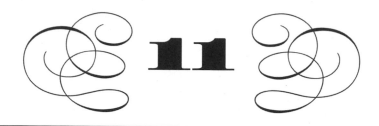

A PRELUDE TO DISFRANCHISEMENT

AFTER THE ELECTION, Butler returned to Washington with hopes of influencing legislation in the final session of the Fifty-fifth Congress. First on his agenda was another effort to reduce the amount paid railroads for carrying mail. In speeches delivered in early 1899 he presented figures purporting to show that the railroads received forty-four times more per pound for carrying the mail than they did for other freight. Ultimately, he argued, the best remedy would be for the government to exercise exclusive ownership over the "transmission of intelligence." The Senate, however, was not convinced, as even Butler's watered-down amendment to retain the current level of railroad pay lost by a vote of forty-five to fifteen; only Populists and a few silver senators supported it.[1]

Butler's fight for a reduction in naval armor costs was equally unsuccessful. He favored lowering the armor price and a government-owned armor plant. Working closely with Benjamin R. Tillman, he helped steer through the Senate a bill reducing the price of armor and containing a tentative provision for a government armor plant. Butler's bill succeeded only because it appealed to friends of a large navy. Nonetheless, the triumph withered in conference. The House did not want the government plant, and Republican Senate conferees did not put up a fight for it. When the session ended, all that remained of Butler's efforts was that the secretary of the navy could not contract for armor for more than three hundred dollars per ton. Butler assumed the armor trust would refuse to make armor for that price, and because there was no alternative source, Congress would capitulate to the manufacturers.[2]

He also offered an amendment to the pension appropriation bill to provide benefits for Confederate veterans. He argued Confederates deserved pensions because before 1865 the Constitution did not plainly prohibit secession. Southerners who fought against the North, therefore, were not traitors. Butler's motivations for the proposal are unclear. Despite a long-standing interest in history, it was unusual for him to spend his time talking about the Civil War. Perhaps he recognized that the recent Spanish-American War had had a unifying effect on the nation and thought his proposal might further reduce sectional feeling. Perhaps he was trying to demonstrate his loyalty to the South in the aftermath of the 1898 white supremacy campaign. Whatever the cause, he did not seek a vote on his amendment.[3]

The leading issue of the session was the recent peace treaty negotiated between Spanish and American representatives in Paris. There was little disagreement about its treatment of Cuba, because the island received independence and was not ceded to the United States. On the other hand, under the bargain the United States obtained the Philippines and thus was now in possession of an expanded overseas "empire." When the treaty came to the Senate in January 1899, Populists played a critical role. Butler and the others rejected European-style imperialism, believing it threatened free government in the United States. Further, the nation already had too many pressing internal problems. In debates just before the treaty vote, Butler stated that the Philippines could not be ruled without giving its inhabitants democratic rights. His newspaper complained that the administration's attitude toward the Philippines "will inject a deadly poison into the very vitals of our Republican form of government." It also described the English writer Rudyard Kipling's recently published "White Man's Burden"—which extolled colonialism—as "an appeal to us to repeal, to discard, and spit upon the great principles of the Declaration of Independence," adding, "The spirit of commercialism," which demanded constant overseas expansion, would eventually lead the United States into China.[4]

Yet Populists Butler, Allen, and Harris voted for the treaty. Because it passed by the razor-thin margin of 57-27, Allen and Butler could have defeated it. Some of Butler's typical allies on economic issues, most notably Tillman and Richard Pettigrew of South Dakota, voted against it. Historians have long speculated on the possible influence of William Jennings Bryan on the Populists. Bryan, although he objected to expansion, supported the treaty because its ratification would end the war, reduce military expenses, and put the issue of Filipino independence squarely before the public, rather than return it to diplomats responsible for renegotiating the treaty.

Butler seems to have approached the subject with the same logic. In fact, before the vote he received a personal letter from Bryan advocating independence for the Philippines after approval of the treaty.[5]

The Senate also debated what policy should govern the Philippines accession. An administration resolution disclaimed any intent to give Filipinos U.S. citizenship or to annex the islands permanently. It vaguely provided that, in "due time," the nation would "make such disposition of the islands as will best promote the interest of the citizens of the United States and the inhabitants of said islands." This did not guarantee independence, and as a result, Senator George F. Hoar of Massachusetts offered an amendment providing that self-rule would be permitted after the creation of "stable" government. Again, Bryan personally asked Butler to support Hoar's amendment. Although Butler complied, the Senate deadlocked, and Republican vice president Garret A. Hobart voted against the proposal. The defeat of the anti-imperialists was complete.[6]

The third session of the Fifty-fifth Congress stands as Butler's least productive session. His efforts on the post office appropriation and the naval bill came to naught. His actions to limit control over the Philippines also went down to defeat, while the proposal for Confederate pensions was not taken seriously. He must have sensed that some of these failures resulted from the decline of Populism. Unfortunately, there was nothing in the national politics of his party that suggested otherwise.

THE GLIMMER OF HOPE in the national Populist Party generated by the Omaha Compromise and Butler's western trip in 1898 evaporated in 1899. First, there was the Barker-Donnelly candidacy. Second, some midroaders, while skeptical of that ticket, continued to oppose any political coalition with Democrats. Third, pro-Bryan Populists, including Butler, did not believe in fighting alone if candidates could be agreed on, although among these Populists there was contention over the precise shape of cooperation. Butler was determined to achieve a coalition with Bryan at its center but with real participation by Populists and other supporters of financial reform. Initially, he hoped most midroaders could be convinced he was right and only troublemakers such as Wharton Barker would be excluded.[7]

As in 1897–98, he still tried to maintain control of the party by avoiding any meeting where there would be a losing or embarrassing confrontation with midroaders. For example, he received an invitation to the annual meeting of the midroad National Reform Press Association but did not attend.

Milton Park, who had been optimistic about the Omaha Compromise six months earlier, was, by February 1899, warning Butler that the movement toward a Barker-dominated party would increase unless they united their forces. By May, Park gave up on Butler and attempted to organize anticooperation Populists without endorsing Barker. For his part, Butler announced that the People's Party executive committee would not meet until the end of 1899 to decide on a date for the presidential nominating convention. This meant any early compromise was impossible.[8]

Butler supported the Omaha Compromise, but he stubbornly, in the face of reasonable views to the contrary, believed it permitted the kind of coalition politics he had supported since 1895. He assumed a majority of Populists agreed, and perhaps he was correct. He also assumed a Populist-Democratic agreement could be made without the difficulties of 1896. Populists would hold their convention first, nominate Bryan (or someone who would resign if Bryan were nominated by Democrats), and then select a non-Democrat for vice president under a platform advocating government money and government ownership of railroads. Because of the potential for disruption, however, this plan would work best if extreme midroaders were exorcised from party councils on the ground that, by supporting the Barker convention, they violated the Omaha Compromise. Butler knew that midroaders divided among themselves, but he failed to appreciate that any formal split was political suicide. Unfortunately, given the fundamental disagreements over strategy, it did not really matter; the ambitions of both Butler and the opponents of Democratic cooperation guaranteed that both Populist defeat and a formal breakup were only a matter of time.[9]

CONDITIONS FOR POPULISM were not much better in North Carolina. With control of the 1899 legislature, Democrats wanted to make sure their recent triumph would last for generations. As a result, the legislature's first action was to eliminate the Populist-Republican local government and election laws. In the future Democratic magistrates selected by a Democratic General Assembly would appoint county commissioners in areas where non-Democrats might prevail. Democrats also enacted a registration law and passed a resolution that sent to voters a constitutional amendment redefining suffrage. Under the registration law, the assembly appointed a state election board, which chose local registrars, all of whom were Democrats. The law also required a new registration for 1900 and allowed registrars to require proof from two voters of each applicant's name, age, and residence. Race was noted in the records, and challenges to eligibility could be made on election day. The law prohibited devices on ballots and differently colored ballots that would have helped those who were illiterate. Ballots cast in the wrong box of the several boxes at each polling place would not be counted. The constitutional amendment, scheduled for consideration in a special general election in August 1900, repudiated universal manhood suffrage. It required voters to pass a literacy test and pay a poll tax although roughly 30 percent of the state's voting-age males and more than half of its black males were illiterate. The amendment, however, included a clause that allowed persons registered before December 1908 to avoid the literacy test if they or their lineal ancestors had been a registered voter before 1867. Democrats claimed this "grandfather clause" skirted the federal Fifteenth Amendment's prohibition of denial of the vote on account of "race, color, or previous condition of servitude."[10]

Suggesting disagreement within their party about the relationship between Populism and black suffrage, Populist reactions to the registration law and the amendment varied. Populists universally condemned the registration law. The *Caucasian* noted that it meant "ballot box thieves can have full license to steal." Reaction to the amendment, however, was less unanimous. One Populist voice that gradually moved in favor of the amendment was the *Progressive Farmer*. Polk's former weekly became increasingly Democratic, primarily because of its new editor, Clarence Poe. The paper did not endorse the amendment in 1899, but it published many letters in favor of it. One pro-amendment Populist wrote, "The negro vote has never been worth anything to us," and therefore the suffrage amendment "does not conflict with nor throw obstacles in the way of our principles." Another wrote that "some of the best Populists I know, say they will vote for it to get rid (as they put it) of the negro, so that a man can be a Populist without being called a 'white-negro.'" Neither the *Progressive Farmer*, the *Hickory Times-Mercury*, nor the *Charlotte People's Paper* reacted negatively to the Democratic effort to disfranchise blacks, although they all bemoaned the potential effect of the amendment on poor whites. In contrast, by the end of the year, Butler had declared against the amendment. He believed that it did not advance white supremacy, it would not remove Democrats' tendency to raise the race issue, and the grandfather clause was unconstitutional. Further, if a court declared the grandfather clause unconstitutional, poor illiterate whites would lose the right to vote. The decision signaled his final break with North Carolina Democrats and provided an opening salvo for the 1900 election.[11]

From the beginning it was doubtful whether Butler's antiamendment pos-

ture could be politically successful. Perhaps he reasoned that it was the only
option. Hal Ayer warned Butler that a reasoned attack on the amendment
ignored reality: The Democracy's election plan "does not mean argument or
discussion; it means riot, slander, abuse, physical violence and general anar-
chy. Their plan now is to red-shirt every town in the state, and to terrorize
voters through the means of such characters as can be hired to wear red-
shirts, drink mean whiskey and raise commotion generally." Although Butler
was unhappy with his conclusions, Ayer correctly described the situation.[12]

Butler spent the summer congressional recess of 1899 at the University of
North Carolina in Chapel Hill, where, at thirty-six, he fulfilled his youthful
ambition to become a lawyer. At the time, admission to the bar in North Carolina required only twelve months of law study, not necessarily in a law school,
and successful performance on a written examination. The summer law
school at the university offered a quick means of preparing for the test.
Courses focused on topics identified by the state supreme court as subject to
testing, including civil procedure, criminal procedure, debtor-creditor law,
real property law, and corporations. After the summer review, Butler passed
the examination and was admitted to the bar at the supreme court's fall session. His new profession suggested not only his long-standing interest in
and study of law, government, and politics but also the more practical consideration that he might need a new job after the next election.[13]

IN RETURNING TO Washington for the Fifty-sixth Congress, Butler planned
his most ambitious Populist assault. He wanted to use the Senate as a platform for the upcoming North Carolina and national elections, which would
determine whether he would remain in office. His first effort was an attack,
with the help of Senator Jeter Pritchard, on North Carolina's new registration law and the proposed suffrage amendment. Although Butler and Pritchard had been political opponents since 1897, by late 1899 the two men perceived that their political survival depended on a renewed alliance. Pritchard,
when Congress convened, introduced a resolution stating that the grandfather clause violated the federal Fourteenth and Fifteenth Amendments.[14]

Butler's 6 February 1900 speech in defense of the resolution focused on
the amendment's unconstitutionality and its effect on poor whites. The legal
issue was whether the grandfather clause violated the Fifteenth Amendment
and, if so, whether the literacy portion of the amendment could survive a
court's finding of unconstitutionality. According to Butler, the grandfather
clause violated the Constitution because it would not "operate equally, im-

partially, and uniformly upon both races." In considering whether the literacy test was severable from the rest of the amendment, Butler argued a court could determine that the legislature intended first to enact a literacy test and then to create a specific exemption from it. In endeavoring to save as much of the law as possible, the court would uphold the literacy test. Such a ruling would disfranchise thousands of "sturdy yeomanry," descendants of "Revolutionary patriots who fought at Kings Mountain, Moores Creek, [and] Guilford Court-House." Even "the good old country darkey who was as faithful and true as steel to our mothers, wives, and sisters during the late war" would lose the right to vote. Remarkably, Butler concluded that African American men had a constitutional right to vote, a highly unusual position for a white southern politician in 1900. Actually, the speech was more campaign ploy than an effort to put the Senate on record against the grandfather clause. Butler did not call for a Senate vote but took great care to coordinate the speech with publicity in North Carolina. Other reform senators, including Allen, Stewart, Teller, and Pettigrew, wrote letters for publication stating that the amendment was unconstitutional.[15]

Another important subject during the session was imperialism, including the continuing war between the United States and independence-minded Filipinos. Butler supported an unsuccessful resolution inquiring whether during the war with Spain the United States had cooperated with Emilio Aguinaldo and the forces of the Philippine Republic. The point was to suggest that McKinley deliberately misled the American public and the Filipinos in order to advance his party's selfish ends. Similarly, Butler introduced amendments intended to advance self-government in Hawaii, and he supported an unsuccessful resolution demanding that the president reveal whether Samoans had been consulted in the recent division of Samoa by Germany and the United States. He also voted for a resolution introduced by Allen providing that constitutional rights be extended to those living in recently acquired Puerto Rico.[16]

Yet the most important topic of the session, especially for Populists, was money. After the bitter contests that lasted through the 1890s, Republican success in the 1898 elections ensured that the GOP would be able to pass a gold standard act. The proposed legislation prompted Butler to make the most complete defense of Populist reform ever uttered in the Senate. It represented his best attempt to distill his understanding of Alliance-Populist reform into specific legislation. The effort began in January 1900, when he introduced what he described as an antitrust resolution. It provided that because Congress had a constitutional duty to regulate interstate commerce, because the regulation of commerce depended on control of the "instruments of commerce," and because the failure to regulate commerce produced private monopolies, Congress should abolish national banks; devise a currency system in which gold, silver, and paper were of an equal and stable value determined by business and population needs; and provide that railroads, telegraphs, and telephones should be owned and operated by the government at cost. Under this proposal "the door of opportunity [will] again be opened, and the era of competition, with equal rights to all and special privileges to none, will be enthroned."[17]

Butler got another opportunity to discuss the antitrust resolution in June, but he was forced to raise the issue in a narrower debate over a House bill intended to strengthen the Sherman Antitrust Act. He complained that the House bill "will not break up trusts, because it will not remove the causes that inevitably produce trusts." The real solution required returning natural monopolies to the people. The Founding Fathers had understood this when they provided in the Constitution that government should issue all money and that highways be open to the public. Through this Jeffersonian policy, "equal opportunities for every individual and every independent business enterprise will be restored; let this be done, and then the old-time economy, simplicity, and purity in politics and government will be restored." The historical appeal did not move Republicans, and Butler's antitrust resolution never came to a vote.[18]

In response to the GOP's gold standard act, Butler introduced a bill that would create money not redeemable in metal and give the government control over money volume. The bill provided for government debts to be paid in paper currency, national banks to deliver all their private notes to the government, and all types of government money to be equal, and it prohibited the government from exchanging one sort of money for another. Although ignored by the majority, the proposal gave Butler an opportunity to make an extended explanation of Populist monetary theory. He contended that the key issues were quantity and who could issue legal tender. He opposed gold because the inadequacy of that supply hurt wealth producers, and a gold standard erroneously relied on the assumption that the value of money depended on what it was made of. What really created value was the relationship between the amount of money in circulation and population and goods; fifty dollars per person, the longtime Populist standard, was an appropriate ratio. Thus "paper is the best material on which to stamp money functions." Nonetheless, his bill provided for gold, silver, and greenbacks, "because then we have less prejudice to combat, and because we accomplish the same thing, except that we waste the raw material in the dollar."[19]

Of course, at the time, Butler's political position was to support Bryan and a silver coalition. Senator Nelson Aldrich of Rhode Island, one of the managers of the McKinley gold bill, perceived the contrast between Butler's bill and the position of silver Democrats, who opposed paper currency and the fifty-dollar benchmark. He asked Butler if he believed in the free and unlimited coinage of silver. Butler said he did not if it meant unlimited inflation. Also, free silver created an unscientific basis for money if the value of silver coins was contingent on the silver mined. Aldrich replied that Bryan supported free silver. Butler answered that Bryan believed in a dollar with unchanging purchasing power. This was satisfactory to him from a political standpoint, because coinage of gold, silver, or paper "is simply a means to that end," and "if we can agree on that principle [that is, unchanged value], then we will discuss the method to secure it." A voice vote silenced Butler's paper money bill. The tally on the GOP gold bill was 46 to 29 in favor, with Butler and the other Populists in the minority.[20]

Butler reintroduced several other Populist proposals during the session. They included a joint resolution providing for direct election of senators, a request that the income tax amendment to the Constitution be placed on the calendar, and a resolution for direct election of the federal judiciary. Although the Senate stifled the resolutions concerning senators and judges, the income tax bill was placed on the next session's schedule. He also reintroduced bills for postal telegraphs, telephones, and postal savings banks, all of which ended up buried in the post office committee. He renewed efforts to reduce railway mail pay, but the Senate overwhelmingly voted down his proposal. When the naval appropriation bill came up, Butler again attacked the amount paid to the armor manufacturers and pushed for a government-owned plant. The naval appropriation bill came back from conference with a provision that allowed the secretary of the navy to pay a price that was "reasonable and equitable." For Butler, this turned "the whole matter absolutely to the Secretary of the Navy and let the Government through him be robbed for the rest of time without limit." The Senate approved the grant to the secretary.[21]

Despite failing to have any of his important proposals enacted during this first session of the Fifty-sixth Congress, Butler effectively presented a complete legislative version of Populism. It was the culmination of more than ten years of reading, thinking, listening, and leadership in the Alliance and the Populist Party. Financial reform and government ownership of "natural monopolies" received a full airing. A concrete package of Populist reform was composed and offered to the Senate. Most important, Butler's antitrust resolution matched the Omaha Platform, reflecting a full expression of his political economy in action. The resolution attempted to expand the economic responsibility of federal government while affirming economic growth through competition, markets, and individual initiative.

IRONICALLY, while Butler defended the whole of Populism in the Senate, destructive infighting in the national Populist Party reached a climax. The midroaders who supported the Omaha Compromise asked him to call a national committee meeting in Chicago in early 1900 to set forth campaign strategy. Meanwhile, Butler conducted a poll among committee members to determine the time and place of the meeting. The survey revealed there were more votes to meet in Lincoln, Nebraska, than in any other city, so he slated a meeting for there. Reactions to this decision depended on whether one supported or opposed Bryan's nomination. Bryan men, such as J. H. Edmisten, were happy the gathering would be in Bryan's hometown, where Bryan supporters were more likely to attend. Butler received many letters and proxies endorsing Bryan and an honorable agreement with Democrats. One writer thought Wharton Barker was "a spy sent from the Republican party to prevent a union of the reform forces," while another favored "keeping middle of roaders out of all our meetings and conventions as I do not consider them Populists." In contrast, anticooperationist John Parker sent a letter to committee members that implied Butler did not have a legitimate reason for holding the meeting in Lincoln.[22]

In the midst of this conflict, *Forum* magazine asked Butler to write an article discussing whether his party would be a factor in the upcoming campaign. In response, Butler first explained the party's principles, including the idea that money should be entirely controlled by the government and that the value of dollars in paper, gold, or silver should be equal. He added that railroads, telephones, and telegraphs should be owned by the people. These goals derived from the Omaha Platform, the chief object of which "was to destroy industrial trusts and to open the door of opportunity for individual enterprise, by restoring the three great instruments of commerce to the people." Turning to politics, Butler argued that the Populist organization had not grown much since 1894 because of the Democratic platform and presidential candidate in 1896. Populist ideas had become more popular, but voters, particularly Democrats, waited to see if their party would retain its 1896 stand. Until Democrats faltered, he surmised, the People's Party would exist primarily as an educator for reform. The article reflected Butler's long-standing belief that Populist principles were correct and enduring but had limited national political meaning.[23]

The Lincoln meeting displayed animosities that had been festering since 1896. It also displayed Butler's unceasing desire to control the strategy of his party, even to the point of squeezing out opponents. Butler, William Allen, James B. Weaver, James Edgerton, and Harry Tracy spoke for the Bryan supporters, while John Parker led the midroad element. The gathering began and ended with a fight over credentials. Butler announced that a preliminary list of legitimate committee members existed, but to be sure that only "real" Populists were on the committee, he would appoint a panel to compose a final list. He selected Weaver, Allen, and Tracy over midroad protests. The panel focused on whether the midroad-held proxies of Populists who participated in the Barker-Donnelly Cincinnati convention in 1898 were valid. Bryan supporters, including Butler, claimed that those persons violated the Omaha Compromise and thus were no longer Populists. The credentials panel agreed, making the proxies worthless. The excommunication forced out moderate midroaders, who now understood they had no chance of directing the national committee away from cooperation. Reportedly, Butler remarked, "It was a bolt here or at the convention, and we preferred that the disturbers show their hand early in the fight." The midroaders called their own national convention for Cincinnati on 9 May, while the Bryan men scheduled nominations for Sioux Falls, South Dakota, also on 9 May.[24]

After Lincoln, both midroaders and Bryan supporters tried unsuccessfully to renew Populist confidence. This work was considerably more difficult for Butler and the Bryan supporters, who offered a plan that resembled the defeated one of 1896. On the other hand, it was the midroaders' great opportunity to demonstrate how a straight ticket could reinvigorate the party and how cooperation could be blamed for the party's ills. Unfortunately, practically no one outside the depleted inner circles cared; the competing campaigns turned into a futile war to defeat other Populists. The battleground focused on the state organizations, as each faction tried to have Populists send delegations only to their convention. Using funds given the Populist committee from boosters of Sioux Falls as repayment for locating the convention there, Butler sent Harry Tracy and J. H. "Cyclone" Davis throughout the South and West to get delegations to South Dakota. Tracy explained to the chairman of the Tennessee party that the Sioux Falls Populists would "reindorse the fundamental principles of the Omaha platform, make direct legislation the leading plank and nominate candidates for president and vice-president and preserve the identity of the party as a separate and distinct organization." This sort of appeal had mixed results. Indiana Populists resolved to boycott Sioux Falls, as would the Georgians. On the other hand, Tracy and Davis believed they could get delegates from Arkansas, Alabama, and Tennessee. Most embarrassing for both factions was the discovery that the Populist Party had ceased to exist in many places, including Maryland, Florida, New York, New Jersey, and South Carolina.[25]

The conventions demonstrated little more than that neither variety of Populism had vanquished the other. In Cincinnati about six hundred delegates endorsed Barker and Donnelly for president and vice president. The platform declared for the initiative and referendum, public ownership and operation of "those means of communication, transportation and production which the people may elect," including railroads, telephone and telegraph lines, and "coal mines, etc." Delegates also favored prohibition of alien ownership of land and irredeemable paper currency, the latter "in sufficient quantity to meet the demands of commerce." For now, however, they were satisfied with "the free and unlimited coinage of both silver and gold at the legal ratio of 16 to 1." The convention also endorsed direct election of senators and federal judges, an income tax, and public ownership of utilities.[26]

Suggesting the continuing impact of regional-based divisions, the Sioux Falls meeting attracted about five hundred mostly western delegates, including a few women. Senator Allen nominated Bryan for the presidency, while Cyclone Davis, a former midroader, gave a speech endorsing Bryan, as did Butler. The platform was longer than the document adopted at Cincinnati. It reaffirmed "adherence to the fundamental principles proclaimed in [the party's] two prior platforms." It demanded "the Lincoln greenback restored, the bonds all paid, and all corporation money forever retired." This meant free coinage of silver and gold, with an increase in silver, silver certificates, and "full legal tender government paper money," replacing all private banknotes, with "total volume so controlled as to maintain at all times a stable money market and a stable price level." The platform supported a graduated income tax, postal savings banks, opposition to land monopoly, public ownership of railroads, municipal ownership of public utilities, and a federal initiative and referendum. It proclaimed federal ownership of "the three great instruments of commerce—money, transportation, and the transmission of intelligence," language undoubtedly selected by Butler, as the only antitrust remedy. In foreign affairs, these Populists wanted freedom for the Philippines. They also defended striking Idaho miners, denounced Asian immigration, and supported direct election of senators. Butler inserted phrasing that condemned "the wholesale system of disfranchisement by coercion and intimidation, adopted in some states."[27]

As in 1896, Bryan Populists divided over how to select a vice president. The convention split among delegates, including Butler, who wanted to nominate the party's own candidate immediately, and those, including James Weaver and William Allen, who wanted to wait and select a committee to go to the upcoming Democratic convention. Butler defended an immediate nomination: "We must not crucify the party under the mistaken idea that this is the best way to elect William Jennings Bryan." He warned, "Let me tell you, if the Democratic Convention goes into New England and puts a man like Sewall on the ticket the battle is lost right now." Weaver, more pragmatically, countered by suggesting that "if you nominate any one here you will never get him" at the Democratic convention. Although the Kansas delegation voted overwhelmingly for Weaver's plan, as did a large portion of the Nebraskans, North Carolinians and the Texans led by Tracy and Davis voted solidly in favor of the party choosing its own nominee. The vote was 262 for Weaver's plan and 492 against. Yet, the Populists who defeated Weaver's proposal did not have a strong candidate for vice president. Minnesotan Charles A. Towne, a Republican who opposed imperialism and supported silver, emerged as the leading contender. Butler and others managed Towne's selection, and Towne accepted.[28]

Butler played an important role at the convention. His efforts for Bryan and Towne succeeded. The platform reflected his ideas on currency, trusts, and government ownership of natural monopolies. Moreover, his speech in favor of Bryan revealed the deep animosity toward the Barker-Donnelly faction. In fact, he separately chastised midroaders, "self-constituted patriots," for wrongly claiming that he and others wanted to turn the party over to the Democrats. By nominating Barker, they were the ones who divided the party and destroyed the Omaha Compromise. Worse, they took Mark Hanna's money.[29]

Butler's broad claims of truer Populism and corruption were as inaccurate as equivalent assertions by midroaders. Contrary to Butler's rhetoric, the two platforms adopted in 1900 demonstrate that Populists, as in 1896, disagreed primarily about political strategy. On government ownership of railroads and government paper money Populists at Sioux Falls and Cincinnati agreed. Both groups also assumed that if government paper was not im-

mediately feasible, free silver and gold would do. Even Bryan, upon notification of the Sioux Falls nomination, recognized "that the Populists believe
in an irredeemable greenback while the Democrats believe in a greenback
redeemable in coin"; politically, however, the difference was meaningless.
Besides the Bryan Populists' greater attack on imperialism, the only difference between the two platforms was the midroaders' vague reference to
public ownership of those means of "production," which "the people may
elect," including "coal mines, etc." This hazy language had no counterpart
in the Alliance platforms or in the Omaha Platform. Nonetheless, Butler
would have supported it if it meant ownership of "natural monopolies,"
which was likely. Additional evidence of congruence among the factions is
that in 1900 former Texas midroaders Harry Tracy and Cyclone Davis supported Bryan, while former Bryan men, such as Ignatius Donnelly, Wharton
Barker, and Davis Waite, were now midroaders.[30]

The Bryan Populist campaign commenced immediately following the
nominations. After being reelected chairman, Butler was once again responsible for organizing national support for a hybrid ticket. Initially, hopes were
high that Democrats would go along with Towne. By the end of May, however, Populists feared Democrats would expressly reject Towne and their
party's paper money plank. More important, many midwesterners, including James Edmisten, the party's vice chairman, regarded Towne as expendable. This view became important when Butler, because of the August suffrage amendment election in North Carolina, was too busy to coordinate a
national campaign and delegated day-to-day operations to Edmisten. Edmisten promptly removed Populist headquarters from Washington to Lincoln.
In fact, Butler was so overwhelmed with North Carolina matters during the
early summer that he missed a critical national committee meeting in July.
Held at the Democratic national convention, Butler hoped it would defend
Towne's candidacy.[31]

When the Democrats gathered for their convention on 4 July, they
spurned Towne. They endorsed a platform that praised free silver and denounced imperialism and trusts. They selected Bryan to head the ticket
against President McKinley, who had already been nominated by the Republicans. They chose Adlai Stevenson of Illinois for the vice presidency. The
Populist leaders gathered at the convention, with Butler absent, did not
present a united front for Towne. Some even thought he should resign,
while others believed he should stay on the ticket and help arrange an 1896
variety of cooperation. Towne met with Bryan and Democratic chairman
James K. Jones, but at first his intentions were unclear.[32]

After the Democratic convention, the North Carolina election kept Butler fully occupied for several weeks. During this time the Towne candidacy disintegrated; Towne abruptly abandoned his nomination in early August. In response, Edmisten called a meeting of the national committee for 27 August. Although only Butler, the party chairman, normally had authority to call such meetings, Edmisten claimed he could act if there was a vacancy on the ticket. Butler, unlike Edmisten, strongly opposed a Populist endorsement of Adlai Stevenson. He responded to Edmisten's call by asking that a meeting not be held and, instead, that there be a referendum on what to do about the vice presidency. Yet Butler soon learned that many midwestern Populists would not mind voting for the entire Democratic ticket, including Stevenson, Grover Cleveland's vice president. Butler began writing for proxies, but many came back endorsing Stevenson. When the national committee met, the pro-Democrats finally achieved the control that escaped them at St. Louis in 1896. During the four-hour struggle, George Washburn moved to have a Populist put on the ticket, while Butler argued that at least the party should not nominate Stevenson. A majority defeated both proposals, and Adlai Stevenson became the Populist nominee.[33]

During the first half of 1900 Butler's party suffered attacks from all directions. In North Carolina, Democrats devised a disfranchisement scheme intended to erase political opposition permanently. In the Senate, a Republican majority embarked on a program of imperialism and financial conservatism. In national politics, the Populist organization shattered into two camps, neither of which reflected Butler's views about proper strategy. One faction seemed to believe Populism could persevere simply by maintaining a separate organization; the other agreed to support whomever Democrats wanted. Through it all Butler articulated his view of Populist economic reform in the Senate and otherwise, opposed North Carolina Democrats' plan for a revolutionary reduction in the electorate and the elimination of local government, helped force the formal splintering of the national Populist Party, and witnessed the takeover of the national organization by midwestern supporters of Bryan. As before, it was not so much the ideology of Populism that presented his greatest trials but the attempt to give that ideology political meaning. Butler's last fight as a Populist was at hand.

THE END OF THE PEOPLE'S PARTY

NORTH CAROLINA Democrats prepared early and often for the 1900 state election, which they scheduled for 2 August. The leading issue was the suffrage amendment to the state constitution, but voters would also elect a governor and the next General Assembly. The key Democratic strategists were Chairman Furnifold Simmons, who had his eye on Butler's Senate seat, and Josephus Daniels, who was on the verge of a national career that would eventually include an appointment to the Cabinet. Simmons arranged the distribution of over one hundred thousand copies of a rousing defense of the suffrage amendment funded by money from friendly businessmen. As early as January, the Democracy inundated the countryside with official literature. Speakers, especially future governors Aycock and Robert B. Glenn, began to travel around the state more than six months before the election. From the beginning, the party also used intimidation. Simmons asked for the names of men who might be doubtful on the amendment and issued a poll book that allowed local leaders to classify every voter in their precinct. Even tax officials passed out Democratic literature, and one merchant dispensed pro-amendment tracts with every purchase. White Supremacy Club members wore red white supremacy buttons ordered by Simmons, while Daniels published the names of prominent antiamendment Populists and Republicans in each county.[1]

In contrast, disagreement and internal disintegration among Populists put Butler's antiamendment campaign on the defensive. Former congressman Harry Skinner, once an outstanding spokesman for reform, now wrote friendly letters to President McKinley protesting prejudice against Republicans and wishing the South "would embrace the potent principles of protection and expansion." Others hesitated to receive antiamendment literature and declined to condemn Democrats openly, "believing fully that they would be boycotted by Democrats, in their business relations." Clarence Poe's *Progressive Farmer* seemed to favor the amendment. More important was Populist racism. The *Charlotte People's Paper* openly endorsed disfranchisement, proclaiming that "so long as the negro scare crow is held up before the people it will be out of the question to get the people—the masses—united for reform." The *Hickory Times-Mercury*, the only prominent Populist paper besides the *Caucasian* that opposed the amendment, promoted a black exodus from the state, partly because it assumed blacks depressed the value of whites' labor. J. F. Click, the editor, also feared that black youths heard "white men and white boys saying many things about well dressed and nice shaped white girls and women they should not hear." As a result, "they get the seeds of sin planted in their natures which grow as they grow, and they never cease longing until they commit or attempt rape." The Populist organization, headed by Cyrus Thompson, was hopelessly disorganized. In January Thompson told Butler the party was penniless. He did not see any grounds for optimism: "This campaign resolves itself into a question of physical force, and we have nothing in sight with which to make the struggle." Curiously, Thompson believed the only way to win was to ignore the amendment. Hal Ayer agreed. He did not contemplate, as Butler seemed to, a fight to "out-do" the Democrats.[2]

Populist disagreement and disengagement meant that the burden of running the campaign against the amendment fell almost entirely on Butler. He assumed it was worth the effort because the amendment would disfranchise up to sixty thousand poorer white voters, thereby effectively ending the Populist Party. Moreover, he wanted to be reelected to the Senate, and these votes, as well as an alliance with Republicans, represented the only route back to Washington. As a result, lacking any hope of a favorable response from Democrats, he abandoned the state-level silver coalition plan that had guided his political strategy in North Carolina since 1895. He commenced the campaign in January 1900 by arguing that Democrats targeted poor whites, as well as blacks, for disfranchisement: "I believe in manhood suffrage and freedom of speech and conscience." His answer to fears of black power was to suggest that if Democrats really opposed "Negro supremacy" they would pass a law barring blacks from office. He flooded the state with his antiamendment Senate speeches and free government seeds.[3]

The campaign got under way in earnest at the three parties' nominating conventions. Democrats met first. Charles B. Aycock, the reigning symbol of white supremacy, easily won the nomination for governor. The platform

reeked of southern "progressivism": Democrats endorsed the disfranchisement amendment, denounced Republican "Negro domination," demanded
an income tax and direct election of senators, pledged a four months' public school term, and criticized the gold standard, imperialism, militarism,
and free railroad passes. More than ten years of Alliance-Populist agitation
had made a difference, but not much.[4]

About three hundred Populists met for their last state convention on 18
April. As they had since 1892, Butler and his allies ran the show. Demonstrating his faith in white supremacy, Butler opponent Harry Skinner criticized delegates for not advocating repeal of the Fourteenth and Fifteenth
Amendments, but the former congressman lacked a large following. The
platform reaffirmed support for the national party's goals, condemned the
election law and the poll tax, and demanded self-government in white counties and white control in black counties, better schools, and harmony between capital and labor. Hedging on the key issue, Populists officially made
the suffrage amendment subject to individual choice while indicating they
thought it was wrong. They also believed that instead of disfranchisement, it
would be better to amend the state constitution to provide that no person
with black ancestry, "to the third generation inclusive," could hold office.
The delegates named a full state ticket with Cyrus Thompson for governor
and endorsed Butler's reelection to the Senate.[5]

The convention demonstrated the disruptive effect of two years of white
supremacy attacks, white Populists' racism, and lingering discomfort over
white cooperation with black voters. Race threatened Populism much more
than silver ever could. The platform gave considerable space to assurances
of Populist devotion to white rule, but there was little in the way of state-level
economic reform. Gone were antitrust proposals, railroad regulation, the
ninety-nine-year lease, a defense of the 6 percent interest law, or any new or
different concrete ideas as to what the state needed. Moreover, the separate
ticket was misleading. Insiders knew Butler-Pritchard rapprochement meant
eventual cooperation with Republicans. The separate ticket existed merely
to create the impression that the poor white man's party—not the party of
Reconstruction and black men—led the fight against the amendment.

Republicans held their convention on 1 May, but even the GOP was not
united. Daniel Russell, the governor, had faded from sight, as he agreed
with Thompson and Ayer that a political fight against the amendment was
hopeless. He suggested blacks refrain from voting. On the other hand, the
Republican leadership under Jeter Pritchard did not accept disfranchisement. Pritchard's platform lauded the gold standard, but it also gave exten-

sive treatment to the election law and the proposed amendment. Republicans accused Democrats of devising a disfranchisement scheme that was an "impudent assault upon the Constitution of the United States." They deplored that suffrage "should be made dependent upon heredity and thus build up an aristocracy of birth," and they condemned the "frauds, robberies, violence and intimidation" that characterized the last election. They nominated a full, but temporary, slate for state offices.[6]

Initially, just after the Populist convention, Butler found it unusually difficult to begin a campaign. The Senate and the troubles of the national party preoccupied him. He did not return to North Carolina to conduct a full-time campaign until early June. Then, although the time was short, he worked tirelessly. He mailed countless optimistic letters to local Populist leaders. He requested precinct chairmen to send information about who had been registered and to petition Democratic election officials for Populist judges of election. Butler often relied on census enumerators for whom he had obtained jobs to gather local information. He impatiently dismissed any excuses for failure, including those of one man who had the impertinence to suggest that his census duties would keep him from campaign work. He also helped effect cooperation, but most Populists and Republicans, as in 1894, 1896, and 1898, cooperated without any encouragement. He and Republican officials engaged in some joint planning, yet the GOP was often not helpful. Republicans, for example, ungraciously assigned Butler the election's most difficult tasks: sending speakers into the east and registering black voters.[7]

Democrats responded to Butler's activities by making the most of their control of the legislature. On 12 June the party took the unprecedented step of convening a special session of the General Assembly, which promptly sank one Populist tactic by revoking the power of the largely Republican superior court judges to order registration of voters until a presumably Democratic jury could hear the registration dispute. The assembly also added a clause to the suffrage amendment indicating its intent to make the grandfather clause inseparable from the literacy test. If one was declared unconstitutional, the other would also fall. This eliminated Butler's legal argument that the literacy test would disfranchise poor whites if a court declared the grandfather clause unconstitutional. Finally, the assembly planned to convene just before the election to prevent any last-minute interferences from the Republican supreme court.[8]

Democrats intensified other strategies. Especially aggressive actions appeared in voter registration. Under the new law, the registration process involved answering, to the satisfaction of a Democratic registrar, questions involving age, residence, and employment. Registrars often excluded Republicans and Populists based on alleged problems with residency. Some registrars asked questions not allowed by statute, such as the name of the president. Intimidation supplemented these official barriers. One Populist reported, "The negroes are so completely frightened by [Democratic] threats that we find it impossible to get them to try to register and many that has [*sic*] been refused registration we can not get them to file their affidavit [of complaint]." Another told Butler that a "mob of masked men about 30 in number" stole the registration book for Honeycutts Township, Sampson County, where Butler grew up and his mother still lived. Butler responded by demanding "the arrest of every registrar at once who refused to register qualified voters." More than forty registrars were arrested, but many Populists opposed the arrests on the ground that they would further inflame angry Democrats.[9]

On 18 July, two weeks before the election, Butler finally and publicly addressed the need for a combined GOP and Populist ticket for state offices. He stated that joint legislative tickets were already set and that Populists had won over three-fourths of those nominations in the east. As for state-level cooperation, it required giving Republicans the governorship; this, in turn, was part of a deal to send Butler back to the Senate. On 24 July, Cyrus Thompson dutifully announced his resignation as the Populist candidate for governor. He stated that keeping Butler in the Senate, writing a new election law, and barring blacks from office were more important than a Populist governor. Butler and Republican chairman Alfred Holton then formalized a ticket for state offices that included eight Populists and three Republicans.[10]

Butler's final role as chairman was to arrange speeches. Populists incessantly called for good speakers. They complained that Democrats appeared "every day and night," while there was no Populist in sight. Butler tried to meet the demand by importing his Texas friends Cyclone Davis, H. S. P. "Stump" Ashby, and Harry Tracy. Yet one Populist told him that "the people here do not want to hear a man from another state." Rather, they wanted Butler. A follower sought to tempt him to Hillsboro with "a brassband and a *Horse Back Parade*," while another argued that it was "an undisputed fact that Marion Butler has more influence with the farmers and laborers of this county than any man in N.C." A Moore County Populist wanted him "if he continues to live. We can't do without *him* and win." Although he made speeches in the western piedmont in June and appeared in Raleigh and a few eastern locations in July, Butler did not make a broad canvass in the east in the last weeks of the campaign, as he planned. Death threats intervened, especially in the east, which was a stronghold of the most violent forms of white supremacy. When he did speak, the speeches tended to be two- and three-hour performances detailing the hypocrisy of the Democrats, the unconstitutionality of the amendment, and the negative effect of the amendment on poor whites. Butler gave his most famous speech at Morganton, where he picked an eleven-year-old boy wearing a white supremacy button out of the crowd and announced that the button "speaks a lie." It "will disfranchise not only you but every poor white boy . . . who is not fortunate enough to get an education and to educate himself to the satisfaction of a Democratic registrar before 1908."[11]

Even more than the 1898 election, the antiamendment campaign illustrated the limits of the Alliance-Populist experience in changing white attitudes toward race. Populists never questioned that the black man was inferior and should be subordinate in politics and otherwise. Butler's contention that fifty thousand blacks would be able to vote while sixty thousand whites would lose that right under the amendment should be considered the crux of antiamendment politics. To be sure, Butler argued and believed that the federal constitution required that blacks be allowed to vote. Although this was a radical position for a white politician, it usually was advanced more as legality than as a matter of moral justice. Given Butler's need for black votes to be reelected, as well as his initial opposition to Republican cooperation in 1896 and 1898, even the constitutional point seemed partly driven by expedience. Equally revealing was Butler and the party's proposal that the state bar blacks from public office. In sharp contrast, Populism instilled a determined opposition to the degradation of poorer whites. The *Caucasian* explained that the amendment was "intended to remove the 'lower classes of whites' forever from politics, thus transferring all political power from the plain honest masses in the country to the town ringster, who would perpetuate his rule by the use of the educated 'town nigger.'" Nothing demonstrated the different attitude toward white and black voting rights more clearly than the Populist effort to attract white millworkers. A Fayetteville man wanted Populists to speak to employees at Holt's Factory and Hope Mills, and Populists in Cleveland and Mecklenburg Counties claimed, "We are working the mill people for all they are worth." Butler himself argued that an expansion of child labor in the mills would increase illiteracy and thus worsen disfranchisement.[12]

During July, Democrats finished the campaign with a flurry of activity. Frantic Populists informed Butler that their opponents accumulated large

Populism's response to Democracy, 1900.
(Courtesy of the North Carolina Division of Archives and History)

stores of arms, threatened speakers with death, planned to destroy cooperation ballots, and stole mail, including Butler's propaganda. One reported that "the democrats are going to try to force the white men to vote the democratic ticket or scare them away. They say they have plenty of rifles ect [*sic*] and if any white man try to instruct a negro they will sure shoot him." A popular Red Shirt tactic in the campaign's last weeks was to prevent Populist speakers from getting off trains or, once off, from speaking. Just before the election Butler ventured into the east, which was fully mobilized by the Democrats. At Warsaw, only a few miles from his wife's ancestral home, and at other towns along the Atlantic Coast Line, Red Shirts waited; they "forcibly, and not too courteously, prevented his getting off the train." When the senator finally did get off, they "tossed [him] back bodily to the platform. All the while shouts of no complimentary nature hit the air."[13]

The Democratic leadership coordinated and inspired the orgy of lies, threats, and violence. As in 1898, the campaign was based on the wholly false idea that opponents of the Democratic Party were also opponents of white supremacy and proponents of "Negro rule," including social equality. Future governor Robert Glenn claimed that Butler advised whipping white men out of the state. Claude Kitchin complained that an old Confederate applied for a Washington job but that Butler and Pritchard had given the position "to a big black Negro weighing over 200 pounds." In more than one hundred speeches Aycock renewed his fascination with the sexual dangers that could be avoided by Democratic rule. Where he spoke, elaborate floats, Red Shirts, women in white dresses, and prominent displays of weapons created a carnival atmosphere in the hot, dusty towns of eastern North Carolina. One Populist described the crowd at Kenansville as half white women and children and half white men brandishing "armed pistols." Blacks kept out of sight. A supporter told Butler that Aycock's brother had been heard to say that the intimidation should be kept up.[14]

Butler's experience in the days before the election symbolized the Populist plight. He issued statements warning that this was the most important election in a century and that the amendment was unconstitutional. But the leading Butler story just before the election had nothing to do with reasoned argument. Instead, it was a personal attack on him by Democratic congressman John D. Bellamy of Wilmington, in which Bellamy called him "the most despicable and contemptible creature in this state," who should be "forcibly expelled" from its borders. Butler's composure burst, and he challenged Bellamy to meet him to begin the "expelling business." This, along with the necessity of gathering an armed guard to escort the United States senator home to vote, indicated the dawning of southern progressivism.[15]

The second of August was a Democratic day. The amendment passed easily, 182,217 to 128,285, and voters elected Aycock governor by an even larger margin. The 1901 legislature would be overwhelmingly Democratic. Election turnout declined about 10 percent from 1896, and black turnout declined by 20 percent. Extreme examples of the effects of the new registration law and intimidation appeared in New Hanover County, where Republican votes dropped from over 2,600 in 1898 to 5 in 1900, and in Richmond County, where the vote for the amendment was 1,636 to 193. Moreover, by one estimate, 37 percent of Populists voted for the amendment. This figure reflects the widespread and deep commitment to white supremacy even among members of the third party. Not surprisingly, intimidation and fraud in the eastern black belt also produced the anomaly of a large black vote in favor of disfranchisement.[16]

Before the election, Butler had asked Populists to record the event for a possible legal challenge. The responses showed that during the election blacks were put in jail, forced to vote for the amendment, and beaten. In Bertie County "a colored man was shot three times the ball passing through his face, and the man, a democrat, who shot him, was brought before [the mayor's court] and fined one cent." African Americans received threatening letters, including one which stated, "As a friend to the colored people I advise you not to vote tomorrow and when you read this tell your neighbor and try to keep him out of trouble as it is sure to come to the colored man that votes tomorrow as we will see him later." A white Lexington Republican told Butler, "They had 47 armed officers—armed with clubs and pistols— on the election ground." Another man reported that Democrats surrounded his store and built a coffin for him. In Robeson County they doused a white man with water, ruining the ballots he carried. In some communities, "bull pens," in which voters were herded into small buildings where no one was allowed to see the counting box except Democratic officials, were used. Cash was a common motivator. The Democratic chairman for the First Congressional District, William B. Rodman, sent checks to registrars, "as a slight testimony of our sincere gratitude" for "the manner in which you conducted your box."[17]

After the election the Populist state organization collapsed. It would play no role in the November elections for president and Congress. All that remained of the organization were a few local units, largely in the western part of the state. The east, apparently, was no longer a place for dissent. Butler's last action as state leader was an attempt to mount a legal challenge to the election. He held a well-attended "Indignation Meeting" in Sampson County, and similar meetings convened in other places. By October, however, he had abandoned the idea of a massive lawsuit.[18]

Although not naïve about politics, the election deeply disturbed Butler. It seemed to thwart his confidence in reform. In a long protest written to the *New York Independent,* he complained that although the Constitution allegedly followed the flag, perhaps "it has gone to the Philippines. . . . [I]t has certainly departed from North Carolina." "Fraud and rascality reigned supreme," and Democrats from Aycock and Daniels down stood for the proposition that violent means justified the end of disfranchisement. National Democrats had read the Declaration of Independence at their convention, but in North Carolina that document "is not considered to apply to negroes nor to white men who do not vote the machine ticket. . . . Unconstitutional regulations have taken the place of the guaranteed right of suffrage and representation; and those in a little brief authority are the masters who select the rulers and servants of the people."[19]

DESPITE THE LOSS in North Carolina, Butler continued to support Bryan in the presidential race. It was difficult, however, to be enthusiastic. Adlai Stevenson, in particular, alienated him and many others. By early September, Butler headed the national Populist Party in name only, as Vice Chairman Edmisten and Secretary Edgerton took over the campaign. They sent out optimistic reports, emphasized imperialism and antitrust, and maintained friendly relations with the Democratic leadership. They ran a campaign in harmony with Bryan's wishes, but it left observers wondering why a separate organization was needed. Nonetheless, Butler advised Populists, except those in North Carolina, to support the ticket, and he gave a number of Bryan speeches in Kansas, Nebraska, and the Dakotas. He argued that Bryan was the only hope for reform.[20]

In North Carolina, when Towne came off the ticket in August, just after the success of disfranchisement, Populists were in no mood to vote for Democrats. Butler asked them to boycott the national election, and one supporter agreed: "Not many of our people through this section will support Stevenson." The lack of a Populist presidential campaign prompted editor J. P. Sossaman of Charlotte, an outspoken supporter of the suffrage amendment and Republican cooperation, to call an 11 October convention to mobilize support for Barker and Donnelly. The *Hickory Times-Mercury* also concluded that the independent Populist ticket was best, largely because it would provide for continued organization. Yet the Barker-Donnelly "convention" attracted only twenty people. On election day Populists seemed to follow Butler's advice to stay home; Barker received a few hundred ballots.[21]

Populists did not fare much better elsewhere, as McKinley won reelection easily. Most important, Bryan lost ground in the heart of western Populism, as Kansas, Nebraska, and South Dakota went for the president. The mid-road ticket also failed, not because it lost, an occurrence that was fully expected, but because it demonstrated there was no significant support for independent Populism. Barker received just over fifty thousand votes; James B. Weaver had captured more than one million in 1892. The performances of Bryan and Barker confirmed the demise of Populism and its various political strategies.[22]

THE ELECTION OF 1900 forced a turning point in Butler's career. The People's Party divided and essentially disappeared. It fell in North Carolina primarily because it was unable to overcome the racism, economic intimidation, and brute force that Democrats used to take over state government. Populism, although posing as a democratic movement, never developed a clear answer to the undemocratic control that seemed inherent in a society based on white supremacy; moreover, it was satisfied with the continuation of white supremacy. Even Butler's important, but limited, conclusion that the Constitution stood for universal manhood suffrage appeared incorrect to a large percentage of the men who abandoned the Democrats for financial and transportation reform in 1892. Butler had tried to eliminate the issue by supporting Democratic cooperation in 1896 and 1898, but opposition in his own party and from anti-Populist Democrats shifted the political balance and produced the counterrevolution of 1900. Ironically, Populist attempts to diminish the significance of race in politics, without challenging white dominance, had actually produced a furious reaction against Populism that eliminated political debate over race. It was the cynical use of white supremacy to achieve something practically all whites agreed about, while destroying economic reform, that so infuriated Butler.

The fate of national Populists, similarly, was affected by internal squabbles, such as over cooperation, but more important were other factors, including the rise of Bryan; the Democrats' acceptance of silver inflation; a gradual improvement in the economy; an increase in the supply of gold and farm prices; racism and sectional politics; the varying needs, events, and personalities of state-level politics; the Populists' weakness among urban workers; and the popularity of McKinley in the Midwest. Together, these doomed the spread of Populism. No ambitious coalition plan or midroad faith—and even supporters of cooperation and midroad politics did not agree about how the respective strategies should be carried out after 1896—could change the many factors that limited Populism's intellectual and political appeal. Most Americans simply did not respond favorably to the agrarian perspective of the party, nor did they view irredeemable currency or government ownership of transportation, the Populists' outstanding proposals, as pivotal political issues in 1890, 1896, or 1900. After 1895, shouting by Populists about corruption and sellouts by other Populists demonstrated only a growing sense of impotence; it had nothing to do with the complex reasons why the movement was dying. The deeper issues were the causes, not the consequences, of the disputes over strategy.

BUTLER'S RETURN TO Washington for the final session of the Fifty-sixth Congress presented his last legislative opportunity. Congress's most important tasks included army reorganization, establishing civil government in the Philippines, defining a relationship with Cuba, and appropriations. Although the session was brief, lasting from December 1900 to early March 1901, Butler was as active as usual.

The Army Reorganization Bill endeavored to modernize the nation's land forces. Prompted partly by the blunders of the Spanish-American War, the bill promised a more efficient staff system and a bigger army. Butler, however, opposed a larger army and reorganization. His criticisms focused on the danger and expense of the proposed peacetime army of one hundred thousand permanent troops. He preferred an old-time volunteer force; the professional soldier fit better in monarchies and other despotisms, he thought, there to "murder, plunder, and oppress." He warned that the bill was "undemocratic and unrepublican and antagonistic to the genius of our institutions," as well as "a radical departure from everything that we have considered distinctly American." It was approved, with Allen and Butler voting against it.[23]

Closely related to the imperialistic implications of the army bill was legislation concerning the Philippines and Cuba. The Philippines bill aimed to give the president broad powers over the islands. Butler and his allies again disagreed and unsuccessfully tried to promote self-government. They wanted to limit the powers of McKinley's officials by enforcing federal constitutional protections, including freedom of religion and trial by jury. As for Cuba, from Butler's perspective the problem was that McKinley wanted the United States to have a right to intervene in Cuban affairs. Butler and others, however, failed to defeat restrictions on Cuban sovereignty.[24]

Appropriation bills dominated much of the session. One of those considered involved the Post Office. Butler, as before, complained about the amount paid railroads for carrying mail and introduced an amendment to trim about 5 percent off a committee proposal for railway pay. He gave a speech that attempted to show that fairness and "business principles" demanded a reduction. The Senate defeated his proposal. Another familiar appropriations matter was naval expense, and Butler again was unable to reduce the amount paid for naval armor. After several years of agitation, he lamented, "We are paying the highest price we have ever paid, with the biggest order that any government ever gave." More novel was his attempt to reduce naval costs by supporting relatively cheap submarines. Although he convinced the Senate to fund three additional submarines, they were dropped in conference.[25]

Butler devoted many of his last hours in the Senate to challenging the election of Furnifold Simmons, who the North Carolina legislature chose as his successor in early 1901. He asked the Senate to reject Simmons because in the recent election Simmons had been responsible for "flagrant frauds and force and crime to override the will of the people." To illustrate this, Butler described his own election day experience in Sampson County. He told the Senate about Red Shirts carrying Winchesters and pistols and about ministers riding at the head of Democratic "anarchists and murderers." Registrars informed voters that their ages were recorded incorrectly and that if they voted they would be guilty of a crime. Democrats switched the order of the six election boxes to confuse, marked a skull and crossbones on the doors of black citizens in his neighborhood, and counted ballots in secret under displays of rifles. A registrar refused to allow a black man to register because he had not completed a ditch-digging job. Most important, Simmons deserved the blame. He devised the tactics and made sure his lackeys carried them out. Predictably, the Senate did not question Simmons's credentials, and he remained there until 1931, becoming one of its most influential members.[26]

Butler's final session reflected many of the broader themes of his Senate career. He spoke often, but few senators listened. His views differed dramatically from those of the majority, and he had little influence on the final shape of legislation. He lost on imperialism and on the army, Post Office, and naval bills. On the other hand, he was among those men who articulated positions challenging the drift of power. He did not simply let the Republicans rule. By 1901, however, many of the questions that were at the forefront of national debate when he was elected in 1895 had been raised and lost. This left him in the ironic position of using much of his time to advocate minimal constitutional rights for persons in overseas possessions or in North Carolina.

Even with the defeats, including the failure to achieve the passage of a single core Populist proposal, the corpus of Butler's Senate work must be evaluated as a substantial accomplishment. Although at the time Populists almost universally recognized his diligent efforts, the consistency of his views and his willingness to put them into legislative form have been ignored or forgotten by historians. In bills, resolutions, and amendments Butler managed to bring Omaha Platform Populism to the Senate. He introduced legislation for directly elected senators and judges, an income tax, irredeemable paper money, a dramatically expanded postal system, and government ownership of railroads. He attacked trusts, corporate greed, and imperialism. He defended universal manhood suffrage. He demanded care in the spending of taxpayer money, particularly to corporations. Although there were several outstanding Populists in Congress, including William Peffer, Jerry Simpson, William Allen, Harry Skinner, and Tom Watson, no other representative of Populism surpassed Butler's record of introducing specific proposals that would have translated the Omaha Platform into law. He offered a broad version of the Populist brief, spending long, lonely, and late hours preparing for hearings, speeches, and votes. Although isolated and preoccupied by the maelstrom over political strategy, as a legislator he was as faithful an advocate as the party could desire.

The demise of the Populist Party brought great bitterness. Nothing was more heart wrenching for Butler than surrendering his Senate seat, particularly given the violent manner in which it had been lost. He loved the Senate and would have been content to spend the rest of his life there. He was only thirty-seven years old in early 1901, yet he would never hold another public office. More personally, his party's collapse, the Democratic coup, and personal criticism from former allies hardened him. There had been few genuine setbacks in his early career, and now it appeared his public life might be at an end even before he entered middle age. Both as a consequence of this disappointment and his own natural seriousness and determination to win, he learned to hate his opponents. Defeat also forced the young reformer to concede that Populism's triumph, which once seemed so close, was indefinitely postponed. These scars, combined with a persistent superconfidence that he was the most able political leader in North Carolina, made him a less attractive leader in 1901 than he had been in 1892. Of course, it is ironic that a man who believed in expanding individual liberty was exceedingly jealous of his own power, a trait he demonstrated in his management of the Populist Party through the middle and late 1890s. On the other hand, there was a direct relationship between his behavior and defeat, and the irony reflected the deeper and more personal consequences of Populist failure. Undoubtedly these harsh consequences were repeated throughout the former strongholds of the People's Party.

PROGRESSIVE ERA HOPES AND
DISAPPOINTMENTS

AFTER THE 1900 election, Butler tried to keep Populist ideas alive. In 1901 his newspaper supported public ownership of railroads, telegraphs, telephones, and public utilities. It demanded an income tax, criticized imperialism, and voiced the complaint that North Carolina Democrats failed to enact a real antitrust law or to tax railroads fully. The strategic problem of the 1890s, however, remained: How could one give these ideas political meaning? Of course, Butler was still chairman of the national and North Carolina Populist Party, but there was little left of those groups. He did not change his belief about the correctness of Populist principles, nor was he willing to abandon public life to the victors. An especially difficult political challenge presented itself because even though the disfranchisement of blacks was now a permanent part of the landscape, a return to the North Carolina Democratic Party was unthinkable. Instead, for his home state he proposed a new coalition that would combine white Populist farmers, Republicans, and another type of producer he extolled in college—manufacturers. The Republican Party, of course, was the only vehicle available to lead this "progressive" coalition. To make the most of retrenchment, Butler reminded his diminished force: "We believe in competition. Let the public own the natural monopolies, and then for the rest, let it be every man for himself."[1]

The transition to twentieth-century politics proved difficult for all Populists, and the roads taken varied as much as the individuals in the party. There were examples of persistence, compromise, and surrender. Some important leaders, including Ignatius Donnelly, Henry Demarest Lloyd of Illinois, and Lorenzo Lewelling, Populist governor of Kansas, died before 1901 or soon thereafter. Among those who survived, Harry Skinner showed Republican leanings as early as 1897, was rewarded with an appointment as U.S. attorney in eastern North Carolina in 1901, and remained a Republican until his death in 1929. William V. Allen dropped from political prominence after he failed to win the Populist nomination for president in 1904; he practiced law in Lincoln and, in 1917, became a state court judge. Tom Watson retired to history writing after the 1896 election but reemerged to run for president as a Populist in 1904 and 1908. He rejoined the Democratic Party in 1910. His subsequent efforts offered a heavy dose of ethnic and religious hatred, focusing on the evils of blacks, Jews, Catholics, and socialists. Watson lost a bid for election to Congress in 1918 but was elected to the Senate in 1920; he died in 1922. Another Populist congressman, Reuben F. Kolb of Alabama, also returned to the Democratic Party. He supported black disfranchisement in 1900, was elected Alabama's commissioner of agriculture in 1910, and lost a Democratic primary for governor in 1914. Frank Doster, the Kansas Populist, entered private law practice, working for a period as an attorney for the Missouri Pacific Railroad. He unsuccessfully ran for the Senate in 1914 as a Democrat and, unlike Tom Watson, supported American involvement with the League of Nations after World War I. H. L. Loucks of South Dakota ran for office as an independent several times after 1900, including for the Senate in 1924. Mary Elizabeth Lease became a Republican supporter of William McKinley and a writer for Joseph Pulitzer's *New York World*. She later endorsed Theodore Roosevelt and prohibition. William Peffer of Kansas returned to the Republican Party before his death in 1912. Milton Park published newspapers, became a fire insurance salesman, and was an adjutant general in the United Confederate Veterans. Fellow Texan J. H. "Cyclone" Davis supported the Prohibition Party in 1904, became a Democrat in 1906, voted for Woodrow Wilson in 1912, and was elected to Congress in 1914. He opposed American involvement in World War I, joined the Ku Klux Klan, and lost a Democratic primary for Congress in 1932. H. S. P. "Stump" Ashby also returned to the Democratic Party. He served in the Oklahoma legislature and died in 1923. Harry Tracy, another Texan, became prominent in the Texas Farmers' Union and rejoined the Democratic Party.[2]

What is most striking about this sample of post-1900 careers, from the perspective of Butler's life, is that practically all the southerners, except Butler and Skinner, made peace with the politics of white supremacy and the Democratic Party. Ironically, this included Watson and the midroad Texans, who in 1896 made so much noise about Butler selling out to the Democrats. Further, most of the southerners mentioned, by returning to the Democracy, had much more successful political careers than Butler. And among them, the more extreme racists, Davis and Watson, represented their states in Washington. Kolb and Ashby held state offices. In contrast, Butler never ran for public office after 1900, unlike many other western or southern Populist leaders, including Watson, Doster, Allen, Kolb, Davis, Ashby, and Loucks. The fate of Populists after 1900 confirms how deeply state-level political issues and loyalties shaped the Populist Party before 1900. Populists in both periods reacted to very different political conditions in the states where they lived. Their political behavior in the twentieth century showed the continuing impact of forces other than reform, and for the Democratic southerners, no force carried more weight than race.[3]

More broadly, the path of Populists in the early twentieth century, including Butler's, sheds considerable light on the relationship between Populism and progressivism. For the Populists themselves, as well as for later historians, the key issue was the extent to which Populism survived into the Progressive Era, including the extent to which progressive reform could be linked to or distinguished from Populism. Historians have offered various interpretations of the relationship between the two reform movements, concluding variously that they had significant connections and that the two were fundamentally different. Recently, Elizabeth Sanders has made a case that "agrarian" congressmen, for the most part Democrats, were leading forces behind Progressive Era legislation in transportation, finance, and agriculture. This clearly links progressive reforms to the earlier rural movements of the 1890s, showing that Populists and progressives had some common goals regarding the relationship between the economy and the government. It also suggests that the Democratic response to Populism in 1896, as well as the Populists' response to the Democrats, had dramatic and long-lasting effects. Further, other studies establish that Populists actively participated in the politics of the early twentieth century and supported progressive reforms. Nonetheless, "agrarian" does not necessarily mean "Populist," and strong evidence also shows the fundamental differences between the two experiences. As C. Vann Woodward put it more than fifty years ago, progressivism "sprouted in the soil that had nourished Populism, but it lacked the agrarian cast and the radical edge that had frightened the middle class away from the earlier movement."[4]

Butler's career is especially useful in comparing the two movements. Between 1901 and 1920 his actions tended to display the sharp differences between the substance of Populism and progressivism, not the similarities. On the other hand, Butler was both a Populist and a progressive, and his career as a progressive politician reveals the common problems of political organization and structure faced by Populists and progressives. Butler continued his obsession with public life, even without seeking office, but his ideas of what kinds of Populist legislation were needed became increasingly less possible, and compromise proposals routinely failed, even in the heyday of progressivism. On occasion, Butler promoted the principles of the Omaha Platform, but by 1910 that doctrine seemed as remote as the Missouri Compromise. His consistent notion of government, state or national, as primarily representing rural producers disappeared as a political force. In North Carolina, the most virulent opponents of Populism—Charles Aycock, Josephus Daniels, and Furnifold Simmons—held power. Other former enemies of Populism, including Theodore Roosevelt, William Taft, and Woodrow Wilson, became president. To be sure, many of the new leaders now wanted better schools, a more flexible currency, a federal income tax, and lower railroad rates. This was certainly a change from the days of Grover Cleveland, but it was starkly different from having Congress set the per capita amount of dollars in circulation and assert government ownership of railroads, telephones, and telegraphs, the core demands of the Populists. Further, the sharp constriction of the southern electorate through disfranchisement dramatically limited the kinds of political coalitions that could be formed to advance reform. Butler, unlike most other southern Populists, freed himself from the numbing effects of defending white supremacy by joining the Republicans rather than the Democrats. Yet he never sought to restore black suffrage. From Butler's vantage, progressivism offered a diminished hope; the path from Populism led to progressivism, but only by way of defeat.[5]

In addition to tolerating disfranchisement and proposing a union with Republicans, after 1900 Butler tried to survive the collapse of his old party through other political maneuvers. First, he began to argue that a high tariff could benefit farmers, industrialists, and southerners. Second, he admitted that the nation's economy had improved since 1893, although he credited the upturn to an increase in money volume. Populist doctrine "always maintained that the substance from which money was made amounted to nothing; it is the quantity on which we had been harping." Indeed, he "never favored the use of that word silver" but supported government paper money and government control over the supply of money. The bottom line was that recent gold strikes accomplished what Populists wanted. When it became necessary, "we will [again] fight for greenbacks instead of bank paper." Finally, Butler announced that imperialism, like disfranchisement, was a settled issue. Although these shifts eased the way to the GOP—and it is difficult to disagree with Butler that political challenges to disfranchisement, protection, gold, and imperialism were doomed—they confirmed the extent to which Populism failed and would differ from "progressivism."[6]

President McKinley's assassination in September 1901 presented an excellent opportunity for Butler to implement his new politics. Theodore Roosevelt (TR), McKinley's successor, had a reputation as a reformer. The *Caucasian* published an editorial on "President Roosevelt and the South" that proclaimed the time was "ripe for building up a strong respectable progressive and liberal party in opposition to the Democratic machine in this state and other southern states." Butler hoped to develop a relationship with the new president and was helped by Senator Jeter Pritchard, who still had two years left in his term. Pritchard, like Butler, recognized the need to reconstruct his party after disfranchisement. He preferred a lily-white GOP with strong ties to industry, but he also favored tossing Populists into the mix. Probably on Pritchard's request, Roosevelt wrote Butler, inquiring about conditions in North Carolina. Butler responded with enthusiasm for Pritchard's plan to replace disfranchised blacks with businessmen and Populists. Textile manufacturers "could organize a movement that would win." Perhaps reflecting on ten years of battling the Democrats without this support, he mused, "North Carolina cannot be carried in any other way."[7]

Butler and Pritchard tried to implement these ideas in the 1902 election. Butler proposed a "citizens ticket composed of all the parties and elements opposed to the Democratic party." Pritchard supported this "Independent" effort, which meant his party accepted both Populists and Democrats upset at their party's nomination of Butler's old friend, the liberal Walter Clark, for chief justice of the state supreme court. The Republican state convention, which excluded blacks and included more urban white businessmen than usual, endorsed Thomas N. Hill, a conservative Democrat who ran an "Independent" campaign against Clark. For the first time since 1890 there was no separate Populist campaign, but Populists tended to support the Republican-Independent movement. Butler participated less in the 1902 contest than in any since 1886. His most important task, at Pritchard's request, was to disclaim any responsibility for Populist criticisms of the 1897 legislature. Pritchard sought reelection to the Senate, and in 1897 Butler had attacked corruption in the legislature, particularly relating to Pritchard's reelection. Butler wrote a public letter admitting he endorsed Cyrus Thompson for the Senate in 1897, not Pritchard, but only because Thompson favored an immediate increase in the money supply. Since then, according to Butler, a "wise and beneficent Providence" solved the quantity problem, and Pritchard was now the right senator for North Carolina.[8]

Despite the coalition, the Republican Party suffered its worst defeat ever. The election law and the constitutional amendment had their intended effect, as one-third of the electorate did not vote. In 1892, Republicans and Populists received about 140,000 votes, and even with widespread intimidation in 1900 almost 130,000 men voted against the constitutional amendment. In 1902, despite an overall population growth of more than 10 percent since 1892, only about 70,000 voted for the Republican-Independent candidates. Democrats even continued to use the white supremacy ploy, arguing that the Independent movement tried to fool white voters into bringing blacks back into power. The reality, according to former Populist J. F. Click, was that of Hickory's 120 eligible African Americans, 2 voted. In Greenville, where African Americans composed a majority, 5 of 787 registered voters were black.[9]

After the election Butler took a genuine break from politics. Pritchard's Senate term ended in March 1903, and Roosevelt appointed him to the Supreme Court of the District of Columbia. Thomas Rollins, Pritchard's son-in-law, became the new GOP chairman. He continued Pritchard's appeal to conservative Democrats, manufacturers, and Populists. Butler, however, lacked a close relation with Rollins. As a result, he focused his limited political efforts on the *Caucasian*. Always financially troubled, the paper achieved some stability in 1903 after a time of particular turmoil. In 1901, Lester, Butler's brother, replaced Hal Ayer as editor. Lester seems to have accepted the task because of a sense of obligation to his older brother. Nonetheless, for more than ten years he performed a difficult job ably, although he rarely satisfied Marion's demanding expectations.[10]

Between 1901 and 1904, Butler did not join the Republican Party and formally held on to his job as chairman of the Bryan wing of the national Populist Party. In September 1901, he received an invitation to a convention of midroad Populists, Bryan Populists, "the liberal Bryan Democrats, the Silver Republicans, the Public Ownership Party of the city of St. Louis, representing more than 30,000 votes, the single taxers and the more liberal wing of the Socialists." Butler did not go, but the attempt at coalition politics, with former senator William V. Allen as one of its leaders, weakly, if ironically, sustained the midroad and Bryan Populist organizations through cooperation. In late 1902, Samuel A. Williams, an Indiana Populist, asked Butler to call another reconciliation meeting between Bryan Populists and the midroad leader John Parker. Butler, however, wanted any settlement to recognize the legitimacy of his organization, not Parker's. As Parker rightly noted, this would kill the prospects for a meaningful reunion.[11]

After several years of straddling, during 1904 Butler moved inexorably away from his old party. He corresponded frequently with Republican E. Carl Duncan (federal internal revenue collector in Raleigh), Rollins, and Pritchard about patronage matters. Roosevelt even invited him to a White House reception and thereafter met regularly with Butler to discuss federal appointments in North Carolina. Apparently TR assumed Butler could help revive GOP fortunes in the state. His failure to shift parties formally, however, caused confusion among Populists. R. L. Strowd told him, "There are thousands of Populists in N.C. awaiting your leadership, [and] if I am not inquisitive I would be glad to have some idea as to the policy that you expect to pursue in the coming campaign." Butler did not attend a 22 February 1904 meeting of Bryan and midroad Populists, which scheduled a presidential nominating convention in Springfield, Illinois, for 4 July. He received an invitation to that convention, but the unused ticket still resides in his personal papers. In Springfield about two hundred die-hard Populists nominated Tom Watson for president and Thomas Tibbles of Nebraska for vice president. Bryan supporters appeared in force; on the first ballot William V. Allen received 319 votes to Watson's 334. The convention reaffirmed previous party platforms.[12]

The two older parties also selected candidates during the summer. Roosevelt received the nomination of the Republicans, combining votes from the Old Guard with those who endorsed his movement toward antitrust enforcement, railroad regulation, and greater friendliness with unions. Democrats selected Alton B. Parker, the chief justice of the New York Court of Appeals. Parker's success indicated that after eight years of Bryan, the Democracy's eastern wing was again ascendant. Many of the Springfield Populists, including Tom Watson, believed this would finally produce the kind of exodus to Populism that Butler had hoped for in 1896. Yet times had changed. Bryan loyally took the stump for Parker; Watson complained that reformers "had no excuse for voting the Democratic ticket" but did anyway.[13]

Theodore Roosevelt became Butler's excuse for not voting for Watson. At first he hoped to aid Roosevelt by secretly helping Watson, thereby reducing any pro-Bryan sentiment that might be reflected in votes for Parker. As a result, Butler adopted the same strategy for which he had viciously attacked midroaders in 1896 and 1900. In September he informed one Populist that he was trying to arrange Watson tickets in northeastern states; he also promised that "our people down in North Carolina will put out an electoral ticket." He reported that he was impressed by Watson sentiment in New York City and predicted Watson would attract the votes of laborers and Single Taxers as well as "some business and professional men." The *Caucasian* reflected Butler's joint Roosevelt-Watson campaign. It printed letters indicating that Populists were becoming Republicans and also published material supporting Watson. The cynicism of the effort appeared in Butler's offer to Roosevelt's campaign manager, George Cortelyou, to induce former Senate colleague Richard Pettigrew to take the stump for Watson for ten thousand dollars. Although Cortelyou wanted to fund some of the Watson campaign, he blandly replied, "Any such figure as that stated is beyond anything which we have in contemplation at the present."[14]

Butler did not publicly reveal his endorsement of Roosevelt until mid-October. He then resigned his position as head of the People's Party and stated that although Populists would have an impact in the West, he expected Roosevelt to win. This was desirable, because "the influences back of the Parker candidacy are so intimately associated with trusts and great corporations that the democratic party could not appeal to the masses." On the other hand, Roosevelt possessed "high courage, sterling honesty, lofty patriotism and rugged independence of character. He has sound progressive ideas, and he does wholesome patriotic things." Butler praised Roosevelt's settling of a labor dispute between anthracite coal miners and operators, the manner in which he was advancing a Central American canal, and his "enforcement of the anti-trust law, while at the same time capital's every right has been protected and conserved in the fullest manner." In late October he gave speeches for Roosevelt in Indiana.[15]

The election results offered Butler considerable grounds for optimism. Roosevelt won easily. Even in North Carolina, a union of former Populists and pro-business whites, now entirely under Republican auspices, produced encouraging results. Republicans received about 38 percent of the state total, up 5 percent from 1902 and only 2 percent less than in 1900. Roosevelt captured approximately eighty-two thousand votes. Beginning a habit that would make Sampson County unique in the eastern part of the state, the former Populist stronghold followed Butler into the GOP.[16]

BUTLER'S REENTRY into politics followed three years of mostly private activity. Needing income, he embarked on several business schemes and began a law practice. He started plying the legal trade in Raleigh in April 1901. Yet the mundane tasks of a general practitioner failed to provide enough excitement or revenue, and his law practice quickly took on a political character. Butler increasingly acted as a lobbyist for legislation or litigated against the government. He soon found that more of this work was in Washington, and he opened an office there in 1902. The next year he abandoned his Raleigh office. The move confirmed a deeper effect of the white supremacy campaigns. Although retaining his North Carolina citizenship, Sampson County property, and Tar Heel political interests, he spent most of the next thirty-five years in the national capital, becoming an exile of sorts from his home state. In his first years in Washington Butler made some money by representing former senators and representatives seeking back pay. He lobbied for the Holland Torpedo Boat, a parcel post bill, and a bill limiting government working hours to eight and providing for overtime pay. He also represented Native American tribes claiming compensation from the government.[17]

After leaving the Senate, Butler's primary home in North Carolina was his wife's family estate, Mount Pleasant, at Elliott in eastern Sampson County. The death of Florence's father in 1905 increased her responsibilities there, and Marion planned to make Mount Pleasant an agricultural showplace. Mount Pleasant embodied Butler's affection for farming, and he spent a good part of each summer on the property. He planted exotic fruit and nut trees, supervised the growing of vegetables, cotton, and grains, and raised hogs and sheep. The farm, worked by black tenants, became a source of interest, experimentation, and pleasure. If the former Alliance president could not play golf in Elliott, as he did in Washington, he might inspect crops, stroll through the woods and fields, read, hunt, or contemplate his next political war with a good cigar and a drink on Mount Pleasant's expansive porches.[18]

BUTLER'S NEW POLITICAL and financial ambitions united in the most spectacular business venture of his career: an effort to collect Reconstruction-era southern bonds that had been repudiated or "readjusted" by southern Democrats. This scheme reflected Butler's burgeoning desire to make money and eventually produced the landmark Supreme Court case *South Dakota v. North Carolina*. More important, it had an enduring effect on his efforts to succeed as a progressive Republican. The plan's author was former governor Daniel L. Russell Jr. Russell knew that many southern state bonds, although their proceeds had been squandered, could be legally valid. However, there existed no means by which to collect on the bonds. The legal barrier was the Eleventh Amendment to the Constitution, which prohibits suits by private citizens against a state in federal court. Of course, a bondholder could bring suit in state court, although there the claim would almost certainly be defeated. Russell's plan was to avoid the Eleventh Amendment by having another sovereign state institute an original jurisdiction claim in the U.S. Supreme Court against the bond-issuing state. To achieve this, Russell would donate a small number of bonds to a willing state and then litigate the claim. Success would create binding Supreme Court precedent allowing bondholders to threaten southern states with massive donations of the now valuable bonds to other states for collection. The southern states, according to Russell's plan, would be willing to settle with the bondholders for lesser sums in order to avoid bankruptcy.[19]

Russell decided the bonds used in a test suit would be those issued to the Western North Carolina Railroad by the North Carolina legislature of 1866–67. The bonds had a par value of $1,000, but in 1879 and 1880 Democrats repudiated bonds issued by the Republican government of 1868–70 and "scaled down" state debt created just before Reconstruction. The scaled-down debt included the Western North Carolina bonds. For these bonds, the state received a good price, the money was actually used for the railroad, and a second mortgage on stock in the state-owned North Carolina Railroad secured the bonds. After 1880, however, Democrats offered only $250 for each $1,000 bond. Although some bondholders sensed this was all they ever would get and surrendered their holdings, Schafer Brothers, a New York investment company, clung to 234 of the Western bonds in anticipation of a better price.[20]

Butler got involved when Russell began looking for a state that would be willing to sue North Carolina. Butler later testified that he first learned of the bonds in the fall of 1900 while in the New York office of Addison Ricaud, a New York lawyer who had been Russell's law partner in Wilmington. In December, while Butler was still a senator and Russell still governor, Russell asked Butler to help states pass donation acts. Butler agreed, and he soon discussed the possibility with Republican senators William Clark of Wyoming, William Chandler of New Hampshire, and William Stewart of Nevada. In early 1901 Butler probably did not know what bonds would be used in a lawsuit. In late January or early February he enlisted Senator Richard Pettigrew to help get the South Dakota legislature to adopt a donation act. A bill was approved, but only after a promise to recompense South Dakota GOP congressman Charles Burke and the state attorney general with proceeds and "fees." Later, Pettigrew, Butler, and Russell entered into a fee agreement to represent Schafer Brothers.[21]

After Schafer Brothers decided to donate ten Western North Carolina bonds to South Dakota in April 1901, Butler and Pettigrew enthusiastically sought other repudiated bonds for future harvest. The now former senators contracted with W. N. Coler and Company, a banking and bond firm, and the North American Trust Company, which agreed to "act as depository, [and] to actively assist in locating and collecting the bonds at their own expense." North American was to "assemble all of the various bonds, which have been issued by any and every state, and which have been repudiated in whole or in part by such state or states respectively." The original plan was to file the South Dakota case in the Supreme Court before the 1901 summer recess, but the state's donation law did not go into effect until June. This meant the case could not be filed until fall. Butler hoped the extra time would allow the North American Trust Company to gather a larger number of bonds. In the meantime, he had little to do with preparing the lawsuit. Russell retained Wheeler Peckham, the brother of Supreme Court justice Rufus Peckham, and they filed South Dakota's petition in mid-November. The action had immediate political implications. Without knowing of Butler and Russell's involvement, Josephus Daniels announced it was a scheme by J. P. Morgan to take over the North Carolina Railroad.[22]

In 1902 Butler met with Russell to discuss strategy; helped arrange for the payment of mounting expenses; performed minor tasks associated with the South Dakota plaintiffs, including assuring the absence of Congressman Burke during the deposition period; and sought more southern bonds. In addition, North Carolina's attorneys uncovered Butler and Russell's involvement and deposed the men. Russell worried the Eleventh Amendment would be fatal if testimony showed South Dakota acted in the interest of a party other than itself, namely, the bondholders. Yet Butler and Russell thought Russell's deposition went well. Butler believed the donation was legitimate and an attempt to suggest any impropriety, particularly regarding his and Russell's involvement with the suit before the expiration of their terms in office, was a political makeweight. At his deposition in December 1902, Butler admitted he knew about the general bond scheme in the winter of 1900–1901. He also testified he became counsel to Schafer Brothers in January 1901, while he was still a senator. He said the donation originated in inquiries he made to Pettigrew about South Dakota's state university while campaigning in the state for Bryan. In December 1900 he had asked Pettigrew if the state had a law that would allow noncash donations to the university. Butler was not questioned about whether he was motivated by the larger bond scheme or whether his connection with Russell had led to a search for

suitable plaintiff states. He did indicate, however, that Pettigrew said Congressman Burke could help secure the state law. As for events after January 1901,
when Schafer Brothers retained him as attorney, Butler invoked attorney-
client privilege.[23]

Butler had tried to advance the legal position that the bond donation was
not intended to benefit private bondholders. Of course it was true that most
of the donation in the lawsuit would go to the University of South Dakota,
but Butler left out the agreement to pay "fees" to South Dakota officials. He
also did not discuss the plan to collect on the more than two hundred remaining Western North Carolina bonds held by Schafer or to collect on
southern bonds generally. From a political standpoint the deposition made
Butler's role in the suit look larger than it was. According to his testimony,
he spearheaded the South Dakota connection and was an attorney for Schafer Brothers, the bondholder. Actually, Russell drafted the act, devised the
scheme, and asked Butler to participate for Schafer Brothers only on specific legislative tasks. Butler's central contribution was his friendship with
South Dakota's Pettigrew.[24]

Russell and Peckham gave oral arguments for South Dakota in the
Supreme Court on 13 April 1903. In November, the Court ordered reargument for 8 January 1904. The anxious plaintiffs speculated that because
only eight justices heard the argument, the Court was evenly divided. After
reargument, it took the justices less than four weeks to determine, by a 5-4
vote, that North Carolina owed South Dakota $27,400, the full par value
plus interest for the ten Western North Carolina bonds donated to South
Dakota. The decision established the important legal principle that when a
state is given the bonds of another state and sues for its own benefit, the
Supreme Court has jurisdiction and can impose liability.[25]

Butler and the bondholders celebrated. The victory seemed partial retribution for past political wrongs. Russell wrote Butler that it "would be well
for the impression to get out" that when the Democrats "walk up and pay
South Dakota her $27,000, you and I will be getting a good slice of it." Nat-
urally, interest in the larger bond project escalated. A representative of the
North American Trust Company told Butler that it was "important to secure
the deposit of all southern bonds outstanding, if it is possible to acquire
them." He believed Butler could furnish a list of the bonds. L. H. Hole of
W. N. Coler and Company wanted to discuss the southern bonds anew now
that the South Dakota case had been favorably decided.[26]

Yet a judgment is worthwhile only if it is collected, and because of the political ramifications of paying for the bonds, North Carolina's Democratic

leadership procrastinated. By early 1904 Josephus Daniels had led a newspaper tirade against Butler and Russell on the bond issue for several years. He even engineered a provision in the 1904 state Democratic platform stating that the party considered the 1879 bond readjustment fair and final. Although not all Democrats, including Governor Aycock, adopted such a stand, Daniels knew that the Supreme Court ordered satisfaction of the judgment by a public sale of one hundred shares of the state's ownership in the North Carolina Railroad, stock that secured the Western railroad bonds. At the current price, these shares would provide about $17,000, considerably less than the $27,400 awarded by the court. The Supreme Court did not consider how or whether it would coerce the payment of a deficiency. North Carolina might either escape paying much of the sum awarded or create indignation by forcing a sale of its property on the steps of the national Capitol. Daniels wanted a forced sale.[27]

By the fall of 1904, however, the trend was away from threats. Governor Aycock arranged a postponement of payment until April 1905. This gave Aycock's successor, Robert Glenn, time to formulate a compromise. Glenn negotiated with the South Dakotans and sought a separate agreement on the bonds still held by Schafer Brothers. Russell responded by directing Butler to have the South Dakota legislature pass a new law providing that all money received in the judgment would be used in purchasing some of the more than two hundred remaining Western North Carolina bonds. According to Russell, South Dakota should be "proud of what she had done and . . . anxious to do more of it"; it should "hit back" at the criticisms of the "States Rights repudiating crowd." Butler had the bill, drafted by Russell, introduced in the South Dakota legislature.[28]

At this crucial stage, the political pendulum swung against Russell and Butler. Although the bill to purchase more bonds passed the South Dakota senate, it bogged down in the house. Butler, on the scene, explained to Russell that "we are doing all we can to overcome" the problem, including providing newspapers from North Carolina that advocated paying the judgment. However, a shift in mid-February dashed all hopes of success. The change among the South Dakotans resulted from actions by Governor Glenn and North Carolina's congressional delegation. On hearing of the latest legislative efforts in South Dakota, Glenn asked Senators Furnifold Simmons and Lee Overman to discuss the matter with their South Dakota colleagues. Their appeal to state comity worked. The South Dakotans preferred not to insult any southern brethren and stopped the bill. Glenn then negotiated a favorable settlement for the remaining bonds held by Schafer

Brothers. The state agreed to pay $892 for each of the outstanding 242 bonds held by Schafer, plus the $2,740 per bond on the ten bonds owned by South Dakota. Although Russell railed at the South Dakota legislature, he consented. Butler, also disappointed, remained optimistic about future gains from other bonds.[29]

In May 1905, North Carolina paid for the Schafer bonds. The complicated fee arrangement left about $41,000 to be distributed among attorneys Russell, Pettigrew, Butler, Ricaud, and Peckham. The battle over who was to get this relatively meager harvest wrecked the coalition. Russell wanted to divide the proceeds in a manner most favorable to him and not as provided in the attorneys' 1901 agreement. He secretly traveled to New York and received a check for the entire amount from Schafer Brothers. On 27 May he wrote Butler, describing what amounted to a new, unilateral settlement between him and the others. It is unclear, however, whether Russell actually paid the sums mentioned in the settlement. Russell's behavior disgusted Butler, particularly what he perceived as Russell's willingness to cheat their associates, and on 31 May he wrote him an extremely hostile letter. On 5 June Russell replied by asking for a bill for Butler's services, and apparently the former governor made some payment. The two, after a rocky relationship that lasted more than eight years, were no longer allies in this or any other matter. Perhaps Butler's anger toward Russell was partly influenced by Pettigrew, who exploded over Russell's failure to distribute the fees according to the 1901 contracts. Butler complained to Peckham that Russell divided up the money as he pleased; if Peckham had received five thousand dollars out of the suit, he had received more than Butler did.[30]

Before and after the conflict with Russell, Butler made strong efforts to collect other repudiated bonds. He initially wanted to discuss a possible alliance with John G. Carlisle, Grover Cleveland's secretary of the treasury, who was also seeking bonds. But, in April 1905, when the Carlisle group made its own solicitation for bonds, Butler prepared a counteradvertisement and placed it in New York papers. This was before the fee disagreement with Russell, and Butler signed the names of W. N. Coler and Co., R. F. Pettigrew, D. L. Russell, and himself to the advertisement. It stated they were "ready to proceed with the collection of all other repudiated bonds of every class, of each state." Because of the breadth of the appeal, with its implication that the committee wanted all bonds, Butler's ad was a terrific political blunder. On Russell's advice, Butler had the names removed from subsequent advertisements. Yet Josephus Daniels had noticed the first version. Daniels proclaimed it proved Butler and Russell hoped to collect fraudulent bonds, including North Carolina's Reconstruction-era "special tax" bonds. Russell responded by stating publicly that the committee was not interested in fraudulent bonds. Whatever Russell's intent, Butler was not so discriminating. In January 1905, Pettigrew informed Butler that he possessed several of the North Carolina "special tax" bonds. Butler did not seem to notice or care about the bonds' questionable background.[31]

Just how long Butler remained interested in such bonds is unclear. Supposedly, in early 1906 W. N. Coler contacted him about pooling resources with the Carlisle group. At this point Butler may have limited the kind of bonds he was willing to collect. He later claimed to have written L. H. Hole of Coler that the bonds being collected by Carlisle were North Carolina "special tax" bonds, which "as I have already explained to you, are fraudulent carpetbag bonds." He would "have nothing to do with their efforts to collect these bonds or any other fraudulent bonds issued by a carpetbag legislature." The record, however, is not clear as to whether Butler wrote this strong language in 1906 or, if so, whether he was willing to live up to it. Just four days after Butler's alleged letter to Hole, Pettigrew told Hole that the South Dakota group, without Russell, "would attend to [the Carlisle Committee's] case for one-half of all they got, on condition that Carlisle help us try the case in the Supreme Court. They have $3,000,000 in North Carolina ['special tax'] bonds." Perhaps Pettigrew and Butler had not discussed prosecuting Carlisle's "special tax" bonds, but perhaps they had.[32]

There is other evidence that Butler did not remove himself from the chase for "carpetbag bonds" until well after 1906. Just a few days after the January 1906 letter to Hole, Pettigrew wrote Butler that he was negotiating with another bondholder for $1 million in repudiated Georgia bonds. In 1908, Butler's law partner, Josiah Vale, expressed interest in a donation of probably the same Georgia bonds to Nevada. During 1908 Butler met with a Canadian who may have been willing to collect Georgia bonds for Great Britain. In early 1909, Hole asked Butler whether it would be advisable to buy $2 million of North Carolina "special tax" bonds for about $8,000. In his reply Butler said nothing about the moral unfitness of the bonds but merely noted that the various classes of bonds were of "very little, if any value, except the last lot." The "last lot" was apparently a group of Wilmington, Charlotte, and Rutherford railroad bonds, which by any reasonable standard were a product of corruption whose proceeds had been squandered. Butler, believing a court would consider what the state received in rendering judgment, which was very little, added that "the whole matter of collecting any of these bonds depends upon having a sufficient quantity of some of the best of the bonds to justify taking action." Apparently Hole, on this advice, refused to acquire the bonds. Butler definitely became uninterested in such bonds by early 1910, and when Hole died later that year, Butler's bond activities came to an end.[33]

The bond affair had more to do with ambition to succeed in a great scheme than anything else. Butler's desire to be in the spotlight was a driving force in this matter as in his political ventures. After all, refashioning an important point of constitutional law and becoming a millionaire were relatively minor projects for a man who wanted to restructure the national money and transportation systems and realign American politics. It is doubtful that Butler saw his actions as unethical. And he did not use his position as senator to advance the scheme. He also rightly believed that North Carolina unfairly "scaled down" the bonds in the South Dakota case, ripping off legitimate investors. As for other Reconstruction bonds, he apparently assumed courts would not award damages to buyers of notoriously fraudulent bonds and that any recovery would only be in proportion to the legitimacy of the bond. Butler's most questionable behavior involved the lobbying and fee arrangements that allowed the South Dakota legislature to be used for a private purpose. Further, he carefully shielded the point from the Supreme Court.

Of only moderate financial and legal success, the bond scheme was most important because of its long-lasting political effect on Butler and the North Carolina Republican Party. Butler's endorsement of the suit and his attempts to collect other bonds associated him with Reconstruction, an event he was too young to have participated in, and made him look antagonistic to his state. In 1919, Democratic historian J. G. deRoulhac Hamilton wrote that although before the case Butler "was not a universally beloved figure," his "part in this business made him possibly the worst hated man in the history of the state and made him henceforth an object of suspicion to thousands who before had for him no particular objection." Robert Durden has shown that most of the Democratic attack was unfair because of a failure to separate the "honest" Schafer bonds from the wasted funds of Reconstruction.[34] Yet Butler could only blame himself for the political consequences. He was the one person representing the bondholders who had public ambitions in North Carolina, but he failed to appreciate the obvious dangers of suing one's own state. The case poisoned his reentry into politics from the beginning and made it less likely that he could be the credible leader of a new progressive coalition.

AFTER THE 1904 election Butler reentered the state political arena in earnest. He told Jeter Pritchard that the political outlook seemed brighter than in Populist days, "and if we carry the state . . . , we will [win] on the solid foundation of a division of the white vote on economic issues and therefore the result will be permanent." For Butler, Roosevelt's popularity and "broad, progressive, and patriotic policies" provided the basis for growth. He also believed the GOP needed to be reorganized, and to that end he focused on improving the party's federal patronage system and creating a daily newspaper. Patronage usually meant choosing postmasters, and Butler became the Washington connection for many appointments, meeting regularly with Roosevelt. However, a contest over which Republicans deserved the ear of the president complicated the task. E. Spencer Blackburn, North Carolina's only Republican congressman, believed his office entitled him to control patronage. For most of 1905 Roosevelt declined Blackburn's ambitions and relied on party chairman Rollins and on Butler.[35]

Also important was establishing the state's only Republican daily. In mid-1905, Butler began to raise funds for a Greensboro paper. He tried to win backing from "business men, including Bankers, Manufacturers, Cotton Mill men and other manufacturers," and he drafted articles of incorporation for the North State Publishing Company. Butler assumed the venture would advance his plan to unite Populists and manufacturers under a "progressive" banner. Former Populists did not offer a reliable source of capital, but many supported the effort. Cyrus Thompson told Butler that he hoped the "paper will accomplish all that we desire it to do," and Butler claimed there were a large number of advance subscriptions "from men who have been Democrats and later were Populists and are now Republicans." This showed that the "class of men who were once active in the Farmers Alliance and People's Party, are now equally anxious to build up the Republican Party."[36]

Yet the newspaper turned out differently from what Butler had planned. Spencer Adams, a Greensboro Republican to whom Butler assigned the task of getting signatures for the corporate charter, incorporated the Industrial Publishing Company, not the North State Publishing Company that Butler promoted. Further, the incorporators did not include the heavy sprinkling of Populists Butler wanted. Instead, they were almost entirely federal office-holders. This did not diminish Butler's optimism about the project. He still went to the Associated Press offices in New York and obtained a valuable news franchise. During preparations to begin publishing, he became the paper's leading advocate. Greensboro's *Industrial News* first appeared on 8

October 1905. Although professionally produced, its pro-tariff, antisocialist stand made rather dull reading. It presented a modest progressive appeal to the middle class, faithfully praising the businessman in politics and reporting on fashion, street crime, and sports. When it did speak for change, such as when it defended Roosevelt's support for railroad regulation, it did so in a manner that reassured businessmen that government regulation was in their interest. As for state government, its editorials argued for better roads and better schools.[37]

Growing tensions over patronage and the attempted Populist participation in the *Industrial News* revealed that not all Republicans welcomed Butler's political revival or his efforts to link Populism, the GOP, Roosevelt, and progressivism. In many ways these tensions resembled the opposition to Alliance influence in the Democratic Party more than fifteen years earlier. They also reflected the disruptive effects of progressivism in both major parties throughout the United States, particularly among Republicans. The first real test of Butler's efforts to reshape the Republican Party in a progressive direction was the 1906 campaign, and Spencer Blackburn emerged as Butler's greatest critic. Prior to the Republican state convention, Blackburn conducted all-out war against Butler. His question was "whether the Republicans of North Carolina propose to accept ex-Senator Marion Butler as their leader and to accept his dictation as to policies, offices, etc." In response, Butler supported a large state convention, not a small crowd that would bicker over patronage, and a "big-name" speaker, preferably Secretary of War William Howard Taft. He also wanted an aggressive new chairman, and Spencer Adams seemed appropriate. Suggesting Butler's growing effectiveness as a Republican, Chairman Thomas Rollins agreed to resign in favor of Adams. Butler also spoke with Taft and Roosevelt and secured Taft for the convention. The rejuvenated former Populist, resurrected from political death at the ripe age of forty-three, told Adams to make it plain "that we expect to have and will have a great state convention, and that this is the beginning of the fight to make North Carolina a republican state."[38]

Butler worked especially hard to secure former Populists, and he was often successful. He offered them "a clean, strong and high-toned fight for the triumph of the progressive principles of the Roosevelt administration." The Sampson County GOP elected him to the Greensboro convention, Lester Butler helped direct Wake County Republicans, and former silver supporter J. J. Mott sought out converts for Roosevelt in Statesville. Editor J. F. Click counted himself as a member of the Populist wing of Republicanism. A Mecklenburg correspondent described fierce factional fighting in the

GOP there, in which Butler was "the bone of contention." Altogether, Butler's reappearance revived some of the old feelings and conflicts of political
insurgence.[39]

The extensive preparations paid dividends at the Republican convention.
Adams won the chairmanship on the first ballot and read a letter from national chairman George Cortelyou proclaiming that party organization "represents not an individual or faction—but the fundamental principles for
which the party stands," an apparent slap at Blackburn. Butler even got the
new Tar Heel GOP to distinguish itself from the pseudoprogressivism of the
Democrats, and the platform reflected this perspective. It praised Roosevelt's efforts to regulate railroad rates, condemned Democrats' failure to
enforce local prohibition laws, contrasted the current national prosperity
with depression under Grover Cleveland, and asked that national banks be
permitted to provide agricultural credit by allowing land to be used as col-
lateral. Most dramatically, the platform claimed that victory for Republicans
"can come from . . . the men of the Farmers' Alliance and the People's party,
to whom alone, or in conjunction with Republicans, the state owes the great
upward movement in railroad regulation, manual education[,] common
school education [and] the preserving care and encouragement of the University, A & M College and other state institutions."[40]

Despite the platform's interesting rhetoric and demands for reform, the
contrast between progressive Republicanism and Populism was as clear as it
had been immediately after disfranchisement. Gone were Populist attacks
on an unjust financial system and calls for government ownership of natural
monopolies. Instead, progressive Republicans promised to run the state
Corporation Commission, which Democrats created in 1901 to replace the
Alliance's Railroad Commission, more "efficiently." Similarly, there was no
request for radical changes in the revenue system, such as with an income
tax. In short, progressive Republicanism in 1906 meant some regulation of
corporations, better schools, and less crime. The GOP promised more government activity than Tar Heel Democrats, but unlike Populists, it did not
demand any dramatic shifting of economic and political power in the interests of producers. Despite Butler's efforts, his new party distinguished itself
from Democracy less on what it might do than on whether it could be
trusted to act. Worse, later events would show that even this accomplishment was highly tenuous, much more so than were similar movements
toward a progressive Republican Party in other states, particularly in the
Midwest.

Nonetheless, Butler campaigned vigorously for the first time since 1900, writing for the GOP press and organizing an ambitious speaking schedule. He contributed a series of unsigned articles on public education to the *Industrial News*, in which he argued that the so-called Education Governor, Charles Aycock, was a fraud. According to Butler, the recent enthusiasm for Aycock's policies came primarily from Democratic state and county officials, "who get the greater part of . . . increased expenditures." His speeches intentionally sought to revive dormant Populists. In Pittsboro "he came . . . to advocate the same principles and reforms which he advocated when he last spoke" there in 1894. He was a Republican now for the practical reason that under Roosevelt the "greatest results could be secured for the protection of equal rights to rich and poor alike, and for the progress and prosperity of all the people." North Carolina Democrats, on the other hand, destroyed local government and did not want meaningful railroad regulation; more broadly, "whenever anyone proposed that the strong arm of the government should be extended to protect the individual and give him an equal opportunity . . . these Democratic leaders would cry out, 'No, that is paternalism; that the best government is that which governs least.' " The opposition party's handbook symbolized Democratic pseudoprogressivism: it "was twice as thick as usual" because "it had twice as much 'nigger' in it."[41]

The lively Republican campaign worried Democrats. A general lack of reform legislation since 1899 and the violent conditions under which Democratic rule was reestablished precluded a persuasive claim that the party stood for progressive economic and political change. Instead, a vitriolic *News and Observer* tried to make Butler's involvement in the *South Dakota* case the principal issue. The party also focused on the continuing danger of black rule, citing various myths about Reconstruction and government in the 1890s. The anti-Butler argument, despite its irrelevance, put the fragile Republicans on the defensive. Republican newspapers, even those which had no great love for Butler, tried to explain that the *South Dakota* case involved Democratic, not Republican, bonds. Butler may have underestimated the effect of the Democratic strategy, as in late October he went on a speaking tour. While he was away, Florence Butler, who accurately perceived the danger, wrote Kemp Battle, Democratic treasurer in 1866 when the state issued the *South Dakota* bonds. She asked Battle about the validity of the bonds. Battle replied that the issuing legislature did not include carpetbaggers. The exchange, which implied Butler had merely sought to collect an honest debt, appeared in several newspapers and as a Republican broadside.[42]

The election results disappointed Republicans. Despite the daily newspaper, a revamped state organization, the addition of former Populists, and a popular president, they lost every congressional race. They also lost some of the few seats they held in the state legislature. Sampson County stayed Republican, but the absence of growth statewide stung. Many of Butler's correspondents ascribed the decline to fraud, which allegedly included more than twenty thousand Democrats who voted without paying their poll tax, as well as "money, liquor, intimidation, ostracism and force." More important, Republicans began to blame each other. Adams and others believed the anti-Butler campaign hurt, while Butler thought Adams had not worked diligently enough to spread the Republicans' reform message.[43]

After the election, Butler's support for progressive Republicanism, combined with his growing belief that Adams betrayed the best interests of the party, devolved into a protracted feud. For the next three years, he tried to overthrow Adams's leadership. The contest was personal and often self-defeating, but it reflected deeper conflict between the conservative and progressive wings of the GOP that had emerged across the nation. Increasingly encouraged by a monumental growth of Republican reform sentiment in Washington, where he lived most of the year, Butler believed he could move the North Carolina party in a direction that would once again make legislation in favor of producers possible. Adams and his supporters, on the other hand, now opposed getting close to Butler or the former Populists. Many were McKinley Republicans, uncomfortable with the reform-oriented president. By 1906 the popular Roosevelt fought regularly with conservatives in his own party in Congress. In addition, such men as Robert La Follette of Wisconsin and Albert B. Cummins of Iowa were connecting the Republican Party to progressive reform in their states. Butler wanted the North Carolina party to follow both Roosevelt and the midwestern models.[44]

To this end he worked desperately to unseat Adams. When the national press reported rumors of a multimillion-dollar slush fund raised by Wall Street to defeat Roosevelt in 1908, he seized on this as the explanation for Adams's lukewarm attitude toward TR. He surmised there was a "barrel of money being spent in the South in trying to defeat the principles and policies of the Republican Party as exemplified by President Roosevelt. I have already uncovered some of the traitors in this deal." When Adams refused to endorse Taft, Roosevelt's handpicked successor for president, Butler warned Roosevelt that "reactionaries" in North Carolina opposed Taft. He wrote Taft that Adams favored an uncommitted delegation from the state to the national convention so that a conservative could be nominated. He gave a May 1907 interview to the *Washington Post* that mentioned the alleged Wall

Street conspiracy and Adams's refusal to endorse Taft. The reader was left to draw the logical conclusion. Two months later, Butler told Roosevelt that Adams was "under the absolute domination of all the corporations in the state, including the railways, the American Tobacco Company, and the Standard Oil Company." For good measure, he claimed Adams recently took bribes while a temporary judge in the Indian Territory.[45]

Butler expressly connected his attack on Adams with both Populism and the Republican progressives. His newspaper promoted Roosevelt's reforms, including a meat inspection act, tariff reduction, and environmental conservation. This needed legislation addressed the "inequitable conditions between the great combinations of invested capital, on the one hand, and between labor and the producer and consumer, on the other hand," which were getting worse. Moreover, after a panic pushed the nation into a recession in late 1907, Butler explained its causes in Populist terms: the economy was growing "faster than the volume of money has increased." Offering an Alliance solution, he suggested that the government "establish bonded warehouses at convenient points and issue warehouse certificates upon products deposited there, up to say 80 percent of the market value of the same, such certificates to circulate as currency, [and] then the currency needed would be automatically created and supplied at the times and places needed." Further returning to his roots, he endorsed government purchase of railroad stock in order to put monopolistic lines under public control. He argued it was consistent for former Populists to be Roosevelt Republicans because Roosevelt "comes nearest to embodying their old principles."[46]

The hard political fact, however, was that most North Carolina Republicans, like most North Carolina Democrats in the 1890s, or most Republicans in the nation, did not hold either Populist or progressive views. As a result, Butler faced a familiar uphill struggle in his party, similar to the one he had lost in 1892. Indeed, the movement of some Tar Heel Republican leaders after 1906 was toward a more strident conservatism. They reacted to the sudden appearance of a faction of Democratic progressives in North Carolina, who helped steer through the 1907 legislature a modest railroad rate reduction, by hoping the Democracy would support more aggressive government and drive frightened conservatives to the GOP. One such Republican assumed Democrats were "Butlerized, Bryanized, Watsonized, and . . . never will recover from the malady." When W. A. Hildebrand, a former Blackburn supporter who disliked Butler, became editor of the *Industrial News* in October 1907, the paper's editorials shifted decisively to the right.

Hildebrand approvingly quoted a conservative Democrat who complained there was "too much Populism in the South."[47]

Thus Butler's problems closely resembled those of progressive Republicans outside North Carolina in 1907, who feared reactionaries would control the party. Roosevelt tried to eliminate the threat by demanding support for Taft in North Carolina and elsewhere. Waving the big stick of patronage, he eventually drove hesitant members of the Tar Heel party into line. In a show of force, he even invited Alfred E. Holton and Harry Skinner to the White House in December 1907 and asked them if Adams and E. Carl Duncan were disloyal to him. Clearly, Roosevelt acted on Butler's suggestion. The question intimidated Adams and Duncan, who quickly declared for Taft.[48]

As the 1908 election approached, Butler offered his most dramatic volley against Adams, which concerned the bribery Butler had privately reported to Roosevelt in July 1907. Adams served as chief justice of the Choctaw and Chickasaw citizenship court, which heard cases in the Indian Territory between 1902 and 1904. Butler's connections in the Senate led to a call in early 1908 by Senator Benjamin R. Tillman for an investigation of the court. The key claim against Adams was that he struck the names of persons entitled to Indian citizenship, and thus federal benefits, from citizenship rolls. This allowed a law firm employed by Native Americans to keep the list small and collect a huge contingency fee, which was calculated from the number of excluded persons. Allegedly, Adams took bribes to remove names. Most important, Butler published an unsigned letter in the *Caucasian* on 1 March 1908, which for the first time publicly suggested Adams took bribes. Well aware of the possibility of a libel suit, he phrased the charge as a news report of the previous day in Congress.[49]

The attack failed to remove Adams. At a spring 1908 GOP meeting intended to develop campaign strategy, Harry Skinner, an Adams ally, introduced a resolution to refer every motion to a platform committee dominated by Adams supporters. Butler tried to fight back by demanding a delay in any action pertaining to the state party, including the selection of a chairman. Believing time was on his side, he wanted those present to select Taft delegates to the national convention and adjourn. After Butler made a virulent personal attack on Skinner, Skinner's resolution was defeated. Before a vote could be taken on Butler's delay proposal, however, the Adams forces moved for the immediate election of a state chairman, which passed easily. Skinner nominated Adams, who was promptly reelected.[50]

After the meeting Butler turned his attention to the presidential nominating convention in Chicago. Despite all the heat he gave Adams about not supporting Taft, he really wanted Roosevelt to run. When Taft received the nomination, Butler, who attended his first national convention since Sioux Falls in 1900, expressed disappointment. Taft's selection was merely "the next best thing that could be done." Although Butler recognized that the Republican platform endorsed many of Roosevelt's reforms, including antitrust enforcement, conservation, and postal savings banks, he thought it was too vague. Roosevelt, "a man who will be a platform within himself," would have remedied the problem. Butler wrote Roosevelt that if he had been "the nominee and the platform," the election would already be won, but now "the result is in doubt."[51]

Next, Butler tried to develop a strategy for the North Carolina nominating convention, his last chance to defeat Adams before the election. This time he planned to eliminate Adams by proposing that the party's nominees should have the power to select a new chairman. Butler thought he found a key supporter in Jeter Pritchard. He hoped Pritchard would resign his judgeship, make the run for governor, and, in the process, dump Adams. The Pritchard moment lasted briefly, in part because Taft told Butler he had "no right to ask [Pritchard] to resign a life office to go into a contest in which he would hold only a temporary office." After Pritchard's exit, J. Elwood Cox, a High Point textile equipment manufacturer and banker, emerged as the likely candidate for governor. Butler perceived Cox's many weaknesses, including his conservatism, inexperience, and lack of canvassing skills. Still, he considered Cox a suitable third or fourth choice, largely because Cox was not close to Adams.[52]

Yet nothing in Butler's plans anticipated Adams's trump card, played against Butler just before the Republican convention. He filed a civil suit for libel, claiming one hundred thousand dollars in damages against Butler, his brother Lester, and the *Caucasian*. Adams's claim focused on the paper's statements about citizenship court corruption. Butler responded that he had published only facts, some of which were privileged because they were taken from the *Congressional Record*. Besides, his paper did not claim the statements were true. The case was pending through the election.[53]

The lawsuit and the Cox candidacy symbolized the waning of Butler's influence between 1906 and 1908, a decline related to broader assaults on Republican progressivism. The Republican convention, held in Charlotte in August 1908, confirmed the trend. Chairman Adams gave an address that denounced Bryan, who was again the Democratic nominee for president, and his "Socialistic doctrine," including government ownership of railroads,

free silver, greenbacks, and government telephones and telegraphs. Not surprisingly, Butler complained that "at least half the delegates in the hall were
former members of the People's party. This fact must have been overlooked
by the chairman, otherwise he would not have gone out of his way to criticize and ridicule some of the chief measures for which that party stood."
The delegates chose Cox for governor, but unhappily for Butler, he refused
to challenge Adams's right to be chairman. Butler's work was reduced to
shaping platform details. He argued that a plank supporting a modest increase in the exemption for property taxes from $25 to $200 was "an insult
to the poor man." He also proposed a local option for alcohol sales, as opposed to the existing statewide ban. Delegates defeated this by 570 to 271, a
vote that suggested the approximate strength of the Butler-Populist forces.[54]

Demonstrating his persistent belief that politics often imposed unpleasant choices, during the election Butler did not disappear. He acted the role
of a good party man. The *Caucasian* supported Cox and wishfully called him
a "progressive" industrial leader. The other Populist remnants agreed, including Cyrus Thompson, J. F. Click and his *Hickory Times-Mercury*, and J. P.
Sossaman, who now published the *Charlotte People's Paper* as the organ of the
Farmers' Union. Nonetheless, the campaign made Butler uncomfortable.
Several reform-minded Democratic papers connected the GOP candidate
with a 1906 antiunion lockout of High Point workers. Cox stilled the controversy by buying off the secretary of the North Carolina Federation of Labor,
but in the meantime, the *Caucasian* had to defend him. Moreover, Butler
probably cringed when Cox wrote him that he was optimistic about the election partly because "the railroad men, so far as I am able to learn, are with
us almost to a man." He instructed Lester that if Cox sent a pro-railroad
statement to the *Caucasian*, to "drop it in the wastebasket." Cox mistakenly
believed "the few railroad votes he will get are more important than the
thousands of laboring and farming votes that he would lose." Butler blamed
Adams and Duncan for Cox's behavior, because "they do not want to see
him elected and are willing to do anything to please the railroads."[55]

Cox, a more conservative state platform, and the absence of Roosevelt
deflated Butler's campaign speeches. After a tour on behalf of Taft in Maryland, Nebraska, Kansas, Missouri, and Oklahoma, he spoke in several western North Carolina towns. His talks consisted primarily of criticisms of Democrats and contained an unusual degree of cynicism. He endorsed local
self-government, better public schools, and railroad rate reductions. Yet he
attacked the Democratic presidential nominee, William Jennings Bryan, on
the ground that Bryan received black delegations in Nebraska and pledged

to reinstate black army troops that Roosevelt had discharged after a racial incident in Brownsville, Texas. Butler considered Bryan's alleged pursuit of the black vote "an insult to the intelligence and manhood of the voters of the South." When speaking in Maryland and the West, he jettisoned the racial stories. There he attacked Bryan as an "opportunist" who offered "crude and ill-digested panaceas" for the nation's ills. In contrast, the GOP was the true labor party, and a vote for Taft would further Roosevelt's progressive policies.[56]

Surprisingly, in November the amorphous Tar Heel GOP appeal tapped antagonism toward Democrats. Taft, who was elected president, and Cox received support from about 45 percent of the electorate, the decade's best showing. The ballots came from a bizarre grouping of anti-Bryan Democrats, former Civil War Unionists, former Populists, Roosevelt progressives, and McKinley Republicans. Taft won a majority of the counties in the western piedmont and mountains and lost to Bryan by only about twenty-two thousand votes. The Republicans also elected 3 congressmen and 40 of the state's 170 legislators, the most since 1896. Only eight years after the cataclysm of 1900, the opposition had cut the Democratic majority in half. Even Roosevelt noticed and told Harry Skinner the result was "the most significant thing in the election."[57]

If Republicans grew hopeful, Butler was not going to let Adams take any credit. Instead, he maintained that progress came from the legacy of Roosevelt, the promise of Taft, and the incompetence of Democrats. He charged that the GOP would have won if not for "the want of intelligent and effective work by the Republican State Chairman." There was more good news. When Butler learned that Congressman-elect John M. Morehead disliked Adams, he believed he had a powerful ally for a new fight. He asked Republicans to rally under a Morehead banner, without Morehead's knowledge. Butler had another reason to restart the battle against Adams. Tired of the delay and the expense of getting his civil libel case to trial, Adams ventured the unusual course of swearing out a complaint of criminal libel against the Butlers. Officials arrested Marion as he went to the polls in Sampson County. Perhaps it was a more civilized tactic than the physical assaults and threats of the 1890s, but it showed that life was also not easy as a Republican.[58]

BETWEEN 1901 AND 1908 Butler struggled to find a place in the "progressive" political environment of the early twentieth century. Theodore Roosevelt offered the brightest hope and explains much of his persistence. Support for Roosevelt meant that he did not have to crawl back to Democracy, as did other southern Populists; furthermore, Butler's daughter remembered that her father admired TR more than any other political figure.[59] Roosevelt promoted progressive reform, was a dynamic individual about the same age as Butler, and was a tough politician who knew how to win. These were attributes Butler ranked highly. Further, the president confronted reactionary factions in his own party, an experience Butler knew well as a Democrat and a Republican. Yet through 1908 Butler could not simply will the North Carolina GOP into a progressive force. Much of his Populist constituency followed him, but like Alliance Democrats in the early 1890s and unlike Republicans in some midwestern states, they could not exert a controlling influence. Instead, his party remained a remarkably convoluted coalition based on hatred of Democracy. Butler tried to promote a reform-oriented union of manufacturers, businessmen, and Populists, but this necessarily produced a circumscribed political position and highlighted the sharp differences between Populism and progressivism. And, after some optimism in 1904 and 1906, even this compromise failed both at the polls and in the party's organization. Political isolation and disappointment also led to desperate deeds. Incessant conspiratorial personal attacks on Spencer Adams revealed a reckless anxiety about his political career and how to salvage it. This, together with the ill-advised bond scheme, engendered countless enemies and reflected poor judgment. To be sure, just as he had assumed some midroad Populists were corrupt, Butler undoubtedly believed Adams took bribes. Yet his attacks placed personal interests above the lofty aims of reform politics. Butler's desire for political relevance increasingly led down a path far removed from the reforms that had propelled him into politics in the first place.

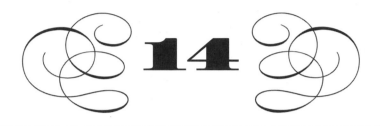

THE FAILURE OF REPUBLICAN
PROGRESSIVISM

BUTLER RENEWED HIS effort to move the North Carolina Republican Party in a progressive direction after the 1908 election. For several reasons, however, this task quickly became frustrating. First, President-elect Taft proved less a reformer than Roosevelt. Second, Butler lost the advantage of the greater personal friendliness he had enjoyed with Roosevelt. Finally, Taft's vision of southern Republicanism focused more on attracting conservative, urban, "respectable" Democrats than on accommodating Populists and Roosevelt progressives. Over the next four years Taft's emphasis on cautious change helped defeat Butler's progressive alternative to Democracy in North Carolina. In many ways the North Carolina situation resembled the decline of reform possibilities in the national GOP. The difference between Taft and Roosevelt appeared as early as December 1908, when Butler wrote the future chief executive and tried to convince him that Spencer Adams opposed reform. Taft's dismissive response spelled trouble: "One of the difficulties that I find in dealing with the politics of the Southern States is the violence and extremity of the statements of one faction in the Republican party in respect to another." It was "impossible to credit [such remarks] as mere statements of simple facts," because they were "colored by the enthusiasm and emphasis of intense factionalism."[1]

Butler's trial for criminal libel also complicated his plans. He spent considerable energy on the defense before it commenced on 29 March 1909 in Greensboro. The charges against Butler rested principally on his newspaper's claim that Adams accepted bribes to keep Native Americans off tribal citizenship lists, but also included the assertion that Adams promised to give a man citizenship if he carried voters in the Indian Territory to the polls.

Unfortunately for Butler, the prosecution decided to focus on the voter issue, which he and his attorneys neglected in the scramble for evidence. To be sure, Butler's lawyers made certain the jury heard about some suspicious coincidences, including Adams's deposit of fifteen thousand dollars in Greensboro banks just after he returned from the Indian Territory and his recent construction of a fifteen-thousand-dollar house. The jury also learned about the bad reputation of Adams and the citizenship courts. Apparently, however, this was not enough to create the requisite doubt in the jurors' minds, and they found Marion and Lester guilty of criminal libel. The Butlers appealed to the state supreme court. When Edward Justice, their trial attorney, became ill, they invited none other than Charles B. Aycock, the former Democratic governor, to pursue the appeal. In the supreme court, Aycock and his partner, Robert W. Winston, argued that Adams had not shown Butler and his brother were responsible for the libels. The justices agreed and reversed the guilty verdicts. Butler considered the result "gratifying" and thought it would prevent a retrial. Although he still wanted legal confirmation of Adams's guilt, the dispute now wearied him. The state seemed to think that it would not retry the criminal case, and Butler hinted that he might accept an "honorable" compromise of the civil suit, such as payment of Adams's legal expenses.[2]

Butler's trial kept Republican infighting in the news, but Taft's political bungling and preference for conservatives had deeper consequences. A leading issue when Taft took office was the appointment of a new federal district judge for eastern North Carolina. Butler supported his brother George, H. F. Seawell, and W. S. O'B. Robinson. In January 1909, Roosevelt chose Seawell, a thirty-four-year-old Carthage lawyer and former Populist. Yet Seawell's nomination went to Congress in the waning days of the Roosevelt administration. Roosevelt's conflicts with the Old Guard had produced ill feeling, and as a result, Seawell's unconfirmed appointment languished in the Capitol when Taft took over. Taft withdrew Seawell on the ground that he was unqualified, compounding the mistake by indicating that he would consider Democrats for the job. Condescendingly, he remarked that he was "not anxious to appoint a Democrat, but I confess I do not find any Republicans there that seem to measure up to the requirements." Part of these requirements were that any Democrat must have had the "right" attitude toward disfranchisement in 1900, meaning support for disfranchisement of illiterates, not blacks, and must have opposed the Democratic impeachment of Republican state supreme court justices David Furches and Robert Douglas in 1901.[3]

Butler tried to convince himself that the new president was not so stupid as to select a member of the opposition. He wrote Taft that "with a strong and growing party of 115,000 Republicans, . . . you will not feel that it is necessary to go outside of the party to find a man for this position." Taft, however, began to give serious consideration to Henry Groves Connor, a Democrat from Wilson serving on the state supreme court. Connor met the litmus test, inasmuch as he had supported disfranchisement, but allegedly for the "right" reason of excluding "ignorant" voters, not blacks, and he had opposed the impeachment of Douglas and Furches. Butler visited Taft in early May, at which time the president asked him about Connor. The former Populist recounted Connor's embarrassment at having been chosen as a Populist-Republican nominee for the state supreme court in 1894; he averred that Connor's rejection of the nomination revealed his subservience to the Democratic Party and "that he was not a man of high moral character."[4]

Confirming Butler's diminished influence, Taft ignored the advice and chose Connor. It was a political error of such gravity that it permanently poisoned feelings for the president. Butler told Lester to write a polite, but critical, *Caucasian* editorial arguing that although "every patriotic citizen has approved of President Taft's idea for the elevation of the judiciary," he had "misapplied the principle," because there were Republican lawyers just as talented as the nominee. The prospect of a Democrat getting a most important political plum shocked Butler's correspondents. Durham attorney William G. Bramham believed "the appointment of a Democrat to this judgeship will be the greatest calamity that has ever befallen the party; and the President will not live to see the time when the party has recovered from the results of his indiscretion." The Republican press tried to restrain itself from denouncing Taft. Its readers suffered social ostracism, economic pressure, even threats and violence at the hands of so-called respectables such as Connor. Taft's apparent discounting of this experience, plus his belief that some Democrats had actually intended simply to disfranchise illiterates, not blacks, revealed his ignorance of the state's history. Taft apparently failed to consider that Connor, as a leader in the 1898 white supremacy campaign and speaker of the state house in 1899, was one of the figures most responsible for Democratic rule in the state. Privately, Butler concluded that Connor's selection was "nothing less than an outrage."[5]

Taft's limitations as a reformer became apparent in other ways. For example, Butler supported Taft's progressive promise to reduce tariff rates. From March until the passage of a new tariff in August 1909, he frequently discussed the bill's legislative progress in the *Caucasian*. It was soon clear, however, that conservative Republicans opposed meaningful tariff reduction, and Butler complained about "the highest protection bill ever proposed in the history of the republican party." Instead, he wanted a "scientific tariff" that would protect workers and consumers, aligning himself with progressive midwestern Republican senators, such as Robert M. La Follette of Wisconsin and Jonathan P. Dolliver of Iowa. Taft managed to get some rates lowered, and the new law provided for a tariff commission, which, it was hoped, would reduce the politics of setting rates. Yet the Payne-Aldrich tariff largely retained the high rates of the 1897 tariff and principally benefited northeastern manufacturers. Most important, it helped destroy the relationship between Taft and the progressive Republicans, placing Taft on the side of reaction. Butler, however, already in a weak political position in North Carolina, was unwilling to denounce the president openly. He squirmed to make the tariff fit a reform model, instructing Lester to write an editorial arguing that although rates had "not been reformed as many of the most progressive Republicans desired it, yet it is a great improvement over the present law." Indeed, all things considered, it was the best "passed in the history of the government." He specifically praised "the corporation tax feature [of the law] and the proposition to submit an income tax amendment [to the Constitution as] very distinct and great progressive steps toward equalizing taxation and regulating corporations."[6]

Despite Taft's mistakes, Butler remained optimistic about the potential for new leadership in the North Carolina party. In late 1908 he hoped that former Populists and an emerging group of anti-Adams Republicans, especially Congressman John Morehead, could be united. Morehead was a cautious progressive of the Taft variety, but he considered Adams and Carl Duncan as machine politicians whose main interest was self-aggrandizement. During 1909 Morehead feuded with Duncan and Adams over patronage, Butler discussed party affairs with Morehead in Washington, and both men made plans to reorganize the party against the "machine" in time for the 1910 election.[7]

In early 1910 Butler implemented a plan to replace Adams as party chairman with Congressman Morehead. The strategy provided a strong motivation to end Adams's libel suits before the state Republican convention. After the supreme court reversed Butler's conviction, neither side seemed sure that the criminal or civil actions would be tried. In March 1910, Adams offered to end the dispute if Butler admitted the statements were false but were honestly published as news without malice. Butler, believing the statements were true, balked. The negotiations took a turn toward resolution

John Motley Morehead: a Progressive Era Bryan.
(Courtesy of the North Carolina Collection, University
of North Carolina at Chapel Hill)

when it appeared the case would be retried, and on 28 July 1910, Adams and
Butler agreed to terminate the matter. In his settlement statement Butler
did not admit that the charges were false but instead indicated they were
published without malice in the belief that they were true. He conceded
that a jury had found them not true. This was no more than a history of the

case. On the other hand, the lawsuit did not bring the crushing shame on Adams that Butler hoped it would, although Adams soon faded permanently from the Republican scene.[8]

With the end of the lawsuit, Butler put his Morehead campaign into high gear. He wrote numerous letters to supporters, hoping to stimulate pro-Morehead sentiment at local conventions. He argued that the party needed a man who could be trusted to advise the president about progressive policy. Thanks to the support of Butler, Thomas Settle, and others, Morehead soon became the likely choice for chairman. On the eve of the convention, however, Carl Duncan decided to defeat the upstart congressman by using the state's military-like phalanx of postmasters. Duncan knew Morehead was a rising star, so he was unwilling to attack him directly. Instead, Butler became his target. Republican newspapers friendly to Duncan mustered an attack on Butler and his purported control of Morehead. They manipulated distrust over Butler's involvement in the bond case, his alleged betrayal of earlier GOP allies, his residence outside the state, and his "questionable" ideology. Especially nasty was a circular that claimed Butler, a "deceiver, a boss, and a traitor who planned to control North Carolina republicanism for private gain," had appeared at the Nash County Republican convention "too full of booze or other dope" to make an effective speech. Butler responded to this and other attacks by sending statements to newspapers describing Morehead as "too big to be bossed by anyone." He was for Morehead "because the tired, disappointed and outraged rank and file of the party from the mountains to the sea are rallying to him because they believe he is able, honest and patriotic."[9]

Butler orchestrated a stunning final assault on Duncan in the weeks before the convention. His hotel room in Morehead City, where he was "vacationing," quickly became cluttered with thousands of pieces of paper, including letters to supporters and vast tabulations of the persuasions of local Republican delegations. He gave a reporter there a pep talk about the promise of Morehead and the treachery of Duncan and Adams. He denied he ran the Morehead campaign, stating he simply desired progressive Republicanism. He then traveled to Greensboro, the site of the Republican convention. Ensconced in a suite at the Guilford Hotel, he received courtesy calls from delegates, roamed the building, and occasionally descended to the hotel's front desk to calculate the latest delegate count. Sporting a fashionable summer suit of white duck, the forty-seven-year-old former senator, still with glossy black hair and a neatly trimmed Vandyke beard, exuded impending success.[10]

The convention gave Butler sweet revenge for the indignities of 1908. Morehead trounced Duncan in the race for chairman, and his acceptance speech emphasized the need for a new party directed by the progressive business element. The platform praised Taft, supported a tariff commission, favored reclamation of federal swamplands, and demanded better education, local control of local government, regulation of corporations, protection of capital and labor, a nonpartisan judiciary, and free school textbooks. Butler made only a brief appearance on the stage, but the plank in the platform concerning free textbooks probably resulted from his influence, and the GOP's support for local self-government and a nonpartisan judiciary had been part of his campaign vocabulary since 1894.[11]

Afterward, he boasted to President Taft that the convention created a "strong, progressive and winning Republican party" and that he was taking up where he had been forced to leave off in 1908 in his effort to make North Carolina a progressive Republican stronghold. Butler threw himself wholeheartedly into the effort. He asked Morehead to run former silver leader J. J. Mott for Congress in the eighth district, develop better organization at the township level, print one hundred thousand copies of Morehead's acceptance speech (five thousand of which Butler would send to his personal mailing list), and emphasize the local self-government issue and the need for a new election law, just as Butler had in 1894. He offered the names of potential speakers for eastern North Carolina, featuring former Populists, including himself. His paper proclaimed that voters would be treated to a "campaign of issues and principles."[12]

As usual, however, Democrats showed less interest in debating principles than in repeating the methods that had kept them in power since 1898. Their leaders feared division between reformers and conservatives in their own ranks, which precluded them from adopting a coherent position on legislation. They were burdened by the party's poor record of reform over the past eleven years and the economic conservatism of Governor William Walton Kitchin. Democrats did, however, seem to agree on negative themes, such as Republican betrayal, racial and otherwise. By September, Josephus Daniels had established the main "ideas" of the Democratic campaign as the need to keep vigilance over disfranchisement and the danger presented by litigation over Reconstruction bonds. Daniels's claim that the Republican campaign slogan should be "Bulter, Booze, Boodle and Bonds" ironically captured the thinness of Democratic progressivism. Daniels even returned to the cartoon presentations that so distinguished his newspaper in the 1890s. The pictures implied that Butler wanted "Negro domination" so he could collect Reconstruction bonds; according to Daniels, a lily-white Republican victory still meant black rule. Democrats also made an effort to associate Butler with unwanted economic regulation, proclaiming that his party's success would mean "Social Degradation and Business Disturbance."[13]

Butler tried to deflate the attacks. He announced that he did not favor the collection of carpetbag bonds. Taking a page from Spencer Adams's book, he even informed Charles Aycock that he wished to bring a libel suit against Daniels, but Aycock replied that he was Daniels's lawyer. He also wanted to help write the party campaign book, particularly a section defending his role with the bonds. When Morehead told him that a committee was not making progress on a book, he published his own pamphlet titled "Cold Facts about Butler and the Bonds." He crisscrossed North Carolina delivering long speeches. Their content indicated the demise of the planned campaign of ideas. Appearing in Charlotte, he denounced Josephus Daniels, a "little contemptible and whining, lying hypocrite," in a manner "hurled into the audience like red-hot canister until the [*News and Observer*] editor . . . was riddled by facts and scorched by Butler's flowing Saxon vocabulary." In Statesville, with a perhaps uncomfortable Vice President James S. Sherman on the podium, he offered more bitter abuse, this time of Senator Furnifold Simmons and Governor Kitchin.[14]

Other Republicans responded with various degrees of enthusiasm to the anti-Butler tirade. Aycock's claim that the Republican Party was a tool of bondholders sufficiently outraged Morehead that he sarcastically informed the former governor that he could not conceive of how that idea originated unless "the proposition has formerly been submitted by these bondholders to the Democrats." Much of the Republican press, however, was dragged into a defense of Butler against its wishes. Although most Republican newspapers took the position that Butler's explanations should settle the matter, practically none openly defended him. The most widely distributed pro-Butler document not emanating from Butler himself was published by Thaddeus Ivey, a former Populist now prominent in the Farmers' Union. It praised Butler's role in the creation of a railroad commission, a woman's college, the 6 percent interest law, rural free delivery, better public education, and postal savings banks.[15]

Particularly revealing of the distress caused by the need to defend Butler were the thoughts of William Garrot Brown, who drafted most of the party's platform. Brown, a sometime Harvard historian living in Asheville, represented the class and ideals of the Taft-Morehead "respectables." He confided to President Taft's secretary that the Populists who had become Republicans

were "troublesome" because they had not adopted "real" Republican principles. Brown did not associate the future of the party, as Butler did, with Populism, progressivism, or Roosevelt's reforms. Instead, he believed growth depended on wealthy businessmen such as Morehead. In fact, the "contingent
of former Populists" was the "least desirable," because it did not aid in the
unceasing need to make the party "respectable." As a result, "Ex-Senator
Butler should receive no recognition [from the administration] in any
form. He is thoroughly discredited with the better people of the state."[16]

As if division in the Republican ranks were not threatening enough, Democrats had a last-minute surprise for the GOP. Throughout the campaign
Butler claimed he was never interested in collecting fraudulent bonds. Yet
just before election day Simmons displayed the 1905 advertisement that
Butler placed in New York papers seeking all varieties of southern bonds.
Precisely why the ad was not brought up before October, as Democrats publicized it in 1905, is unclear. At any rate, the Democratic press trumpeted
the "discovery" as proof that Butler was a liar and, equally important, that he
still wanted to collect bonds.[17]

Not to be outdone, Butler offered his own parting shot before the election. He hired the Raleigh Academy of Music and dared Simmons or Daniels
to show up. When the audience in the nearly full hall was seated, he launched
into a remarkable critique of the Democrats' progressive record and a defense of himself. Governor Kitchin had promised an effective antitrust law,
but no trust feared the one that had been passed. As a result, Democrats
"dare not face the people and say where they stand on the great live economic issues." Turning to the "slanderous" attacks about the bonds, Butler
stated that the *South Dakota* case involved bonds issued by a Democratic legislature. As for the now infamous 1905 advertisement, he agreed to the broad
language because he assumed any bonds submitted would be evaluated for
their soundness and that fraudulent carpetbag bonds would be refused. He
stopped the advertisement after learning that some of the bonds accepted
were fraudulent, telling L. H. Hole of Coler and Company that he would
have nothing to do with those bonds. These statements were misleading at
best. Fortunately, at this point almost all the other characters in the Supreme Court drama, including Daniel Russell, were dead.[18]

Butler then addressed economic and political reform in a spectacular
manner that demonstrated both his adherence to Populist ideas and his
frustration with twentieth-century politics. Although the year was 1910 and
this was a Republican speech, he argued that the desired end, equal economic opportunity, could be achieved only through the Populists' Omaha

Platform: "It was first necessary that every instrument of commerce and every other natural monopoly should be controlled and used by the National Government as an instrument of government for the benefit of all and for the protection of all." The instruments of commerce were "money, transportation, and the transmission of intelligence," and the Constitution's Commerce Clause obligated the government to take over these "instruments." Reliving the 1890s, he discussed the quantity theory of money, said it did not matter what money was made of, and stated that its volume should be determined by the needs of the population and of business. He poured anger on the political boundaries that prevented these changes. His career demonstrated how the "trusts and malefactors of great wealth have their tools and agents in both parties and are trying to control both." Arguing that a reform coalition based on Populism could be fashioned in the Republican Party, he asked voters "to put love of State and Country above party prejudice, and rally together to control the organization of one of these parties— the party of progressive policies and constructive statesmanship—so that we might use that great militant organization for the preservation of our liberties and for the progress and prosperity of all the people." In essence, it was the same message of reform and coalition political strategy Butler had offered since the early 1890s.[19]

Despite the exhausting five-hour performance, voters seemed as uninterested in Populism and reform politics as they had been twenty years earlier. All the Republican candidates for Congress lost, and only twenty-seven Republicans were elected to the legislature, the lowest number ever. Election totals indicated that the Republican vote had declined by about thirteen thousand since 1908, while the Democratic vote had risen by about five thousand. The result suggested that some of the persons who voted for Taft in 1908 did not choose to associate with the Morehead-Butler leadership and that Democratic progressives certainly did not seek common ground with progressive Republicans.[20] Butler offered several explanations for Republican decline. He viewed it as part of a national movement away from his party, which reflected dissatisfaction about failed tariff reform and perceived differences between Taft and Roosevelt on reform matters. In short, the movement of the country was toward reform, and progressives disliked Taft. On a more basic level, Butler believed the Democratic Party in North Carolina also used its control over the election process to produce a fraudulent count, including the "normal" Democratic tactics of "intimidation, force, bribery, [and] whiskey."[21]

AFTER THE ELECTION a host of seemingly intractable problems beset the GOP. Instead of putting aside debilitating differences, Republicans renewed old disagreements. Duncan, the national Republican committeeman, and Morehead, the state chairman, continued their conflict, this time in a protracted struggle over federal jobs. As before, Taft was at the center of the problem. He had always been quick to criticize southern Republicans as patronage hungry, but by 1911 he was worrying about his renomination, and in North Carolina, as in other states, he manipulated through patronage both the reactionary and progressive factions to advance his candidacy. Meanwhile, outside North Carolina, the insurgency of progressive Republicans rose to a crescendo. As a result, Butler's political problem, reminiscent of the 1896 campaign, was deciding how to deal with intense factionalism in his own party as well as differing degrees of reform in national and state politics.[22] Initially, he tried to coordinate federal and state Republican politics by arguing that Roosevelt would not run for president in 1912 and that Taft would be the party's progressive nominee. This allowed him to seek solidarity between the Populist and Morehead groups, the latter of which stood steadfastly behind Taft. Butler also continued to portray Taft as a progressive: He "has passed more great reform measures during the first two years of his administration . . . than has ever occurred before in the administration of any president," and he correctly pursued antitrust suits against the oil, lumber, beef, tobacco, and harvester companies.[23]

Because of national trends, Butler still displayed optimism about progressive reform. He made significant improvements in the *Caucasian*, which he now hoped to make the banner newspaper of North Carolina progressivism. In 1911 it advocated compulsory labor arbitration, universal white suffrage, free textbooks, an end to railroad freight rate discrimination, a tariff commission, local self-government, postal savings banks, direct election of senators, a ten-hour workday, an end to night work for women, the Mexican revolution, reduction of railway mail pay, the initiative and referendum, the recall of judges, conservation, government life insurance and old-age pensions, and stronger antitrust laws. It gave extensive attention to the founding of the National Progressive Republican League, led by Robert La Follette, in January 1911. Butler endorsed all the league's demands, including direct election of party convention delegates, increased corporate regulation, and financial reform.[24]

The optimism seems to have been bolstered by a continued faith in Populism, as he increasingly viewed the newer movement as a vindication of the earlier cause. Repeating his words from 1892, he declared Congress had a duty to impose government ownership of "any natural monopoly which is an instrument of commerce." His paper promoted the subtreasury as a means of making the currency supply more flexible. He proposed a government-owned steamship line and, pending the inevitable failure of railroad regulation, government ownership of railroads. He argued gold money was an "accidental standard." He became interested in the Farmers' Union, and although he did not join the organization, his paper made favorable references to it and endorsed its proposals, many of which resembled those of the Alliance.[25]

Despite Butler's efforts to link Taft, Populism, Morehead, and surging Republican progressivism, a formal splintering of the Tar Heel GOP became imminent in late 1911. At first it appeared that patronage alone would be the catalyst. Distress signals, damning Taft, poured in to Butler daily from an angry Tar Heel rank and file. Butler and Morehead urged their followers to be patient and prepare for the election year, when Duncan could be replaced as the national committeeman. Butler, who now wanted Duncan's job, recognized that Taft sought "to hold every member of the National Committee[, including Duncan,] under his thumb until after the next [National] Convention meets." In early 1912, he and Morehead began soliciting local party organizations for support.[26]

Their efforts fell into confusion with the sudden appearance of the Roosevelt for President movement, a cause that quickly overwhelmed squabbles over federal jobs. Much as elsewhere in the nation, North Carolina's early Roosevelt supporters were a political hodgepodge. They included genuine admirers of TR, persons disappointed with Taft's patronage policies, and Republicans who disliked the Taft-oriented state leadership, including Morehead and Butler. Its most important figure was Richmond Pearson, one of the original leaders in the Populist-Republican cooperation of 1894. The Asheville Republican had spent almost all the 1900–1910 decade as Roosevelt's minister to Persia, Greece, and Montenegro. In 1912 he was back in North Carolina, encouraging Roosevelt to make the run and successfully tapping dissatisfaction with Taft's patronage policy. Roosevelt wrote Pearson that because of Taft's putting North Carolina offices "on the auction block, it has been evident that we can win only by getting our friends united and insisting upon the expression of the public will."[27]

Roosevelt formally announced his candidacy in February 1912. Because Morehead and Butler had stood by Taft, their original strategy collapsed. This became clear at a banquet hosted by Morehead on 28 February. Morehead invited more than five hundred guests, including Butler, assuming that the dinner would reflect a rousing commitment to defeating Duncan and reelecting Taft. Morehead drafted an elaborate speech, which Butler helped prepare. Butler was also scheduled to give a short talk. Held literally hours after Roosevelt's announcement that he intended to run, however, the mood was so pro-Roosevelt that Morehead did not even attempt to wring a resolution from the group supporting Taft's reelection.[28]

Butler must have felt as if he were back in 1892, as presidential politics again disrupted well-laid plans. Consistent with his reaction to Grover Cleveland's candidacy, he responded that his state organization should stay out of the presidential fight and send uninstructed delegates to the national convention. Republicans ought to concentrate on supporting Morehead and unseating Duncan. Butler knew that defending the unpopular Taft would be suicidal. Further, his personal inclinations were in favor of Roosevelt. On the other hand, based on his experiences in the nineties, he distrusted the North Carolina leaders of the Roosevelt movement. They were not true progressives, and besides, "[Richmond] Pearson's performance would [not] result in anything but a fiasco, for a man like him would queer even a popular and winning movement." Even more disheartening, Duncan used the Roosevelt boom to help himself. W. A. Hildebrand, conservative editor of the *Greensboro Daily News*, wrote Roosevelt that "Duncan has at last seen the light" and, despite an earlier pledge for Taft, would support TR. Duncan, however, hedged all bets, for soon after this apparent shift he went to Washington and defended his loyalty to Taft. Pearson also allied with Duncan, although he doubted Duncan's ability to run the Roosevelt campaign in the east. Altogether, Roosevelt, Duncan, and Pearson, albeit strange bedfellows, revolutionized North Carolina Republican politics.[29]

In the face of these developments Morehead tried to stabilize his tottering organization. He was among the few leading Republicans who honestly preferred Taft to Roosevelt. To his credit, he initially kept his gaze fixed on the need to depose Duncan. Morehead characterized this cause as a fight against machine rule, including local determination of patronage appointments. Like Butler, he wanted to avoid a confrontation on the presidential issue and preferred an uninstructed delegation to the national convention. Wishfully, he tried to deflate the Roosevelt stampede by claiming that "Colonel Roosevelt will withdraw before the convention, thoroughly satisfied with the progress his candidacy has made for 1916."[30]

Despite his support for Morehead, the Roosevelt frenzy soon affected Butler. By April he believed most Republicans did not regard the success of both Roosevelt and Morehead as contradictory. Newspaper reports of dual

endorsements of Roosevelt and Morehead by county organizations corrob-
orated these perceptions. As a result, his newspaper moved from a position
of neutrality in presidential politics to a celebration of Roosevelt's successes
in Republican primaries outside North Carolina. Butler proclaimed the primary wins reflected a desire for change "that would bring the government
nearer the people and eliminate boss rule, which is another name for the
domination of special interest at the expense of the wealth producers."[31]

This revised strategy fell apart at a Republican meeting on 15 May. Because many Republicans believed Morehead was tainted by his support for
Taft, Morehead turned over the proceedings to Zebulon Vance Walser, a
leader in the Roosevelt campaign. Butler tried to show his loyalty to Roosevelt by announcing that he had believed in the same principles TR endorsed for more than twenty years. Ironically, some thought he had been
too hesitant, and he and Morehead lost on practically every ensuing vote.
Butler desperately wanted to be one of the at-large delegates to the national
convention in Chicago, but Tom Owens, the pro-Roosevelt editor of the
Clinton News-Dispatch, defeated him. The other at-large delegates were Cyrus
Thompson, Richmond Pearson, and Walser, former Populists or Republicans who had supported cooperation with Populists in the 1890s. Pearson
soundly defeated Butler in the contest for national committeeman. The
only development that partially saved Butler's plan was a fierce but successful battle to adjourn before a vote could be taken to replace Morehead as
chairman.[32]

Butler reacted to the setback by denouncing Pearson. Pearson bargained
with Duncan and "claimed to be the personal representative of Col. Roosevelt, [and] organized and tried to jab through a revolutionary scheme to
kick Mr. Morehead out." Nonetheless, Butler thought the party could be put
in a proper posture when it met to select state-level candidates after the national convention. Unfortunately for the Morehead-Butler coalition, when
Butler asked Morehead for a conference to discuss this strategy, Morehead
indicated that he planned to remain "quiescent" until after the presidential
nomination. If Roosevelt won he might become "permanently quiescent."
The reason for Morehead's gloom was clear. The Tar Heel press and rank
and file ardently favored TR. All but one delegate to Chicago, including Butler, endorsed the former president. Their railroad car carried a bold banner
identifying it as "The N.C. Roosevelt special—the Old North State Delegates Solid for the Honest Chieftain—Teddy Roosevelt. Down with the
bosses. Let the people rule."[33]

At the Chicago convention the Taft organization had the upper hand.

Pro-Taft decisions from the national committee awarded almost all the contested seats to Taft supporters. Taft men challenged Butler's seat, along with three others from North Carolina. After it became apparent that Roosevelt would lose the contests, the colonel advised his delegates to abstain from participation. Taft's nomination followed, but Roosevelt did not accept defeat. After the Republicans adjourned he promised to continue his campaign.[34] Most North Carolina Republicans sided with Roosevelt. Many who attended the convention denounced the "high-handed" tactics of Taft's managers, who did "dishonest and contemptible work." They had no intention of voting for Taft. Some former Populists, including J. F. Click, thought "a new party is coming. It has to head off wild socialism on the one extreme and tyrannical financialism on the other." Yet others pleaded for unity under Taft. The *Union Republican* argued that Roosevelt could not win, while the *Burlington State Dispatch* declared, "There is such a thing as progressing too far, [and this is] what has happened to the Progressives." Butler agreed with Taft's critics, but he still believed Morehead could lead the party. He focused his attack on Duncan, whose votes as national committeeman helped seat Taft contestants at Chicago. Taft himself praised Duncan's work as "magnificent. It has touched me more than I can tell you and it is with pride and satisfaction in you that I write to express myself. I thank you more than I can say and send you all my best wishes."[35] Butler initially proposed to hold the state party together by ignoring the Chicago result. He wanted Roosevelt presidential electors and a state ticket under Morehead. The plan resembled his unsuccessful attempt in 1892 to support the Populist presidential candidate, James Weaver, while remaining an Alliance Democrat for purposes of state politics. Roosevelt men, including Butler, Pearson, and Walser, took a step in this direction when they met on 8 July. They decided not to form a third party but to lead a "Roosevelt Republican" campaign and present their own slate of presidential electors.[36]

In the midst of this turmoil, Butler visited Roosevelt at Oyster Bay, New York. Attempting a direct link between Populism and progressivism, the former Populist chairman and Alliance president spoke with Roosevelt about the agrarian revolt. Roosevelt listened, at least, and asked Butler to send him a copy of the 1892 Omaha Platform. Butler loyally supported Roosevelt after 1904, but for the same political reasons he supported Bryan in the 1890s. Actually, the two men held very different views about economics. Roosevelt conceded the necessity of large business organization and decried the wastefulness of excessive competition. He believed the increased responsibilities of government would allow it to serve as a paternalistic regu-

lator of an orderly industrial state. Roosevelt's message was also a moral crusade against materialism. Butler, in contrast, demanded government ownership of the "instruments of commerce" in order to restore equality of opportunity within the marketplace. He had much greater faith in competition
once monopolies were nationalized and much less faith in the ability of
elites to manage large businesses or government fairly. His perspective was
more democratic and more individualistic than Roosevelt's, although it implicitly conceded large-scale business organization. Butler had long endorsed
economic combination among market actors, most obviously through agricultural cooperatives. Yet he ultimately rested his reform on the desirability
of ensuring the fair pursuit of self-interest by "wealth producers." As a result,
Butler's conclusions more resembled the pro-producer progressivism of
Robert La Follette. Nonetheless, as a politician Butler recognized that Roosevelt believed the federal government had to play a decisive role in controlling private power in order to benefit workers. He could also win. Much as
with Bryan, this was enough to command Butler's support.[37]

Roosevelt's North Carolina supporters faced many challenges. In late July
Roosevelt played midroad Populist and decided that hybrid "Roosevelt Republican" movements would not be acceptable. A separate Progressive Party
organization from each state should send delegates to a Roosevelt convention in Chicago. The concept did not impress Pearson, Walser, or Butler,
who did not respond to the call for a local third party. James N. Williamson,
however, answered and held a slimly attended meeting that organized the
North Carolina Progressive Party.[38] These events caused Morehead and his
supporters to try to defeat the Pearson-Butler bid to recast the state party in
Roosevelt's image. At an executive committee meeting on 7 August, Taft
supporters reenacted another drama of the Populist era by adopting resolutions reminiscent of Furnifold Simmons's pro–Grover Cleveland proscrip-
tions of 1892. The committee barred opponents of Taft from all local nominating conventions and from the state convention. The ban was a surprise,
as Pearson, Walser, and Butler had not bothered to attend the executive
committee meeting.[39]

The chaotic reactions to the ban signaled the GOP's impending collapse.
It angered Roosevelt's Republican supporters, who made up between 80
and 90 percent of the party. They simply ignored it, attended local Republican conventions, and selected Roosevelt delegates to the state convention.
Perhaps recalling the options of the 1890s, Pearson spoke in favor of a cooperation deal between Roosevelt Republicans and Progressives. Even Roosevelt dropped his midroad posture and became a cooperationist after real-

izing that the "Taft men in N.C. are acting with the infamy which characterized the action of the Taft men in Chicago." Carl Duncan indicated that although, like Pearson, he was willing to discard Morehead, he would not oppose Taft. Progressive Party leader Williamson considered cooperation, but
he did not want anything to do with Butler. Chairman Morehead initially
told Pearson that perhaps there could be some cooperation between Taft
and Roosevelt Republicans on state and local tickets, but he later changed
his mind. Butler thought Morehead would not exclude Roosevelt Republicans from the state convention. He told Pearson there should be a statewide
primary for presidential electors, which TR would win, and unity on state
candidates. Nonetheless, if Morehead acted unfairly, there would be "nothing to do but organize a separate convention and appeal to the people of
the state to stand by us."[40]

These disparate forces appeared at the GOP's nominating convention in
Charlotte on 4 September. First, meeting apart from the convention, the
pro-Taft executive committee, by a vote of 8 to 6, unseated all Republicans
who supported Roosevelt. It then employed local police to prevent those
who would not pledge their votes to Taft from entering the hall. In the convention, Morehead declared Pearson's national committeeman's seat vacant
and, incredibly, to unite the Taft forces, asked that Carl Duncan fill it. The
delegates duly elected Duncan and nominated Thomas Settle for governor.
Morehead, although disgusted with Taft's political incompetence, seems to
have believed that these bullying methods were the only way to save the Taft
candidacy, and he preferred Taft, with his faults, to Roosevelt.[41]

The Roosevelt Republicans had little choice except to find another hall.
Their task was complicated by the fact that two days earlier the North Carolina Progressive Party nominated a full state ticket headed by the former
Populist Cyrus Thompson for governor. It had adopted a lengthy platform,
which called for primary elections, better public schools, higher teacher
pay, a state board of health, a parole system, better treatment of prisoners,
a fairer tax system, antitrust legislation, state control of water power, workers' compensation, and the creation of land banks. Butler, like other Roosevelt supporters, was excluded from the Taft convention, and he attended
the Roosevelt Republican meeting. Although he detested the work of the
Taft men, he proposed a harmony conference with Morehead. However,
there was so much bitterness that the suggestion was easily defeated. Butler
also tried to squash a resolution endorsing Cyrus Thompson as the Roosevelt Republican candidate for governor, but this also was voted down. He
knew Thompson would not be able to unite the party. Perhaps he was ap-

peased when Thompson sent a telegram saying that he was not interested in running. Under Pearson's direction, the Roosevelt Republicans denounced Taft, praised Roosevelt, selected Zebulon Walser as their candidate for governor, and planned a cooperation conference with the Progressives.[42]

Butler achieved greater success at a subsequent meeting of Progressives and Roosevelt Republicans. Along with Pearson, he helped defeat a proposed merger of the Progressive and Roosevelt Republican organizations. The groups agreed to a cooperative presidential ticket with Roosevelt as its standard-bearer. As for state races, they offered a unity ticket and platform. The convention nominated Iredell Meares, a former Democrat who had played a role in the white supremacy movement in Wilmington in 1898, for governor. The platform generally mirrored the Progressives' earlier product but eliminated their call for state control of water power and added Butler's demand for a secret ballot.[43]

The Roosevelt coalition existed only because of TR's popularity. Most of its members seemed to think the new organizations resulted from an unfortunate necessity of circumstance; their deeper loyalty remained with the Republican Party. As a result, despite personal appearances by Roosevelt in North Carolina, which attracted huge crowds, the Progressive–Roosevelt Republican campaign limped along halfheartedly. The coalition had limited press support. The *Caucasian*, the *Hickory Times-Mercury*, the *Clinton News-Dispatch*, and the *Burlington State Dispatch* endorsed both Roosevelt and the combination state ticket. The state's largest GOP paper, the *Union Republican*, supported Taft and the regular organization, and the *Greensboro Daily News* opted for Roosevelt, but timidly. At the local level a confusing maze of regular Republican, Roosevelt, and Progressive organizations developed. In some places, including Sampson County, there were no regular Republican tickets. In other counties, Roosevelt and regular Republicans cooperated.[44]

After the nominations, Butler withdrew from the contest. He declined invitations to speak, except for one appearance in Clinton three days before the election. He knew Republicans could not win, and he opposed waging a hostile campaign that would permanently divide the party. His newspaper refrained from attacking Taft. Instead, it proclaimed Roosevelt as the heir to Populism: "We are delighted that Col. Roosevelt has adopted the whole People's Party Platform, and we shall live in hopes that he shall be more faithful in living up to its principles than those who in the past have stolen one or more planks therefrom." The *Caucasian* also pointed out that Tom Watson supported Roosevelt and that TR's success would mean government ownership of all "natural monopolies." In contrast, the Democratic nominee, Woodrow Wilson, "went out of his way to sneer at labor and at the farmers of the country, and upheld the position of the monopoly and capitalistic class."[45]

The election confirmed the disastrous effect of the Taft presidency. Taft polled only about 12 percent of the state's total, which meant that in four years he accomplished the incredible feat of losing 70 percent of his support. Roosevelt won majorities in several mountain counties and in Sampson County. In fact, Butler's Sampson County and Tom Watson's McDuffie County, Georgia, represented practically the only rural, nonhill counties in the South to vote for Roosevelt. More ominous for North Carolina Republicanism, its representation in the legislature sunk from twenty-three to twenty, and Republicans failed to elect a single congressman. Worst of all, the split in Republican ranks sent Wilson to the White House.[46]

BETWEEN 1908 AND 1912 Butler continued his effort to construct a progressive Republican Party based on Populist principles. Success eluded him primarily because Populists constituted a small and diminishing force within the GOP. Nonetheless, Butler managed to help elect John Morehead state party chairman in 1910. The alliance of former Populists and the millionaire Morehead, however, presented severe limitations in terms of offering an alternative to conservative Democratic rule. These limitations far exceeded those of Republican-Populist cooperation in the 1890s and demonstrated the constriction of political discourse that followed disfranchisement. Butler's intellectual isolation appeared most clearly in his Populist Raleigh speech in November 1910, where he promoted Populism in the absence of any organized support for its principles. Further, even the moderate coalition that included Morehead and Butler fell apart as a result of division in the national GOP, Taft's political failure, and Roosevelt's decision to run for president in 1912. As in the Populist era, presidential politics deeply affected North Carolina, stimulating party factionalism and suddenly creating new leaders and even a new political party. Similarly, it sounded the death knell of Butler's efforts to bring Populism into the Progressive Era.

FADING MEMORIES

BUTLER KNEW THAT the 1912 election caused the GOP to enter a holding stage. Publicly, he supported TR's policy of maintaining separate Progressive and Republican forces after the election because the "progressive party is the only hope to liberate the people of the South from the incompetent, extravagant and tyrannical yoke of the Democratic machine that has dominated my state and all the other southern states." Yet triumph was unlikely. Perhaps the greatest symbol of Butler's new pessimism was the decision, in May 1913, to stop publishing the *Caucasian*. The paper enjoyed some good years between 1908 and 1912, increasing its circulation to nearly five thousand. By early 1913, however, Lester wanted to quit, and no one else seemed interested in working in a politically hostile environment for little pay. The demise of the *Caucasian*, at the acme of white supremacy, was ironic. A leading reform paper for more than twenty-five years, its death dramatically narrowed journalistic opinion in North Carolina.[1]

The fallout from 1912 lasted through several elections. In 1914 the Taft men tried to reunite the party. Morehead and Duncan asked Zebulon Walser, for the Progressives, and Charles Cowles, for the Roosevelt Republicans, to attend a joint meeting. Walser and Cowles rejected the overture, and two Republican conventions were held. First, a sparse joint gathering of forty-eight Progressives and Roosevelt Republicans accomplished little. As for the regular Republican organization, Frank Linney of Boone replaced the retiring Morehead as chairman, but Morehead and Carl Duncan remained the key leaders. In the demoralized campaign that followed, the most encouraging news was that local Roosevelt and Taft Republicans developed cooperative tickets. Progressive Party organizations ceased to exist in some counties. The third party's only congressional candidate, in the piedmont's Fifth District, suffered the ignominy of getting a mere four hundred votes, less than the nominee of the Socialist Party. Butler refrained from practically all political activity. When Sampson's Roosevelt Republicans considered sending a delegation to the regular convention, he advised that it would be a mistake. Instead, he thought Republicans should cooperate at the local level to preserve the Roosevelt parties until 1916.[2]

Motivated by the possibility of again supporting Roosevelt and the everlasting appeal of political warfare, after the election Butler showed a renewed interest in politics. He lashed out at Democrats' "high taxes," "general extravagance," and the mismanagement of the public school system. A renewed attack on Duncan made it clear that Butler also hoped to revive the antimachine theme. Skillfully, he used correspondence to appeal to both the Roosevelt and Taft wings of the party. He agreed with the Progressive Walser that the 1915 Democratic legislature had been "extremely reactionary," while he told Morehead ally Gilliam Grissom that North Carolina was a naturally high tariff state. Roosevelt was important to Butler's strategy. The former Populist wanted to use the popularity of the former president to return the GOP to the hopeful condition of 1910. As before, this would require disposing of Duncan, who sought reelection as national committeeman. Unfortunately for Butler, his political clout was increasingly limited, and Morehead thought he could achieve unity without Butler's interference. Undaunted, Butler stormed into Raleigh before the 1916 GOP convention and held a rally for his followers, which included almost two hundred delegates. He came to defeat the men who had sundered the party in 1912, especially Duncan. He demanded equal representation of Taft and Roosevelt supporters among the at-large delegates to the national convention. The Butler caucus aimed to split the Taft men by proposing that Morehead could bring the party together against Duncan.[3]

At the convention, Butler's thirty years of political experience paid off. The moment of truth occurred when, while he was out of the hall, Duncan tried to elect delegates to the national convention that opposed a compromise between Roosevelt and Taft forces. When Butler returned he asked the convention to elect a new national committeeman first. After denouncing Duncan as a traitor, he endorsed Morehead for the job. Duncan responded that Butler planned to take over the party and that before the convention Morehead agreed to get rid of Butler. After Butler roused his supporters to jeers and hisses, Duncan left the platform. Morehead solemnly rose and stated that he wanted the party united and that he could hardly refuse a clear demand from the faithful. The delegates named him the new national

committeeman. Butler also served on the GOP's platform committee; the re-
sulting document advocated several of his long-standing demands, including fair elections, a national rural credit system, and immigration restriction. The waning of economic progressivism, however, meant there was no
reference to antitrust enforcement or corporate regulation.[4]

Butler's political expertise did not accomplish much of substance. To be
sure, Duncan went down to defeat, and the Roosevelt revolt was partly vindicated. Yet to win it had been necessary to combine with "respectables," the
same men who adopted machine tactics in 1912 to save Taft. The frenzied
1916 Republican convention confirmed the exceedingly short-term ideological impact of the Progressive Party and the tenuousness of progressive Republicanism in North Carolina. Apparently, the most Butler could hope for
now was to defeat that element of the party which was most objectionable.
The ensuing election also confirmed progressivism's declining relevance.
Democrats revived the Butler, bonds, and "Negro domination" themes,
while the *Charlotte Observer* criticized even the mild reforms proposed in the
Republican platform. Demonstrating the negligible effect Populism and
progressivism had on the rhetoric of interparty politics, Democratic chairman Thomas P. Warren surmised that a return to Republicanism "will bring
to North Carolina a repetition of scandal, corruption and extravagance that
characterized their administrations during Reconstruction days." As voters
went to the polls, the *News and Observer*, still owned by the "progressive" Josephus Daniels, who was now in Woodrow Wilson's cabinet as secretary of the
navy, headlined that Cuba wanted to sue on North Carolina bonds.[5]

During the contest Butler made his last effort for Roosevelt. He promised
Roosevelt's manager, George Perkins, that he could have the North Carolina delegation to the national convention for TR. He wrote Roosevelt and
seems to have met with him in New York. The former president, however,
did not win the Republican nomination and declined to run as a Progressive. Butler stood by him until the end. At the nominating convention, nine
of Roosevelt's sixty-five first-ballot votes came from North Carolina; Butler
seconded his nomination. When the former president shifted his support to
Henry Cabot Lodge, Butler and six other North Carolinians loyally followed,
despite the absurdity of a Populist supporting the Massachusetts reactionary.
Although Charles Evans Hughes's nomination facilitated a reunion of Old
Guard and Progressive elements, Butler was disappointed. He complained
to Roosevelt that "we made the best fight we knew how but somebody flunked
between one and three last Saturday morning." Whatever that meant, Butler
assured TR of his continuing importance.[6]

Butler's actions in the ensuing campaign were anticlimactic. He published several tracts, which attacked national Democrats for not defending Americans in Mexico and, in the European war, for surrendering to British violations of international law. As for North Carolina, he criticized high taxes, poor management, and deprived schools. He wrote a widely circulated article arguing that Hughes should be elected because of his reform accomplishments while governor of New York. He went to Ohio, Missouri, and Indiana to make speeches for Hughes. In the end, North Carolina Republicans regained most of the strength they had lost in 1912, as Hughes won about 42 percent of the vote and Republican representation in the assembly increased to thirty. Still, since 1904 Republican support had remained stagnant at between 40 and 45 percent of the electorate. As a result, where to obtain the votes needed for a majority was just as much a problem in 1916 as it had been when Butler joined the party. Composed of an odd coalition of persons repelled by the various moods of Democracy from the Civil War through progressivism, the GOP faced permanent defeat unless political boundaries could be dramatically redefined.[7]

Conditions during the later years of the 1910–19 decade did not suggest imminent realignment. In 1917 Butler criticized President Wilson's manner of prosecuting the European conflict and argued Republicans could gain by espousing a patriotic antiwar agenda. The draft and the threat to civil liberties particularly upset him. The state Republican leadership, however, rejected this approach, and the 1918 contest was unusually dull. Butler attended the strangely harmonious state convention, where delegates nominated Morehead for the U.S. Senate and Butler earned a spot on the platform committee. Importantly, the delegates declared for women's suffrage, which Democrats opposed, and opposed discrimination in the pay of male and female teachers. The platform directly reflected Butler's influence through demands for a nonpartisan judiciary; improvement in the Federal Farm Loan program, which established Federal Land Banks to make loans on farm mortgages; fertilizer price control; and a fair election law. Butler gave a short speech that condemned Wilson for not conducting the war on a nonpartisan basis. The subsequent campaign, however, because of the war, avoided an active canvass. This was not helpful to the minority, and Republicans slid to the usual defeat.[8]

At the conclusion of World War I in late 1918, the national Republican Party approached a crossroads, and much to Butler's disgust, the impetus was to cast aside entirely the Roosevelt-Progressive legacy. Even in North Carolina there was an attack on "progressive Republicans" published in an

Asheville paper, which Butler traced to Morehead's group. The editorial, appearing in the summer of 1919, reflected hysteria over communist revolution in Russia and the broader fallout from Populism, progressivism, and Roosevelt. It claimed that progressives were "tainted with socialism and bolshevism." Publicly, Butler condemned this as "a gratuitous insult to over half of the [Republican] party," which included former members of the Alliance and People's Party. Privately, he castigated Morehead, because the "business crowd with who he runs and with whom he makes his money" would "rather keep the kind of legislation which they get from the Simmons machine at Raleigh, than risk a Republican legislature." If Morehead could dominate the assembly, "he would try to make it beat the Simmons' legislature in passing reactionary laws to suit his business associates which would alienate labor, farmers, and average voters."[9]

Despite the demise of progressivism, the likelihood of Republican success in the 1920 presidential election rekindled some of Butler's political enthusiasm. A local movement to support Jeter Pritchard for president also helped. The idea was to improve the southern Republican Party by having Pritchard, now a federal appeals court judge, become the GOP's vice presidential nominee. Another source for hope was the Republican state convention, held in March 1920, which suggested a decline in former bitterness. Even Butler thought it best finally to declare a truce with Duncan, whose political savvy he respected and whose dislike for Morehead was now useful. As a result, the delegates selected Butler, Morehead, Duncan, and Frank Linney as the "Big Four" at-large delegates to the national convention. Butler, Morehead, and Duncan even stood before the cheering crowd and shook hands. The delegates chose Linney as party chairman, Morehead as national committeeman, and John J. Parker for governor. The "harmony," however, was shallow. Afterward, Butler wrote Duncan a terse note stating he had done his part "for a square deal and for the good of the party, without any trade or *quid pro quo*, but now I expect reciprocation in the same spirit." Separately, he complained about the weakness of the Republican platform, particularly on labor, the income tax, and education. Still trying to inject a reform spirit into the party, he asked Parker to take a stand on labor's right to protect itself through "organized collective bargaining." Whatever position Parker adopted, it would "not lose you a single vote from the cotton-mill crowd," because the manufacturers did not want a Republican governor or legislature. Instead, "the only way you can be elected is to get the independent dissatisfied farmer and labor vote."[10]

As for the national GOP convention, Butler supported Pritchard's token bid, but initially he was undecided about his real choice for president. Dominated by conservatives looking for a pliable, popular candidate, the 1920 Chicago convention represented everything a former Populist should loathe. On the first ballot Pritchard received twenty-one of North Carolina's twenty-two votes. Butler placed Pritchard's name in nomination and voted for him on the first two ballots. He then shifted, first to Senator Hiram Johnson of California and then to Senator James Watson of Indiana. After the fourth ballot the convention temporarily adjourned, and a handful of party leaders fastened on Senator Warren G. Harding of Ohio as the most available man. Harding's supporters used Butler, Duncan, and Pritchard as functionaries in passing the word to North Carolinians that Harding was it. Pritchard told Butler to use a telegram from him supporting Harding "judiciously and strictly confidentially." After Harding's selection, Butler recalled the late-night meeting of party leaders after the fourth ballot and stated he agreed with the decision to shift to Harding. The flabbergasted *Clinton Sampson Democrat* thought the fact that "ex-Populists [would] vote for Harding and his platform [was] a marvel." Butler, however, believed Harding could be persuaded to support programs beneficial to farmers, and he reasoned the Ohioan, at least, was better than the Democratic opposition. A meeting with Harding further encouraged him. Butler's agricultural interests came up, and he and Harding took a liking to each other. Harding even asked Butler what he might say about farming in his acceptance speech. The former Alliance president replied he should convince the farmer that he understood "the conditions under which he labored to do his duty during the world war, and that you feel agriculture must be made more remunerative, and the conditions of country life less onerous, both as a matter of justice and as the only effective way to increase production." He also implored Harding to address the need for the Federal Reserve Board to improve farm credit.[11]

Butler's activity persisted after the convention. He tried to get his party to establish a separate southern headquarters. He argued it should be led by a southern man, perhaps himself, and located in a southern city. Butler pleaded his case to Harding; to Harry Daugherty, Harding's closest political adviser; and to Will Hays, the Republican national chairman. Although Harding seems to have brought the idea to Hays's attention, Hays told Butler that a southern headquarters outside of Washington would be impossible. More than one of Butler's correspondents assumed the decision was motivated by Hays's desire to accommodate black Republicans. The setback did not remove Butler from the contest. He prepared literature for the national committee. He made speeches in North Carolina and published campaign tracts for Harding. His principal message was that the Wilson administration was a failure and that Harding would be better for farmers. For example, the Democratic Federal Reserve Board had recently increased its lending rate, which was followed by a downward spiral of agricultural prices. Butler suggested Harding would end deflation and Republicans would favor state legislation to promote cotton and tobacco cooperative warehouses.[12]

North Carolina Republicans ran a relatively strong campaign, but Democrats successfully repeated tried-and-true practices. The GOP's U.S. Senate candidate, Alfred E. Holton, came out for workers' compensation, which Democrats opposed. The *Union Republican* made appeals to the Farmers' Union and the State Federation of Labor. Yet Democrats again relied on racial themes, stimulated this time by recently enacted women's suffrage. One fraudulent party circular, titled "A Challenge to White Men and Women of North Carolina," was allegedly written by a member of the "Colored Women's Rights Association for Colored Women." Signed "Yours for negro liberty," the document advised black women to vote and to hold secret night meetings and, most fantastical, claimed "there are plenty of white Republicans that will help us." Democrats advanced the fable about Harding's black ancestry. The racist propaganda, paeans to the Red Shirt glories of 1898 and 1900, and personal attacks on Butler by the Democrats' candidate for governor, Cameron Morrison, elicited a defensive reply. John Parker, the candidate for governor, in a statement that later helped prevent his confirmation to the U.S. Supreme Court, declared that Republicans did not seek to enfranchise blacks. Yet neither reassurances nor the Harding landslide resulted in significant improvement in Republican fortunes. The party polled 40 percent of the vote, and Harding carried several counties, including Sampson, but Republican representation in the General Assembly increased only from thirty-seven to thirty-eight.[13]

The Harding triumph prompted Butler to begin a campaign for appointment as secretary of agriculture. Although unsuccessful, he secured many recommendations, a flood of which poured into Harding's headquarters. Those who spoke in favor of Butler included Edwin A. Alderman, president of the University of Virginia, who recalled Butler's advocacy of education in the 1880s; Jeter Pritchard, who described him as a man of "unimpeachable personal character"; W. A. Graham, North Carolina's commissioner of agriculture; and Democratic congressman Claude Kitchin, who stated he had known Butler for twenty years and had "met no man during my public life, possessing a clearer and stronger intellect." North Carolina chief justice Walter Clark; Harry Woodburn Chase, president of the University of North Car-

olina; and Charles W. Dabney, a leader in Southern education, endorsed
him. Butler was also supported by most of the progressive wing of North
Carolina Republicanism. Prominent members of the Farmers' Alliance and
the Farmers' Union, as well as southern Republican leaders and several federal judges, governors, and senators, promoted his candidacy.[14]

On the other hand, a few of Butler's enemies conducted a countercam-
paign. One wrote that he made "inexcusable mistakes" during the 1890s,
which resulted in "race conflicts and race riots." Another thought him an
"infamous scoundrel" who undermined Republican success in North Carolina. He would be better as "ambassador to Hades and then I am confident
he would be persona non grata to his satanic majesty." Senator Simmons
thought it a disgrace that any Democrat could support Butler. Governor
Thomas Bickett brought up the bond case. One newspaper described the
former Populist as unqualified because he had made "speeches against the
[world] war" and had used the Alliance "to put the state under negro domination." Republicans in the 1921 legislature recommended Morehead, not
Butler, for a cabinet spot, and Morehead coldly told Butler he would not
support him.[15]

After the 1920 election Butler settled into an unusual semiretirement
from politics. The toll of time, including death and retirement, encouraged
a less confrontational posture. In the early 1920s, Carl Duncan and Jeter
Pritchard died, Linney abruptly resigned as state chairman, and Morehead
resigned as national committeeman. Most important, Harding's presidency
destroyed any ideological basis for new leadership in the state GOP. Butler
failed to appear at the boring 1922 state convention, which lasted only four
hours. The new chairman, William G. Bramham of Durham, a lawyer and
minor league baseball executive, reflected the emerging urban, piedmont,
pro-manufacturing orientation of the party. The GOP platform repeated
tired demands for better schools and roads, lower taxes, and free elections.
Apathy and defeat marked the ensuing campaign, as party representation in
the assembly reached a new low, declining from thirty-eight to twelve.[16]

By mid-1923, however, furious about persistent failure, Butler resurrected
his political interests and aimed his venom at Chairman Bramham. Butler's
complaints matched those he had offered since 1905: The leadership hap-
pily dispensed federal patronage and did not know how to conduct the kind
of grassroots appeal to workers and farmers that was necessary to win. Butler proposed to reconstitute the executive committee with county leaders
and give them power to elect the state chairman. Not surprisingly, the challenge did not generate much excitement. As Bramham told Butler's brother

George, Butler himself proposed the current manner of electing chairmen in 1916 in order to eliminate Carl Duncan. A deeper problem, which Butler ignored, was that even with a revamped organization, it was unlikely that reform-minded Republicans could make a persuasive attack on the "unprogressive" policies of Democrats. Not only did conservatives dominate the national Republican Party, but now the North Carolina Democratic Party actually promoted expanded public responsibility. This "business progressivism" earned the state its reputation as the "Wisconsin of the South." Democrats advanced unprecedented sums for roads, longer school terms, and public health. The legislature drastically altered the tax code, most significantly through income taxes. None of this had radical aims, and none of it approached the levels of state ownership that Butler and the Populists had desired. On the other hand, Democrats used state power and money to advance public goals. Ironically, because of events in the history of the Democratic Party that could trace their origin back to Butler's support for Bryan in 1896, the limited time Republicans had to claim the mantle of government activism was over. Even Butler, tongue in cheek, told Governor Cameron Morrison that he would vote for Democratic gubernatorial candidate Angus McLean if McLean supported a massive bond issue to improve North Carolina's ocean ports.[17]

Nonetheless, it was far too late to consider a change in parties, so the sixty-year-old Butler executed his attack on Bramham. He commenced a letter-writing blitz to convince the faithful that the leadership cared only about patronage. In response, baseball commissioner Bramham showed he also could play a mean game of political hardball. He did not want to change the party organization and would not compromise. He warned Isaac Meekins, a Butler ally, that he would drive Butler from the party in disgrace. He planned to tear off "the mask of political, professional and social hypocracy [sic] from this modern Dr. Jeckel [sic] and Mr. Hyde." If Butler continued, Bramham proposed to humiliate him by the publication of two affidavits.[18]

The contents of Bramham's affidavits are uncertain. One probably related to alleged improper business practices. Just after Calvin Coolidge became president in August 1923, Butler promoted himself as a potential ambassador to Mexico. He had engaged in business in Mexico since the early years of the century, and his interests included oil, cement, and water power. About this time Butler discussed some of his Mexican projects with the corrupt secretary of the interior Albert B. Fall. Perhaps Butler wanted to use Fall's influence to arrange favorable treatment in Mexico. More important, it is possible that Butler suggested using the ambassadorship for personal gain. He seems to have told Meekins of his ideas and expressed similar sentiments to Bramham in a meeting. As Meekins put it, at the meeting Butler began talking about "going to Mexico," and "seeing just what you were leading up to, I took the privilege of interrupting you and suggesting to you right there in Mr. Bramham's presence, that you leave out all that sort of thing." Butler continued to elaborate, however, and his statements probably formed the basis of Bramham's first affidavit. As for the other affidavit, it is possible that Bramham claimed Butler was a public drunk. Bramham's letter to Meekins referred to Butler as a "self-confessed crook and debaucher." Certainly Butler enjoyed his liquor and by the 1920s was a frequent drinker.[19]

In the end, Butler did not clearly address the charges, Bramham did not carry out his threat, and the election proceeded without a nasty confrontation. When learning of Bramham's reaction to his Mexican comments, Butler asked Meekins if Bramham was "damnfool enough to think that I meant what I said." He even attended the 1924 state convention and introduced a resolution to change the party organization, which lost by a close vote. Yet he refused to come to the platform or make a speech for his proposal. Further, leaving the hall early, he did not participate in the convention after the vote. Predictably, Butler did not have a prominent role in the ensuing campaign, although he attended the national GOP convention as a member of the North Carolina Coolidge delegation and participated in a controversy over the Republican platform that would have put the party, symbolically, in favor of black suffrage in the South. Butler met with members of the platform committee and helped squelch a plank favored by black delegates. He thought the proposal would allow southern Democrats to raise white fears. After the convention Butler contemplated campaigning in the Midwest to help counter Robert La Follette's independent run for president, but it is doubtful that he did. Instead, he remarked privately that La Follette's principles resembled those of William Jennings Bryan. The 1924 election did not drastically change GOP prospects in North Carolina, as Calvin Coolidge won 40 percent of the vote, and Republican representation in the assembly rose from twelve to twenty-three. One of the new state house members was Edward F. Butler, Marion's son.[20]

Following the 1924 contest it became apparent that Butler's interest in politics had become a hobby, a parody of his years as a Populist and progressive. Despite Bramham's threats, and perhaps encouraged by a generational shift, Butler renewed his meaningless attack on the GOP's organization. Now the sons of the leading men of the 1890–1920 era competed for positions held by their fathers, and Butler implored them to rise up and overthrow the Bramham "machine." Butler's attack seemed an absurd remnant of an earlier era. He tried to evoke the memory of Populism and Roosevelt by declaring that "the Great Battle of Armageddon Is On," describing his effort as a "fight to redeem our party from the blighting clutches of the pie-counter machine." Many Republicans laughed. A satirical response came from George Flow, a Monroe lawyer, who was "dead sure that if the main-spring of [the state organization's] motives, the secret instructions, the clandestine assembling of juntas, liaisons, agreements, promises, and all of the damnable elements belonging to stratagems and treasons and conspiracies were written upon the sky in figures of fire, that the people of the State, irrespective of political affiliations, would rise up in their sovereign might and hurl to hell the whole motley crew and consign their memories to eternal infamy." Bramham was less amused. In a veiled reference to his earlier threat, he claimed Butler was not "so pure or virtuous as they claim, politically or otherwise."[21]

Unfazed, Butler made a mark on the 1926 campaign. At the state convention he held a caucus attended by three hundred persons that featured a speech by Marion Butler Jr., a Winston-Salem attorney. The next day, however, delegates met the senior Butler's reorganization plan with loud hisses. Nonetheless, they approved an alternate system under which four members of the party executive committee were elected from each congressional district. Butler and his forces endorsed the new state chairman, Brownlow Jackson of Hendersonville. The convention nominated several candidates supported by Butler, including his brother George for state chief justice. During the election he pleaded with Jackson to engage in grassroots organizing and to get Republican women to the polls. He contributed to Republican newspapers, typically arguing for a new election law. He held a dinner for North Carolina's candidates in Washington, which featured the national GOP chairman. Butler had been interested in appealing to women since 1920, and he complained loudly when women did not receive equal voting membership on the executive committee. Moreover, local organizing by women, Butler thought, was necessary for success. In November, however, the party took the usual losses, suffering a decline from twenty-three to nineteen seats in the legislature.[22]

The 1928 election further confirmed Butler's ideological and strategic isolation, signaling that the real potential of North Carolina Republicanism lay in reaction, not reform. The presidential race focused on the personal characteristics of the Democratic nominee, Governor Alfred E. Smith of New York. The Catholic Smith, who opposed Prohibition and resided in New York City, symbolized evil to many Tar Heel Democrats, including Senator

Furnifold Simmons. Republicans recognized the possibilities of the Catholic and Prohibition issues as early as 1927, when one told Butler, "All we have to do [to win] is to let the Democrats handle the Catholic–Ku Klux fight, and we go along about our own business and get out the Republican vote of the state." Despite this negative environment, Butler faithfully supported the Republican candidate, Herbert Hoover, the engineer, former progressive, and businessman who served Harding and Coolidge as secretary of commerce. He wrote letters claiming Hoover would promote prosperity, help the farmer, and break up the Democratic South. He sent pro-Hoover essays to newspapers, solicited the national party for funds for North Carolina, and again encouraged party leaders to register women. In an interview with the *New York Times*, he argued that the central problem in North Carolina was the need to lessen the tax burden on land, an old Alliance issue. Yet Butler's economic appeal was out of step with other opponents of Al Smith. The state GOP organization treated him as an undesirable. One of Hoover's workers in North Carolina was told, "Whenever his name is mentioned down here one thinks immediately 'Butler-Bonds-Nigger Domination.' He made himself very unpopular years ago in demanding redemption of the carpetbagger bonds."[23]

Ironically, the Smith furor produced Republican success, suggesting the persistent weakness of economic arguments in North Carolina politics. Hoover, in fact, was the only Republican to win North Carolina's electoral votes between 1868 and 1968. Voters also elected Charles Jonas and George Pritchard, Jeter's son, to Congress, and Republicans captured forty-seven seats in the legislature, the most since 1897. The margin of success, however, came from anti-Catholic Democrats. As a result, Republican voters included descendants of Civil War Unionists, piedmont manufacturers and professionals, Roosevelt Progressives, former Populists, and Furnifold Simmons's bigots. This combination agreed only about its dislike for Smith and did not survive the election. Butler, still looking for realignment on economic issues, concluded that the campaign had not been properly conducted and that an opportunity for permanent growth had been lost.[24]

Butler participated in his last political battles in the context of the Great Depression, a cataclysm that crushed the GOP while pointing the way to its rebirth. In 1930 he focused on supporting his brother George in the Republican Senate primary and saving the nomination of John J. Parker to the United States Supreme Court. In the Senate primary, Butler pled with western Republicans to vote for his brother and against George Pritchard. Apparently this refreshed unpleasant memories of the 1897 Butler-Pritchard contest; Pritchard won easily. In the general election, his party suffered an unmitigated disaster, as economic conditions cost it 20 percent of its members and reduced its representation in the legislature to an all-time low of seven. The defeat of John Parker's nomination to the Supreme Court underscored the collapse. Butler considered the federal appeals court judge from Charlotte and former Republican candidate for governor an able asset. When Hoover sent Parker's name to the Senate in March 1930, Butler wrote several senators expressing his confidence in Parker. The most dramatic attack on the nomination came from the National Association for the Advancement of Colored People (NAACP), which focused on Parker's apparent approval of black disfranchisement in the 1920 race for governor. Butler told senators that Parker's remarks had to be understood in the context of decades-long Democratic attempts to manipulate white prejudice. According to Butler, Parker actually tried to eschew racial politics. Seeking credibility, he assured Senator George Norris that he had "always been a pronounced advocate for equal justice to the colored race, and that they have always looked upon me as a staunch and fearless friend," particularly for his opposition to disfranchisement in 1900. Butler's defense of Parker demonstrated his differences with other North Carolina Republicans, who sneeringly identified Parker's enemies as "labor unions, negroes, and communists." Butler, in contrast, tried to stress what he viewed as the irony of the NAACP's complaint, which condemned Parker for trying to direct attention away from Democrats' obsession with white supremacy. Yet Butler also seemed unsympathetic to the fact that by 1930 many African Americans would not accept exclusion as an alternative to race-baiting. The Senate defeated Parker's bid in a close vote.[25]

Evidence suggests that Butler initially failed to perceive the political effects of the depression. Contemplating the 1932 contest, he optimistically told his brother George that there was "every indication that [economic] conditions will soon begin to improve. Even if the mills did not open on full time until a week before the election, it would mean the certain election of Hoover." Further, he seemed to have little interest in the North Carolina party, choosing to skip the state convention. He was more active in the presidential race, serving as a delegate to the national convention, which nominated Hoover, and giving about a dozen speeches for Hoover in Missouri, Tennessee, Maryland, and Kentucky. Butler told his listeners that the administration could not be blamed for the depression and that the president was doing everything he could. He praised Hoover's "great reconstruction program," including "self-liquidating" public works projects and Home Loan Banks. As for Franklin D. Roosevelt (FDR), the Democratic candidate, Butler complained he was "simply making promises in glittering generalities for better times in the future." Butler's defense of Hoover, like most of his politics after 1912, reflected Republican partisanship, yet it was not unrelated to Populism. He did not promote "rugged individualism" but instead talked about where the Hoover government intervened to help. Similarly, he thought FDR a "clean, cultured, liberal, forward-looking American citizen," who, as president, would benefit from Hoover's relief measures. In literature he received from the national Republican Speakers Bureau, Butler underlined those parts which supported Home Loan Banks and which criticized Roosevelt's vagueness. He left unmarked those passages which declared "sound money is based on gold" and which blamed the panic of the 1890s on the "assault on our currency system" by those who favored free silver. As always, political behavior reflected choices and complexity. In the end, the magnitude of Hoover's defeat surprised him. He believed voters, particularly the unemployed, rejected Hoover more than they endorsed Roosevelt. North Carolina's GOP practically disintegrated, as its candidate for governor won only about 28 percent of the vote.[26]

In a fine testament to Butler's dogged persistence, even after the ascension of the New Deal he participated in minor ways in the 1934 and 1936 elections. The year 1934 saw yet another self-defeating dispute over state party leadership, this time featuring Chairman James Duncan and Edward Butler, who, following literally in his father's footsteps, became the leader of a faction seeking to depose the Duncan group. The whole affair, with second-generation Duncans, Butlers, Pritchards, Moreheads, and Linneys fighting over party power, was fascinating but unrelated to earlier battles over progressivism. Still, the elder Butler, now past seventy, had not missed many political fights since his student days in Chapel Hill, and he could not resist joining the fray. At the state convention, with an old-fashioned collar, a "huge shock of bristling white hair, an over-size white Van Dyke [beard], . . . and a portentious [sic] stomach," the veteran of almost fifty years of party politics "bobbed up" and in two minutes seized the convention "by the nape of the neck." He strode to the platform, surrounded by ominous silence, and proclaimed the party could capitalize on the blunders of the New Deal. He moved that the new chairman be elected for a two-year term. Duncan agreed to step down, and William Meekins became chairman. Butler did little else after the convention, and predictably, the Republicans performed dismally at the polls.[27]

By 1936 the state party revealed its future by taking a strident anti–New Deal approach. Many Republicans thought Roosevelt's legislation pushed the nation toward fascism or communism, and this fear provided new vigor. Butler was uncomfortable with some of the New Deal and some of the Republican critique; he made only a limited appearance in the contest. At the state convention, his last, Republicans picked John Morehead's former aide, Gilliam Grissom, to run for governor and reelected William Meekins state chairman. Butler sat on the platform and made a brief speech, vaguely proposing that if the national Republicans could not win, "we ought to go out of business." On the other hand, he did not attend the national convention or campaign for Alfred M. Landon, the party's presidential nominee. The party met yet another decisive defeat in the fall. Of course, defeat in North Carolina should not have been a surprise. By the end of his political career, Butler's party had won control of the state legislature only four times in thirty-four elections—a span of almost fifty years. Moreover, all those victories occurred before 1897.[28]

Between 1912 and 1938, Butler moved to the fringes of politics. The hopeful period in which he joined and tried to shape the GOP was over by 1920. After that, it was unclear what could be accomplished. To be sure, like an addict clinging desperately to his habit, Butler participated in party activities at national and state levels year after year. He had an unending desire to engage in politics that traced at least back to his youth. Piles of letters were sent and received, and hours of meetings occupied his time. Although he made failing attempts for appointments as a director of Harding's southern campaign, secretary of agriculture, and ambassador to Mexico, during this long period he never sought elected office for himself, although going to the state legislature from Sampson County would have been easy enough. Equally important, after 1920, political action became increasingly removed from earlier demands for populist economic reform. The separation between Populist ideology and politics, which began with the splintering of the Alliance in 1891–92, expanded until the two had little connection. The process of seeking success on issues on which a majority could be constructed, begun in the 1890s, shrunk to inane intraparty battles over who would control the state Republican organization. And even when a major shift in politics occurred, in the 1930s, it came from sources and took directions that were largely displeasing to the former Populist. A most intriguing aspect of this part of Butler's political career is his persistence in the face of continued defeat. It was as if Butler simply could not stop attending conventions or speaking to crowds on behalf of Hoover or Harding, just as he had done for Weaver and Bryan many years earlier. Yet the image of Butler, at sixty-nine, standing in front of an audience and discussing farm relief on behalf of Herbert Hoover seems more consistent with than different from the image of the same man speaking as an Alliance lecturer in 1889. Both suggest not simply an obsession with political methods in an organized party but also some deeper faith that the political system was actually worth the time, that participating in and even leading was a grand thing that should not and could not be abandoned, even when others laughed and there was no possibility of public office. In the waning time of his life, a significant part of Butler's story is that the will to participate, to have one's say, lived on even after the message itself lacked political meaning. The result is simultaneously pathetic and appealing.

AFTER 1912, the distinction between Butler's politics and ideology appeared most clearly in his activities outside the party. In contrast to the political arena, where he showed loyalty to the GOP, here he was able to promote his understanding of the Populist creed without restrictions. First, before the adoption of the federal Farm Loan Act of 1916, several of his public writings focused on the need for a federal system of agricultural credit. Much as in the 1890s, he argued that the national banking system failed to provide adequate credit. He kept a close watch on the farm loan proposal in Congress, writing Representative Carter Glass of Virginia and former Populist J. H. "Cyclone" Davis, now a Democratic congressman from Texas, in support of a bill. He endorsed long-term loans at low interest as well as loans to renters interested in buying land. The bill that became law did not tackle the tenant problem, but it set up a federally backed system for farm loans.[29]

Persistent Populism also allowed Butler to criticize other "accomplishments" of the Progressive Era. Butler believed that neither Republicans nor Democrats had a real program to combat monopolies. He denounced the notion that mere regulation of natural monopolies would ever work, because monopolists would simply control the administrative agencies responsible for enforcing regulation. He particularly objected to Republican and Democratic methods of regulating railroads. This regulation tended to be "either smothered or killed by the long delay[s in enforcement], or by inefficient enforcement." He also condemned the Federal Reserve Act, passed in 1913, as "not a remedy[;] it is at best a doubtful compromise with the money trust." Instead, he thought it would be better if the government increased the amount of money in circulation by allowing farmers to capitalize their land through government-issued bonds. Further, he advocated public town markets in order to facilitate direct bargaining between producers and consumers, because individual farmers were not in a financial position to develop cooperative markets on their own. He traced these ideas to the Alliance's subtreasury plan.[30]

Butler also attempted more theoretical approaches to political economy, writing at length in the middle and late years of the 1910–19 decade about the differences between Populism and socialism. He conceded that in the 1890s he was "impressed with [the socialists'] earnest and honest sincerity of purpose for social justice as the ultimate goal," and he wanted to cooperate with them in politics to achieve this end. Still, their economic position was "fundamentally unsound." He was especially bothered by the notion of equal income. More preferable was that all persons should be "equal as [to their] natural rights, and there is social justice when the law preserves these rights unimpaired." Government should strive to create equal opportunity, not mandate equal reward: "To reach the greatest state of development, each individual must have an incentive for full mental and physical effort." The socialist system would remove incentive "and the result would be to chloroform effort, to paralyze progress, and produce a degree of social injustice beyond anything from which the race had yet suffered and escaped." He stressed the necessity of the private corporation to economic growth, believing the country would benefit from more corporations, as long as they were not monopolistic.[31]

Butler recalled that Populism specifically rejected socialism. Populism sought to destroy the grip of the "capitalistic class" with the Omaha Platform, which declared that land, currency, transportation, and the "transmission of intelligence" were natural monopolies and "should be used as public functions for the benefit of all." Further, "after these reforms had been secured, that if there were still any monopolies left, due to the existence of a natural cause, like the limited deposit of iron or coal, that then each such monopoly should also be taken charge of by the people and used for the good of all." Butler believed the average laborer rejected socialism because he did not "want to remove the capitalist from his back in order that his place may be taken by the worthless drones at the other end of society" who failed to use their talents as producers.[32]

Perhaps because these Populist-based arguments had limited political relevance, Butler became interested in the work of organizations other than political parties. In 1917 he appeared before the feeble remains of the Tar Heel Farmers' Alliance, making several speeches. At this time he wrote A. C. Townley, leader of the North Dakota Non-Partisan League, a group devoted to state-owned warehouses and banks, and endorsed "the platform you present, as I understand it." He pondered a Non-Partisan League in North Carolina, telling Townley that the largely Republican organization would succeed in a state "ripe for revolt against the Democratic party." He also corresponded with the National Public Ownership League, a quasi-socialist organization.[33]

Persistent Populism also influenced Butler's opposition to President Woodrow Wilson's foreign policy. Before American entry into the First World War, Butler criticized what he perceived as the administration's unequal treatment of Germany and Great Britain, arguing that Britain ignored the United States' right of free trade. He sympathized with Wilson's fight against German submarines, but he complained about the harm caused to farmers, particularly cotton growers, by the president's failure to demand a free flow of noncontraband materials. This did not mean Butler opposed preparation for the war or, once the United States joined the effort, American triumph. Still, he concluded the conflict did not present a just cause because its European victors would use the outcome to grab land. Butler also attacked war revenue and the threat to civil liberties. Writing Senators Hiram Johnson and Robert La Follette that "the rich munitions factories and other 'War Shylocks' have escaped their burden," he demanded that the rich pay more of the costs. He was also unhappy about the administration's actions toward dissenters. He attacked the Espionage Act, which limited free speech, and thought the police breakup of a peace meeting in New York particularly ironic, because it seemed "a strange thing that people should be arrested . . . for attending a meeting where Peace, Democracy, and Liberty were the slogans." Butler's views caused tensions with his law partner, Josiah Vale, who complained that "there has been a tendency on your part towards a [N]on-[P]artisan campaign in North Carolina, with a view of drifting towards, or gathering in the socialists."[34]

Although Butler invested considerable time in politics and political writing, he also had to earn a living. He maintained his Washington law practice, which consisted primarily of claims against the government and lobbying for legislation. He also continued to develop Mount Pleasant, in Sampson County, where he and his family spent summers. In an important sense the farm represented a practical expression of the Alliance ideal. At Mount Pleasant he was not a lawyer or politician but a bona fide farmer. He grew cotton, tobacco, and corn; planted nut trees; and oversaw the production of fruits, vegetables, and livestock. Rural progressivism prevailed: Before 1920 a generator produced electric power for the home; the family hired a full-time superintendent fresh from the A & M College in Raleigh; and Butler bought perhaps the first Ford tractor ever sold in the state.[35]

For most of the year, however, Butler and his family lived in a house at 2200 R Street in northwest Washington. He and Florence participated in many community activities, and all five of their children went to school in the capital. Here also the spirit of reform prevailed. Drawing on his long-standing support for education, Butler was interested in the district's public school system, and in 1916 he testified before a congressional committee that the duties of the district school board should not be transferred to the city's Board of Commissioners because it would politicize the schools. He attended St. Thomas Episcopal Church and taught Sunday school. Butler believed his church should concern itself with social uplift, sponsor city missions, and promote "civic righteousness." Suggesting his sense that religion and reform politics mixed, one of his Sunday school lessons in 1915 asked, What "five verses of the Old Testament have recently been quoted by President Wilson and Ex-President Roosevelt to support their position on 'preparedness' "?[36]

Butler participated in several important efforts to improve cooperative agricultural marketing. Driven by the collapse in cotton prices in 1920, the American Cotton Association spearheaded a marketing movement; Butler was present at the group's founding. He also lobbied for the federal Capper-Volstead Act of 1922, which exempted agricultural cooperatives from the antitrust laws. He contributed to cotton and tobacco cooperative efforts in North Carolina, including the construction of a cooperative warehouse in Sampson County, where he encouraged farmers to sign contracts reducing acreage and pledging their crops to the co-op. His reasons for supporting cooperation derived from the Alliance. In an article about the Tobacco Growers' Cooperative Marketing Association, Butler argued that migration from farms and tenancy resulted from poverty caused by farmers' lack of control over marketing. The only solution was cooperative action, which dispensed with intermediaries and allowed farmers to set their own prices. This was a position he had articulated for more than thirty years.[37]

In the early 1920s Butler led another ambitious scheme to benefit farmers. He and Frederick E. Engstrum, an engineer and head of the Newport Shipbuilding Company, made a lease and construction bid for the federally owned Muscle Shoals water power project in Alabama. The government built nitrate plants for wartime explosives at the site; in 1921 it completed most of the work on a large dam on the Tennessee River to provide electricity for the plants. Objecting to the idea of a new and large government operation in peacetime, President Harding proposed to lease the property to private interests. The most famous offer came from Henry Ford, but Butler and Engstrum made a determined effort to defeat the automobile maker. The Butler-Engstrum proposal was to lease the property for fifty years, to increase nitrate production, to sell the nitrate as fertilizer at a price set by the government, and to sell the surplus electricity for profit.[38]

Although the plan had plenty of room for personal gain, Butler envisioned it as a boon to American farmers. He told a congressional committee that "we propose to carry out a great public purpose to result in a great public good, and we guarantee the Government a definite rental for the lease, that rental to increase as more power is developed." If Congress did not think the plan would most efficiently carry out the government's original aim in building the plant, to produce nitrates, then it should run the project itself. Butler was deeply attached to the idea. He told a cooperative leader that he did "not want any better monument for myself than to be able to develop . . . Muscle Shoals so as to help make agriculture more profitable." To better their chances, Butler and Engstrum secured the services of General George Goethals, the builder of the Panama Canal. Butler also publicized the project to agricultural publishers throughout the nation. Although some elements in Congress liked the farming emphasis, it was rejected. The status of the property, which remained in government hands, was not finally decided until the 1930s, long after Butler's interest in it had ended.[39]

In the late 1920s and early 1930s Butler wrote extensively about the persistent farm depression. Once again he turned to the Alliance and Populism for guidance. In 1928 he opposed the federal McNary-Haugen Bill and a separate "export debentures plan" endorsed by the Grange. McNary-Haugen and the debenture plan sought to raise crop prices by granting federal protections to compensate farmers for lower overseas prices. Butler disagreed with them partly because he thought they would increase production when it did not need to be increased and partly because he had more faith in the market and the ability of an adequate money supply and cooperatives to control production, lower costs, and generate fair prices. For these reasons he supported Hoover's Agricultural Marketing Act. The 1929 law created the Federal Farm Board and gave it $500 million to lend to cooperatives to help control production and prices. Butler argued that the board would eliminate the greedy middleman, return profit to the farmer, and benefit the consumer. By 1931, however, with huge cotton surpluses in warehouses, below-cost prices, and board losses of more than $100 million, it was obvious that this version of government-sponsored cooperation did not work. In response, Butler unsuccessfully asked the chairman of the Farm Board to support legislation based on the Alliance's subtreasury idea. He wanted the government to pay farmers eighty to ninety cents per dollar of the market value of their crops and then sell the staples in equal monthly installments, with the average price going to the farmer.[40]

After FDR's election in 1932, Butler applied a Populist critique to the New Deal. Specifically, he objected to its haphazard quality as well as the unwarranted manner in which government acted in the market. Although he did not participate in rejuvenated demands for silver money, his criticisms had nothing to do with opposition to government action and a lot to do with Populism. In late 1933 he praised Senator William E. Borah for expounding a quantity theory of money. Butler thought it "heartening and inspiring to have a man [as prominent as Borah] state the truth about money, the most vital instrument of commerce." Butler's age showed when he added, "From the beginning the unorganized millions of wealth-producers have been continuously robbed by the few organized Shylocks and gambling money changers who were described by Theodore Roosevelt as the 'Malefactors of Great Wealth.'" He asked Borah to rally the "progressive congressmen" and enact a law that would guarantee the dollar equal value over time. Perhaps reflecting on his career, he remarked that although many persons knew the true "nature and function of money, . . . they have wasted their time and efforts by crying aloud in the wilderness."[41]

The best demonstration of Butler's application of Populism to the depression was his 1933 testimony to the Senate and House committees considering the National Industrial Recovery Act. Butler showed up without invitation as a public witness and was given five minutes by the busy Senate committee. As in the 1890s, however, he ignored impatient senators from the older parties and made a lengthy presentation. He focused on the portion of the bill that provided $3.3 billion for public works. Although impressed with its intent, he thought the amount and the restrictions on the money's use were inappropriate. He proposed that the appropriation be at least $5 billion, a figure endorsed by the American Federation of Labor, or better yet, "Congress should not limit the sum to be used by the President." He also thought expenditures should not be limited to "public business and for public purposes" but that the president should be given "unlimited discretion" to distribute the money to "any self-liquidating [private] project or business which will increase employment, which will reasonably produce revenue, and which shall be deemed to be primarily and essentially for the improvement of public interests and for public benefit." This was the subtreasury plan with a vengeance.[42]

Butler also criticized the Reconstruction Finance Corporation (RFC), Hoover's loan program for business. The government wasted RFC money on "a few big businesses at the top." These companies were "so frightfully over-capitalized and . . . have been so miserably managed that they can never pay dividends on their watered stock except by charging an oppressive and ru-inous rate upon the millions of people who need and deserve better service at less cost." The new legislation, by contrast, should reach smaller enter-prises, where a larger volume of the money would be put into circulation. It would be a mistake not "to stimulate existing business, [and] vitalize the idle brains and labor everywhere, which are waiting and anxious to start needed new business."[43]

Several years later Butler criticized Roosevelt's Agricultural Adjustment Administration Acts. In particular, the former Allianceman opposed paying farmers not to produce. This was a "false and ruinous policy of 'scarcity and destruction' under which vast sums of money have been borrowed at the ex-pense of the taxpayers with which to pay a bonus to those who will agree to produce less." It flew directly in the face of the Alliance creed, which denied that farmers' losses were due to overproduction. Instead, Populist remedies, including fairer marketing conditions, generated by freight rate reductions, cooperatives, and currency reform, would create farm profits by reducing costs and raising prices. This could be accomplished if the government would lend "its credit to our producers at a very low interest rate. Such a pol-icy will never be a burden of one dollar to the taxpayer, because the money so loaned will be a lien on the products produced and this will be self-liquidated each year."[44]

In the end, Butler saw relief from the depressions of the 1890s and the 1930s in similar terms. Recovery depended on sound currency policy, fair taxation, and use of spending power to bind producers to the government through credit. Loans would flush money into the economy and stimulate consumption so as to produce higher prices and a steady demand for goods. The Populist strategy discouraged government in competitive business, Washington superagencies, and intrusive taxation. Nonetheless, it assumed government had a responsibility to bring the nation out of a depression. Butler's Populist remedy would free competitive energies through public ownership of natural monopolies and government credit. It would save the market, private industry, and the small landowning farmer. In the 1930s, Populism allowed Butler to promote revolutionary federal loans while also demanding an end to the New Deal's "crazy experiments, to stop wild spend-ing, to lower the cost of living, and to reduce taxes."[45]

Of course, the critique seemed out of place in an era that offered a choice between bureaucratic liberals and antigovernment conservatives. This was a larger consequence of the failure of Populism. Charles Jonas, Butler's most frequent political correspondent in the mid-1930s and a Republican progressive, perceived the dilemma. An opponent of the New Deal, Jonas also regretted the response of the Republican Party. He told Butler the GOP should rededicate itself to the "humanitarian purposes that induced Lincoln and his associates to form the party." He complained that voters thought the Republican leadership "not only reactionary but wholly materialistic and completely out of tune with twentieth century conditions and progress." The party should convince the public that it was "not tied fast to the DuPonts, the Liberty League and every other selfish interest in the country." However, more than thirty years after the Democrats' white supremacy campaigns, race complicated the analysis. Suggesting another path to Republican success, Jonas regretted his party's failure to treat its white southern members with respect because of a desire to manipulate black delegates to national conventions. According to Jonas, Republicans must attract white southerners if they were to survive against the "New Deal party."[46]

Butler revealed his consistent ideology more subtly in an increased concern about history. In 1929, after he stopped going to Sampson County for extended visits, he donated a large amount of newspapers, pamphlets, and other personal material to the newly constructed University of North Carolina Library in Chapel Hill. It is possible that he was motivated by a comment from his nephew, Algernon, who later became a federal judge. While a student at Duke University and at Chapel Hill in the mid-1920s, the younger Butler complained that his history professors taught a "Negro domination" interpretation of the 1890s. In addition, a new generation of historians asked Butler to recount his Populist experience. C. Vann Woodward, William A. Mabry, and William DuBose Sheldon, all of whom were working on doctoral dissertations, contacted him for information about Populism.[47]

He also developed a plan, undertaken in 1932 and 1933, to write a history of the People's Party. He prepared a reading list, which included standard scholarly works, such as Frank McVey's *Populist Movement*; writings of Solon Buck; J. D. Barnhart's *History of the Nebraska Farmer's Alliance and People's Party*; John Hicks's new history of Populism; Simeon DeLapp's Trinity College bachelor's thesis, "The Populist Party in North Carolina"; and J. G. de-Roulhac Hamilton's *North Carolina since 1860*. Butler's notes on Hicks and Hamilton indicate great pride in Populism. He did not focus on politics but stressed the importance of Alliance lecturers and the Alliance press, the buy-

Survivors of the Class of 1885, fifty years later. Marion Butler is second
from the right. (Courtesy of the North Carolina Collection,
University of North Carolina at Chapel Hill)

ing and selling of cooperatives, the relationship between the lack of federally sponsored credit and the failure of the cooperatives, the connection between private cooperative failure and the demand for railroad regulation,
the subtreasury, government ownership of railroads, and the need for elas-
tic, not metal-based, currency, which would respond to business needs and
be backed by the government's goodwill. As for state matters, he cited
Hamilton's discussion of the party's demands for better public education.
Butler the historian summarized the causes of the Alliance as "railroad discrimination and oppression, . . . high rates of interest, the extortions of the
middle men[,] and . . . the scarcity of money and credit."[48]

The contrast between Butler's political activities and his activities outside
the political arena were stark. In politics, although scorned by most of his
fellow North Carolina Republicans, he persisted in hopeless squabbles as
progressivism vanished and was replaced by Harding, Hoover, and reaction
against the New Deal. Outside politics, on the other hand, he condemned
administration policy during World War I, ran a model farm, participated in
progressive causes in his home and church, applauded the Non-Partisan
League, promoted the expansion of government financing of agriculture,

participated in the strengthening of agricultural cooperatives, supported an unlimited government loan program for business and agriculture during the depression, and wrote about Populism, even reviewing university scholarship on the topic and planning a book that would stress the economic correctness of the Alliance and the People's Party. Although the behavior might appear schizophrenic, it was merely an extreme application of the dilemma that had always characterized Butler's political life: How can one engage in politics and at the same time promote one's (personal and unpopular) beliefs? Butler had never accepted the part of the lonely, alienated dissenter. He enjoyed the political game too much. At the same time, however, he was unwilling to admit Populism was dead because he was so sure of its enduring value. Perhaps if he just kept talking and writing about it, and perhaps if he promoted it, it might live on. Nothing demonstrates this perspective on private and public duty better than the seventy-year-old "has-been" busying himself with scholarship on Populism or lecturing fresh-faced New Dealers about massive government loans.

BUTLER NEVER FINISHED the book, preferring to spend his last years in part-time law practice and political dabbling. Death did not come suddenly. In late 1937 he entered a sanatorium in suburban Takoma Park, Maryland, for debilitating kidney disease. After several months of ineffective treatment, he died on 3 June 1938, two weeks after his seventy-fifth birthday. The death, not surprisingly, did not produce an outpouring of public grief. Although Florence received many condolences from Washington friends, including members of Congress, Butler died an old man after a long illness. The only Republicans of statewide importance who attended his funeral were, appropriately, Charles and Harvey Jonas, H. F. Seawell, and Jake Newell, the scant remains of Populism and progressive Republicanism. After the Episcopal rites, a reading of Tennyson's "Crossing the Bar," and a rendition of "Rock of Ages," the body was laid to rest.[49]

Reports of Butler's death reflected the political chasm that separated the 1930s from the 1890s. There was no sense of the opportunities that had been lost or the purpose of the battles Butler waged. Obituaries appeared in all the major newspapers in North Carolina and Washington and in the *New York Times*. The Washington and New York notices were bland statements issued by the family that mentioned the easily understood highlights of his legislative career: RFD, postal savings banks, support for public schools, and the 6 percent interest law. The North Carolina press offered equally incomplete, but more politically charged, remarks. The *Union Republican* used the opportunity to render a contemporary attack on the opposition. Butler deserved credit because he earned the hatred of Democrats, who "stole the state" in 1898 and enacted the "infamous election law." Another modern perspective appeared in the *News and Observer*. Still owned by Josephus Daniels, it described Butler as a "stormy petrel" and vaguely explained his defeat in the nineties as the result of "political bitterness." Although it mentioned his support for public education, ideas were deemphasized; Butler appeared as a prominent politician. The *Greensboro Daily News*, which Butler helped establish in 1905, tried to be analytic. It published an editorial by William Bost, the *News*'s Democratic Raleigh reporter. Bost surmised that the "Butler biography can be easily written. He was the creature of calamity. He varied his style none whatsoever, but the country changed its own." Bost correctly perceived a difference between the 1890s and 1930s, yet he lacked an understanding of its significance. To him, change was a matter of "style."[50]

Wholly missing from his or any other death notice was Butler's faith in the Populists' Omaha Platform. As a result, no one saw that its contents were the substantive thread that bound together his career as an Alliance Democrat, Populist, and Republican. Contemporaries did not perceive that Butler's continuing political failure, as opposed to his ideological consistency, reflected the rejection of the Populist ideal and demonstrated the immense institutional barriers to the change it favored. Obviously, Butler's public loyalty to the Republican Party after 1912 and his bizarre insistence on futile political activity in the 1920s and 1930s contributed to the confusion. It was not easy, even for him, to put his political support for candidates as different as Tom Watson, Theodore Roosevelt, Warren Harding, and Herbert Hoover in a coherent package. Yet during his last decades Butler faithfully represented the last of a generation of politicians who believed politics should focus on economic arguments to small producers, who in turn should assert their political supremacy and demand that the government advance their goals without substituting elite bureaucracies for elected representatives. Butler and his followers did not believe in cultural politics or balancing the concerns of interest groups. Their democracy was directed to producers and their economic rights. If the producer received financial justice, government performed its purpose. The readers of Butler's obituaries, living in a world where landowning small producers had been refashioned as wage-earning consumers, where successful Left politics had come to mean bureaucratic agencies, and where conservatism was an apology for private wealth and power, could not comprehend Butler. American Populism died with him.

NOTES

Abbreviations

BP	Marion Butler Papers, Southern Historical Collection, Wilson Library, University of North Carolina, Chapel Hill, N.C.
Duke	Manuscript Department, Perkins Library, Duke University, Durham, N.C.
ECU	Manuscript Collection, J. Y. Joyner Library, East Carolina University, Greenville, N.C.
LC	Manuscript Division, Library of Congress, Washington, D.C.
MB	Marion Butler
MHS	Minnesota Historical Society, St. Paul, Minn.
NCC	North Carolina Collection, Wilson Library, University of North Carolina, Chapel Hill, N.C.
NCDAH	North Carolina Division of Archives and History, Raleigh, N.C.
OHS	Ohio Historical Society, Columbus, Ohio
SHC	Southern Historical Collection, Wilson Library, University of North Carolina, Chapel Hill, N.C.
SHSW	State Historical Society of Wisconsin, Madison, Wis.
UA	University Archives, Wilson Library, University of North Carolina, Chapel Hill, N.C.

Introduction

1. My own writings about Butler include a three-part article, "The Making of a Populist: Marion Butler, 1863–1895," published in 1985 in the *North Carolina Historical Review*, and "Marion Butler and the Populist Ideal, 1863–1938," a Ph.D. dissertation completed at the University of Wisconsin in 1990. In the 1980s and 1990s there were several short sketches of Butler in print, including one cowritten by Butler and James B. Lloyd in Samuel A. Ashe et al., eds., *Biographical History of North Carolina*. Others, by Theodore Saloutos and Robert Durden, had been published in Allen Johnson et al., eds., *Dictionary of American Biography*, and William S. Powell, ed., *Dictionary of North Carolina Biography*, respectively. The *National Cyclopedia of American Biography*, *Who Was Who in America*, and the *Biographical Directory of the American Congress* also contained brief biographies.

By 2002 specific studies of North Carolina Populism had undergone significant development, but most provided limited information about Butler. The original work, by Sim DeLapp, a future ally of Senator Jesse Helms, is a 1922 Trinity College (later Duke University) undergraduate thesis that concentrates on the potential for opposition to Democrats. Florence Emeline Smith's 1929 dissertation, despite an interview with Butler, yields only a little more insight. In his 1971 dissertation, "New South Populism: North Carolina, 1884–1900," Phillip R. Muller makes an interesting point about the relationship between agrarians and New South ideology but does not discern changes in the Alliance after 1890 or accurately portray Butler's development. After my dissertation about Butler, three other dissertations addressed North Carolina Populism. First, Craig Thurtell's 1998 "The Fusion Insurgency in North Carolina," although not just about Populism, contains valuable information about the stock law debate and the activities of African Americans before 1897. In my opinion, however, it does not provide much new information about Butler. James M. Beeby's solid 1999 dissertation, "Revolt of the Tar Heelers: A Socio-Political History of the North Carolina Populist Party, 1892–1901," contains a wealth of useful information and insight about the party, particularly in a chapter using election contest testimony from 1894. This portion of the dissertation has been published separately as "'Equal Rights to All and Special Privileges to None': Grass-Roots Populism in North Carolina" in the *North Carolina Historical Review*. Beeby, however, adds little to what was already written about Butler, partly because he, understandably, does not address national Populist politics in any detail. In his dissertation, "Righteous Indignation: Religion and Populism in North Carolina, 1886–1906" (2000), Joseph W. Creech Jr. uncovers a huge amount of information about the religious ideas of Alliance members and Populists, using such previously untapped sources as religious publications and church records, mostly for the years before 1892. Yet he does not address Butler's career in a novel manner, at least as already described in my dissertation or those of Beeby or Thurtell. Suggestive of the point is Creech's claim that Lawrence Goodwyn "is notably sympathetic to Marion Butler, casting him as being pure in motive but slight in political savvy and experience" (55 n. 43).

There have also been a number of important published and unpublished studies on North Carolina politics in the Populist era. They include Helen G. Edmonds's *The Negro and Fusion Politics in North Carolina* (1951); Eric Anderson's *Race and Politics in North Carolina, 1872–1901: The Black Second* (1981); Jeffrey J. Crow and Robert F. Durden's *Maverick Republican in the Old North State: A Political Biography of Daniel L. Russell* (1977); Dwight B. Billings's *Planters and the Making of a "New South": Class, Politics, and Development in North Carolina, 1865–1900* (1979); Paul D. Escott's *Many Excellent People: Power and Privilege in North Carolina, 1850–1900* (1985); Glenda E. Gilmore's *Gender and Jim Crow: Women and the Politics of White Supremacy in North Carolina, 1896–1920* (1996); John H. Haley's *Charles N. Hunter and Race Relations in North Carolina* (1987); J. G. deRoulhac Hamilton's *North Carolina since 1860* (1919); James L. Leloudis's *Schooling the New South: Pedagogy, Self, and Society in North Carolina, 1880–1920* (1996); Frenise Logan's *The Negro in North Carolina, 1876–1894* (1964); William Mabry's *The Negro in North Carolina Politics since Reconstruction* (1940); Stuart Noblin's *Leonidas La Fayette Polk: Agrarian Crusader* (1949); Lala Carr Steelman's *The North Carolina Farmers' Alliance: A Political History, 1887–1893* (1985); Joseph F. Steelman's dissertation, "The Progressive Era in North Carolina, 1884–1917" (1955); and

Alan B. Bromberg's dissertation, "'Pure Democracy and White Supremacy': The Redeemer Period in North Carolina, 1876–1894" (1977). Although the volume and range of these studies suggest the maturity of the field and I have benefited from each, few of them, except the works by Lala Steelman, Crow and Durden, Bromberg, and Joseph Steelman, illuminate much about Butler's life. None of them, moreover, focus on Butler's ideology or the relationship between his ideology and political strategy during the 1890s or later.

Historians of the national Alliance movement and Populism generally have treated Butler in the context of his activities in the 1896 presidential election, leaving out his career before and after that time. This is as true of Robert F. Durden's *The Climax of Populism: The Election of 1896* (1965) as it is of Lawrence Goodwyn's *Democratic Promise: The Populist Moment in America* (1976), C. Vann Woodward's *Tom Watson: Agrarian Rebel* (1938) and *Origins of the New South, 1877–1913* (1951), and Robert McMath's *American Populism: A Social History, 1877–1898* (1993). Other studies of particular use to me in studying Butler include Carl Degler, *The Other South* (1974); Paul W. Glad, *McKinley, Bryan, and the People* (1964); Gretchen Ritter, *Goldbugs and Greenbacks: The Antimonopoly Tradition and the Politics of Finance in America, 1865–1896* (1997); Stanley Jones, *The Presidential Election of 1896* (1964); Theodore Mitchell, *Political Education in the Southern Farmers' Alliance, 1887–1900* (1987); Jeffrey Ostler, *Prairie Populism: The Fate of Agrarian Radicalism in Kansas, Nebraska, and Iowa, 1880–1892* (1993); Bruce Palmer, *"Man over Money": The Southern Populist Critique of American Capitalism* (1980); Steven Hahn, *The Roots of Southern Populism: Yeoman Farmers and the Transformation of the Georgia Upcountry, 1850–1890* (1983); Shawn Kantor, *Politics and Property Rights: The Closing of the Open Range in the Postbellum South* (1998); Barton C. Shaw, *The Wool-Hat Boys: Georgia's Populist Party* (1984); Gene Clanton, *Congressional Populism and the Crisis of the 1890s* (1998); and Peter Argersinger, *The Limits of Agrarian Radicalism: Western Populism and American Politics* (1995). Where most pertinent, I address the wide-ranging ideas and disagreements in these books about Populism and Butler elsewhere in this introduction and throughout the text.

Two books by Norman Pollack deserve special note: *The Just Polity: Populism, Law, and Human Welfare* (1987) and *The Humane Economy: Populism, Capitalism, and Democracy* (1990). Both are important studies of Populist political and economic ideas. Pollack takes a biographical approach, focusing on a small group of leading Populists. Butler is not among those given greatest attention, but Pollack has some interesting things to say about him. He indicates that he prepared a lengthy study of Butler's Populist years in the 1960s, largely because it was necessary as part of a larger project in evaluating Populism to put focused effort into one person's experience (*Just Polity*, 14–15). He briefly mentions Butler's gradual transformation and education in Alliance and Populist ideas and the exercise of those beliefs in public office (350–51 nn. 25, 26). Therefore, he states, Butler "merits a careful treatment in his own right, beyond the disputes of historians, as a disciplined theorist and political strategist" (350 n. 25). I agree and have tried, apart from this introduction, to limit historiographical debates and let Butler's story develop outside those limitations.

2. Goodwyn, *Democratic Promise*, 442–45. The perspective seems to hold. In a 1999 article in the *Journal of American History* that restates several myths about Populism,

Mark Voss-Hubbard writes: "Careful studies of the Farmers' Alliance and People's party, for example, have shown the stance of leaders figured crucially in the movement's history. The conservatism of leaders in North Carolina and Alabama—men such as Marion Butler and Reuben F. Kolb—shaped the free-silver, pro—William Jennings Bryan cast of those states' Populist movements. By the same token the radicalism and independence of men such as Charles Macune and Tom Watson invigorated 'mid-road' Populism in Texas and Georgia" (144). As discussed below, despite the "careful studies," Butler was not a conservative, North Carolina's Populist movement was not characterized by a silver cast, Tom Watson supported William Jennings Bryan and was more conservative than Butler, Charles Macune did not last even one election as a Populist, and many Texas "mid-roaders" supported fusion with William McKinley.

3. Woodward, *Tom Watson*, 288, 315–18, 327–29; Woodward, *Origins of the New South*, 275–76, 282, 287–88.

4. Durden, *Climax of Populism*.

5. McMath, *American Populism*, 197; Palmer, "Harry Tracy," ‹http://www.tsha.utexas.edu/handbook/online›.

6. Goodwyn, *Democratic Promise*, 558–59.

7. *Wadesboro Plow Boy*, 13 Nov. 1895.

8. Woodward, *Origins of the New South*, 282; *Caucasian*, 20 June 1895; *Progressive Farmer*, 18, 25 June 1895; *Clinton Sampson Democrat*, 20 June 1895; *Charlotte Daily Observer*, 13, 14 June 1895. Goodwyn made the same omissions; see *Democratic Promise*, 440.

9. Peter Argersinger is one of Populism's outstanding historians and has done innovative and excellent work on the politics of the era. Unfortunately, his 1999 short biography of Marion Butler in Garraty and Carnes, *American National Biography* (4:99–100), reflects the kind of true-and-false Populist dichotomy that continues to limit Populist history. Inexplicably, Argersinger spends more time talking about Butler's career as a Republican and a lawyer than as an Allianceman and Populist senator. The sketch contains several misleading or inaccurate statements, such as that Butler "narrowed his views in an attempt to maintain his political relevance" as a Republican (Butler necessarily changed his strategy, but he did not change his belief that Populist principles should be enacted into law) and that after 1900 he was "specializing" as a lawyer for "corporations seeking federal contracts" (Butler was more often involved in lawsuits, occasionally on behalf of Native Americans, against the government). More important are the omissions. At no point does Argersinger mention Butler's Alliance education or his lifelong admiration for the Omaha Platform. Considering that Butler was president of the national Alliance and the only Populist United States senator from the South, those high-level attachments deserve some explanation. Argersinger also does not address racism and its impact on Butler's ideas or political career. To omit, even in a very brief sketch, that Butler supported voting rights for blacks in North Carolina in 1900, a decision that helped destroy his political career, is to misjudge both Butler and the context of southern Populist politics. Instead, Argersinger states that the 1899 Democratic legislature disfranchised "many of [fusion's] political voters" without making it clear that most (or any) of those vot-

ers were black or that Butler opposed the legislation. In contrast, one might compare Argersinger's glowing sketch of William Peffer in Garraty and Carnes, *American National Biography*. Perhaps I might summarize Peffer's political career as primarily that of a Democrat-hater: He joined the GOP at its founding in 1854, hesitated to leave the Republican Party in the late 1880s although its goals clearly contrasted with those of the Alliance, naturally opposed fusion with Democrats except when it seemed expedient not to do so, and returned to a Republican Party controlled by conservatives as soon as Populism fell into decline. But, then again, that might be a bit simplistic (and wrong). The point is not that all Populists were alike but that one cannot lump every Populist who supported cooperation or opposed cooperation (Butler and Peffer actually supported both kinds of strategy during their careers) into some preordained ideological category. Further, the failure to treat race when describing southern Populists or comparing them with western Populists is most problematic.

Chapter 1

1. Ashe et al., *Biographical History*, 6:477—94; Crow, "Thomas Settle Jr."; Dowd, *Vance*, 142—62; Shirley, *Zebulon Vance*, 72—85; Hamilton, *North Carolina since 1860*, 189—90; *Vance and Settle: Their Record as Public Men*, NCC.

2. Ashe et al., *Biographical History*, 8:81—82.

3. Bizzell, *Sampson County*; De Bow, *Statistical View*, 288—89; Clay, Orr, and Stuart, *North Carolina Atlas*, 15—17; Seventh Census, 1850: Sampson County, Social Statistics Schedule, NCDAH.

4. Powell, *North Carolina Gazetteer*, 110; *Clinton Independent*; Eighth Census, 1860: Sampson County, Social Statistics Schedule, NCDAH.

5. Bizzell, *Sampson County*, 67—68; *North Carolina Votes*, 88, 193.

6. Tenth Census, 1880: Sampson County, Population Schedule, 12, NCDAH; Johnson et al., *Dictionary of American Biography*, 12:78—79; Ashe et al., *Biographical History*, 8:81—90; Powell, *Dictionary of North Carolina Biography*, 1:291—92; *National Cyclopedia of American Biography*, 47:431—33; *Who Was Who in America*, 177; *Biographical Directory of the American Congress*, 639; Clay, Orr, and Stuart, *North Carolina Atlas*, 14—17; First Census, 1790: Sampson County, Population Schedule, 115; Second Census, 1800: Sampson County, Population Schedule, 525; Third Census, 1810: Sampson County, Population Schedule, 161; all in NCDAH; *Roster of the Soldiers from North Carolina*, 320—21.

7. First Census, 1790: Sampson County, Population Schedule, 115; Sixth Census, 1840: Sampson County, Population Schedule, 188; both in NCDAH; Bizzell, *Sampson County*, 334; Seventh Census, 1850: Sampson County, Free Inhabitants Schedule, 749; Seventh Census, 1850: Sampson County, Agricultural Schedule, 477; both in NCDAH.

8. Bizzell, *Sampson County*, 334; Fifth Census, 1830: Sampson County, Population Schedule, 188; Seventh Census, 1850: Sampson County, Free Inhabitants Schedule, 749; Seventh Census, 1850: Sampson County, Agricultural Schedule, 477; Seventh Census, 1850: Sampson County, Slave Schedule, 152—54; Sampson County Deeds,

Grantee Index, book 33, 448; book 34, 339; book 35, 96; Eighth Census, 1860: Sampson County, Free Inhabitants Schedule, 21, 108–10; all in NCDAH.

9. Pocahontas Butler Woodson, interview, 20, 27 Sept. 1986; *Clinton Sampson Democrat*, 24 Aug. 1895.

10. Eighth Census, 1860: Sampson County, Agricultural Schedule, 45; Eighth Census, 1860: Sampson County, Slave Schedule, 13; Works Progress Administration, Survey of pre-1914 Cemetery Records; all in NCDAH; Bizzell, *Sampson County*, 334–35.

11. Ninth Census, 1870: Sampson County, Agricultural Schedule, 1–2, NCDAH.

12. Sampson County Tax List, 1877, NCDAH; Pocahontas Butler Woodson, interview, 20, 27 Sept. 1986; MB to American Historical Society, 18 Feb. 1931, BP; Tenth Census, 1880: Sampson County, Agricultural Schedule, 6; Sampson County Tax List, 1882; both in NCDAH.

13. *History of Salemburg Baptist Church*; MB to American Historical Society, 18 Feb. 1931, BP; Wiles, "Marion Butler"; Pocahontas Butler Woodson, interview, 20, 27 Sept. 1986; Simpson, "Education in Sampson County," 26–29; U.S. Census Office, *Statistics of the Population . . . from the Original Returns of the Ninth Census*, 424, 633; *Sash and the Sabre, Dunn State's Voice*, 1 Aug. 1934; Bizzell, *Sampson County*, 96, 111; *Clinton Sampson Republic*. Butler later chose his mother's denomination and was an active church member. In the early 1890s his newspaper frequently published sermons, including those of the Reverend Thomas Dixon Jr., an Alliance supporter. See also Creech, "Righteous Indignation," 221–22, 231 n. 33, 493.

14. Bizzell, *Sampson County*, 111; *Clinton Sampson Republic; Fayetteville Observer*, 23 Dec. 1886.

15. Ashe et al., *Biographical History*, 8:82; *News and Observer*, 8 Oct. 1922, 3 June 1938. While researching this biography, I tried to collect information about Butler's personal life and personality, but usually the search was unsuccessful, largely because of his unwillingness or inability to articulate information about his family or himself during his life. Interviews with nephews, nieces, and a daughter gave only minor insights, basically confirming Butler's very formal presence and elevated remoteness even from family members. One nephew recalled being turned out of Butler's home in Washington during a hurricane; Butler expected him to hitchhike back to North Carolina despite the storm. Noticing that C. Vann Woodward had cited in his biography of Tom Watson an interview with Butler in the 1930s, I wrote him a letter, hoping to learn something about Butler's manner. Woodward promptly responded that he had destroyed the notes for the interview, but he did recall that Butler was "stuffy and uncommunicative" (C. Vann Woodward to James L. Hunt, 30 Mar. 1991, in possession of the author). The record of Butler's life retains plenty of speeches, editorials, and lawsuits but frustratingly little of his life outside public affairs. Based on my research it seems fair to conclude that there really was not very much in his life, including his marriage to Florence Faison, that did not have at least some connection to public issues and politics.

16. Bode, *Protestantism and the New South*, 20–25; Lefler and Newsome, *North Carolina*, 534–37, 542; Brabham, "Defining the American University"; Battle, *History of the University of North Carolina*, 2:214–20; Leloudis, *Schooling the New South*, 55–60;

Catalogue of the University of North Carolina at Chapel Hill, 1883–1884, 13, 16; Student Reports, 1875–85, 46, 51, 56, 61, 66, 70, 79, UA.

17. Dialectic Society Periodical Register, 1881–85, 60, 113, 159; Library Journal of the Dialectic Society, 1882–86, 105, 271; both in UA.

18. Battle, *History of the University of North Carolina*, 1:72–78, 410; *Catalogue of the Members of the Dialectic Society*, 5–6, 12–31; York, "Dialectic and Philanthropic Societies' Contributions."

19. Dialectic Society Minutes, 12 Sept. 1881, 4 Mar. 1882, 2 Feb., 1, 7 Sept. 1883, 4 Sept. 1884, 27 Feb. 1885, UA; Battle, *History of the University of North Carolina*, 2:269–71, 296; *Catalogue of the Members of the Dialectic Society*, 38–43.

20. Dialectic Society Minutes, 16 Oct. 1883, 15 Feb., 5 Sept., 10 Oct. 1884, 16 Jan. 1885, UA.

21. Junior Debate, 4 June 1884, Dialectic Society Papers, UA.

22. MB, essay, "Past and Present Phases in Teutonic Character and Literature," 4 Apr. 1884, and Junior Debate, 4 June 1884, Dialectic Society Papers, UA.

23. MB, "Hour's Need"; "Chapel Hill Speech" [1885], BP; Dialectic Society Minutes, 22 Apr. 1885, UA.

24. *Charlotte Daily Observer*, 25 Jan. 1895.

25. *Alumni History*; Coates, *Legal Education*, 15–33; Ashe et al., *Biographical History*, 8:81–82.

26. Insurance Policy, 14 July 1888, BP; Will of Wiley Butler, Estates Records Office, Sampson County Courthouse, Clinton, N.C.; Bizzell, *Sampson County*, 334–35; Sampson County Tax List, 1887, NCDAH (Marion Butler possessed no real property and $225 worth of personal property); *Catalogue of the University of North Carolina at Chapel Hill, 1881–1882*, 20–21, 38, 40; University of North Carolina Treasurer to MB, 27 June 1916, BP.

27. Bizzell, *Sampson County*, 96, 111; *Caucasian*, 4 Nov. 1886; *Fayetteville Observer*, 26 Dec. 1886, 2 June 1887, 10, 24 May 1888.

28. *Fayetteville Observer*, 23 Dec. 1886, 2 June 1887, 24 May 1888.

29. Gilbert and Warren, "Teachers' Assembly," 7, 34, 49, 80, 95, 122; *Proceedings of the North Carolina Teachers' Assembly* (1884), 8–9; *Proceedings of the North Carolina Teachers' Assembly* (1887), 26; E. P. Moses to MB, 14 July 1896, BP; *Caucasian*, 22 Jan. 1891.

Chapter 2

1. Hicks, *Populist Revolt*, 54–95; Turner, "Understanding the Populists"; McMath, *Populist Vanguard*, 3–35.

2. Hicks, "Farmers' Alliance in North Carolina"; Steelman, *North Carolina Farmers' Alliance*, 1–24.

3. Hughes and Cain, *American Economic History*, 261–68, 381–85; Thurtell, "Fusion Insurgency in North Carolina," 29–30, 33; Mitchell, *Political Education in the Southern Farmers' Alliance*, 24–46.

4. Hughes and Cain, *American Economic History*, 298–99.

5. Steelman, *North Carolina Farmers' Alliance*, 10–15; Noblin, *Leonidas La Fayette Polk*; Thurtell, "Fusion Insurgency in North Carolina," 40–46, 95–96; *Progressive Farmer*, 29 Sept. 1886.

6. McMath, *Populist Vanguard*, 161–63; Steelman, *North Carolina Farmers' Alliance*, 16–17.

7. Bizzell, *Sampson County*, 37–38, 118–19; *Agriculture of the United States in 1860*, 108–9; *Report on the Statistics of Agriculture in the United States*, 170, 395; Steelman, *North Carolina Farmers' Alliance*, 1.

8. *Progressive Farmer*, 5 Jan., 2, 9 Feb., 6, 13, 20, 27 Mar., 3, 24 Apr. 1888; Thurtell, "Fusion Insurgency in North Carolina," 76.

9. *Progressive Farmer*, 3, 24 Apr. 1888; Ashe et al., *Biographical History*, 8:81–83; Knights of Honor Insurance Policy, 14 July 1888; Masonic Fair Circular, 11 Apr. 1898; both in BP.

10. *Fayetteville Observer*, 24 May 1888; *Caucasian*, 1 Mar. 1888, 28 Feb. 1889; Sampson County Tax List, 1888, 1889, NCDAH; *N. W. Ayer and Son's Newspaper Annual* (1887), 666; *N. W. Ayer and Son's Newspaper Annual* (1888), 376.

11. North Carolina Farmers' State Alliance Minute Book, 1887–1893, 32, North Carolina Farmers' State Alliance Papers, NCDAH; *Progressive Farmer*, 24 Apr., 14, 28 Aug., 11 Sept., 18 Dec. 1888.

12. *Progressive Farmer*, 3, 24 July 1888.

13. Ibid., 22 May, 14 Aug. 1888.

14. Ibid., 4 Sept. 1888; Bromberg, "'Pure Democracy and White Supremacy,'" 1–386; Steelman, "Progressive Era in North Carolina," 1–56.

15. *News and Observer*, 8, 15, 22 Oct. 1922; *Fayetteville Observer*, 31 May 1888; Cheney, *North Carolina Government*, 455, 466–67.

16. *Caucasian*, 28 Feb., 7, 14 Mar., 11 Apr., 16, 23 May, 6 June, 8 Aug., 21 Nov. 1889, 2 Jan. 1890; McMath, *Populist Vanguard*, 54–59.

17. *Caucasian*, 28 Feb., 7, 14 Mar., 18 Apr., 5 Dec. 1889.

18. Hicks, *Populist Revolt*, 427–28; McMath, *Populist Vanguard*, 87–89; *Washington National Economist*, 14 Dec. 1889; Steelman, *North Carolina Farmers' Alliance*, 56–58.

19. Steelman, *North Carolina Farmers' Alliance*, 67–125; Bromberg, "'Worst Muddle'"; *Proceedings of the Third Annual Session*, 12–13; *Proceedings of the Fourth Annual Session*, 30–35.

20. *News and Observer*, 23 Aug. 1890; *Caucasian*, 23 Jan., 3, 10 Apr., 1, 22 May, 28 Aug., 25 Sept. 1890.

21. The outstanding history of the Alliance's role as educator is Mitchell, *Political Education in the Southern Farmers' Alliance*. Ironically, although Butler, given his roles as a teacher, Alliance lecturer, editor, president of the North Carolina and national Alliances, Populist United States senator, and chairman of the national Populist Party, is arguably the greatest example of the success of Alliance indoctrination, this aspect of his life is not discussed by Mitchell and other historians who have described the educational powers of the Alliance. Part of the reason is that Butler himself never gave a succinct account of his personal experiences. Instead, it has to be dug out of his weekly newspaper columns and rare public statements that were published

in other newspapers between 1889 and 1892. This was clearly a gradual transformation, shaped by face-to-face dealings with Alliance members, readings of Alliance "lessons," increasing political hostility to Alliance ideas, and a growing crisis in the economy. Obviously, in 1888 and after, Butler could have decided to disagree with Alliance proposals, agree with them, or agree with some and disagree with others. What is most remarkable is that he unhesitatingly, immediately, and publicly endorsed all Alliance proposals. As will be seen, however, he did not synthesize the proposals and articulate their broader purposes until the winter of 1891–92. As it turned out, this personal journey was short and relatively easy compared with another task he gave himself: devising a national political strategy to enact the proposals into law.

22. *Caucasian*, 23 Jan., 6, 13 Feb., 13, 20 Mar., 1 May, 21 Aug. 1890.

23. Ibid., 6, 20 Feb., 6 Mar., 24 July 1890; *Fayetteville Observer*, 24 July 1890; *News and Observer*, 25 July 1890.

24. Sampson County Tax List, 1889, NCDAH; *News and Observer*, 8, 15 Oct. 1922; MB to W. M. Neal, 18 Apr. 1921, BP; *Caucasian*, 11, 18, 25 Sept. 1890; *Daily State Chronicle*, 12 Sept. 1890.

25. *Daily State Chronicle*, 12 Sept. 1890; *Washington National Economist*, 27 Sept. 1890; Sampson County Miscellaneous Records (Elections), 1878–1926, NCDAH; *Caucasian*, 30 Oct., 6 Nov. 1890; *News and Observer*, 15 Oct. 1922.

26. *Caucasian*, 1, 8 Jan. 1891; *Daily State Chronicle*, 6 Jan. 1891; *News and Observer*, 16 Jan. 1891.

27. *Caucasian*, 11 Sept. 1890, 15 Jan. 1891; *Journal of the Senate . . . of North Carolina* (1891), 77–78, 86; *Laws and Resolutions of the State of North Carolina* (1891), 651; Steelman, *North Carolina Farmers' Alliance*, 126–31, 138–39.

28. *Caucasian*, 15 Jan. 1891; MB to W. M. Neal, 18 Apr. 1921, BP; *News and Observer*, 8, 18, 20, 28 Jan., 8, 10, 20 Feb. 1891; *Progressive Farmer*, 20 Jan. 1891; Steelman, *North Carolina Farmers' Alliance*, 141–49; *Journal of the Senate . . . of North Carolina* (1891), 132; *Laws and Resolutions of the State of North Carolina* (1891), 270, 303, 304, 313–14; *Daily State Chronicle*, 19, 20 Feb. 1891; *Caucasian*, 26 Feb. 1891.

29. Much later, Butler admitted that the commission had "not functioned up to the expectations of myself and others who created" it. MB to W. M. Neal, 18 Apr. 1921, BP.

30. *News and Observer*, 15, 29 Jan., 28 Feb. 1891; *Daily State Chronicle*, 27 Feb., 8 Mar. 1891; *Journal of the Senate . . . of North Carolina* (1891), 247, 556.

31. *News and Observer*, 11, 13, 19 Jan., 6 Feb. 1891; *Caucasian*, 15, 29 Jan. 1891; *Journal of the Senate . . . of North Carolina* (1891), 75, 86, 243, 337; Walter Clark to MB, 13 Feb. 1891, BP.

32. *Trinity College Country Life*, Sept. 1890; *Caucasian*, 22 Jan. 1891; *Journal of the Senate . . . of North Carolina* (1891), 148, 157, 166; Steelman, *North Carolina Farmers' Alliance*, 156–57.

33. Steelman, *North Carolina Farmers' Alliance*, 162–65.

Chapter 3

1. McMath, *Populist Vanguard,* 90–133.

2. Ibid.; Steelman, *North Carolina Farmers' Alliance,* 171–83. An effective discussion of the importance of local political structure to third-party politics in Kansas, Nebraska, and Iowa is Ostler, *Prairie Populism.*

3. *Wilmington Messenger,* 25 Oct., 1 Nov. 1890; Faulkner, "Samuel A'Court Ashe," 155–88; J. A. Graham to E. A. Thorne, 23 May 1891, Thorne Papers, Duke; *Taylorsville Index,* 30 Apr., 14, 21 Aug., 11 Sept., 16 Oct., 10 Nov. 1891; *Trinity College Country Life,* Mar., Apr. 1891.

4. *Caucasian,* 19 Feb., 21 May, 2, 23 July 1891.

5. Ibid., 18, 25 June, 16 July, 17, 24 Sept. 1891; *Tarboro Farmers' Advocate,* 2 Sept. 1891; *Progressive Farmer,* 3 Nov. 1891.

6. *Caucasian,* 16 July 1891; *Proceedings of the Fifth Annual Session;* Steelman, *North Carolina Farmers' Alliance,* 185–87.

7. *Caucasian,* 20, 27 Aug. 1891; *Washington National Economist,* 22 Aug. 1891; T. B. Long to L. L. Polk, 3 Aug. 1891, L. P. Denmark Papers, NCDAH; Minutes, 1887–1893, 212, 214, 234–35, 244–45, 248–49, North Carolina Farmers' State Alliance Papers, NCDAH; *Fayetteville Observer,* 20 Aug. 1891; *News and Observer,* 14, 15 Aug. 1891; *Tarboro Farmers' Advocate,* 27 Apr. 1892; *Progressive Farmer,* 18 Aug., 1 Sept. 1891.

8. *Tarboro Farmers' Advocate,* 2 Sept., 21 Oct., 4 Nov. 1891; *Progressive Farmer,* 29 Sept., 13 Oct., 3 Nov. 1891; *Caucasian,* 8 Oct., 17 Dec. 1891; MB to E. Carr, 1891, Carr Papers, ECU; Steelman, *North Carolina Farmers' Alliance,* 175–76; McMath, *Populist Vanguard,* 118–19; Minutes, 1887–1893, 264, 306–7, 329–31, North Carolina Farmers' State Alliance Papers, NCDAH.

9. *Caucasian,* 19, 26 Nov. 1891, 25 Feb. 1892; *Tarboro Farmers' Advocate,* 25 Nov., 9 Dec. 1891, 16 Mar. 1892; *Progressive Farmer,* 17 Nov., 8, 15, 22 Dec. 1891, 16 Feb., 1 Mar. 1892; McMath, *Populist Vanguard,* 129–31; Hicks, *Populist Revolt,* 223–27, 436–39; *Washington National Economist,* 20, 27 Feb., 5 Mar. 1892; Steelman, *North Carolina Farmers' Alliance,* 191–93.

10. *Progressive Farmer,* 22 Mar., 5 Apr. 1892; *Caucasian,* 7 Apr. 1892.

11. *Goldsboro Headlight,* 21 Apr. 1892; *Tarboro Farmers' Advocate,* 3 Mar., 27 Apr. 1892; *Progressive Farmer,* 3 Nov. 1891, 5 Apr. 1892; J. W. Edwards to J. W. Denmark, 26 Apr. 1892, J. W. Denmark Papers, NCDAH; *Caucasian,* 15 Oct. 1891, 7, 14 Jan., 11 Feb., 10 Mar. 1892.

12. *Progressive Farmer,* 3 Nov. 1891, 5 Apr. 1892; *Caucasian,* 7 Jan., 10 Mar., 2 June 1892. Two significant analyses of Populist thought, drawing from the writings of Populists leaders, make a similar point about the purpose of Populist economic reform; see Pollack, *Just Polity* and *Humane Economy.* Although briefly noting Butler's views, Pollack focuses primarily on the writings of William Peffer, James Weaver, Ignatius Donnelly, W. Scott Morgan, James H. Davis, Thomas E. Watson, Thomas L. Nugent, and Frank Doster. For a focus on these issues through judicial Populism, with a similar conclusion, see Hunt, "Populism, Law, and the Corporation."

13. Steelman, *North Carolina Farmers' Alliance,* 182–84; *Caucasian,* 31 Mar., 28 Apr., 5 May 1892; *Tarboro Farmers' Advocate,* 23 Mar. 1892; *Progressive Farmer,* 22 Mar. 1892.

14. *Progressive Farmer,* 22 Mar., 3 May 1892; L. L. Polk to J. W. Denmark, 27 Apr. 1892, J. W. Denmark Papers, NCDAH; J. D. Ezzell to L. L. Polk, 22 Apr. 1892; H. H. Boyce to L. L. Polk, 4 Apr. 1892; J. W. Edwards to L. L. Polk, 26 Apr. 1892; all in Polk Papers, SHC; *Salisbury Carolina Watchman,* 5 May 1892; *Washington National Economist,* 14 May 1892.

15. J. W. Edwards to L. L. Polk, 26 Apr. 1892, and A. L. Swinson to L. L. Polk, 10, 19 Apr. 1892, Polk Papers, SHC; *Progressive Farmer,* 19 Apr. 1892; *Hickory Mercury,* 6 Apr. 1892; *Tarboro Farmers' Advocate,* 13 Apr. 1892.

16. E. Carr to G. E. Hunt, 28 May 1892, Carr Papers, ECU; S. F. Telfair to J. B. Grimes, 25 Apr. 1892, Grimes Papers, SHC; *Progressive Farmer,* 10, 31 May 1892; *Daily State Chronicle,* 4 May 1892; Steelman, *North Carolina Farmers' Alliance,* 193–96.

17. *News and Observer,* 11 Sept., 4 Oct. 1891, 23, 29 Apr. 1892; *Fayetteville Observer,* 5 May 1892; *Hertford Perquimans Record,* 27 Apr. 1892; *Daily State Chronicle,* 14, 17, 18 May 1892; *Wilmington Messenger,* 12 May 1892; W. M. Robbins to S. A. Ashe, 7 Apr. 1892, and T. H. Sutton to S. A. Ashe, 28 Mar. 1892, Ashe Papers, NCDAH; *Progressive Farmer,* 3, 10 May 1892; *Elizabeth City Economist-Falcon,* 8, 29 Mar., 3, 17 May 1892; J. C. Robinson to J. B. Grimes, 14 May 1892, Grimes Papers, SHC; *Charlotte Daily Observer,* 17 May 1892; T. J. Jarvis to E. C. Smith, 5 Apr. 1892, Smith Papers, Duke; Steelman, *North Carolina Farmers' Alliance,* 202–4.

18. *Washington National Economist,* 2 July 1892; *Raleigh Special Informer,* 22 June 1892; *News and Observer,* 18 May 1892; *Fayetteville Observer,* 26 May 1892; *Caucasian,* 9 June 1892; *Daily State Chronicle,* 17, 18 May 1892; *Progressive Farmer,* 24 May 1892; *Charlotte Daily Observer,* 18 May 1892; Steelman, *North Carolina Farmers' Alliance,* 208–9.

19. *Charlotte Daily Observer,* 19 May 1892; *News and Observer,* 19 May 1892; *Salisbury Carolina Watchman,* 19 May 1892; Steelman, *North Carolina Farmers' Alliance,* 209–10.

20. *Caucasian,* 26 May, 2, 9 June 1892; R. J. Powell to E. Carr, 26 May 1892, Carr Papers, ECU; *Progressive Farmer,* 24 May 1892; Noblin, *Leonidas La Fayette Polk,* 281; *Tarboro Farmers' Advocate,* 25 May 1892; *Salisbury Carolina Watchman,* 9 June 1892.

21. *Fisherman and Farmer,* 20 May 1892; *Charlotte Daily Observer,* 20 May 1892; *Elizabeth City Economist-Falcon,* 24 May 1892.

22. *Charlotte Daily Observer,* 20 May 1892; *Progressive Farmer,* 24 May 1892; *Union Republican,* 26 May 1892.

23. Noblin, *Leonidas La Fayette Polk,* 277–98; *Union Republican,* 2 June 1892; *Progressive Farmer,* 7 June 1892; *Washington National Economist,* 4 June, 2, 16 July 1892; Steelman, *North Carolina Farmers' Alliance,* 214–16; *Raleigh Special Informer,* 22 June 1892; *Caucasian,* 16 June 1892.

24. *Progressive Farmer,* 31 May, 7, 14, 21 June, 19, 26 July 1892; *Hertford Perquimans Record,* 15 June 1892; *Tarboro Farmers' Advocate,* 1, 15 June, 6 July 1892; *Salisbury Carolina Watchman,* 23 June, 7 July 1892; *Mountain Home Journal,* 15 July 1892; McMath, *Populist Vanguard,* 195; Hicks, *Populist Revolt,* 231–37, 439–44. An article that seeks to quantify the failure of Populists to attract Alliancemen without discussion of long-standing ideological divisions is Redding, "Failed Populism—Movement-Party Disjuncture in North Carolina."

25. *Progressive Farmer,* 31 May 1892; *Caucasian,* 12 May, 2 June, 14 July, 4 Aug. 1892;

MB to Elias Carr, 7 June, 8 July 1892, and MB to S. B. Alexander, 9 July 1892, Carr Papers, ECU; Minutes, 1887–1893, 308, North Carolina Farmers' State Alliance Papers, NCDAH; McMath, *Populist Vanguard*, 138–39.

26. MB to E. Carr, 7 June 1892, and MB to S. B. Alexander, 9 July 1892, Carr Papers, ECU; *Caucasian*, 23 July 1892; *Wilmington Messenger*, 21 July 1892.

27. *Caucasian*, 23 June, 7, 14, 21 July 1892; *Raleigh Special Informer*, 22 June 1892; J. W. Denmark to L. L. Polk, 2, 6 June 1892, and A. L. Swinson to L. L. Polk, 1 June 1892, Polk Papers, SHC; *Goldsboro Headlight*, 21 July 1892.

28. *Charlotte Daily Observer*, 24, 26, 27, 31 July 1892; *News and Observer*, 20, 21, 23 July 1892, 15 Oct. 1922; *Fayetteville Observer*, 28 July, 4 Aug. 1892; *Goldsboro Headlight*, 28 July 1892; *Wilmington Messenger*, 27, 28, 29, 30 July 1892; Steelman, *North Carolina Farmers' Alliance*, 224–25; *Caucasian*, 28 July, 11 Aug. 1892.

29. Daniels, *Tar Heel Editor*, 385–87. Beeby, "Revolt of the Tar Heelers," 79–80, points out that Populist organization existed in Sampson County as early as 7 July.

Chapter 4

1. *Caucasian*, 11 Aug. 1892; *Charlotte Daily Observer*, 12 Aug. 1892; *Hickory Mercury*, 24 Aug. 1892; *Proceedings of the Sixth Annual Session*, 2, 4–7; Smith, "Populist Movement in North Carolina," 93; Centre Alliance Minute Book, 27 Aug. 1892, Johnson Papers, Duke.

2. *Proceedings of the Sixth Annual Session*, 10–11, 20–21, 23–25, 28–29, 33–35; J. W. Denmark to O. W. Sutton, 16 Sept. 1892, J. W. Denmark Papers, NCDAH.

3. *Hickory Mercury*, 24 Aug. 1892; *Progressive Farmer*, 23 Aug. 1892; *Union Republican*, 18 Aug. 1892; *Fayetteville Observer*, 25 Aug. 1892; *News and Observer*, 17 Aug. 1892; *Washington National Economist*, 20 Aug. 1892; *Charlotte Daily Observer*, 17 Aug. 1892; *Caucasian*, 18, 25 Aug. 1892; *Salisbury Carolina Watchman*, 18 Aug. 1892; Steelman, *North Carolina Farmers' Alliance*, 247–49; *Greensboro Daily News*, 15 Oct. 1916; *Goldsboro Headlight*, 13 Oct. 1892; Ashe et al., *Biographical History*, 3:478–80; Beeby, "Revolt of the Tar Heelers," 99.

4. *N. W. Ayer and Son's Newspaper Annual* (1891), 537–46; *Tarboro Farmers' Advocate*, 3 Aug. 1892; *Henderson Vance Farmer*, 20 Sept. 1892; *Whitakers Rattler*, 6 Aug. 1892; *Hickory Mercury*, 29 June, 24 Aug. 1892.

5. *Caucasian*, 25 Aug., 1, 29 Sept., 27 Oct. 1892; *Tarboro Farmers' Advocate*, 2 Nov. 1892; *Goldsboro Headlight*, 13 Oct. 1892.

6. *Caucasian*, 11, 25 Aug., 1, 22 Sept., 27 Oct., 3 Nov. 1892; *Raleigh Signal*, 11 Aug., 6, 13, 27 Oct. 1892; *Washington National Economist*, 8 Oct. 1892; *Fayetteville Observer*, 25 Aug. 1892; *Progressive Farmer*, 8 Nov. 1892; G. E. Butler to O. J. Peterson, 27 Jan. 1933, BP.

7. *Henderson Vance Farmer*, 20 Sept. 1892; *Washington National Economist*, 8 Oct. 1892; *Tarboro Farmers' Advocate*, 5, 19 Oct. 1892; *Progressive Farmer*, 6, 13, 27 Sept., 4, 11, 25 Oct., 1 Nov. 1892; *Caucasian*, 29 Sept. 1892; *Salisbury Carolina Watchman*, 29 Sept. 1892; *Hickory Mercury*, 14 Sept. 1892; *Union Republican*, 22 Sept., 27 Oct. 1892; *Patron and Gleaner*, 27 Oct. 1892; *Fayetteville Observer*, 6 Oct. 1892.

8. *Progressive Farmer*, 13, 20 Sept., 4, 11, 25 Oct. 1892; *Union Republican*, 22 Sept. 1892; *Fayetteville Observer*, 6 Oct. 1892; *Tarboro Farmers' Advocate*, 19 Oct. 1892; MB to

J. W. Denmark, 6 Sept. 1892, J. W. Denmark Papers, NCDAH. (Butler admonished Denmark to keep the Omaha Platform in the *Progressive Farmer.* "I often refer to it. It is not in any paper and many of the people have not seen it.") Two important books by Norman Pollack, *The Just Polity: Populism, Law, and Human Welfare* and *The Humane Economy: Populism, Capitalism, and Democracy,* mentioned above, portray the intellectual substance of Populist economic and political ideas. Pollack indicates Butler's ideas were within the mainstream of Populist thought, when compared with those of other leading Populist politicians. By the 1892 campaign Butler had already received his Alliance education. As a result, his most important tasks were to educate others and encourage new political behavior. His speeches reflect both the Populist ideas described by Pollack and a strategy to give them political meaning.

9. *Goldsboro Headlight,* 22 Sept., 3 Nov. 1892; *Hickory Mercury,* 14 Sept. 1892; *Salisbury Carolina Watchman,* 8 Sept. 1892; *Raleigh Signal,* 22 Sept. 1892; *Progressive Farmer,* 27 Sept. 1892; *Charlotte Observer,* 28 Oct. 1892; Orr, *Charles Brantley Aycock,* 93–94; MB to L. Butler, 25 Apr. 1934, BP.

10. Bromberg, "'Pure Democracy and White Supremacy'"; Anderson, *Race and Politics in North Carolina;* J. B. Stephens to T. Settle, 22 June 1892, Settle Papers, SHC; Hicks, *Populist Revolt,* 245–49; Steelman, "Vicissitudes of Republican Party Politics"; *Raleigh Signal,* 5, 12 May, 2, 16 June, 21 July, 18 Aug. 1892; Steelman, *North Carolina Farmers' Alliance,* 229–30.

11. Steelman, *North Carolina Farmers' Alliance,* 232–44; Schlup, "Adlai Stevenson and the 1892 Campaign"; *Goldsboro Headlight,* 1 Sept. 1892; *Wilmington Messenger,* 5 Aug. 1892; *Elizabeth City Economist-Falcon,* 16, 23 Aug. 1892; *Fisherman and Farmer,* 19 Aug., 2 Sept. 1892; *News and Observer,* 17 Aug. 1892; K. Battle to S. A. Ashe, 23 May 1892, and T. J. Jarvis to S. A. Ashe, 26 Sept. 1892, Ashe Papers, NCDAH; L. W. McMullan to W. B. Rodman, 20 Aug. 1892, Rodman Papers, ECU; H. G. Tilley to T. Settle, 9 Aug. 1892, and S. O. Wilson to T. Settle, 17 Sept. 1892, Settle Papers, SHC; *Elizabeth City North Carolinian,* 7 Sept., 12, 26 Oct. 1892; *Union Republican,* 3 Nov. 1892; *Raleigh Signal,* 15 Sept. 1892; *Washington National Economist,* 8 Oct. 1892; Kousser, *Shaping of Southern Politics,* 183.

12. *Hertford Perquimans Record,* 14 Sept., 12 Oct. 1892; *Fayetteville Observer,* 15, 29 Sept., 6 Oct. 1892; *Elizabeth City Economist-Falcon,* 16, 23 Aug. 1892; *Fisherman and Farmer,* 19 Aug. 1892; *News and Observer,* 20, 29, 30 Oct. 1892; Steelman, *North Carolina Farmers' Alliance,* 255–57; *Progressive Farmer,* 27 Sept., 25 Oct. 1892; *Henderson Vance Farmer,* 20 Sept. 1892; *Goldsboro Headlight,* 8 Sept., 3 Nov. 1892; *Weekly State Chronicle,* 30 Aug. 1892; *Raleigh North Carolinian,* 9 Sept. 1892; *Caucasian,* 1, 8, 29 Sept. 1892; *Charlotte Daily Observer,* 6, 8 Oct. 1892.

13. Steelman, *North Carolina Farmers' Alliance,* 258–62; Kousser, *Shaping of Southern Politics,* 185–86.

14. *News and Observer,* 9 Nov. 1892; Steelman, *North Carolina Farmers' Alliance,* 262–64; *Caucasian,* 10 Nov., 1 Dec. 1892; W. E. Clarke to C. Thompson, 20 Nov. 1892, Thompson Papers, SHC.

15. After the election Butler again contended that the nomination of a state ticket had been a mistake and that Weaver could have won without Populist state candidates. *Caucasian,* 1 Dec. 1892.

16. Ibid., 10 Nov., 1 Dec. 1892; *Washington National Economist*, 26 Nov., 10 Dec. 1892; *Progressive Farmer*, 22 Nov. 1892; McMath, *Populist Vanguard*, 144–46.

17. *Caucasian*, 23 Feb., 2, 9, 30 Mar., 24 Aug. 1893; *Progressive Farmer*, 21, 28 Feb. 1893; *News and Observer*, 16 Feb. 1893; *Bill to Be Entitled an Act for the Relief of the Stockholders of the State Alliance Business Fund*, NCC; Steelman, *North Carolina Farmers' Alliance*, 265–66; Hamilton, *North Carolina since 1860*, 242; Centre Alliance Minute Book, 14 Feb. 1893, Johnson Papers, Duke.

18. *Proceedings of the Seventh Annual Session*, 4–9, 16; *Proceedings of the Sixth Annual Session*, 9; *Proceedings of the Eighth Annual Session*, 12; *Caucasian*, 5, 12, 19 Oct., 19 Nov. 1893; *Progressive Farmer*, 15 Aug. 1893.

19. *Caucasian*, 2, 9, 23 Mar., 11 May 1893; *Progressive Farmer*, 23 Feb. 1893; Hicks, *Populist Revolt*, 301–20.

20. Hicks, *Populist Revolt*, 305–20; Hollingsworth, *Whirligig of Politics*, 11–19.

21. *Caucasian*, 18 May, 20 July, 3 Aug., 21, 28 Sept., 12, 26 Oct. 1893.

22. *Caucasian*, 5 Jan., 9 Feb., 9, 23 Mar., 4, 18, 25 May, 8, 22, 29 June, 30 July, 31 Aug., 7, 14 Sept., 23, 30 Nov., 21 Dec. 1893; *Progressive Farmer*, 19 Dec. 1893.

23. *Laws and Resolutions of the State of North Carolina* (1889), chap. 278; *Caucasian*, 5 Jan., 9 Feb., 16, 23, 30 Mar., 4, 11, 18, 25 May, 7, 14, 28 Sept., 5, 12 Oct., 16, 23, 30 Nov., 21 Dec. 1893.

Chapter 5

1. MB to T. Settle, 2 Feb., 1 Mar., 16 Sept., 23 Nov., 8, 17, 29 Dec. 1893, Settle Papers, SHC; MB to R. Pearson, 16 Feb. 1893, Pearson Papers, SHC; *Caucasian*, 16 Nov. 1893; *Fayetteville Observer*, 1 Dec. 1892.

2. MB to R. Pearson, 3 Mar. 1893, Pearson Papers, SHC; *Progressive Farmer*, 8 Aug. 1893; *Caucasian*, 18 May 1893; MB to T. Settle, 23 Aug. 1893, Settle Papers, SHC.

3. *Caucasian*, 26 Jan., 2, 16 Feb., 9, 16, 23 Mar., 9 Sept. 1893; *Washington National Economist*, 25 Feb. 1893; MB to T. Settle, 11 Oct. 1893, Settle Papers, SHC; *Goldsboro Headlight*, 2, 9 Feb. 1893; *Tarboro Farmers' Advocate*, 7 Dec. 1892.

4. *Caucasian*, 26 Jan., 2, 16 Feb., 9, 16, 23 Mar., 9 Sept. 1893; MB to T. Settle, 11 Oct. 1893, Settle Papers, SHC; *Goldsboro Headlight*, 2, 9 Feb. 1893.

5. Sampson County Marriage Register, 1892–1908, Sampson County Courthouse, Clinton, N.C.; F. Faison to MB, 16 June 1891, BP; Bizzell, *Sampson County*, 404; Pocahontas Butler Woodson, interview, 20, 27 Sept. 1986; Moore, interview, 16 July 1985; Thomas D. Woodson, interview, 20, 27 Sept. 1986; *Caucasian*, 28 June 1894. Florence Faison is a fascinating person who deserves more biographical attention. Some of her personal papers, which I consulted for this book, have been preserved in the Southern Historical Collection. Interviews with family members provided other information. Yet details of her relationship with Butler, particularly her specific impact on his activities, as well as about her political views, are difficult to describe because of a lack of evidence. I did not find any significant information about her interaction with other Alliance or Populist figures. A great deal of her papers concerns her work for the United Daughters of the Confederacy. One problem is that

very little correspondence exists between the two after their marriage. Apparently, the couple was rarely separated for any length of time; they both went to Washington, for example, when Butler became a United States senator. Yet there are many suggestions of the political aspects of the relationship: they attended political meetings together; "family time" included reading political items in newspapers; Faison wrote former University of North Carolina president Kemp Battle a highly publicized letter during the tense 1906 election; and Butler supported proportional representation of Republican women, such as Faison, on GOP committees after 1920. The marriage seems to have worked well partly because both Butler and Faison equally enjoyed politics.

6. *Progressive Farmer*, 13, 20, 27 Feb. 1894; *Proceedings of the Fourth Annual Session*, 13; *Proceedings of the Seventh Annual Session*, 13–41; H. W. Ayer to MB, 3 Apr. 1894, BP; *Proceedings of the Eighth Annual Session*, 8–27; *Proceedings of the Ninth Annual Session*; *Caucasian*, 15, 22 Feb. 1894; McMath, *Populist Vanguard*, 148.

7. *Caucasian*, 15, 22 Feb., 17 May, 7 June, 19 July 1894; *Progressive Farmer*, 5, 19 June, 10 July 1894; McMath, *Populist Vanguard*, 148.

8. MB to R. Pearson, 22 Jan., 19 Feb., 17 May, 12 June 1894, Pearson Papers, SHC; R. Pearson to T. Settle, 1 Mar. 1894, and MB to T. Settle, 24 Jan., 23 June, 28 Aug. 1894, Settle Papers, SHC.

9. MB to R. Pearson, 17 May, 18, 25 June 1894, Pearson Papers, SHC; H. Skinner to T. Settle, 27 Feb. 1894, Settle Papers, SHC; *Caucasian*, 11 Jan., 15, 29 Mar., 5 Apr., 28 June 1894; *Progressive Farmer*, 20 Mar., 22 May, 26 June 1894; *Hertford Perquimans Record*, 24 Mar. 1894. On the biracial aspects of Reconstruction, see, for example, Edwards, *Gendered Strife*, 190–92, 225–28, and Escott, *Many Excellent People*, 136–70. For an interesting discussion of Populist efforts to deal with Democratic fraud in the 1894 election, including cooperation with Republicans, see Beeby, "Revolt of the Tar Heelers," 248–73.

10. Hicks, *Populist Revolt*, 321–22; Hollingsworth, *Whirligig of Politics*, 23–26; *Caucasian*, 4 Jan., 1, 15 Feb., 8, 15, 29 Mar., 5, 12, 26 Apr., 3, 10, 24 May, 12 July, 23, 30 Aug., 11, 18 Oct. 1894; *Progressive Farmer*, 23 Jan., 15 May 1894; Ingle, "Southern Democrat at Large."

11. *Caucasian*, 31 May, 21, 28 June 1894; *Progressive Farmer*, 26 June, 24 July, 7 Aug. 1894; MB to C. Thompson, 22 May, 16, 26 June 1894, Thompson Papers, SHC; Steelman, "Republican Party Strategists," 257–60; *Union Republican*, 2, 9 Aug. 1894; *Charlotte Daily Observer*, 31 July, 1 Aug. 1894.

12. *News-Observer-Chronicle*, 2 Aug. 1894; *Union Republican*, 9 Aug. 1894; *Caucasian*, 2 Aug. 1894; *Charlotte Daily Observer*, 2 Aug. 1894.

13. *Caucasian*, 2 Aug. 1894.

14. Ibid.; *Progressive Farmer*, 7 Aug. 1894.

15. Faulkner, "Silver Fusion Politics," 234–41; *Caucasian*, 16 Aug. 1894; *News-Observer-Chronicle*, 9 Aug. 1894; Bromberg, "'Pure Democracy and White Supremacy,'" 540–42, 550–52; Winston, "Chief Justice Shepherd."

16. Steelman, "Republican Party Strategists," 246–69; D. M. Furches to Editor, *Union Republican*, 7 Apr. 1894; MB to T. Settle, 19 Aug. 1894, Settle Papers, SHC;

Union Republican, 26 July, 2, 9, 30 Aug., 6, 13 Sept. 1894; *Progressive Farmer,* 4 Sept. 1894; *Caucasian,* 30 Aug., 6 Sept. 1894; A. E. Holton to J. G. Ramsey, 16 Sept. 1894, Ramsey Papers, SHC.

17. *Hertford Perquimans Record,* 27 June, 31 Oct. 1894; *Granville County Reformer,* 21 June 1894; *Pinnacle Era,* 26 July 1894; *Progressive Farmer,* 4 Sept., 23, 30 Oct. 1894; *Caucasian,* 12 Apr., 9, 16 Aug., 6 Sept., 4, 11 Oct., 8 Nov. 1894.

18. Muller, "New South Populism," 93–94; *Progressive Farmer,* 11, 18, 25 Sept., 2, 9, 16, 23 Oct. 1894; *Caucasian,* 23 Aug., 13 Sept., 25 Oct. 1894; "My Day in Court," Montgomery Papers, SHC.

19. *Caucasian,* 4 Jan., 23, 30 Aug., 6 Sept., 25 Oct. 1894; J. B. Lloyd to C. Thompson, 5 June 1894, Thompson Papers, SHC.

20. *Caucasian,* 30 Aug., 4 Oct. 1894; *Progressive Farmer,* 31 July, 11, 25 Sept., 16 Oct. 1894; Robert Smith, "Rhetorical Analysis of the Populist Movement," 134–91.

21. *Caucasian,* 18, 25 Oct. 1894.

22. *News and Observer,* 31 Aug., 10, 12, 14, 23 Oct., 2 Nov. 1894; Daniels, *Editor in Politics,* 85–101; *Raleigh North Carolinian,* 20 Sept. 1894; *Clinton Sampson Democrat,* 18 Oct. 1894; *Fayetteville Observer,* 19 July 1894; *Democratic Hand-Book, 1894,* 78–79; *Fisherman and Farmer,* 10 Aug. 1894; *Durham Daily Globe,* 3 Nov. 1894; *Caucasian,* 18 Oct. 1894.

23. *News and Observer,* 14, 17, 26, 30 Oct., 2, 3 Nov. 1894; *Charlotte Daily Observer,* 11, 13, 16, 19, 20, 25 Oct. 1894; *Reidsville Webster's Weekly,* 6 Sept., 4 Oct. 1894; *Fayetteville Observer,* 1 Nov. 1894; *Fisherman and Farmer,* 14 Sept. 1894; *Raleigh North Carolinian,* 18, 25 Oct., 1 Nov. 1894; *Wilmington Messenger,* 26 Oct. 1894.

24. J. P. Leach to M. J. Hawkins, 10 Nov. 1894; W. B. Faison to M. J. Hawkins, 3 Nov. 1894; J. H. Pou to M. J. Hawkins, 5 Nov. 1894; Circulars from J. H. Pou, 26, 31 Oct. 1894; all in Hawkins Papers, NCDAH; B. F. Rogers to E. Carr, 11 Nov. 1894, Carr Papers, ECU; H. Harding to W. B. Rodman, 9 Oct. 1894; M. M. Alexander to W. B. Rodman, 29 Oct. 1894; W. B. Rodman to J. H. Pou, 3 Oct. 1894; W. B. Rodman to Z. Cradle, 25 Oct. 1894; all in Rodman Papers, ECU. For a more detailed discussion of Democratic methods, based on evidence from election challenges in two congressional districts, see Beeby, "Revolt of the Tar Heelers," 248–73.

25. James H. Pou to M. J. Hawkins, 5 Nov. 1894, Hawkins Papers, NCDAH; Bromberg, "'Pure Democracy and White Supremacy,'" 553.

26. *Caucasian,* 15 Nov. 1894; *News and Observer,* 11, 13, 15 Nov. 1894.

27. *Caucasian,* 13, 27 Dec. 1894; *News and Observer,* 13, 18, 28 Dec. 1894.

28. *Caucasian,* 27 Dec. 1894; *News and Observer,* 13, 15 Dec. 1894; G. Butler to MB, 7 Feb. 1905, BP; A. E. Holton to B. N. Duke, 10 Nov. 1894; B. N. Duke to W. F. Strowd, 10 Nov. 1894; B. N. Duke to W. H. Worth, 17 Dec. 1894; W. F. Strowd to B. N. Duke, 12 Nov. 1894; J. Daniels to B. N. Duke, 19 June 1894; all in Duke Papers, Duke.

29. *Progressive Farmer,* 20 Nov. 1894; *News and Observer,* 11 Dec. 1894. For additional evidence of grassroots support for cooperation, see Beeby, "Revolt of the Tar Heelers," 233–37.

Chapter 6

1. *Caucasian*, 17 Jan. 1895; *Wadesboro Plow Boy*, 9 Jan. 1895; Steelman, "Progressive Era in North Carolina," 119–24; Trelease, "Fusion Legislatures"; *Public Laws and Resolutions of the State of North Carolina*, chap. 159. Peter H. Argersinger has shown the costs to Populists, including cooperationists, of not controlling the election machinery. See "'A Place on the Ballot.'"

2. Steelman, "Progressive Era in North Carolina," 3–4, 120; *Public Laws and Resolutions of the State of North Carolina*, chaps. 86, 121, 135, 157, 352.

3. R. L. Reinhart to M. W. Ransom, 12 Nov. 1894, Ransom Papers, SHC; *Caucasian*, 24 Jan., 28 Feb. 1895; *News and Observer*, 15, 16, 17, 23 Jan., 23 Feb. 1895; *Wadesboro Plow Boy*, 30 Jan. 1895.

4. *Caucasian*, 28 Feb. 1895; *Progressive Farmer*, 12 Mar. 1895; *Wadesboro Plow Boy*, 9, 30 Jan., 13 Feb. 1895; *Union Republican*, 31 Jan. 1895.

5. *Caucasian*, 17, 24, 31 Jan., 21 Feb. 1895; *News and Observer*, 13, 31 Jan., 9, 13, 23 Feb., 15 Mar. 1895; *Wadesboro Plow Boy*, 9, 30 Jan., 13 Feb. 1895; Bode, *Protestantism and the New South*, 32–38; Daniels, *Editor in Politics*, 102–11; Thurtell, "Fusion Insurgency in North Carolina," 244.

6. B. N. Duke to T. Settle, 14, 16, 22 Nov. 1894, 14 Feb. 1895; B. N. Duke to MB, 2 Jan. 1895; MB to B. N. Duke, 14 Jan. 1895; B. N. Duke to W. H. Worth, 19 Jan. 1895; all in Duke Papers, Duke.

7. W. W. Fuller to J. E. Stagg, 8 Jan. 1895; J. E. Stagg to B. N. Duke, 1 Feb. 1895; B. N. Duke to J. B. Duke, 10 Nov. 1895; T. Settle to B. N. Duke, 11, 15 Feb. 1895; W. H. Worth to B. N. Duke, 12, 19 Jan., 18 Feb., 5, 6 Mar. 1895; B. N. Duke to MB, 14 Feb. 1895; all in Duke Papers, Duke; *Public Laws and Resolutions of the State of North Carolina*, chap. 116; *Journal of the Senate . . . of North Carolina* (1895), 197, 366.

8. W. H. Worth to B. N. Duke, 12, 19 Jan., 18 Feb., 5, 6 Mar. 1895, Duke Papers, Duke; *Journal of the Senate . . . of North Carolina* (1895), 197, 366.

9. *Caucasian*, 10, 31 Jan., 7, 28 Feb., 14, 28 Mar., 4 Apr. 1895; *Progressive Farmer*, 12 Mar. 1895; *News and Observer*, 19 Mar. 1895; *Charlotte Daily Observer*, 17 Jan. 1895.

10. *Caucasian*, 21 Mar. 1895; *Raleigh Daily Caucasian*, 5 Mar. 1895; *News and Observer*, 12 Mar. 1895; W. H. Worth to B. N. Duke, 13 Feb. 1895, and Caucasian Publishing Company to B. N. Duke, 5 Mar. 1895, Duke Papers, Duke; H. W. Ayer to J. B. Grimes, 31 July 1893, Grimes Papers, SHC.

11. *Wadesboro Plow Boy*, 13 Feb. 1895; *Progressive Farmer*, 12, 26 Feb. 1895; *News and Observer*, 5, 6, 9 Feb. 1895; *Caucasian*, 14 Feb. 1895; McMath, *Populist Vanguard*, 148.

12. *Progressive Farmer*, 12 Feb. 1895, 18 Feb. 1896; North Carolina Farmers' State Alliance Day Book, 297, 310, 321, North Carolina Farmers' State Alliance Papers, NCDAH; McMath, *Populist Vanguard*, 148.

13. *Clinton Sampson Democrat*, 22 Aug. 1895; *Caucasian*, 8, 22 Aug. 1895; *Proceedings of the Ninth Annual Session*, 18.

14. See Silverman, "Silver Movement," 249–318.

15. In addition to Silverman, ibid., see Jones, *Election of 1896*, 18–35.

16. *Raleigh North Carolinian*, 10 Jan. 1895; *Caucasian*, 4 July 1895.

17. *Caucasian*, 23 May 1895.

18. Ibid., 18 Apr., 23, 30 May, 4, 20 June, 4 July 1895; *Progressive Farmer*, 9 Apr. 1895.

19. Watson wrote, "Let us drop the sub-treasury . . . [and] let us [also] deliver our land plank from the suspicion of socialism." *Wadesboro Plow Boy*, 13 Nov. 1895.

20. Jones, *Election of 1896*, 50–73; Silverman, "Silver Movement," 384–85; *Caucasian*, 4, 20 June 1895; *Progressive Farmer*, 11, 18, 25 June 1895; *Clinton Sampson Democrat*, 20 June 1895; H. Jones to MB, 31 May 1895, BP; MB to C. Thompson, 28 May 1895, Thompson Papers, SHC; *Charlotte Observer*, 13, 14 June 1895. Compare Goodwyn, *Democratic Promise*, 440, and Woodward, *Origins of the New South*, 282, which omit Butler's references to the Omaha Platform.

21. *News and Observer*, 28 Nov. 1894, 12, 16, 17, 20, 24 Apr. 1895; *Caucasian*, 20 June, 26 Sept., 17 Oct. 1895; J. Caldwell to E. C. Smith, 1 Oct. 1895, Smith Papers, Duke.

22. *Fayetteville Observer*, 22 Aug. 1895; *Caucasian*, 4, 20 June, 4 July, 29 Aug., 26 Sept. 1895; *Progressive Farmer*, 3 Sept., 1 Oct. 1895; H. Jones to MB, 27 Aug. 1895, and S. Whitaker to MB, 29 Aug. 1895, BP; Faulkner, "Silver Fusion Politics," 242–44; *Clinton Sampson Democrat*, 3 Oct. 1895; *News and Observer*, 26 Sept. 1895; *Charlotte Observer*, 26 Sept. 1895; *Wilmington Messenger*, 26 Sept. 1895. Lawrence Goodwyn incorrectly suggests the Raleigh convention indicated Butler's narrow commitment to silver; see *Democratic Promise*, 444–45, 667.

23. *Caucasian*, 21 Nov. 1895; *Wadesboro Plow Boy*, 13 Nov. 1895. The standard study of the Senate in this period is Rothman, *Politics and Power*. Populism in Congress has been the subject of study, but Butler's career is not addressed in detail. See Clanton, *Congressional Populism*; Clanton, "'Hayseed Socialism' on the Hill"; and Argersinger, "'No Rights on This Floor.'"

24. *Congressional Directory* (1892), 310–17; *Congressional Directory* (1893), 324–31; *Congressional Directory* (1896), 323–30.

25. Johnson et al., *Dictionary of American Biography*, 1:241, 7:393; Tipton, "William V. Allen"; Argersinger, *Populism and Politics*.

26. *Caucasian*, 31 Oct. 1895; *Congressional Record*, 54th Cong., 1st sess., 421, 425; Peffer, *Populism*, 106–8.

27. *Congressional Record*, 54th Cong., 1st sess., 339, 452, 6905, 6906.

28. Ibid., appendix, 377–94. Butler's newspaper also described the support for gold as partly the result of a "London Jew syndicate." It labeled the Rothschilds "Money shark Jews." Many of these statements seem to have been written by Hal Ayer. Yet some of Butler's speeches given in 1895 reflect the theme, at least for Jews perceived as part of the money power. *Caucasian*, 4, 18 Apr., 23 May, 20 June, 22, 29 Aug., 3 Sept. 1895.

29. *Congressional Record*, 54th Cong., 1st sess., appendix, 377–94.

30. *Congressional Record*, 54th Cong., 1st sess., 3420, 4650–51, 5783.

31. Ibid., 335, 2913, 3651, 3751, 5155; U.S. Congress, Senate Committee on Post Offices and Post Roads, *Report of Hearings regarding Postal Telegraphy*.

32. *Congressional Record*, 54th Cong., 1st sess., 3663, 3671; Fuller, *R.F.D.*, 17–35; Fuller, "Populists and the Post Office."

33. *Congressional Record*, 54th Cong., 1st sess., 611, 5993, 6391.

34. Ibid., 609–11, 5994.

35. *Progressive Farmer*, 14, 21, 28 Jan., 28 Apr., 9 June 1896; *Warren Plains People's Paper*, 14 Feb. 1896; *Wadesboro Plow Boy*, 8, 22 Jan. 1896; *Hillsboro Alliance Weekly*, 7 Jan., 8 May 1896; *Caucasian*, 2, 9 Jan., 16 Mar., 7 May, 4 June 1896; *Dallas Southern Mercury*, 18 June 1896.

Chapter 7

1. *Caucasian*, 30 Jan., 6, 13 Feb. 1896; MB to N. Gibbon, 6 Jan. 1896, and MB to J. A. Simms, 17 Feb. 1896, BP; *Wadesboro Plow Boy*, 12 Feb. 1896.

2. *Wadesboro Plow Boy*, 12 Feb. 1896; *Progressive Farmer*, 3 Mar. 1896; *Warren Plains People's Paper*, 14 Feb. 1896; *Caucasian*, 6, 13 Feb. 1896.

3. *Wadesboro Plow Boy*, 18 Mar., 8 Apr. 1896; *Progressive Farmer*, 10, 17 Mar., 7 Apr. 1896; *Salisbury Carolina Watchman*, 7 Apr. 1896; *Caucasian*, 5, 12 Mar. 1896.

4. *Caucasian*, 9, 23 Apr., 7 May 1896; *Progressive Farmer*, 7, 21 Apr. 1896; *Wadesboro Plow Boy*, 8 Apr. 1896; *Wilmington Messenger*, 17, 18 Apr. 1896; *Kings Mountain Progressive Reformer*, 23 Apr. 1896; *News and Observer*, 18 Apr. 1896; *Charlotte Observer*, 16, 17, 18 Apr. 1896; J. E. Fowler to MB, 20 Apr. 1896, BP.

5. W. H. Kitchin to MB, 20 Apr. 1896; W. A. Guthrie to MB, 30 Apr. 1896; H. H. Paddison to MB, 23 Apr. 1896; Y. C. Morton to MB, 30 Apr. 1896; R. B. Kinsey to MB, 1 May 1896; C. Thompson to MB, 2 May 1896; C. A. Nash to MB, 24 Apr. 1896; A. J. Moye to MB, 30 Apr. 1896; all in BP; *Progressive Farmer*, 21, 28 Apr., 5, 12 May 1896; *Caucasian*, 14 May 1896.

6. *Elizabeth City North Carolinian*, 11, 25 Mar., 22, 29 Apr., 6 May 1896; *Union Republican*, 12, 19 Mar., 23, 30 Apr. 1896; *News and Observer*, 15 Apr. 1896; R. Pearson to W. H. Worth, 25 Apr. 1896, Pearson Papers, SHC; W. E. Clarke to T. Settle, 16, 22 Apr. 1896, Settle Papers, SHC; *Hickory Press*, 9 Apr., 21 May 1896; T. J. Jarvis to E. C. Smith, 13 Apr. 1896, and R. B. Davis to E. C. Smith, 6, 15 Apr., 4 May 1896, Smith Papers, Duke; MB to F. A. Olds, 24 Mar. 1896, Olds Papers, NCDAH; *Elizabeth City Economist*, 8, 15 May 1896; *Clinton Sampson Democrat*, 23 Apr. 1896.

7. T. E. Watson to MB, 23, 28 Dec. 1895, BP.

8. *New York Times*, 5, 13, 18 Jan. 1896; J. E. Stealy to MB, 10 Jan. 1896, BP; *Caucasian*, 6 Feb. 1896.

9. *Caucasian*, 30 Jan. 1896; W. Barker to I. Donnelly, 19 Mar. 1896, Donnelly Papers, MHS; *Progressive Farmer*, 11 Feb. 1896.

10. *Progressive Farmer*, 4 Feb. 1896; MB to E. Light, 7 Feb. 1896, and MB to R. K. Bryan Jr., 14 Apr. 1896, BP.

11. MB, "Why the South Wants Free Coinage of Silver."

12. Glad, *McKinley, Bryan, and the People*, 95–112; Jones, *Election of 1896*, 91–98, 172, 176.

13. H. E. Taubeneck to I. Donnelly, 15 May 1896, Donnelly Papers, MHS; W. H. Kitchin to MB, 5 June 1896; W. A. Guthrie to MB, 23 June 1896; J. J. Mott to MB, 21 June 1896; H. E. Taubeneck to MB, 2 July 1896; all in BP; MB to W. J. Peele, 1 July 1896, Peele Papers, SHC; Durden, *Climax of Populism*, 17–18; Jones, *Election of 1896*, 204–11; *Caucasian*, 25 June 1896.

14. *Caucasian,* 25 June 1896; *Progressive Farmer,* 7 July 1896.

15. Crow and Durden, *Maverick Republican,* 61–62.

16. Steelman, "Progressive Era in North Carolina," 138–39; Faulkner, "Silver Fusion Politics," 245–46; R. B. Davis to E. C. Smith, 3, 10, 22 June 1896, Smith Papers, Duke; *Fisherman and Farmer,* 12 June 1896.

17. MB to D. Russell, 15 July 1896; D. C. Pearson to D. Russell, 22 July 1896; J. Young to D. Russell, 6 Aug. 1896; R. Pearson to D. Russell, 22 July 1896; R. A. Cobb to D. Russell, 17 July 1896; all in Russell Papers, SHC; *Patron and Gleaner,* 23 July 1896; *Elizabeth City Economist,* 24 July 1896.

18. A survey of the convention is Glad, *McKinley, Bryan, and the People,* 131–41.

19. *Progressive Farmer,* 9 June 1896; *Topeka Farmers' Advocate,* 15 July 1896; D. Waite to I. Donnelly, 12 July 1896, Donnelly Papers, MHS; Jones, *Election of 1896,* 244–45; Peffer, *Populism,* 146–47.

20. MB to S. A. Ashe, 13 July 1896, Ashe Papers, NCDAH; MB to W. J. Peele, 8 July 1896, Peele Papers, SHC; *Caucasian,* 16, 23 July 1896.

21. W. J. Peele to MB, 18, 20 July 1896, BP; Durden, *Climax of Populism,* 23.

22. *Progressive Farmer,* 14 July 1896; *Dallas Southern Mercury,* 5 Mar., 9 July 1896; *News and Observer,* 21 July 1896; *Caucasian,* 23 July 1896.

23. Jones, *Election of 1896,* 255; *News and Observer,* 22 July 1896; *Washington Post,* 22 July 1896; *New York Times,* 22 July 1896.

24. *News and Observer,* 23 July 1896; *Caucasian,* 30 July 1896; *Washington Post,* 23 July 1896; *New York Times,* 23 July 1896.

25. Durden, *Climax of Populism,* 33.

26. *News and Observer,* 24 July 1896; *New York Times,* 24 July 1896; Durden, *Climax of Populism,* 33–34; Jones, *Election of 1896,* 256.

27. *News and Observer,* 25 July 1896; *Caucasian,* 30 July 1896; *Washington Post,* 25 July 1896.

28. *News and Observer,* 25 July 1896; Goodwyn, *Democratic Promise,* 482–83; Jones, *Election of 1896,* 250–60.

29. *News and Observer,* 25 July 1896; *Caucasian,* 30 July 1896; *People's Party Paper,* 31 July 1896; Woodward, *Tom Watson,* 303–5.

30. Durden, *Climax of Populism,* 114; *People's Party Paper,* 31 July 1896; *Caucasian,* 30 July 1896.

31. *New York Times,* 26 July 1896.

32. Of course, variety among state Populism is an old idea, reflected in historians as different as John Hicks and Lawrence Goodwyn. What I emphasize here is the importance of strategic concerns as distinct from ideological differences, although the significance of that issue has already been confirmed by considerable state-level work. All historians of Populism owe Worth Robert Miller a great debt because of his creation and maintenance of a comprehensive annotated bibliography on Populism on his Website ‹http://history.smsu.edu/wrmiller›. On the point at issue, even the structure of the bibliography, which is arranged by subject, suggests the highly localized characteristics of Populism. Writings about prominent Populist states, for example, such as Alabama, Georgia, Kansas, Nebraska, North Carolina, and Texas, are much more extensive than writings on other states. Some large states, such as New

York and Massachusetts, do not even warrant a separate entry. More important, the substance of state-level studies, much of it written in the past twenty years, has documented a nearly endless variety in strategy and success, especially in the most important Populist states. See, for example, Ostler, *Prairie Populism*, and Argersinger, *Limits of Agrarian Radicalism*, on political structure and institutional concerns in Kansas, Nebraska, and Iowa. On the Texas party's strategic behavior in 1896, see Cantrell, *Kenneth and John B. Rayner*, 233–41. Barton Shaw's *Wool-Hat Boys* describes the complicating effect of factions and personalities in Georgia, as does William Warren Rogers's *One-Gallused Rebellion* in Alabama. In *Ben Tillman*, Stephen Kantrowitz discusses the Tillman phenomenon in South Carolina and its consequences for a third party there. Equally unique conditions in far western Populism are presented in Robert W. Larson, *Populism in the Mountain West*, and James E. Wright, *Politics of Populism* (Colorado). Of course this is only the tip of the historiographical iceberg, as Miller's bibliography, which lists hundreds of state- and local-level citations, shows. The larger point, for the biographer of Butler, is how Butler perceived and tried to deal with the intense local political forces that had such a devastating effect on his attempts to build a national party, particularly in presidential elections.

33. *News and Observer*, 26 July 1896.

Chapter 8

1. *News and Observer*, 14 Aug. 1896; J. H. Pou to W. B. Rodman, 3 July 1896, Rodman Papers, ECU; *Elizabeth City Economist*, 7, 14 Aug. 1896; *Patron and Gleaner*, 6, 13 Aug. 1896; *Hickory Press*, 6 Aug. 1896; *Wilmington Messenger*, 13 Aug. 1896; *Goldsboro Headlight*, 6 Aug. 1896; *Greenville King's Weekly*, 7 Aug. 1896; *Fayetteville Observer*, 6 Aug. 1896; C. S. Donaldson to T. Settle, 10 Aug. 1896, Settle Papers, SHC; *Moravian Falls Yellow Jacket*, Aug. 1896; *Union Republican*, 27 Aug. 1896; B. N. Duke to D. Russell, 12 Aug. 1896, Duke Papers, Duke.

2. *Progressive Farmer*, 4 Aug. 1896; C. Thompson to J. Ramsey, 7 Aug. 1896, and J. W. Mewborne to J. Ramsey, 8 Aug. 1896, J. W. Denmark Papers, NCDAH.

3. *News and Observer*, 14 Aug. 1896.

4. Steelman, "Progressive Era in North Carolina," 133–34; O. H. Dockery to MB, 10 Aug. 1896, BP; *News and Observer*, 14 Aug. 1896; *Caucasian*, 20 Aug. 1896.

5. *News and Observer*, 14, 15 Aug. 1896; *Caucasian*, 20 Aug. 1896; *Patron and Gleaner*, 20 Aug. 1896.

6. *Progressive Farmer*, 18 Aug. 1896.

7. *Caucasian*, 20 Aug. 1896; *Patron and Gleaner*, 20 Aug. 1896; *Hickory Press*, 20 Aug. 1896; *Union Republican*, 20, 27 Aug. 1896; *Elizabeth City North Carolinian*, 19, 26 Aug. 1896; *Progressive Farmer*, 25 Aug. 1896.

8. H. Ayer to R. Pearson, 31 Aug. 1896, Pearson Papers, SHC; A. E. Holton to T. Settle, 24 Aug. 1896, and M. M. Corbett to T. Settle, 31 Aug. 1896, Settle Papers, SHC; *Patron and Gleaner*, 3, 10 Sept. 1896; H. Ayer to MB, 1, 4 Sept. 1896; J. W. Shook to MB, 3 Sept. 1896; MB to Z. V. Walser, 1 Sept. 1896; G. Hunt to MB, 29 Aug. 1896; H. Ayer to MB, 4 Sept. 1896; J. J. Mott to MB, 2 Sept. 1896; all in BP; W. B. Rodman to W. H. Lucas, 13 Oct. 1896, Rodman Papers, ECU.

9. H. Ayer to C. Thompson, 1 Sept. 1896, Thompson Papers, SHC; *Patron and Gleaner*, 10 Sept. 1896; *Charlotte Daily Observer*, 11, 12 Sept. 1896; *Elizabeth City North Carolinian*, 16 Sept. 1896; *Caucasian*, 17 Sept. 1896; *Progressive Farmer*, 15 Sept. 1896; *Union Republican*, 17 Sept. 1896; *Clinton Sampson Democrat*, 17 Sept. 1896; H. Ayer to MB, 11 Sept. 1896, BP.

10. *Progressive Farmer*, 22 Sept. 1896; *Clinton Sampson Democrat*, 10 Sept. 1896; Hal Ayer Circular, 1896, and J. B. Lloyd to MB, 15, 19, 22, 30 Sept. 1896, BP.

11. J. A. Spruill to W. B. Rodman, 29 Aug. 1896; J. S. Winfield to W. B. Rodman, 19 Sept. 1896; H. T. King to W. B. Rodman, 9 Oct. 1896; W. B. Rodman to W. S. Paul, 16 Sept. 1896; all in Rodman Papers, ECU; *Reidsville Webster's Weekly*, 17 Sept., 22 Oct. 1896; *Elizabeth City Economist*, 9 Oct. 1896; C. B. Aycock to MB, 19 Oct. 1896; MB to C. J. Faulkner, 17 Oct. 1896; W. J. Peele to MB, 24 Oct. 1896; H. Ayer to MB, 6, 10 Oct. 1896; W. H. Worth to MB, 6, 8 Oct. 1896; all in BP; *News and Observer*, 13, 14, 15, 16 Oct. 1896; *Greenville King's Weekly*, 16 Oct. 1896; *Charlotte Daily Observer*, 14 Oct. 1896; *Caucasian*, 15 Oct. 1896; *Fayetteville Observer*, 22 Oct. 1896; *Union Republican*, 22 Oct. 1896; *Patron and Gleaner*, 15, 22 Oct. 1896.

12. H. Ayer to MB, 6 Oct. 1896; W. J. Peele to MB, 27 Oct. 1896; B. F. Keith to MB, 13, 29 Oct. 1896; W. A. Guthrie to MB, 16 Oct. 1896; all in BP; Ayer, *To the Populist Voters of the Eighteenth Senatorial District*, NCC; *Wadesboro Plow Boy*, 21 Oct. 1896; *Clinton Sampson Democrat*, 15 Oct. 1896; *Progressive Farmer*, 29 Oct. 1896; Guthrie, *Supplemental Address to the People's Party Voters*, NCC.

13. H. Ayer to MB, 6 Oct. 1896, BP; *Caucasian*, 15 Oct. 1896; *Wilmington Messenger*, 14 Oct. 1896.

14. *Caucasian*, 6 Aug. 1896.

15. Ibid., 27 Aug. 1896; *Progressive Farmer*, 25 Aug. 1896; W. S. Morgan to MB, 5 Aug. 1896; A. W. C. Weeks to MB, 2 Aug. 1896; T. E. Watson to MB, 28 July, 8 Aug. 1896; all in BP; Durden, *Climax of Populism*, 54–57.

16. *Dallas Southern Mercury*, 6 Aug. 1896; MB to J. Bradley, 25 Aug. 1896, BP; *Topeka Farmers' Advocate*, 5 Aug. 1896.

17. H. W. Reed to MB, 25, 27 Aug. 1896; MB to L. C. Bateman, 25 Aug. 1896; MB to C. E. Sugg, 25 Aug. 1896; T. E. Watson to MB, 24, 25 Aug. 1896; all in BP; *Caucasian*, 27 Aug. 1896; Durden, *Climax of Populism*, 59–60.

18. MB to J. E. Bradley, 25 Aug. 1896; MB to T. E. Watson, 27 Aug. 1896; MB to H. W. Reed, 27 Aug. 1896; H. W. Reed to MB, 30 Aug. 1896; MB to J. M. Patterson, 28 Aug. 1896; MB to D. H. L. Banser, 31 Aug. 1896; MB to T. E. Thayer, 1 Sept. 1896; MB to L. H. Weller, 27 Aug. 1896; all in BP; MB, Circular, [1896], Weller Papers, SHSW.

19. MB to G. B. Deans, 31 Aug. 1896; MB to H. Moore, 31 Aug. 1896; MB to J. Parker, 28 Aug. 1896; MB to J. D. Bray, 28 Aug. 1896; MB to G. L. Spence, 29 Aug. 1896; MB to J. S. Anderson, 29 Aug. 1896; MB to J. Bradley, 26 Aug. 1896; MB to P. H. Blake, 27 Aug. 1896; all in BP; *Progressive Farmer*, 25 Aug. 1896.

20. H. W. Reed to MB, 29 Aug. 1896; T. E. Watson to MB, 25 Aug., 1 Sept. 1896; MB to W. V. Allen, 5, 11, 12, 14 Sept. 1896; all in BP; *People's Party Paper*, 4, 18 Sept. 1896; *Progressive Farmer*, 22 Sept. 1896.

21. *Dallas Southern Mercury*, 17, 24 Sept. 1896.

22. MB to J. H. Boyd, 21 Sept. 1896; MB to B. P. Baker, 1 Sept. 1896; MB to T. K. Massie, 2 Sept. 1896; MB to J. Parker, 5 Sept. 1896; MB to N. E. Baker, 3 Sept. 1896; MB to J. S. McDonald, 8 Sept. 1896; MB to J. R. Holton, 7 Sept. 1896; MB to R. D. Richardson, 18 Sept. 1896; MB to W. C. Hyatt, 19 Sept. 1896; F. H. Hoover to W. Barker, 12 Sept. 1896; MB to E. Debs, 12 Sept. 1896; MB to G. Washburn, 18 Sept. 1896; MB to T. G. McHaven, 14 Sept. 1896; all in BP; *New York Times*, 25 Sept. 1896.

23. Woodward, *Tom Watson*, 318-25; Durden, *Climax of Populism*, 90-92; MB to T. E. Watson, 8 Sept. 1896, and MB to G. Washburn, 15 Sept. 1896, BP.

24. H. W. Reed to MB, 17 Sept. 1896; MB to T. E. Watson, 22 Sept. 1896; MB to H. W. Bridenthal, 21 Sept. 1896; MB to G. Washburn, 28 Sept. 1896; MB to C. F. Taylor, 25 Sept. 1896; all in BP.

25. T. E. Watson to MB, 27 Sept. 1896, BP; Woodward, *Tom Watson*, 323-25.

26. MB to H. W. Reed, 29 Sept. 1896; MB to C. F. Taylor, 25 Sept. 1896; MB to G. Washburn, 18, 24, 29 Sept. 1896; MB to T. E. Watson, 30 Sept. 1896; all in BP.

27. MB to M. C. Rankin, 11, 17 Sept., 9 Oct. 1896; MB to R. G. Scott, 31 Aug. 1896; MB to J. K. Brunt, 29 Aug. 1896; MB to F. K. Lane, 28 Aug. 1896; MB to T. E. Watson, 22 Sept. 1896; MB to H. W. Reed, 18 Sept. 1896; MB to G. Washburn, 11 Sept. 1896; MB to C. J. Faulkner, 17 Oct. 1896; MB to E. Boyce, 5 Oct. 1896; W. H. Worth to MB, 12 Sept., 2 Oct. 1896; R. C. Rivers to MB, 8 June 1896; MB to W. R. Hearst, 8 Oct. 1896; MB to J. R. Sovereign, 26 Sept. 1896; all in BP; J. A. Edgerton to I. Donnelly, 3 Oct. 1896, Donnelly Papers, MHS.

28. *People's Party Paper*, 2, 9, 30 Oct. 1896; *Dallas Southern Mercury*, 15 Oct. 1896; *Progressive Farmer*, 13, 20 Oct. 1896; J. A. Tatts to MB, 3 Oct. 1896, and R. Kolb to MB, 20 Oct. 1896, BP.

29. H. W. Reed to MB, 7, 9 Oct. 1896; MB to G. Washburn, 8 Sept., 3, 5, 6, 24 Oct. 1896; MB to J. Haskell, 7 Sept. 1896; MB to R. Kolb, 21 Sept. 1896; MB to J. H. Burnham, 21 Sept. 1896; MB to J. K. Jones, 5, 21 Sept. 1896; MB to S. S. Field, 25 Sept. 1896; MB to J. K. Jones, 22 Oct. 1896; all in BP; Durden, *Climax of Populism*, 72-78, 114. Butler persuaded Ignatius Donnelly to issue a statement supporting the Bryan-Watson ticket. He wrote Donnelly: "The individual voter is governed too much, as a rule, by his local surroundings. He is apt to be guided much by local prejudices, and fail to comprehend in a crisis like this what his full duty is, and what the responsibilities are that attach to his action or non-action" (MB to I. Donnelly, 18 Sept. 1896, BP).

30. *Progressive Farmer*, 14 Oct. 1896; W. J. Peele to MB, 24 Oct. 1896, BP; E. P. Howell to T. E. Watson, 17 Oct. 1896, Watson Papers, SHC; Durden, *Climax of Populism*, 114-20.

31. MB to G. Washburn, 22 Oct. 1896; MB to C. F. Taylor, 19 Oct. 1896; F. H. Hoover to T. E. Watson, 19 Oct. 1896; MB to G. Washburn, 22 Oct. 1896; all in BP; Durden, *Climax of Populism*, 122-23; *Caucasian*, 3 Dec. 1896.

32. MB to T. E. Watson, 26 Oct. 1896, BP; *Caucasian*, 3 Dec. 1896.

33. T. E. Watson to MB, 28 Oct. 1896; MB to H. W. Reed, 2 Nov. 1896; F. H. Hoover to J. T. Willets, 31 Oct. 1896; all in BP; *People's Party Paper*, 20 Nov. 1896; *Caucasian*, 5 Nov. 1896; *Progressive Farmer*, 3 Nov. 1896.

34. *Progressive Farmer*, 27 Oct. 1896; *Caucasian*, 29 Oct. 1896.

35. Durden, *Climax of Populism*, 126-27; Glad, *McKinley, Bryan, and the People*,

189–209; Hicks, *Populist Revolt*, 377; Hamilton, *North Carolina since 1860*, 261–62; S. R. Mason to MB, 10 Nov. 1896, BP.

36. *Clinton Sampson Democrat*, 26 Nov. 1896; *Topeka Farmers' Advocate*, 11 Nov. 1896; *New York Times*, 8 Nov. 1896; MB to W. J. Peele, 9 Nov. 1896, Peele Papers, SHC.

37. MB, "Some Facts the Public Should Know," Dec. 1896, BP; *People's Party Paper*, 20 Nov. 1896.

38. *Topeka Farmers' Advocate*, 11 Nov. 1896; *People's Party Paper*, 13, 20 Nov. 1896; *Dallas Southern Mercury*, 5, 19, 26 Nov. 1896.

39. *Caucasian*, 19 Nov. 1896; *Clinton Sampson Democrat*, 19 Nov. 1896; *Progressive Farmer*, 17 Nov. 1896; J. H. Sherrill to MB, 12 Nov. 1896, and J. F. Click to MB, 18, 19 Nov. 1896, BP.

Chapter 9

1. H. Skinner to C. Thompson, 12 Nov. 1896, and J. C. Pritchard to C. Thompson, 26 Dec. 1896, Thompson Papers, SHC; T. C. McCrary to J. G. Ramsey, 24 Nov. 1896, Ramsey Papers, SHC; Crow and Durden, *Maverick Republican*, 79–81; Hamilton, *North Carolina since 1860*, 260; *Caucasian*, 10 Dec. 1896, 14 Jan. 1897; M. L. Mott to D. Russell, 3 Dec. 1896, BP; *Patron and Gleaner*, 7, 21 Jan. 1897; *New York Times*, 4 Jan. 1897; *News and Observer*, 9, 10 Jan. 1897; *Raleigh Daily Tribune*, 16 Jan. 1897. Perhaps Chairman James K. Jones of the Democratic national committee sent Butler money to fight Pritchard's nomination. See J. M. Devine to MB, 10 Jan. 1897, BP.

2. *Raleigh Gazette*, 2 Jan. 1897; *Elizabeth City North Carolinian*, 13 Jan., 3 Feb. 1897; *New York Times*, 21 Jan. 1897; *Raleigh Daily Tribune*, 16, 21 Jan. 1897; *Pittsboro Chatham Citizen*, 18 Feb. 1897; *Union Republican*, 14 Jan. 1897; *News and Observer*, 9, 10 Jan. 1897; *Caucasian*, 14 Jan. 1897; *Patron and Gleaner*, 21 Jan. 1897.

3. *Elizabeth City Economist*, 15 Jan. 1897; *News and Observer*, 10 Jan. 1897; *Fayetteville Observer*, 14 Jan. 1897; *New York Times*, 21 Jan. 1897; *Raleigh Daily Tribune*, 21 Jan. 1897; *Pittsboro Chatham Citizen*, 18 Feb. 1897; *Union Republican*, 14 Jan. 1897; *Progressive Farmer*, 26 Jan. 1897; J. Duckett to MB, 7 Jan. 1897; W. J. Peele to MB, 1 Jan. 1897; G. L. Hardison to MB, 1 July 1897, 25 June 1906; MB to G. Washburn, 5 Feb. 1897; MB to Mrs. Marion Butler, 25 Jan. 1897; Response to *Charlotte Observer*, Mar. 1916; all in BP; *Wadesboro Plow Boy*, 13 Jan. 1897; *Caucasian*, 7, 14, 21 Jan. 1897.

4. *Progressive Farmer*, 26 Jan., 9 Feb. 1897; *Fayetteville Observer*, 21 Jan. 1897; *Elizabeth City Economist*, 22 Jan. 1897; *Caucasian*, 4, 11 Feb. 1897; MB to G. Washburn, 5 Feb. 1897, BP; Hamilton, *North Carolina since 1860*, 265; *Patron and Gleaner*, 28 Jan. 1897; *Raleigh Daily Tribune*, 22, 27, 28, 29 Jan. 1897; *Wadesboro Plow Boy*, 13 Feb. 1897; *Raleigh Gazette*, 13 Feb. 1897.

5. G. Butler to MB, 29 Jan., 18, 28 Feb., 7 Apr. 1897; W. Clark to MB, 30 Jan., 11, 22 Feb. 1897; W. S. Pearson to MB, 14 Feb. 1897; all in BP; Trelease, "Fusion Legislatures," 280–309; Crow and Durden, *Maverick Republican*, 78–86, 90; *Caucasian*, 11 Feb. 1897; *Clinton Sampson Democrat*, 11, 18 Feb. 1897.

6. *Raleigh Daily Tribune*, 4 Feb. 1897; Crow and Durden, *Maverick Republican*, 85–89; Trelease, "Fusion Legislatures," 301–4; J. F. Click to MB, 23 Feb. 1897; T. S.

Sutton to MB, 30 Jan. 1897; G. Butler to MB, 18 Feb. 1897; MB to J. H. Ferris, 11 Mar. 1897; all in BP.

7. *Raleigh Daily Tribune*, 20 Mar. 1897; G. Butler to MB, 28 Feb., 1 Mar. 1897, and W. E. Fountain to MB, 2, 5 Mar., 2 Apr. 1897, BP; Crow and Durden, *Maverick Republican*, 93–95.

8. "Address of Populist Congressional Caucus," [1897], BP.

9. Rothman, *Politics and Power*, 96–98; Ginger, *Age of Excess*, 195; Leech, *Days of McKinley*, 140–41; *Congressional Record*, 55th Cong., 1st sess., 1573, 1576, 1589–92, 1594, 1617–20, 1745–46, 1752, 1790–91, 1793–94, 1811, 1832, 1854–61, 1874–75, 1902–3, 1948, 1958, 2013–14, 2016, 2138–39, 2151, 2165–66, 2173–74, 2185–87, 2384, 2386–87, 2430, 2438, 2446, 2772–73, 2909; Typescript, 21 May 1897, BP.

10. *Congressional Record*, 54th Cong., 2d sess., index, 38; *Congressional Record*, 55th Cong., 1st sess., index, 41; *Congressional Record*, 54th Cong., 2d sess., 2096–97, 2407–15, 2436–48; U.S. Congress, Senate Committee on Post Offices and Post Roads, *Senate Minority Rep. 1517*; MB to C. F. Taylor, 16 Nov. 1897, BP; *Congressional Record*, 55th Cong., 1st sess., 795–98, 992–93, 1049, 1083–84, 1440, 2414, 2552; Fuller, *American Mail*, 138–39, 157–87. Much later, Butler recalled that he worked to nationalize natural monopolies but he knew he did not have the votes to succeed. He then "attempted to secure certain minor [e.g., postal] reforms, where I hoped to meet less organized resistance." MB to E. J. Ridgway, 2 Apr. 1914, BP.

11. *Congressional Record*, 54th Cong., 2d sess., 241, 246, 395, 1937–38, 2080, 2081–83, 2089, 2186, 2337, 2340; *Congressional Record*, 55th Cong., 1st sess., 69–70, 1041, 1084, 1440, 1492–96, 1899, 1926, 2625, 2874, 2951.

12. Hicks, *Populist Revolt*, 380–81; I. Donnelly to MB, 28 Nov. 1896, and MB to I. Donnelly, 10 Dec. 1896, Donnelly Papers, MHS.

13. Hicks, *Populist Revolt*, 380–81; *People's Party Paper*, 7 July 1897; M. O'Neill to MB, 28 Jan. 1897; J. Edgerton to MB, 28 Jan. 1897; G. Washburn to MB, 30 Jan. 1897; H. Tracy to MB, 1 Feb. 1897; all in BP.

14. MB to J. Rosenheimer, 5 Feb. 1897; M. E. O'Neill to MB, 10 Feb. 1897; MB to A. Rozelle, 9, 16 Feb. 1897; MB to S. F. Norton, 16 Feb. 1897; J. H. Briedenthal to MB, 9, 17 Feb. 1897; MB to G. Washburn, 14, 30 Jan., 5 Feb. 1897; G. Washburn to MB, 30 Jan., 24 Feb., 3 Mar. 1897; J. R. Sovereign to MB, 16 Feb. 1897; J. M. Glass to MB, 13 Feb. 1897; MB to C. Vincent, 5 Feb. 1897; all in BP; *New York Times*, 11 Jan. 1897; *Wadesboro Plow Boy*, 17 Feb. 1897.

15. G. Washburn to MB, 24 Feb., 3 Mar. 1897, and J. R. Sovereign to MB, 25 Feb. 1897, BP; Hicks, *Populist Revolt*, 380–81; *New York Times*, 23 Feb. 1897.

16. F. Burkitt to MB, 26 Feb. 1897; MB to G. Washburn, 9 Mar. 1897; MB to C. M. Walter, 8 Feb. 1897; C. Taylor to MB, 9 Jan. 1897; List of Committeemen, Jan. 1897; MB to J. McDowell, 25 Mar. 1897; all in BP.

17. MB to M. Page, 28 Mar. 1897; MB to J. A. Edgerton, 11 Mar. 1897; MB Circular to People's Party National Committee, 13 Mar. 1897; MB to J. Sutherland, 7 Apr. 1897; MB to F. Burkitt, 16 Mar. 1897; MB to J. H. Ferris, 7 Apr. 1897; R. Kolb to MB, 14 June 1897; J. R. Sovereign to MB, 29 Apr., 17 May 1897; C. Vincent to MB, 30 May

1897; H. W. Reed to MB, 30 Apr. 1897; J. R. Sovereign to M. Park, 16 Apr. 1897; E. Pomeroy to MB, 27 June 1897; all in BP; *Caucasian*, 8, 15 Apr., 1 July 1897.

18. *New York Times*, 19, 20 Apr. 1897; *Progressive Farmer*, 8 June, 10 Aug. 1897; Hicks, *Populist Revolt*, 381–82; *People's Party Paper*, 9 July, 12 Nov. 1897; *Topeka Farmers' Advocate*, 14 July 1897; *Caucasian*, 22 July 1897; R. Schilling to MB, 9 July 1897; C. Vincent to MB, 9 July 1897; A. H. Cardin to MB, 10 July 1897; G. Washburn to MB, 31 July 1897; M. Howard to MB, 13 Aug. 1897; M. Park to MB, 16 Aug. 1897; all in BP; I. Donnelly to MB, 28 Nov. 1896, Donnelly Papers, MHS.

19. *New York Times*, 20 Apr. 1897; *Caucasian*, 15 July 1897; *Wadesboro Plow Boy*, 7 July 1897; J. K. Jones to MB, 1 June 1897, BP.

20. *Wadesboro Plow Boy*, 17, 24 Mar., 28 Apr. 1897; *Salisbury Carolina Watchman*, 10 June, 12 Aug. 1897; *Hickory Mercury*, 22 Sept. 1897; W. A. Barbrey to MB, 12 Dec. 1897; L. C. Caldwell to MB, 13 June 1897; G. Butler to MB, 12 Dec. 1897; J. Graham to MB, 17 Apr. 1897; D. Russell to MB, 5 May, 12 June, 24 July, 20 Dec. 1897; J. H. Pearson to MB, 26 Dec. 1897; S. A. Asbury to MB, 19 June 1897; all in BP; *Raleigh Hayseeder*, 14 Oct., 4, 11, 25 Nov., 9 Dec. 1897; Crow and Durden, *Maverick Republican*, 97–110.

21. Handbill, Wadesboro Speech, 12 Aug. 1897; C. Vincent to MB, 17 Sept. 1897; MB to W. J. Peele, 12 Oct. 1897; all in BP; *Raleigh Gazette*, 21 Aug. 1897; *Progressive Farmer*, 17 Aug. 1897; *Hickory Mercury*, 11, 18, 25 Aug. 1897; *Caucasian*, 13 May, 3, 17 June, 12, 19 Aug., 16 Sept., 14, 21, 28 Oct., 4, 18 Nov., 16 Dec. 1897.

22. Hamilton, *North Carolina since 1860*, 279–80; *Caucasian*, 19 Aug., 23, 30 Sept., 7 Oct. 1897; *Raleigh Gazette*, 21 Aug. 1897; Morrison, *Josephus Daniels Says*, 103–4; Thurtell, "Fusion Insurgency in North Carolina," 312.

23. *Caucasian*, 16, 30 Sept., 7 Oct., 25 Nov., 2, 9, 16 Dec. 1897; Steelman, "Progressive Era in North Carolina," 156–58; *Asheville Daily Gazette*, 23 Nov. 1897; *Hickory Mercury*, 24 Nov., 8, 15 Dec. 1897; *Raleigh Hayseeder*, 25 Nov. 1897; B. F. Keith to MB, 29 Nov. 1897, and J. F. Click to MB, 30 Nov. 1897, BP.

24. *Congressional Record*, 55th Cong., 2d sess., 23, 110–14, 310, 961, 2069, 5535–36; Fuller, *American Mail*, 178–84.

25. *Congressional Record*, 55th Cong., 2d sess., 961, 2404, 4609–19.

26. Ibid., 4687, 4696–97, 4703, 4719–20, 4755–60.

27. Ibid., 310, 430–31, 1572.

28. Hicks, *American Nation*, 308–13; Ginger, *Age of Excess*, 196–200; *Caucasian*, 16 Dec. 1897, 24 Feb., 10 Mar., 7 Apr. 1898. Contrasting views of Populists and the war are Woodward, *Origins of the New South*, 369; Shaw, *Wool-Hat Boys*, 193–94; and Hicks, *Populist Revolt*, 389–90.

29. *Congressional Record*, 55th Cong., 2d sess., 3703, 3731–33; Leech, *Days of McKinley*, 186–87; Hicks, *American Nation*, 310–13; Ginger, *Age of Excess*, 201.

30. Leech, *Days of McKinley*, 186–89; *Congressional Record*, 55th Cong., 2d sess., 4035–41, 4069; *Caucasian*, 21 Apr. 1898.

31. *Congressional Record*, 55th Cong., 2d sess., 4341, appendix, 468–89; W. Clark to MB, 14 Apr. 1898, BP; *Caucasian*, 5 May, 7 June 1898.

32. *Congressional Record*, 55th Cong., 2d sess., appendix, 468–89.

Chapter 10

1. J. P. Buchanan to MB, 9 Jan. 1898; H. W. Reed to MB, 14 Dec. 1897; E. G. Brown to MB, 5 Jan. 1898; J. Bell to MB, 5 Jan. 1898; MB to J. C. Young, 3 Mar. 1898; all in BP; *People's Party Paper*, 21 Jan. 1898; Hicks, *Populist Revolt*, 382–83; *New York Times*, 16 Feb. 1898; *Caucasian*, 24 Feb., 12 May 1898; *Progressive Farmer*, 3 May 1898.

2. MB, "Trusts—the Causes That Produce Them—the Remedy."

3. J. R. Brown to MB, 18 Apr. 1898, and A. S. Brown to MB, 23 Mar. 1898, BP.

4. E. Pomeroy to MB, 25 May 1898, and T. F. Keleher to MB, 11 June 1898, BP; Hicks, *Populist Revolt*, 383–85; *New York Times*, 16, 17 June 1898; *Caucasian*, 23 June 1898.

5. "Petition," 16 June 1898; G. Butler to MB, 21 June 1898; M. Caldwell to MB, 22 June 1898; all in BP; *Caucasian*, 23 June 1898; *New York Times*, 18 June 1898; *Hickory Times-Mercury*, 22 June 1898; *Caucasian*, 23 June 1898; *Dallas Southern Mercury*, 23 June 1898; *New York Times*, 18 June 1898.

6. W. Barker to L. Weller, 29 June, 7 July 1898, Weller Papers, SHSW; *New York Times*, 2 July 1898; *Progressive Farmer*, 14 June, 5 July 1898; H. Tracy to MB, 4, 11 July 1898; H. Tracy to J. H. Ferris, 9 July 1898; G. Washburn to MB, 13 July 1898; M. Park to J. H. Ferris, 1 Aug. 1898; J. H. Ferris to MB, 11 July 1898; J. H. Ferris to Editor of the *Caucasian*, 14 July 1898; H. L. Bentley to MB, 8 July 1898; all in BP; *Caucasian*, 30 June, 7 July 1898.

7. C. F. Taylor to MB, 14 July 1898; E. Pomeroy to C. F. Taylor, 24 July 1898; E. Pomeroy to H. L. Bentley, 31 July 1898; H. Tracy to J. H. Ferris, 9 July 1898; all in BP.

8. MB to M. Park, 26 July 1898; M. Park to MB, 8 Aug. 1898; J. H. Davis to MB, 9 Aug. 1898; H. Tracy to MB, 14 Aug. 1898; J. Bell to MB, 17 Aug. 1898; H. D. Wood to MB, 28 Aug. 1898; E. Pomeroy to MB, 24 Aug. 1898; M. Park to W. S. Morgan, 9 Sept. 1898; L. Mantle to MB, 2 Oct. 1898; all in BP; *Caucasian*, 1, 9 Sept. 1898; *Hickory Times-Mercury*, 31 Aug. 1898.

9. *New York Times*, 24 July, 31 Aug. 1898; E. Pomeroy to MB, 19 Sept. 1898, BP; *Progressive Farmer*, 13 Sept. 1898; *Caucasian*, 22 Sept. 1898; Hicks, *Populist Revolt*, 385–87.

10. Hicks, *Populist Revolt*, 393–96; Shaw, *Wool-Hat Boys*, 195–96.

11. *Caucasian*, 10 Feb., 3 Mar., 7, 14, 28 Apr. 1898; *Hickory Times-Mercury*, 9 Mar. 1898; *Progressive Farmer*, 3 May 1898; J. F. Click to MB, 11 Jan. 1898; B. F. Keith to MB, 26 Feb. 1898; R. C. Rivers to MB, 1, 10 Mar. 1898; R. B. Davis to MB, 12 Mar. 1898; H. Ayer to MB, 17 Jan., 23 Feb. 1898; M. Caldwell to MB, 17 Feb. 1898; all in BP.

12. *Raleigh Hayseeder*, 20, 27 Jan., 17 Feb., 17 Mar. 1898; *Pittsboro Chatham Citizen*, 27 Apr. 1898; *Progressive Farmer*, 12 Apr., 10 May 1898; *Charlotte People's Paper*, 25 Feb., 4 Mar., 8, 15 Apr., 6, 20 May 1898; *Hickory Times-Mercury*, 23 Mar., 27 Apr., 4 May 1898; J. F. Click to MB, 19 Mar. 1898; "Populist Conference," 16 Mar. 1898; "Clipping" [1898 Conference]; M. Caldwell to MB, 18 Mar. 1898; G. Butler to MB, 3 May 1898; J. W. Mayo to MB, 10 Jan. 1898; W. J. Leary to MB, 29 Apr. 1898; T. H. Sutton to MB, 31 Jan. 1898; R. C. Rivers to MB, 17 Mar. 1898; all in BP.

13. *Elizabeth City North Carolinian*, 4, 25 May 1898; *Hickory Press*, 21 Jan., 31 Mar., 5 Apr. 1898; *Raleigh Gazette*, 1 Jan., 22 Feb. 1898; Crow and Durden, *Maverick Republi-*

can, 111 — 22; *Raleigh Hayseeder*, 13, 27 Jan. 1898; W. L. Person to MB, 7 Feb., 12 Mar. 1898; W. Clark to MB, 28 Feb., 23 Mar. 1898; J. H. Pearson to MB, 3 Mar. 1898; L. C. Caldwell to MB, 13 Jan., 9 Mar. 1898; B. F. Keith to MB, 15 Apr. 1898; C. H. Utley to MB, 26 Mar. 1898; D. L. Russell to MB, 20, 30 Apr. 1898; R. Hancock to MB, 15 Jan. 1898; J. S. Basnight to MB, 13 Jan. 1898; R. B. Davis to MB, 21 Feb., 12 Mar. 1898; all in BP.

14. E. J. Hale to MB, 18 Feb., 7 Mar. 1898, and W. Clark to MB, 28 Apr. 1898, BP; C. Manly to Dear Sir, 19 Apr. 1898; W. B. Rodman to E. J. Hale, 31 Oct. 1897; W. B. Rodman to Dear Sir, 22 Nov. 1897; all in Rodman Papers, ECU; Steelman, "Progressive Era in North Carolina," 158 — 80; *Caucasian*, 3, 10 Mar., 5 May 1898; *Reidsville Webster's Weekly*, 14 Apr., 5, 12, 19 May 1898; C. B. Aycock to R. B. Creecy, 9 May 1898, Creecy Papers, NCDAH.

15. *Caucasian*, 7, 14 Apr., 19 May 1898; *Hickory Times-Mercury*, 23 Mar., 25 May 1898; J. McDuffie to MB, 2 May 1898; M. Caldwell to MB, 11 Apr., 2, 7 May 1898; B. F. Keith to MB, 7 May 1898; J. J. Rodgers to MB, 6 May 1898; all in BP; *News and Observer*, 17, 18 May 1898; *Raleigh Morning Post*, 17, 18 May 1898; *Asheville Daily Gazette*, 19, 20 May 1898; *Wilmington Messenger*, 18 May 1898; *Charlotte Observer*, 18 May 1898; *Raleigh Home Rule*, 26 May 1898; *Elizabeth City Economist*, 20 May 1898; *Progressive Farmer*, 24 May 1898; *Fisherman and Farmer*, 20 May 1898; *Pittsboro Chatham Citizen*, 25 May 1898.

16. *Hickory Times-Mercury*, 25 May 1898; *Charlotte People's Paper*, 27 May 1898; *News and Observer*, 19, 26 May 1898; *Fayetteville Observer*, 19, 26 May 1898; *Patron and Gleaner*, 26 May 1898; *Greenville King's Weekly*, 27 May 1898; *Elizabeth City Economist*, 27 May 1898; *Charlotte Observer*, 20, 22, 25 May 1898; *Wilmington Messenger*, 18, 21, 26 May 1898; W. A. Guthrie to MB, 20, 24 May 1898; J. M. King to MB, 25 May 1898; W. W. Barker to MB, 20 May 1898; M. Caldwell to MB, 23 May 1898; J. B. Lloyd to MB, 21 May 1898; all in BP; *Is the Democratic Party Honest?*, NCC; *Caucasian*, 16 June 1898; *Raleigh Morning Post*, 25 May 1898.

17. *Progressive Farmer*, 31 May 1898; *Caucasian*, 2 June 1898; *Asheville Daily Gazette*, 26, 28 May 1898.

18. *Hickory Times-Mercury*, 1 June 1898; *Caucasian*, 4 Aug. 1898; J. H. Sherrill to MB, 30 May 1898; J. F. Click to MB, 26 June 1898; C. Thompson to MB, 3 June, 21 July 1898; W. F. Strowd to MB, 7, 21 July 1898; E. A. Moye to MB, 20 June, 4 July 1898; W. J. Leary to MB, 29 July 1898; B. F. Keith to MB, 8 July 1898; J. Z. Green to MB, 8 July 1898; all in BP.

19. J. W. Lassiter to MB, 24 June 1898; J. F. Click to MB, 26 June 1898; W. S. Bailey to MB, 7 June 1898; J. W. F. Mitchell to MB, 30 May 1898; J. T. B. Hoover to MB, 30 May 1898; M. Caldwell to MB, 30 May 1898; all in BP; *Raleigh Home Rule*, 16, 30 June, 4 Aug. 1898; *Asheville Daily Gazette*, 21, 22, 23 July, 1 Sept. 1898; Crow and Durden, *Maverick Republican*, 124 — 25; *Union Republican*, 28 July 1898.

20. W. H. Standin to MB, 23 July 1898; R. C. Rivers to MB, 6 Aug. 1898; J. H. Sherrill to MB, 8 Sept. 1898; H. J. Doxey to MB, 29 Aug. 1898; all in BP; *Caucasian*, 28 July 1898; *Raleigh Home Rule*, 4 Aug. 1898; *Elizabeth City North Carolinian*, 17 Aug., 7 Sept. 1898; C. Thompson to R. Pearson, Pearson Papers, SHC; *Greenville King's Weekly*, 6 Sept. 1898; *Union Republican*, 8 Sept. 1898; *Asheville Daily Gazette*, 2, 3 Sept. 1898;

Hickory Times-Mercury, 1 Sept. 1898; *Progressive Farmer*, 13 Sept. 1898; *Raleigh Morning Post*, 30 Aug., 1, 2 Sept. 1898; *News and Observer*, 2 Sept. 1898.

21. *Greenville King's Weekly*, 7 Oct. 1898; *News and Observer*, 25, 26 Oct. 1898; *Elizabeth City Economist*, 14 Oct., 4 Nov. 1898; *Goldsboro Headlight*, 3 Nov. 1898; F. Simmons to W. B. Rodman, 29 July 1898, Rodman Papers, ECU. On the 1898 election, see, for example, Crow and Durden, *Maverick Republican*, 117–37; Steelman, "Progressive Era in North Carolina," 150–80; Hamilton, *North Carolina since 1860*, 272–99; Edmonds, *The Negro and Fusion Politics*, 148–77; Rippy, *Furnifold Simmons*, 23–29; Wooley, "Race and Politics"; Richard L. Watson Jr., "Furnifold M. Simmons and the Politics of White Supremacy," in Crow, Escott, and Flynn, *Race, Class, and Politics*, 126–72; Gilmore, *Gender and Jim Crow*, 82–118.

22. *Asheville Daily Gazette*, 6 Sept. 1898; *Reidsville Webster's Weekly*, 29 Sept., 6, 13 Oct. 1898; *Fayetteville Observer*, 15, 22 Sept., 6 Oct. 1898; *Caucasian*, 29 Sept. 1898; *Greenville King's Weekly*, 7 Oct., 15 Nov. 1898; *Populist Handbook Answered*, NCC.

23. Several important recent studies of late-nineteenth-century North and South Carolina show the importance of gender to politics. See, for example, Kantrowitz, *Ben Tillman*; Gilmore, *Gender and Jim Crow*, and Edwards, *Gendered Strife*. One of these historians, Stephen Kantrowitz, has suggested that the "study of gender may constitute the 'missing piece' in developing a new, compelling political synthesis of the period" (*Ben Tillman*, 312 n. 1). Yet assuming the importance of gender to politics broadly understood, its explanatory force for Populism as a distinct political force seems limited, at least for North Carolina. Glenda Gilmore's book, for example, despite its considerable attention to state politics in the 1890s, contains no analysis of male Populist attitudes toward women. As for Butler, she implies only that gender affected his career because a Democratic nickname for him, "Mary Ann," was an attempt to suggest he was a homosexual (*Gender and Jim Crow*, 98). There does not seem to be any direct evidence for this conclusion, and at any rate, Democrats also labeled Butler a crook, a liar, a boss, and practically every other masculine vice they could conceive. Democrats ridiculed Populists using a range of arguments, and Populists responded in kind. The lack of any substantial distinction between white Populists and Democrats on gender issues is worth emphasizing because Populism was the greatest organized uprising against Democracy between Reconstruction and the 1960s. If gender was not an important factor in that uprising, then gender's ability to produce a new synthesis of political history seems unlikely, unless Populism is relegated to irrelevance. In contrast, real differences existed on issues of political economy. The hypocritical, contrived political tactics of Josephus Daniels and Charles Aycock were not motivated by any sincere belief that Democrats differed with white Populists about gender; in fact, they were intended to make the most of agreement.

Perhaps a tentative assessment of the role of gender in North Carolina Populism should take into account the important distinction between party politics and politics more broadly considered. For example, historians of Populism and the Alliance have long recognized the significance of women in the movement. Worth Robert Miller's bibliography of Populism lists about forty articles, books, and graduate theses on the relationship between women and Populism. Yet the effects of women on party politics were not always meaningful. In North Carolina, there was ambivalence among Alliancemen about women's "place." Lala Steelman found that although women made up between one-third and one-half of Alliance members in some counties, in other counties Alliance units were all male, sometimes based on express policies of exclusion (*North Carolina Farmers' Alliance*, 19). Even if some women found a home in the Alliance, in the transfer of the movement from the Alliance to the People's Party, as Robert McMath observed, "the role of women actually diminished" (*American Populism*, 127). By the late 1890s, if one focuses on policy disagreement among organized parties as one way of measuring political conflict, gender did not operate to distinguish North Carolina Populism from its competitors.

24. Hamilton, *North Carolina since 1860*, 287; *Greenville King's Weekly*, 25 Nov. 1898; *News and Observer*, 2 Nov. 1898; T. F. Winston to J. H. Small, 3 Sept. 1898, and S. B. Spruill to J. H. Small, 1 Oct. 1898, Small Papers, SHC; A. M. Scales to W. D. Hardin, 13 Oct. 1898, Hardin Papers, Duke; F. Simmons to W. B. Rodman, 13 Oct. 1898, Rodman Papers, ECU. For an interpretation of such arguments in a state where there was no effective Populist Party to contest them, see Kantrowitz, "Ben Tillman and Hendrix McLane."

25. *Caucasian*, 8, 29 Sept., 6, 20 Oct. 1898; *Hickory Times-Mercury*, 21, 28 Sept. 1898; *Progressive Farmer*, 4, 25 Oct. 1898; *Charlotte People's Paper*, 10 Sept., 4 Nov. 1898; 1898 Speech, Bright Papers, NCDAH; *Dr. Thompson's Great Speech*, NCC; R. C. Rivers to MB, 12 Sept. 1898, and C. Thompson to J. B. Lloyd, 22 Sept. 1898, BP; A. E. Holton to R. Pearson, 22 Sept. 1898, Pearson Papers, SHC; *People's Party Handbook of Facts*, NCC.

26. *Is the Democratic Party Honest?*, and *No. 12—Democrats on the Run*, NCC; *Caucasian*, 27 Oct. 1898; *Progressive Farmer*, 25 Oct. 1898.

27. J. Z. Green to MB, 27 Sept. 1898; A. C. Shuford to MB, 26 Sept. 1898; C. Thompson to MB, 22 Oct. 1898; J. Pritchard to MB, 31 Oct. 1898; Clipping from *Danville Register*, 22 Sept. 1898; J. B. Lloyd to MB, 29 Sept. 1898; all in BP; *Raleigh Home Rule*, 29 Sept., 20 Oct. 1898; *Hickory Times-Mercury*, 5 Oct. 1898; *Progressive Farmer*, 11 Oct. 1898; *Charlotte Observer*, 6 Nov. 1898; *Caucasian*, 22, 29 Sept., 27 Oct. 1898; *Elizabeth City North Carolinian*, 20 Oct. 1898; *Charlotte People's Paper*, 7 Oct. 1898; *Asheville Daily Gazette*, 8 Nov. 1898.

28. Clipping from *Danville Register*, 22 Sept. 1898, BP; *Progressive Farmer*, 11 Oct. 1898; *Caucasian*, 27 Oct. 1898; *Raleigh Home Rule*, 13 Oct. 1898.

29. Although recent histories, such as those by Stephen Kantrowitz and Glenda Gilmore, demonstrate the reactionary use of gender and race by Democratic politicians, Butler's interests were a restructuring of the national party system and the enactment of federal legislation according to the Populist economic program. Everything else, including race, took a back seat to these concerns. During his life he commented very infrequently about the public or private roles of women. In his fifty-year political career he supported higher education for women; he welcomed women into the Alliance; he opposed women's suffrage until World War I; he opposed the use of white male fears of black rapists for political purposes; he favored the death penalty for rapists; he supported Progressive Era legislation to improve working conditions for women; after 1920, he supported mandatory proportional representation

of women (50 percent) on state Republican governing committees; and after 1920, he actively tried to interest male North Carolina Republicans in the greater mobilization of (white) Republican women. In short, to him gender was unimportant as a political issue, at least before North Carolina women obtained the right to vote. Given his organizational orientation, this is not surprising. Only when women could have a direct impact on an election did he view them as politically meaningful. Beyond his public positions, Butler's relationship with women is simultaneously unexciting and difficult to assess, largely because of his and others' silence. As already noted, he apparently had a long and happy marriage, partly because he and his wife, Florence Faison, shared an interest in politics. Yet evidence on the marriage, as well as on Faison's political influence, is scattered and anecdotal; it is addressed elsewhere in the biography whenever there was information to support it. He seems to have been fairly close to his mother, but information is sorely lacking on the details of that relationship. His daughters seemed more attached to him than his sons. His first daughter, Pocahontas, admired him greatly, although in an interview with her I sensed considerable formality, which fits with Butler's general personality. He corresponded with women about Republican politics after 1920, trying to get them involved in the party. Overall, Butler adopted some "progressive" views, such as on education and, after 1920, political activity, but in general he accepted that woman's role was primarily domestic and thus irrelevant to his political party activities. In contrast to Charles Aycock and Ben Tillman, he did not express insecurities about protecting white women from black rapists, probably more out of the self-confidence that characterized his general personality and the belief that such claims were deceptive and offered by economic conservatives than from any doubts that black men wanted to rape white women.

30. *Caucasian*, 13 Nov. 1898; B. Cade to MB, 19 Oct. 1898; D. L. Russell to MB, 26 Sept. 1898; B. R. Tillman to MB, 1 Nov. 1898; J. H. Small to MB, 17 Oct., 2 Nov. 1898; all in BP; F. Simmons to W. B. Rodman, 3 Oct. 1898, Rodman Papers, ECU.

31. E. A. Moye to MB, 12, 29 Sept. 1898; W. A. Guthrie to MB, 22 Sept. 1898; W. F. Strowd to MB, 27 Sept. 1898; J. B. Lloyd to MB, 11 Aug., 23, 24 Sept., 14, 15 Oct. 1898; B. F. Keith to MB, 17, 26 Oct. 1898; J. M. King to MB, 25 Oct. 1898; S. H. Bright to MB, 15 Oct. 1898; E. J. Faison to MB, 19 Oct. 1898; MB to C. S. Garner, 8 Oct. 1898; W. P. Craven to MB, 21 May 1898; W. E. Fountain to MB, 9 Aug. 1898; all in BP; *Goldsboro Headlight*, 22 Sept. 1898; *Elizabeth City North Carolinian*, 2 Nov. 1898; *Hickory Times-Mercury*, 2 Nov. 1898; B. H. Thompson to W. B. Rodman, 2 July 1898, Rodman Papers, ECU; *Raleigh Home Rule*, 27 Oct. 1898; *Union Republican*, 27 Oct. 1898; J. Sprunt to D. L. Russell, 24 Oct. 1898, and D. L. Russell to J. Sprunt, 4 Nov. 1898, Sprunt Papers, Duke; *Raleigh Gazette*, 18 Feb. 1898; *Elizabeth City Economist*, 4 Nov. 1898.

32. Kousser, *Shaping of Southern Politics*, 186, 193−94; T. J. Jarvis to S. A. Ashe, 25 Nov. 1898, Ashe Papers, NCDAH; F. Simmons to W. B. Rodman, 17 Nov. 1898, Rodman Papers, ECU; W. Leigh to J. S. Cunningham, 12 Nov. 1898, Cunningham Papers, Duke; M. M. Marshall to J. Daniels, 9 Nov. 1898, Daniels Papers, LC; *News and Observer*, 23, 25 Oct. 1898; A. M. Waddell to E. A. Oldham, 6 Dec. 1898, Oldham Pa-

pers, Duke. There are many accounts of the Wilmington Race Riot. See, for example, Hamilton, *North Carolina since 1860*, 291–97; Memoir of Thomas Clawson [1942], Clawson Papers, Duke; Cronly Family Papers, Duke; Prather, *We Have Taken a City*.

33. B. F. Keith to MB, 17 Nov., 12 Dec. 1898; F. T. Jones to MB, 10 Dec. 1898; J. B. Lloyd to MB, 13 Nov. 1898; J. F. Click to MB, 13 Nov. 1898; MB to J. S. Mitchell, 12 Nov. 1898; all in BP; *Pittsboro Chatham Citizen*, 16 Nov. 1898; *Hickory Times-Mercury*, 9, 16 Nov. 1898; *Caucasian*, 10, 17, 24 Nov. 1898.

Chapter 11

1. *Congressional Record*, 55th Cong., 3d sess., appendix, 175–97; ibid., 2095–98, 2131–33.

2. *Congressional Record*, 55th Cong., 3d sess., 2633–36, 2732–35, 2845–51, 2862–65.

3. *Caucasian*, 2, 16 Feb. 1899; *Congressional Record*, 55th Cong., 3d sess., 1203–4, 1074–80.

4. Hicks, *American Nation*, 330–32; *Congressional Record*, 55th Cong., 3d sess., 565–66, 799–802, 847–48; *Caucasian*, 2, 23 Feb., 16 Mar., 25 May, 28 Sept. 1899.

5. *Journal of the Executive Committee of the Senate*, 183–84; W. J. Bryan to MB, 30 Jan. 1899, BP; Glad, *Trumpet Soundeth*, 72–75; Coletta, "Bryan, McKinley, and the Treaty of Paris."

6. W. J. Bryan to MB, 13 Feb. 1899, BP; *Congressional Record*, 55th Cong., 3d sess., 1487–88, 1845–48; Glad, *Trumpet Soundeth*, 74–75; Welch, *George Frisbie Hoar*, 221–50.

7. J. Jones to MB, 31 Jan. 1899, and J. H. Davis to MB, 8 May 1899, BP.

8. J. H. Ferriss to MB, 14 Jan. 1899; M. Park to MB, 16 Feb. 1899; S. Williams to MB, 27 Apr., 19 May 1899; all in BP; J. A. Parker to L. Weller, 20 Apr. 1899, and M. Park to L. Weller, 21 June 1899, Weller Papers, SHSW; *Caucasian*, 6, 27 Apr. 1899; *New York Times*, 18 May 1899; *Dallas Southern Mercury*, 25 May, 1 June 1899; Hicks, *Populist Revolt*, 396–98.

9. J. H. Davis to MB, 8 May 1899; E. Pomeroy to MB, 3 Aug. 1899; S. Smith to MB, 5 Aug. 1899; J. A. Edmisten to MB, 18 Oct. 1899; H. Tracy to MB, 18 Oct. 1899; S. Williams to MB, 5, 6, 19 May 1899; H. L. Bentley to MB, 12 June 1899; all in BP; *Caucasian*, 19 Oct. 1899.

10. Hamilton, *North Carolina since 1860*, 299–301; Edmonds, *The Negro and Fusion Politics*, 178–93; Steelman, "Progressive Era in North Carolina," 197–206; Kousser, *Shaping of Southern Politics*, 190–91; Roller, "Republican Party of North Carolina," 20.

11. *Caucasian*, 23 Feb., 9, 16 Mar., 28 June, 13 July, 24, 31 Aug., 28 Sept., 23 Nov., 7 Dec. 1899; *Hickory Times-Mercury*, 5 Apr., 17 May, 20 Dec. 1899; *Reidsville Webster's Weekly*, 11 May 1899; *Progressive Farmer*, 14, 21 Mar., 9 May 1899; *Charlotte People's Paper*, 6 Oct. 1899; *Rockingham Anglo-Saxon*, 5 Oct. 1899; R. B. Davis to MB, 12 Dec. 1899; MB to My Dear Sir, 23 Nov. 1899; B. F. Keith to MB, 23 Dec. 1899; M. Caldwell to MB, 20 Dec. 1899; all in BP.

12. H. Ayer to MB, 29, 30 Dec. 1899, and M. Caldwell to MB, 20 Dec. 1899, BP.

13. *Code of North Carolina*, chap. 4, secs. 17, 20; Coates, "Story of the Law School," 19–21, 29; Law School Notes, box 56, vol. 3, BP.

14. *Congressional Record*, 56th Cong., 1st sess., 233, 441, 1063.

15. Ibid., 1544–57; *Caucasian*, 5 Jan., 1, 8, 15, 22 Feb., 8 Mar. 1900; *Rockingham Anglo-Saxon*, 18 Jan., 1 Feb. 1900; *Asheville Daily Gazette*, 23, 25 Jan., 9 Feb. 1900; *Hickory Times-Mercury*, 21 Feb. 1900; MB to W. J. Peele, 25 Feb. 1900; R. F. Pettigrew to MB, 23 Jan. 1900; W. Allen to MB, 29 Jan. 1900; all in BP.

16. *Congressional Record*, 56th Cong., 1st sess., 378–79, 853–54, 1295, 2250, 2256, 2316, 2965–66; Leech, *Days of McKinley*, 482–88; Hicks, *American Nation*, 347.

17. Hicks, *American Nation*, 277; *Congressional Record*, 56th Cong., 1st sess., 735–36.

18. *Congressional Record*, 56th Cong., 1st sess., 6663–70.

19. Ibid., 1712–24, 2538–45; *Caucasian*, 15 Feb. 1900.

20. *Congressional Record*, 56th Cong., 1st sess., 1826–35, 2541, 2586–88, 2590, 2812.

21. Ibid., 601, 631, 664, 702, 2250–56, 2316–18, 4206–7, 5107, 5481–83, 5639, 5642–43, 5736–37, 5744–45, 5791–92, 6034, 6356, 6368–69, 6378, 6441, 6796–98.

22. J. Parker to MB, 28 Dec. 1899; J. Parker to My Dear Sir, 9 Dec. 1899, 30 Jan. 1900; W. Allen to MB, 3 Jan. 1900; MB to Members, People's Party National Committee, 27 Jan. 1900; J. H. Edmisten to MB, 25 Jan., 5 Feb. 1900; G. Washburn to MB, 20 Jan. 1900; A. H. Cardin to MB, 31 Jan. 1900; T. T. Rinder to MB, 29 Jan. 1900; J. H. McDowell to MB, 1 Feb. 1900; T. F. Keleher to MB, 3 Feb. 1900; all in BP; Circular, 19 Feb. 1900, Weller Papers, SHSW; Hicks, *Populist Revolt*, 396–97; *New York Times*, 6 Jan. 1900; *Asheville Daily Gazette*, 26 Jan. 1900.

23. MB, "People's Party."

24. *Caucasian*, 16, 23 Feb., 1 Mar. 1900; *New York Times*, 19, 20, 21 Feb. 1900; *Charlotte People's Paper*, 23 Feb., 16, 30 Mar. 1900; Circular, 19 Feb. 1900, Weller Papers, SHSW; J. H. Edmisten to MB, 5 Dec. 1899; "The Omaha Agreement Sustained," 20 Feb. 1900; MB to W. J. Peele, 25 Feb. 1900; W. Clark to MB, 24 Mar. 1900; all in BP.

25. J. H. Davis to MB, 21 Feb., 21 Apr. 1900; B. Lien to MB, 6 Mar. 1900; J. A. Edgerton to MB, 12, 16 Mar., 9, 24 Apr. 1900; H. Tracy to MB, 14, 18 Mar., 17 Apr. 1900; C. M. Walter to MB, 2 Mar. 1900; T. C. Jenkins to MB, 19 Mar. 1900; all in BP; *Caucasian*, 8 Mar. 1900.

26. *New York Times*, 6, 9, 11 May 1900; Hicks, *Populist Revolt*, 399–400.

27. *New York Times*, 11 May 1900; *Washington Post*, 11 May 1900; J. A. Edgerton to MB, 9 Apr. 1900, BP.

28. *New York Times*, 11 May 1900; *Washington Post*, 9, 11 May 1900; *Caucasian*, 24 May 1900; J. A. Edgerton to MB, 13 Apr. 1900; J. H. Edmisten to MB, 20 Apr. 1900; C. A. Towne to MB, 1, 12 May 1900; all in BP. For more detail on Towne, see Schlup, "Charles A. Towne."

29. *Caucasian*, 17, 24 May 1900; *New York Times*, 10 May 1900; *Charlotte People's Paper*, 18 May 1900.

30. *New York Times*, 24 Aug. 1900.

31. *Caucasian*, 17 May 1900; H. Preyer to MB, 14 May 1900; J. A. Edgerton to MB,

21, 29 May, 20 Aug. 1900; H. Tracy to MB, 20, 25 May 1900; J. H. Davis to MB, 18 May 1900; J. H. Edmisten to MB, 24, 25 May 1900; G. H. Shibley to MB, 18 May 1900; G. Washburn to MB, 2 June 1900; MB to N. Fitzgerald, 14 June 1900; W. M. Dersher to MB, 15 June 1900; W. H. Robb to MB, 15 May 1900; all in BP.

32. Roseboom, *Presidential Elections*, 326–27; Leech, *Days of McKinley*, 542–43; *New York Times*, 9 July 1900; *Caucasian*, 12 July 1900; Coletta, *William Jennings Bryan*, 238–62.

33. *New York Times*, 28 July, 4, 10, 28 Aug. 1900; J. A. Edgerton to MB, 20 Aug. 1900; G. Washburn to MB, 11 Aug. 1900; T. T. Rinder to MB, 11 Aug. 1900; R. F. Pettigrew to MB, 16 Aug. 1900; J. Field to MB, 18 Aug. 1900; W. R. King to MB, 19 Aug. 1900; C. Thompson to MB, 22 Aug. 1900; J. H. Calderhead to MB, 23 Aug. 1900; all in BP; *Hickory Times-Mercury*, 22, 29 Aug. 1900.

Chapter 12

1. F. M. Simmons to Dear Sir, 23 Mar., 18 Dec. 1899, 3 Jan., 23 Feb., 14 Mar. 1900, and J. Daniels Circular, 22 Jan. 1900, Rodman Papers, ECU; S. A. Ashe to T. F. Davidson, 22 Jan. 1900, Davidson Papers, SHC; B. F. Keith to MB, 17 Feb. 1900; W. F. Tally to MB, 5 Feb. 1900; E. H. Morris to MB, 21 Mar. 1900; all in BP; Cotten, "Negro Disfranchisement in North Carolina."

2. H. Skinner to W. McKinley, 2 Nov. 1899, McKinley Papers, LC; W. J. Peele to MB, 23, 28 Feb. 1900; J. H. Caldwell to MB (1900; folder 118[b]); G. Hunt to MB, 18 Jan. 1900; H. Ayer to MB, 10 Mar. 1900; J. F. Click to MB, 8, 23 Mar. 1900; C. Thompson to MB, 4, 22 Jan., 13 Mar. 1900; B. F. Keith to MB, 12 Mar. 1900; all in BP; *Progressive Farmer*, 9 May 1899; *Charlotte People's Paper*, 9, 16 Feb. 1900; *Fayetteville Observer*, 19 Apr. 1900; *Elizabeth City North Carolinian*, 26 Apr. 1900; *Elizabeth City Economist*, 20 Apr. 1900; *Caucasian*, 11 Jan., 1 Feb., 5, 12 Apr. 1900; *Hickory Times-Mercury*, 4 Apr., 20 Dec. 1899, 10, 24 Jan. 1900.

3. *Hickory Times-Mercury*, 24 Jan. 1900; *Caucasian*, 4, 25 Jan., 1, 8 Feb. 1900; W. J. Leary to MB, 24 Jan. 1900; MB to My Dear Sir, 22 Jan. 1900; C. Thompson to MB, 24 Feb. 1900; R. C. Rivers to MB, 8 Mar. 1900; all in BP; J. R. Cooper to W. B. Rodman, 21 Mar. 1900, Rodman Papers, ECU.

4. *Caucasian*, 12 Apr. 1900; *Asheville Daily Gazette*, 12 Apr. 1900; Lefler, *North Carolina History Told by Contemporaries*, 404–5.

5. *Hickory Times-Mercury*, 21 Feb., 25 Apr. 1900; *Asheville Daily Gazette*, 18 Apr. 1900; *Caucasian*, 19 Apr. 1900; *News and Observer*, 18, 19 Apr. 1900; *Charlotte Daily Observer*, 19, 20 Apr. 1900.

6. *News and Observer*, 3 May 1900; Crow and Durden, *Maverick Republican*, 138–55; Hamilton, *North Carolina since 1860*, 309; Roller, "Republican Party of North Carolina," 22–26; Lefler, *North Carolina History Told by Contemporaries*, 405–7; *Asheville Daily Gazette*, 2, 3 May 1900; *Caucasian*, 3 May 1900.

7. *News and Observer*, 19, 26 Apr. 1900; H. Ayer to MB, 10 Mar. 1900; R. B. Davis to MB, 26, 29 Apr., 28 May, 11 June 1900; A. E. Holton to MB, 26 Apr., 18 May 1900; C. Dick to MB, 21 May 1900; W. S. Hyams to MB, 29 May, 27 June 1900; L. L. Jenkins to MB, 29 May 1900; W. K. Pigford to MB, 16 May 1900; H. F. Seawell to MB, 31 May

1900; N. Reid to MB, 6 June 1900; B. F. Keith to MB, 2, 21, 28 June 1900; W. H. Hoover to MB, 25 June 1900; R. B. Davis to A. B. Bradley, 15 June 1900; R. Bender to MB, 28 June 1900; F. Mahoney to MB, 25 June 1900; W. F. Sessoms to MB, 26 June 1900; A. C. Shuford to MB, 22 June 1900; J. B. Schulken to MB, 28 June 1900; J. B. Lloyd to MB, 18 June 1900; all in BP; *Hickory Times-Mercury*, 20 June, 4 July 1900; *Elizabeth City North Carolinian*, 24 May, 21 June, 12, 19 July 1900; *Reidsville Webster's Weekly*, 28 June 1900.

8. Hamilton, *North Carolina since 1860*, 309-10, 313; C. Bell to MB, 29 June 1900, and H. C. Foster to MB, 18 June 1900, BP; W. H. Cooper to W. B. Rodman, 9 July 1900, Rodman Papers, ECU.

9. F. M. Simmons to Dear Sir, 2, 6, 25, 26 June 1900, Rodman Papers, ECU; *Charlotte People's Paper*, 15 June 1900; F. Carr to MB, 7 June 1900; B. P. Long to MB, 26 June 1900; W. S. Bailey to MB, 1 July 1900; D. C. Farabow to MB, 26 July 1900; G. F. Walker to MB, 20 July 1900; W. E. Lindsay to MB, 17 July 1900; C. C. Fagan to H. Ayer, 13 July 1900; A. E. Holton to MB, 17 July 1900; W. F. Sessoms to MB, 23 July 1900; W. R. White to MB, 14, 16 July 1900; "The Law on Registration and Challenges," 23 July 1900; Circular, 24 July 1900; "Here Is the Proof," 14 July 1900; Circular, 27 July 1900; MB to My Dear Sir, 26 July 1900; "Another Important Letter (No. 6)," 31 July 1900; all in BP; *Instructions to Judges of Election*, NCC.

10. MB to W. R. Dixon, 18 July 1900; MB to My Dear Sir, 18 July 1900; W. P. Lyon to MB, 23 July 1900; R. Nowland to MB, 22 July 1900; C. Dockery to MB, 15 July 1900; C. Thompson, "Personal Letter," 24 July 1900; all in BP; *New York Times*, 30 July 1900; *Caucasian*, 26 July 1900; *Progressive Farmer*, 3 July 1900.

11. W. B. Gibson to H. Ayer, 24 July 1900; J. E. Person to H. Ayer, 12 July 1900; R. L. Burns to MB, 25 July 1900; J. E. Kelley to MB, 13 July 1900; H. Ayer to R. C. Hill, 20 July 1900; H. Tracy to MB, 25, 28 July 1900; J. H. Sherrill to MB, 24 July 1900; T. Turner to MB, 20 July 1900; J. E. Carpenter to H. Ayer, 11 July 1900; R. C. Hill to H. Ayer, 21 July 1900; H. F. Seawell to C. E. Taylor, 21 July 1900; H. Ayer to D. W. Patrick, 19 June 1900; G. Butler to MB, 24 July 1900; C. E. Taylor to MB, 21 July 1900; A. B. Winder to MB, 25 July 1900; R. A. Cobb to MB, 21 June 1900; all in BP; *Caucasian*, 5, 12, 26 July 1900; *Hickory Times-Mercury*, 25 July 1900; Cowden, "H. S. P. Ashby."

12. J. R. Jenkins to MB, 23 July 1900; J. S. Basnight to H. Ayer, 23 July 1900; D. C. Downing to MB, 11 July 1900; J. P. Sossaman to MB, 26 July 1900; J. H. Quinn to MB, 11 July 1900; all in BP; *Caucasian*, 28 June, 12, 19, 26 July, 2 Aug. 1900; *Charlotte People's Paper*, 6 July 1900; *Progressive Farmer*, 26 June 1900.

13. H. F. Seawell to MB, 26 July 1900; J. E. Person to MB, 26 July 1900; B. F. Keith to MB, 28 July 1900; W. J. Leary to MB, 30 July 1900; R. D. Paschall to MB, 21 July 1900; W. H. Brown to MB, 5 July 1900; A. B. Winner to MB, 25 July 1900; R. W. Blackman to MB, 28 July 1900; "Another Important Letter (No. 6)," 31 July 1900; all in BP; *Charlotte People's Paper*, 13 July 1900; *New York Times*, 31 July 1900; *Charlotte Daily Observer*, 1 Aug. 1900.

14. S. L. Gibson to MB, 17 July 1900; B. F. Keith to MB, 27 July 1900; M. Ward to MB, 16 July 1900; T. Jones to MB, 26 July 1900; all in BP; *Rockingham Anglo-Saxon*, 5 July 1900; A. R. Smith Journal, 31 July 1900, Smith Papers, ECU; Steelman, "Progressive Era in North Carolina," 219-21.

15. *Caucasian*, 26 July, 2 Aug. 1900; *Asheville Daily Gazette*, 3 Aug. 1900; *Hickory Times-Mercury*, 15 Aug. 1900; MB to J. D. Bellamy, 1 Aug. 1900, BP.

16. Kousser, *Shaping of Southern Politics*, 193–95; Hamilton, *North Carolina since 1860*, 311; Crow and Durden, *Maverick Republican*, 156–57; *Union Republican*, 9 Aug. 1900; *Rockingham Anglo-Saxon*, 9 Aug. 1900.

17. *Hickory Times-Mercury*, 8 Aug. 1900; *Caucasian*, 9 Aug. 1900; *Asheville Daily Gazette*, 4 Aug. 1900; J. T. Haywood to MB, 10 Aug. 1900; McGidden to MB, 13 Aug. 1900; Z. V. Walser to MB, 4 Aug. 1900; S. Holmes to MB, 6 Aug. 1900; R. R. Harris to MB, 2 Aug. 1900; K. Parker to MB, 3 Aug. 1900; S. S. Strother to MB, 3 Aug. 1900; H. Tracy to MB, 10 Aug. 1900; H. S. P. Ashby to MB, 7 Aug. 1900; N. McRae to MB, 3 Aug. 1900; all in BP; W. B. Rodman to D. P. Overton, 3 Aug. 1900, Rodman Papers, ECU.

18. *Caucasian*, 16 Aug., 27 Sept., 4 Oct. 1900; *Hickory Times-Mercury*, 19 Sept., 10, 17, 24 Oct. 1900; *Charlotte People's Paper*, 17 Aug., 5 Oct. 1900; D. A. Long to MB, 6 Aug. 1900; N. C. Cooper to MB, 6 Aug. 1900; J. C. Pritchard to MB, 12 Aug. 1900; R. A. Cobb to MB, 22 Aug. 1900; Z. V. Walser to MB, 30 Aug. 1900; Circular, People's Party State Committee, 4 Aug. 1900; all in BP.

19. *Caucasian*, 30 Aug. 1900; MB, "Election in North Carolina."

20. *New York Times*, 2, 28 Sept., 14 Oct. 1900; *Caucasian*, 13 Sept., 8 Nov. 1900; *Hickory Times-Mercury*, 12 Sept., 24, 31 Oct. 1900; *Charlotte People's Paper*, 21 Sept., 5 Oct. 1900; E. Corsen to MB, 18 Sept. 1900, and "Dates for Senator Butler," 1 Oct. 1900, South Dakota People's Party State Central Committee, BP.

21. *Caucasian*, 6 Sept., 25 Oct. 1900; *Hickory Times-Mercury*, 19 Sept., 10, 17, 24 Oct., 7, 14, 21 Nov. 1900; *Charlotte People's Paper*, 14, 28 Sept. 1900; *Progressive Farmer*, 16 Oct. 1900; J. P. Sossaman to *Caucasian*, 21 Sept. 1900; A. C. Shuford to MB, 3 Sept. 1900; J. H. Sherrill to MB, 1 Sept. 1900; all in BP.

22. Roseboom, *Presidential Elections*, 332–33; Hicks, *Populist Revolt*, 400; W. Barker to L. Weller, 22 Sept. 1900, and A. W. C. Weeks to L. Weller, 18, 22 Sept. 1900, Weller Papers, SHSW; *New York Times*, 30 Dec. 1900.

23. Hicks, *American Nation*, 348–49; Leech, *Days of McKinley*, 568; Millis, *Arms and Men*, 173–81; *Congressional Record*, 56th Cong., 2d sess., appendix, 166–70; ibid., 853–54, 1176–77, 1662–66, 1727–31.

24. Leech, *Days of McKinley*, 568–69; *Congressional Record*, 56th Cong., 2d sess., 2955, 2972–73, 2977, 3136–39, 3144–55; Hicks, *American Nation*, 340–41.

25. *Congressional Record*, 56th Cong., 2d sess., appendix, 271–88; ibid., 2124–25, 2128, 2188–90, 2207–10, 2252–53, 2209–10, 2684, 2751–52, 2818–19, 3511–14.

26. *Congressional Record*, 56th Cong., 2d sess., appendix, 360–65; ibid., 1597; *Caucasian*, 7 Mar. 1901.

Chapter 13

1. J. S. Basnight to MB, 10 Oct. 1901; J. F. Click to MB, 20 Nov. 1901; D. C. Downing to MB, 23 Oct. 1901; J. F. Foard to MB, 29 Mar. 1901; W. J. Leary to MB, 11 Nov. 1901; MB to T. Mann, 28 Sept. 1901; all in BP; *Charlotte People's Paper*, 4 Jan. 1901; *Caucasian*, 17, 24, 31 Jan., 7, 14, 21 Feb., 28 Mar., 18 Apr., 16 May, 4, 18, 25 July, 1 Aug., 3, 10 Oct., 7 Nov. 1901; *New York Times*, 30 June 1901.

2. Information about Populists is from Garraty, *American National Biography*, 17:627–28; 1:351; 4:99–100; 20:20–21; 14:290–91; 22:800–802; 6:730–32; 12:876–77; 6:777–78; 13:938–40; 13:788–89; 13:334–35; 13:555–56; Powell, *Dictionary of North Carolina Biography*, 5:355–56; Tyler, *New Handbook of Texas*, 5:57. A description of the Texans' compromise with Democracy is Miller, "Building a Progressive Coalition in Texas."

3. Despite decades of writing about Populism, there has been very little systematic study of the experience of individual Populist leaders after 1900. The lingering image in the literature is of a semirational, embittered Tom Watson. Yet Watson after 1900 seems no more typical of post-Populism than he was typical of Populism during the 1890s. At a minimum, Butler's sanity and resistance to the lure of white supremacy provide a useful counterpoint.

4. Sanders, *Roots of Reform*, 3–4; Woodward, *Origins of the New South*, 371.

5. The literature on Progressive Era politics is generally less strident than that on the Alliance and Populism, revealing greater ambivalence. Dewey Grantham's history of southern progressivism, for example, refers to it as the "reconciliation of progress and tradition." Yet from the standpoint of political history, the difference seems unjustified. Ironically, while references to "movement cultures" and social histories of Populism invigorated Populist studies, a similar retreat from core-level political analysis of progressivism frequently has led to confusion about progressivism. Recently, Alonzo Hamby made the persuasive observation that progressivism "can be understood only as a *political movement* that addressed ideas, impulses, and issues stemming from the modernization of American society" ("Progressivism: A Century of Change and Rebirth," 41). Butler allows a focus of the study of progressivism around politics. His progressive activities after 1900 were not motivated by status anxiety or based in any urban social or cultural movements; his career also does not fit easily into simplistic theoretical models of capitalist development. Nor were Butler's views about reform changed much during the period. Instead, his actions reflected the same kind of complex political concerns about party organization and economic legislation present in the 1890s. Butler's efforts to reinvent himself as a Republican displayed the broad political similarities between the Populist attempt to construct a political majority and progressive attempts to achieve the same goal. The meaning of democracy, the function of the political party, the regulatory role of government, and the relation between the states and Washington were all central issues on which Butler acted as a Populist and a progressive. As in the 1890s, politics, and not the program of reform, proved Butler's greatest challenge. Butler's life offers yet another justification for placing political history, particularly the history of state and local political organization, at the center of both Populist and progressive studies.

6. *Caucasian*, 2, 23, 30 May, 6, 20 June, 18, 25 July 1901.

7. Ibid., 19, 26 Sept., 17, 24 Oct. 1901; Roller, "Republican Party of North Carolina," 65–66, 93; MB to T. Roosevelt, 4 Oct. 1901, Roosevelt Papers, LC.

8. W. J. Leary to MB, 13, 17 June 1902; J. H. Quinn to MB, 3 June 1902; J. C. Pritchard to MB, 21 July, 3, 18 Sept., 1, 18, 23 Oct. 1902; J. F. Click to MB, 2 Sept. 1902; "Butler for Pritchard," 22 Sept. 1902; W. J. Flowers to MB, 11 Oct. 1902; W. F. Sessoms to MB, 26 Sept. 1902; all in BP; Roller, "Republican Party of North Car-

olina," 70–92; Hamilton, *North Carolina since 1860*, 330–33; Steelman, "Progressive Era in North Carolina," 401–3; *Hickory Times-Mercury*, 25 June, 17, 24 Sept., 15 Oct. 1902; *Asheville Daily Gazette*, 18 Oct. 1902; Steelman, "Republican Party Politics in North Carolina, 1902."

9. Hamilton, *North Carolina since 1860*, 333; Roller, "Republican Party of North Carolina," 90–92; *Hickory Times-Mercury*, 5 Nov. 1902; N. Kirkman to Dear John, 9 Nov. 1902, Hardin Papers, Duke.

10. J. C. Pritchard to MB, 29 Aug. 1903; MB to P. P. W. Plyler, 10 Mar. 1903; L. Butler to MB, 10 Sept. 1901, 23 Oct., 6 Nov. 1902; G. Butler to MB, 9 Jan. 1902; all in BP; *Caucasian*, 16 Apr. 1903; Roller, "Republican Party of North Carolina," 113–23; Butler, interview, 20 July 1987.

11. J. H. Cook to MB, 5 Sept. 1901; H. Tracy to MB, 1 Mar. 1902; S. A. Williams to MB, 17 Oct. 1902, 16, 27 Jan., 10, 13 Feb. 1903; J. A. Parker to MB, 2, 19 Jan. 1903; J. H. McConnell to MB, 16 Feb. 1903; G. Brown to MB, 13 May 1903; W. N. Hill to MB, 22 May 1903; all in BP; Hicks, *Populist Revolt*, 402.

12. E. C. Duncan to MB, 12 Jan., 2 Feb. 1904; D. L. Russell to MB, 18, 23, 30 Jan. 1904; D. L. Russell to W. S. O'B. Robinson, 23 Jan. 1904; B. F. Keith to MB, 22 Jan. 1904; V. S. Lusk to MB, 13 Mar. 1904; MB to J. H. Gore, 21 Mar. 1904; J. C. Pritchard to MB, 20 July 1904; T. Rollins to MB, 30 Jan. 1904; G. Cortelyou to MB, 3 Feb. 1903; J. F. Click to MB, 5 July 1904; R. L. Strowd to MB, 4 Apr. 1904; S. W. Williams to MB, 26 Feb. 1904; S. A. Lowrance to MB, 9 Feb. 1904; J. H. Edmisten to MB, 13 Apr. 1904; all in BP; MB to D. L. Russell, Russell Papers, SHC; Roller, "Republican Party of North Carolina," 141–43; *Caucasian*, 14 Jan., 14 Apr., 19 May, 2 June, 14 July 1904; Hicks, *Populist Revolt*, 402; Woodward, *Tom Watson*, 357–64.

13. Roseboom, *Presidential Elections*, 338–41; Woodward, *Tom Watson*, 358–68.

14. R. F. Pettigrew to MB, 19 Aug. 1904; S. A. Lowrance to MB, 31 Aug. 1904; H. M. McDonald to MB, 31 Aug., 3 Sept. 1904; W. N. Hill to MB, 5, 6 Sept. 1904; P. P. W. Plyler to MB, 7 Sept. 1904; MB to J. H. Ferris, 8 Sept. 1904; J. H. Ferris to MB, 16, 23 Sept. 1904; MB to L. Butler, 6 Oct. 1904; W. L. Scott to MB, 23 Sept. 1904; MB to R. F. Pettigrew, 27 Sept. 1904; MB to G. Cortelyou, 27 Sept. 1904; G. Cortelyou to MB, 29 Sept., 11 Oct. 1904; J. C. Pritchard to MB, 27 Sept. 1904; E. C. Duncan to MB, 29 Sept. 1904; "Your Obedient Servants to the President," 12 Oct. 1904; H. B. Wall to MB, 17 Feb. 1905; all in BP; *Caucasian*, 29 Sept., 6, 13, 27 Oct., 3 Nov. 1904; W. Clark to T. Watson, 23 Aug. 1904, and J. B. Lloyd to T. Watson, 23 Aug. 1904, Watson Papers, SHC.

15. *Caucasian*, 13, 27 Oct. 1904; Schedules, Indiana Republican State Committee, 25, 26 Oct. 1904, BP.

16. Kousser, *Shaping of Southern Politics*, 195; Roseboom, *Presidential Elections*, 344; Roller, "Republican Party of North Carolina," 153; *Caucasian*, 10 Nov. 1904; *Hickory Times-Mercury*, 11 Nov. 1908.

17. H. D. Lyman to MB, 3 June 1901; "Lease," 1 Jan. 1901 to 1 Jan. 1902; MB to C. L. Joyner, 20 June 1901; MB to J. L. Harrington, 6 May 1901; MB to W. B. Lane, 19 Apr. 1901; A. Rutherford to MB, 21 Sept. 1901; Petition, North Carolina Supreme Court, Aug. 1902; Box 19, folders 153, 157; P. M. Wilson to MB, 25 Mar. 1902; MB to H. Alexander, 17 Apr. 1902; MB to D. L. Russell, 26 Apr. 1902; Contract, Apr. 1902; W.

D. Merritt to MB, 14 Apr. 1902; C. N. Bennett to MB, 4 Apr. 1903; "Legal Agree-ment," 23 Jan., 15 Dec. 1903; J. M. Vale to MB, 1 Aug. 1904; Contract, Choctaw Cot-ton Co., 23 Apr. 1902; W. B. Pringer to MB, 26 Feb. 1903; Memorandum, 1 July 1904; Bill regarding Ute Indians, 16 Nov. 1903; W. M. Hazlett to MB, 4 Dec. 1903; W. A. Jones to J. M. Vale, 28 Jan. 1902; MB to R. F. Pettigrew, 23, 25 Apr., 20, 21, 26 June 1902; J. L. Cowles to MB, 17 Jan. 1903; all in BP; *Caucasian*, 11 Apr., 27 June 1901; MB to J. L. Cowles, 3 Apr. 1903, Cowles Papers, SHC.

18. MB to J. Faison, 12 May 1905; B. F. Byrd to MB, 1 Mar. 1907; MB to Mrs. E. L. Faison, 17 Apr. 1908; MB to Mrs. P. V. Bumgardner, 5 Oct. 1908; MB to W. H. Bum-gardner, 25 Nov. 1907; all in BP.

19. Durden, *Reconstruction Bonds*, 3−62; Hamilton, *North Carolina since 1860*, 323−30; Orth, *Judicial Power of the United States*.

20. Durden, *Reconstruction Bonds*, 22−62.

21. Ibid., 47−50; Deposition of MB, 15 Dec. 1902, BP; MB to D. L. Russell, 11, 18 Jan., 19, 25, 26 Feb., 11 Mar. 1901, and D. L. Russell to MB, 30 Jan. 1901, Russell Pa-pers, SHC.

22. Durden, *Reconstruction Bonds*, 52−62, 65−71; MB to D. L. Russell, 13, 18, 25 Apr., 13, 19 May, 25, 29 Oct., 11 Nov. 1901, and J. W. Murphy to D. L. Russell, 4 May 1901, Russell Papers, SHC; D. L. Russell to MB, 23 Apr. 1901; D. K. Thorne to MB, 16 Apr. 1901; Folder 152; Legal Agreement, 6 Sept. 1901; all in BP; *Caucasian*, 21 Nov. 1901.

23. MB to D. L. Russell, 20 Feb., 8 Dec. 1902, and D. L. Russell to MB, 17 Mar., 16, 19 Apr. 1902, Russell Papers, SHC; D. L. Russell to MB, 4 Dec. 1901, 21 Sept., 21 Nov. 1902; MB to R. W. Stewart, 10 Feb. 1902; R. W. Stewart to MB, 1 Feb. 1902; D. L. Rus-sell to Horner and Stewart, 4 Aug. 1902; Deposition of MB, 15 Dec. 1902; all in BP; Durden, *Reconstruction Bonds*, 97.

24. Durden, *Reconstruction Bonds*, 98−100.

25. W. N. Coler and Co. to MB, 30 Jan. 1903, and D. L. Russell to MB, 23 Nov. 1903, BP; MB to D. L. Russell, 23 Jan., 19 Mar., 2 Apr. 1903, Russell Papers, SHC; Durden, *Reconstruction Bonds*, 108−22.

26. D. L. Russell to MB, 19 Oct. 1903, 2 Feb. 1904; W. Peckham to MB, 1, 4 Feb. 1904; F. C. Prest to MB, 19 Feb. 1904; L. H. Hole to MB, 19 Feb. 1904; all in BP; MB to D. L. Russell, 16 Oct. 1903, Russell Papers, SHC.

27. Durden, *Reconstruction Bonds*, 122−46.

28. MB to D. L. Russell, 30 Sept. 1904, 26 Jan. 1905, and D. L. Russell to MB, 21, 23 Dec. 1904, Russell Papers, SHC; L. H. Hole to MB, 19 Oct. 1904, and D. L. Rus-sell to MB, 23 Jan., 4 Feb. 1905, BP; Durden, *Reconstruction Bonds*, 147−54.

29. D. L. Russell to MB, 31 Jan. 1905, and MB to D. L. Russell, 16, 18, 22 Feb. 1905, Russell Papers, SHC; Durden, *Reconstruction Bonds*, 188−209; D. L. Russell to MB, 1 Feb., 14 Mar. 1905, and R. F. Pettigrew to MB, 15 Feb. 1905, BP.

30. Agreement, 27 May 1905; R. F. Pettigrew to D. L. Russell, 10 June 1905; D. L. Russell to MB, 5 Aug. 1905; all in Russell Papers, SHC; Durden, *Reconstruction Bonds*, 211−19; D. L. Russell to MB, 27 May, 5 June 1905; MB to D. L. Russell, 31 May 1905; C. H. Burke to MB, 28 June 1905; R. F. Pettigrew to D. L. Russell, 28 July 1905; MB to W. Peckham, 16 Aug., 20 Sept. 1905; J. M. Vale to D. L. Russell, 16 Sept. 1905; all in BP.

31. MB to A. Ricaud, 2 Apr. 1905; D. L. Russell to MB, 24 Mar. 1905; A. Ricaud to D. L. Russell, 13 Apr. 1905; MB to D. L. Russell, 28 Apr., 1, 20 May 1905; D. L. Russell to J. G. Carlisle, 27 July 1906; all in Russell Papers, SHC; Hamilton, *North Carolina since 1860*, 327; Durden, *Reconstruction Bonds*, 219−27; R. F. Pettigrew to MB, 18 Jan. 1905; MB to R. F. Pettigrew, 20 Jan., June 1905; D. L. Russell to MB, 23 Jan. 1905; all in BP.

32. W. N. Coler and Co. to MB, 12 Jan. 1906; MB to L. H. Hole, 15 Jan. 1906; R. F. Pettigrew to MB, 18 Jan. 1906; J. J. Cushing to MB, 31 Jan. 1906; E. J. Best to MB, 23 June 1906; all in BP. The letter to Hole that supposedly exonerated Butler from "bad" bond contact was not widely publicized by Butler until 1910, after Hole's death, when it was used to defend Butler from charges by Democrats. See MB to W. N. Coler and Co., 8 Sept. 1910; W. N. Coler and Co. to MB, 6 Sept. 1910; MB to C. J. Harding, 25 Jan. 1911; all in BP. Nonetheless, there is a telegram in the Butler papers in which Butler states that he has "no connection with the [Carlisle] syndicate or with any effort to collect the carpet-bag bonds." MB to R. L. Strowd, box 52, folder 542 [May 1906?], BP.

33. R. F. Pettigrew to MB, 19 Jan. 1906; J. J. Cushing to MB, 18 July 1907; J. M. Vale to L. H. Hole, 2 Apr. 1908; L. H. Hole to MB, 23 June, 29 July, 8 Aug. 1908, 4 Feb. 1909; MB to L. H. Hole, 24 June, 8 Aug. 1908, 5 Feb. 1909; W. N. Coler and Co. to MB, 12 July 1910; J. G. Capers to MB, 28 Sept. 1910; MB to C. H. Burke, 16 Jan. 1909; all in BP.

34. Hamilton, *North Carolina since 1860*, 326; Durden, *Reconstruction Bonds*, 26−27.

35. MB to J. C. Pritchard, 15 Nov. 1904, 23 Jan., 18 Feb. 1905; J. C. Pritchard to MB, 6 Dec. 1904, 9 Jan. 1905; T. Rollins to MB, 17 Dec. 1904; E. C. Duncan to MB, 11 Mar., 11 Apr. 1905; Petition to President, 10 Mar. 1905; G. Butler to MB, 18 Mar. 1905; MB to W. A. Montgomery, 15 May 1905; T. Glenn to MB, 17 June 1905; all in BP.

36. T. Glenn to MB, 2, 8, 9, 13 May 1905; L. E. Cox to MB, 20 May 1905; A. E. Holton to MB, 20 May 1905; T. Rollins to MB, 22 May 1905; MB to D. L. Gore, 26 May 1905; Agreement, North State Publishing Company, May 1905; C. Thompson to MB, 25 May 1905; MB to L. Butler, 20 May 1905; MB to G. Butler, 19 May 1905; all in BP.

37. T. Glenn to MB, 13 May 1905; MB to M. Stone, 17 May 1905; J. E. Cox to MB, 24 May 1905; R. H. McNeill to MB, 25 May 1905; MB to S. Adams, 26 May 1905; MB to A. E. Holton, 26 May 1905; MB to D. L. Gore, 26 May 1905; S. Adams to MB, 31 May 1905; Certificate of Incorporation, Industrial Publishing Company, 31 May 1905; R. D. Douglas to MB, 5, 11 June 1905; MB to J. C. Pritchard, 1 June 1905; S. Adams to MB, 6 June 1905; Application for Associated Press Membership, 1 June 1905; all in BP; Roller, "Republican Party of North Carolina," 158−73; *Daily Industrial News*, 8, 13, 14, 20, 24 Oct., 3 Nov. 1905.

38. *Weekly Tar Heel*, 25 Jan., 15 Feb., 15, 29 Mar., 5, 12 Apr., 31 May 1906; MB to J. C. Pritchard, 9 May 1906; J. A. Sims to MB, 5 May 1906; T. Rollins to Z. V. Walser, 14 May 1906; Z. V. Walser to MB, 9 May 1906; T. Rollins to MB, 21 May 1906; MB to T. Rollins, 12 May 1906; MB to S. Adams, 28 May 1906; all in BP; T. Roosevelt to T.

Rollins, 31 May 1906, Roosevelt Papers, LC; *Asheboro Randolph Bulletin*, 31 May 1906; *Caucasian*, 17 May 1906.

39. N. M. Jones to MB, 29 May 1906; MB to B. T. Person, 8 June 1906; MB to C. C. Vann, 11 June 1906; MB to T. D. Hewitt, 11 June 1906; E. C. Duncan to MB, 15 June 1906; J. J. Brinson to MB, 2 July 1906; W. McAulay to MB, 25 June 1906; L. Butler to MB, 26 June 1906; G. Butler to MB, 2 July 1906; B. F. Keith to MB, 29 June 1906; J. J. Mott to MB, 3 July 1906; J. J. Brinson to MB, 2 July 1906; A. J. Hunter to MB, 9 July 1906; J. F. Click to MB, 9 July 1906; all in BP; *Caucasian*, 21, 28 July 1906; *Union Republican*, 28 June 1906.

40. MB to T. T. Hicks, 26 June 1906; G. Butler to MB, 27 June 1906; S. Adams to Z. V. Walser, 6 July 1906; all in BP; *Asheboro Randolph Bulletin*, 12 July 1906; *News and Observer*, 8 July 1906; *Charlotte Daily Observer*, 9, 10, 11, 12 July 1906; R. M. Douglas to W. H. Taft, 8 July 1906, Taft Papers, LC; *Union Republican*, 12 July 1906; *Caucasian*, 12 July 1906; Morrison, *Josephus Daniels Says*, 227–35.

41. Education Articles, box 21, folder 183; H. T. Chapin to MB, 21 Aug. 1906; J. Leach to MB, 17 Sept. 1906; J. W. Mewborne to MB, 18 Sept. 1906; J. Q. A. Wood to MB, 22 Sept. 1906; W. S. Pearson to MB, 22 Sept. 1906; H. F. Seawell to S. Adams, 3 Oct. 1906; S. Adams to MB, 2 Oct. 1906; W. A. Montgomery to MB, 3 Nov. 1906; all in BP; *Caucasian*, 3 May, 30 Aug., 13, 27 Sept., 4, 11, 18 Oct. 1906.

42. C. D. Holland to MB, 27 Aug. 1906, BP; *Henderson Gold Leaf*, 25 Oct. 1906; *Reidsville Webster's Weekly*, 11 Oct. 1906; *News and Observer*, 8, 9, 11 July, 26 Oct. 1906; *Union Republican*, 1 Nov. 1906; *Weekly Tar Heel*, 4 Oct. 1906; *Asheboro Randolph Bulletin*, 25 Oct. 1906; Broadside, 27 Oct. 1906; Indiana Republican State Committee to MB, 24 Oct. 1906; K. Battle to Mrs. Marion Butler, 27 Oct. 1906; all in BP; *Caucasian*, 1 Nov. 1906.

43. G. Butler to MB, 9 Nov. 1906; S. Adams to MB, 19 Nov. 1906; J. F. Click to MB, 8 Nov. 1906; all in BP; R. M. Douglas to W. H. Taft, 3 Nov., 21 Dec. 1906, Taft Papers, LC; *Weekly Tar Heel*, 6 Dec. 1906.

44. MB to E. C. Duncan, 27 Mar. 1907; MB to P. L. Baker, 16 Mar. 1907; MB to J. Pritchard, 26 Mar. 1907; MB to M. L. Mott, 9 Apr. 1907; T. Rollins to MB, 20 Apr. 1907; all in BP; Roller, "Republican Party of North Carolina," 191–97; *Twice-a-Week Tar Heel*, 15 Mar., 9 Apr. 1907; *Asheboro Randolph Bulletin*, 9 May 1907; Cooper, *Warrior and the Priest*, 69–88, 109–18; Mowry, *Theodore Roosevelt and the Progressive Movement*, 13–35.

45. MB to T. Rollins, 24 Apr. 1907; MB to J. P. Leach, 27 Apr. 1907; MB to G. Butler, 8 May 1907; MB to T. Rollins, 16 May 1907; MB to T. Roosevelt, 8 May, 17 July 1907; MB to H. Cruikshank, 13 May 1907; R. L. Strowd to MB, 15 May 1907; W. H. Taft to MB, 17 May 1907; W. S. O'B. Robinson to S. Adams, 14 May 1907; S. D. Johnson to MB, 14 May 1907; MB to R. D. Douglas, 16 May 1907; MB to F. H. Hoover, 17 May 1907; H. Cruikshank to MB, 17 May 1907; MB to W. S. O'B. Robinson, 17 June 1907; all in BP; MB to W. H. Taft, 16 May 1907, Taft Papers, LC; *Washington Post*, 11, 12 May 1907; *Asheboro Randolph Bulletin*, 6, 27 June 1907; *Union Republican*, 20 June 1907; *Twice-a-Week Tar Heel*, 26 Apr., 7, 14, 21 May, 11 June 1907; MB, *An Open Letter*, 31 July 1907, NCC. Butler was able to cultivate a very good relationship with the pres-

ident. Even the *New York Times* described Butler as Roosevelt's "Administration General for the South," who consulted with southern Republicans for Roosevelt. Butler sent Roosevelt a pair of riding gloves for Christmas in 1907. *New York Times*, 27 Apr. 1907; MB to T. Roosevelt, 24 Dec. 1907, BP.

46. MB to J. D. Grady, 18 May 1907, BP; *Caucasian*, 3, 24 Jan., 2, 23 May, 2 June, 11, 18, 25 July, 1, 8 Aug., 12, 19 Sept., 10, 17 Oct., 7, 28 Nov. 1907; *New York Times*, 5 Aug. 1907.

47. *Twice-a-Week Tar Heel*, 18 June, 10, 20 Sept., 1 Oct. 1907; *Asheboro Randolph Bulletin*, 1, 29 Aug. 1907; Roller, "Republican Party of North Carolina," 195−204; *Daily Industrial News*, 30 Jan., 10 Mar., 1 May, 13 Oct. 1907.

48. Roller, "Republican Party of North Carolina," 204−5; S. Adams to W. H. Taft, 23 Dec. 1907, 7 Jan. 1908, and W. H. Taft to S. Adams, 26 Dec. 1907, Taft Papers, LC; *Caucasian*, 2 Jan. 1908; *Union Republican*, 12 Mar. 1908; *Daily Industrial News*, 31 Jan., 23 Feb. 1908. On Roosevelt's support for Taft and opposition from conservatives, see Mowry, *Theodore Roosevelt and the Progressive Movement*, 29−32.

49. MB to Gilbert and Barnes, 24 Dec. 1907, and MB to Southern Newspaper Union, 1 Mar. 1908, BP; *Charlotte Daily Observer*, 12 Mar. 1908; *Caucasian*, 5 Mar. 1908.

50. L. Butler to MB, 21 Mar. 1908; W. S. O'B. Robinson to MB, 21 Mar., 28 Apr. 1908; MB to L. Butler, 27 Mar. 1908; MB to G. Butler, 14 Mar. 1908; all in BP; R. M. Douglas to W. H. Taft, 25 Mar. 1908, and S. Adams to W. H. Taft, 2 Apr. 1908, Taft Papers, LC; MB to T. Roosevelt, 3 July 1908, Roosevelt Papers, LC; J. C. Stancill to W. G. Briggs, 21 Apr. 1908, Briggs Papers, SHC; *Daily Industrial News*, 24, 30 Apr., 11 May 1908; *Caucasian*, 16 Apr., 7, 14 May 1908; *Union Republican*, 7 May 1908; *Asheboro Randolph Bulletin*, 7 May 1908; MB, *Republican State Convention*, NCC.

51. *Caucasian*, 14, 21, 28 May, 4, 25 June 1908; MB to W. Loeb, 16 June 1908, and MB to T. Roosevelt, 21 June 1908, Roosevelt Papers, LC; S. Adams to W. H. Taft, 2 Apr., 23 June, 4, 13 July 1908, and E. C. Duncan to W. H. Taft, 5 June, 1 July 1908, Taft Papers, LC.

52. MB to M. G. Gregory, 16 June 1908; MB to E. B. Frost, 29 June 1908; MB to T. Roosevelt, 3 July 1908; C. Thompson to MB, 21 Aug. 1908; T. Rollins to MB, 10 July 1908; L. Butler to MB, 30 July 1908; J. H. Holt to MB, 14 Aug. 1908; all in BP; *Caucasian*, 9 July 1908; MB to W. H. Taft, 8, 18 Aug. 1908; J. C. Pritchard to MB, 3 Aug. 1908; R. S. Mebane to MB, 14 Aug. 1908; I. Meares to MB, 13 Aug. 1908; T. Settle to W. H. Taft, 16 Aug. 1908; A. E. Holton to MB, 3 Aug. 1908; H. Skinner to W. H. Taft, 22 July 1908; H. Skinner to T. Roosevelt, 22 July 1908; W. H. Taft to MB, 10 Aug. 1908; J. C. Pritchard to W. H. Taft, 14 Aug. 1908; J. C. Pritchard to MB, 14 Aug. 1908; W. H. Taft to J. C. Pritchard, 17 Aug. 1908; all in Taft Papers, LC; MB to C. Thompson, 6 Aug. 1908, Thompson Papers, SHC; J. E. Williamson to J. E. Cox, 6 July 1908; D. H. Blair to J. E. Cox, 9 July, 21 Aug. 1908; MB to J. E. Cox, 5 Aug. 1908; all in Cox Papers, Duke; *Daily Industrial News*, 30 July 1908; *Asheboro Randolph Bulletin*, 23 July 1908; Steelman, "Jonathan Elwood Cox"; Roller, "Republican Party of North Carolina," 209−13.

53. W. Ballinger to MB, 27 Aug. 1908; Answer, Sept. 1908; W. S. O'B. Robinson to MB, 31 Aug. 1908; W. J. Justice to MB, 10, 14 Sept., 9 Oct. 1908; A. Cruce to MB, 21

Oct. 1908; MB to W. P. Bynum, 4 Sept. 1908; G. Butler to MB, 7 Sept. 1908; all in BP.

54. *News and Observer*, 27, 28 Aug. 1908; *Daily Industrial News*, 27 Aug. 1908; *Caucasian*, 3 Sept. 1908; *Charlotte Daily Observer*, 26, 27, 28 Aug. 1908; Roller, "Republican Party of North Carolina," 213–14.

55. *Caucasian*, 3, 10 Sept. 1908; J. P. Sossaman to J. E. Cox, 28 Aug. 1908; L. Butler to J. E. Cox, 31 Aug. 1908; H. Skinner to J. E. Cox, 29 Aug. 1908; C. Thompson to J. E. Cox, 31 Aug. 1908; MB to J. E. Cox, 12 Sept. 1908; all in Cox Papers, Duke; J. E. Cox to MB, 15 Sept. 1908, and MB to L. Butler, 24 Sept. 1908, BP.

56. MB to L. Butler, 21 Sept., 8 Oct. 1908; MB to G. Butler, 22 Sept., 5 Oct. 1908; MB to F. Butler, 31 Oct. 1908; MB to R. F. Pettigrew, 25 Sept. 1908; all in BP; *Caucasian*, 16 Apr., 30 July, 6, 13 Aug., 17, 24 Sept., 8, 15, 22, 29 Oct. 1908; *Hickory Times-Mercury*, 30 Sept., 21, 28 Oct. 1908.

57. Roller, "Republican Party of North Carolina," 216–17; *Caucasian*, 12 Nov. 1908; J. C. Pritchard to W. H. Taft, 6 Nov. 1908, and S. Adams to W. H. Taft, 14 Dec. 1908, Taft Papers, LC; T. Roosevelt to MB, 10 Nov. 1908, and T. Roosevelt to H. Skinner, 12 Nov. 1908, Roosevelt Papers, LC.

58. *Caucasian*, 5, 12, 19, 26 Nov. 1908; *Daily Industrial News*, 15, 17, 26 Nov. 1908; A. E. Holton to W. H. Taft, 9 Jan. 1909, Taft Papers, LC; Roller, "Republican Party of North Carolina," 218–23; L. Butler to MB, 23 Nov. 1908; MB to L. Butler, 23 Nov. 1908; J. F. Wray to MB, 8 Nov. 1908; MB to J. F. Wray, 18 Nov. 1908; A. E. Holton to MB, 21 Nov. 1908; MB to W. P. Bynum, 24 Nov. 1908; G. Butler to MB, 24 Nov. 1908; Evidence (Criminal Court), Oct. 1908; all in BP.

59. Pocahontas Butler Woodson, interview, 20, 27 Sept. 1986.

Chapter 14

1. Cooper, *Warrior and the Priest*, 232–33; Coletta, *William Howard Taft*, 1–20; Steelman, "Republicanism in North Carolina," 158–60; Roller, "Republican Party of North Carolina," 227–28; MB to W. H. Taft, 4 Dec. 1908; W. H. Taft to MB, 7 Dec. 1908; S. Adams to W. H. Taft, 14 Dec. 1908; J. R. Joyce to S. Adams, 11 Dec. 1908; all in Taft Papers, LC.

2. MB to F. Carter, 16 Dec. 1908; W. Ballinger to MB, 15 Dec. 1908; L. Butler to MB, 15 Dec. 1908, 10 Feb. 1909; J. Vale to MB, 21, 22, 29, 30 Jan., 1, 2, 10, 11, 21 Feb., 10, 24 Mar., 14 Dec. 1909; MB to J. Vale, 28 Jan., 1, 5, 8 Feb. 1909; MB to J. Wilson, 19 Feb. 1909; W. S. O'B. Robinson to MB, 6 Feb., 9 Apr., 11 Dec. 1909; MB to W. S. O'B. Robinson, 3 Feb. 1909; Challenge to Depositions, 12 Feb. 1909; MB to E. J. Justice, 29 Mar. 1909; MB to L. Butler, 19 Apr. 1909; Statement of Case for Appeal, 25 Apr. 1909; Justice and Broadhurst to MB, 9 Apr., 10 May 1909; J. Vale to A. C. Cruce, 9 Apr. 1909; MB to T. L. Wright, 23 Apr. 1909; W. S. Thompson to MB, 30 Apr. 1909; W. Ballinger to E. J. Justice, 10 May 1909; MB to Justice and Broadhurst, 24 May 1909; L. Butler to MB, 28 May 1909; Aycock and Winston to L. Butler, 19 Oct. 1909; MB to Justice and Broadhurst, 20 Oct. 1909; E. D. Broadhurst to MB, 26 Aug., 22 Oct., 5 Nov. 1909; MB to E. D. Broadhurst, 25 Oct. 1909; L. Butler to MB, 25 Oct. 1909; E. J. Justice to M. Ballinger, 11 May 1909; MB to E. D. Broadhurst, 4 Nov. 1909; MB to W. S. O'B. Robinson, 4 Nov. 1909; MB to W. R. Blakemore, 4 Nov. 1909; MB to

Aycock and Winston, 8, 10 Nov. 1909; H. W. Blakeslee to MB, 15 Nov. 1909; all in BP; *Caucasian*, 8, 23 Apr., 6, 13, 20, 27 May 1909; *Hickory Times-Mercury*, 18 Nov. 1908; *State v. Butler*, 151 N.C. 672 (1909).

3. *Caucasian*, 28 Dec. 1908, 7, 14, 28 Jan. 1909; MB to C. B. Aycock, 21 Dec. 1908; MB to W. A. Montgomery, 22 Dec. 1908; J. C. Pritchard to MB, 24 Dec. 1908; J. A. Smith to MB, 30 Dec. 1908; W. S. O'B. Robinson to MB, 5 Jan. 1909; R. M. Douglas to MB, 16 Jan. 1909; T. T. Hicks to MB, 21 Apr. 1909; MB to A. E. Holton, 8 Jan. 1909; J. J. Mott to MB, 12 Jan. 1909; MB to T. Roosevelt, 28 Dec. 1908, 4, 12 Jan. 1909; MB to W. S. O'B. Robinson, 13 Jan. 1909; MB to G. Butler, 19 Apr. 1909; MB to W. H. Taft, 22, 27 Mar. 1909; all in BP; W. H. Taft to J. M. Morehead, 22 Dec. 1908, 23 Mar. 1909; W. H. Taft to J. C. Pritchard, 29 Mar. 1909; J. M. Morehead to W. H. Taft, 24 Mar., 2 Apr. 1909; all in Taft Papers, LC; Roller, "Republican Party of North Carolina," 229–39; Mowry, *Era of Theodore Roosevelt*, 222–25.

4. MB to W. H. Taft, 22 Mar. 1909, Taft Papers, LC; MB to W. S. O'B. Robinson, 16 Apr. 1909; MB to G. Butler, 19 Apr. 1909; L. Butler to MB, 23 Apr., 2, 3 May 1909; MB to Justice and Broadhurst, 23 Apr. 1909; MB to W. H. Taft, 7 May 1909; all in BP; *Caucasian*, 29 Apr. 1909.

5. MB to L. Butler, 12 May 1909; J. F. Click to MB, 24 Apr., 11 May 1909; W. G. Bramham to MB, 24 Apr. 1909; W. S. O'B. Robinson to MB, 11 June 1909; MB to C. A. Jonas, 23 June 1909; all in BP; *Charlotte Daily Observer*, 11 May 1909; *Caucasian*, 13 May, 3, 10 June, 1 July 1909; *Union Republican*, 13 May 1909; *Asheboro Randolph Bulletin*, 13, 20 May 1909; Roller, "Republican Party of North Carolina," 235–36; Steelman, "Republicanism in North Carolina," 160–61.

6. *Caucasian*, 11 Mar., 22, 29 Apr., 12, 19 Aug. 1909; MB to L. Butler, 5 Aug. 1909, BP. For a survey of the conflict between Taft and the progressives on the tariff, see Mowry, *Theodore Roosevelt and the Progressive Movement*, 36–65.

7. MB to W. H. Taft, 6 Jan. 1909, and J. M. Morehead to W. H. Taft, 11 Sept. 1909, Taft Papers, LC; MB to W. H. Taft, 20 Jan. 1909; W. H. Taft to MB, 8, 31 Jan. 1909; MB to D. A. Tompkins, 23 Jan. 1909; MB to J. M. Morehead, 24 Dec. 1908, 29 Apr. 1909; J. M. Morehead to MB, 30 Dec. 1908; L. Butler to MB, 14 Jan., 25 June 1909; MB to R. M. Douglas, 4, 16 Dec. 1909; MB to J. Newell, 19 Nov. 1909; MB to L. Butler, 23 Nov. 1909; all in BP; D. A. Tompkins to J. E. Cox, 31 Dec. 1908, and D. Blair to J. E. Cox, [1908], Cox Papers, Duke; *Caucasian*, 24 Dec. 1908; Steelman, "John Motley Morehead," 162–63; Roller, "Republicanism in North Carolina," 243–47.

8. A. E. Holton to J. M. Morehead, 2 Mar. 1910; T. Settle to W. G. Brown, 4 Mar. 1910; J. M. Morehead to W. G. Brown, 8, 12 Mar. 1910; all in Brown Papers, Duke; Steelman, "Republicanism in North Carolina," 163–64; Roller, "Republican Party of North Carolina," 247–48; *Caucasian*, 21, 28 Apr., 2, 9 June 1910; MB to G. Butler, 2, 18 Feb. 1910; MB to J. J. Mott, 1 Mar. 1910; MB to J. F. Click, 29 Mar. 1910; Justice and Broadhurst to W. S. O'B. Robinson, 4 Mar. 1910; MB to Justice and Broadhurst, 10 Feb., 11, 16 Mar. 1910; E. J. Justice to MB, 14 Mar. 1910; MB to J. Vale, 19 Mar., 28 July 1910; J. Vale to R. M. Douglas, 2 Apr. 1910; R. M. Douglas to J. Vale, 6 Apr. 1910; W. S. O'B. Robinson to C. D. Benbow, 9 Apr. 1910; MB to W. S. O'B. Robinson, 6, 8, 20 May 1910; Justice and Broadhurst to MB, 31 May, 22, 25, 29 July 1910; C. D. Benbow to MB, 28 May 1910; MB to C. D. Benbow, 1 June 1910; J. Vale to MB, 27 July 1910;

Agreement [28 July 1910]; all in BP. In late 1910 Adams entered the Keeley Institute, perhaps for treatment of alcoholism, and tried to commit suicide by cutting his throat. E. L. Summerell to MB, 9 Jan. 1911; B. T. Person to MB, 3 Jan. 1911; J. Newell to MB, 10 Jan. 1911; all in BP.

9. R. A. Kohloss to MB, 1 July 1910; MB to My Dear Sir [1910]; R. G. White to Dear Gov., 21 July 1910; MB to G. Grissom, 21, 22 July 1910; "Morehead's Reply to a False and Malicious Attack," July 1910; all in BP; MB to J. E. Ramsey, 15 July 1910, Ramsey Papers, SHC; *Caucasian*, 7, 14, 21, 28 July 1910; W. G. Briggs to E. J. D. Boykin, 1 July 1910, and Circular, 16 July 1910, Briggs Papers, SHC; Roller, "Republican Party of North Carolina," 251–53; Steelman, "Republicanism in North Carolina," 164–65; *Marion Butler: Who Is Trying to Capture the Approaching Republican State Convention*, NCC.

10. B. F. Keith to MB, 3 Aug. 1910, BP; *Caucasian*, 4, 18 Aug. 1910; *Burlington State Dispatch*, 3 Aug. 1910; *Charlotte Daily Observer*, 5, 10 Aug. 1910; *News and Observer*, 7, 8, 10, 11 Aug. 1910; *Charlotte Evening Chronicle*, 10 Aug. 1910; *Greensboro Daily News*, 10 Aug. 1910.

11. *Greensboro Daily News*, 11 Aug. 1910; *Caucasian*, 11, 18 Aug. 1910; *Union Republican*, 11 Aug. 1910; *Charlotte Daily Observer*, 11 Aug. 1910; *Hickory Times-Mercury*, 17 Aug. 1910; *Burlington State Dispatch*, 17 Aug. 1910; *Clinton News-Dispatch*, 18 Aug. 1910; *Charlotte Evening Chronicle*, 11 Aug. 1910; *News and Observer*, 11 Aug. 1910; W. G. Brown to A. P. Andrews, 22 Sept. 1910, Brown Papers, Duke; Steelman, "Republicanism in North Carolina," 166–67.

12. MB to C. Norton, 13 Aug. 1910; MB to W. H. Taft, 15 Aug. 1910; MB to J. M. Morehead, 13, 15, 29, 31 Aug., 7 Sept. 1910; MB to G. Grissom, 1, 7 Sept. 1910; J. M. Morehead to MB, 24 Aug. 1910; J. M. Morehead to W. H. Taft, 29 Aug. 1910; MB to G. L. Hardison, 7 Sept. 1910; all in BP; *Caucasian*, 25 Aug., 1 Sept. 1910.

13. Steelman, "Trials of a Republican State Chairman," 31–36; Durden, *Reconstruction Bonds*, 244–53; Steelman, "Progressive Era in North Carolina," 429–30; *News and Observer*, 11 Aug. 1910; *Henderson Gold Leaf*, 6 Oct. 1910; *Reidsville Webster's Weekly*, 28 Oct., 11 Nov. 1910; *Chapters from the Republican Hand-book*, and *Butler in His Own Mirror*, NCC; J. S. Basnight to MB, 14 Oct. 1910, BP; "A Mighty Protest by North Carolinians" [1910], Nunn Papers, Duke; *Charlotte Evening Chronicle*, 25 Oct. 1910.

14. MB to Aycock and Winston, 8 Sept. 1910; Aycock and Winston to MB, 16 Sept. 1910; MB to J. M. Morehead, 15, 17, 28 Sept. 1910; W. A. Montgomery to MB, 16 Sept. 1910; G. Butler to MB, 17 Sept. 1910; G. Grissom to MB, 17, 27 Sept. 1910; MB to A. E. Holton, 17 Sept. 1910; J. M. Morehead to MB, 20 Sept. 1910; MB to G. Grissom, 27, 28 Sept., 9 Oct. 1910; all in BP; *Burlington State Dispatch*, 31 Aug., 7, 14 Sept. 1910; *Caucasian*, 8, 15, 29 Sept., 6, 13, 20, 27 Oct. 1910; *Greensboro Daily News*, 18, 23, 29 Oct., 4 Nov. 1910; *Charlotte Evening Chronicle*, 3 Oct. 1910.

15. J. M. Morehead to C. B. Aycock, 7 Oct. 1910, and J. J. Mott to J. Daniels, 20 Oct. 1910, BP; *Union Republican*, 13, 20, 27 Oct., 3 Nov. 1910; *Hickory Times-Mercury*, 5, 12, 26 Oct. 1910; *Asheboro Randolph Bulletin*, 20, 27 Oct. 1910; *Moravian Falls Yellow Jacket*, 13, 27 Oct. 1910; *Greensboro Daily News*, 7, 13, 18, 23 Oct. 1910; *Burlington State Dispatch*, 5, 12, 19, 26 Oct. 1910; *Caucasian*, 3 Nov. 1910.

16. W. G. Brown to C. Norton, 13 Oct. 1910, Brown Papers, Duke. The letter was

apparently read to an approving Taft. C. Norton to W. G. Brown, 3 Nov. 1910, ibid.

17. *Charlotte Daily Observer*, 27 Oct. 1910; *Charlotte Evening Chronicle*, 27 Oct. 1910; *News and Observer*, 4, 5 Nov. 1910.

18. MB to F. M. Simmons, 17 Oct. 1910, BP; *Greensboro Daily News*, 2, 5 Nov. 1910; *Marion Butler's Raleigh Speech*, NCC; *Charlotte Evening Chronicle*, 4, 5 Nov. 1910.

19. *Marion Butler's Raleigh Speech*, NCC.

20. Roller, "Republican Party of North Carolina," 263–64; Steelman, "Trials of a Republican State Chairman," 35–36.

21. *Caucasian*, 10, 17, 24 Nov., 1, 15 Dec. 1910; MB to A. M. Clarke, 17 Nov. 1910; C. E. Fuller to MB, 21 Nov. 1910; C. Thompson to MB, 18 Nov. 1910; G. Grissom to MB, 22 Nov., 2 Dec. 1910; MB to R. A. Kohloss, 23 Nov. 1910; MB to G. Grissom, 28 Nov. 1910; J. S. Morris to MB, 28 Nov. 1910; all in BP. The divide between Taft and progressives, along with its negative effect in the 1910 elections on Butler's party nationwide, is detailed in Mowry, *Theodore Roosevelt and the Progressive Movement*, 88–119, 155–56.

22. Steelman, "Trials of a Republican State Chairman," 36–42; Roller, "Republican Party of North Carolina," 265–78; J. M. Morehead to C. D. Hilles, 23 Mar. 1911, Taft Papers, LC; Mowry, *Theodore Roosevelt and the Progressive Movement*, 128–30. On the limited Democratic achievements after 1911, see Steelman, "Progressive Era in North Carolina," 318–98.

23. *Caucasian*, 5 Jan., 9 Feb., 16 Mar., 13, 20 Apr., 11, 25 May, 1, 15, 29 June 1911.

24. Ibid., 5, 26 Jan., 9, 23 Feb., 2 Mar., 13, 20 Apr., 1, 8, 29 June 1911; MB to G. L. Steele, 15 Feb. 1911, BP.

25. *Caucasian*, 6, 20, 27 July, 3 Aug., 19 Oct., 9, 16, 23, 30 Nov. 1911; MB to Spurgeon, 14 Oct. 1911, and *Washington Post*, interview [1911], BP; MB to C. D. Wilkie, 11 Nov. 1911, Briggs Papers, SHC.

26. MB to G. Grissom, 7 July, 9 Dec. 1911; MB to A. S. Mitchell, 7 July 1911; G. Grissom to MB, 12 July 1911, 13 Jan. 1912; J. M. Morehead to MB, 25 Sept. 1911, 4 Jan. 1912; MB to J. M. Morehead, 10 Oct., 11 Nov., 1, 9, 15 Dec. 1911, 2 Jan. 1912; MB to G. L. Hardison, 24 Oct. 1911; MB to E. W. Hill, 6 Dec. 1911; J. M. Morehead to C. D. Hilles, 13, 20 Dec. 1911; MB to G. Davis, 15 Dec. 1911; *Washington Post*, interview [1911]; MB to F. P. Tucker, 6 Jan. 1912; MB to I. Warwick, 25 Jan. 1912; W. S. Clayton to MB, 16 Feb. 1912; all in BP; MB to C. D. Hilles, 16 Sept. 1911, and J. M. Morehead to C. D. Hilles, 5 Sept., 27 Nov. 1911, Taft Papers, LC; J. M. Morehead to W. G. Brown, 14 Nov., 1 Dec. 1911, and W. G. Brown to G. Grissom, 2 Jan. 1912, Brown Papers, Duke; *Caucasian*, 15 Feb., 17 Aug., 26 Oct., 2, 16, 30 Nov. 1911.

27. *Clinton News-Dispatch*, 26 Oct. 1911; J. N. Williamson to T. Roosevelt, 23 Dec. 1911; R. Pearson to T. Roosevelt, 8 Jan., 3 Feb. 1912; A. V. Dockery to T. Roosevelt, 11 Jan., 16 Feb. 1912; all in Roosevelt Papers, LC; Steelman, "Richmond Pearson," 122–23; T. Roosevelt to R. Pearson, 30 Jan., 2 Mar. 1912, Pearson Papers, SHC; G. Grissom to MB, 24 Feb. 1912, and Clipping, *Asheville News-Gazette*, 4 Feb. 1912, BP; *Caucasian*, 15, 22 Feb. 1912; Mowry, *Theodore Roosevelt and the Progressive Movement*, 202–4.

28. Steelman, "Trials of a Republican State Chairman," 40–41; T. Settle to W. G. Brown, 26 Jan. 1912, Brown Papers, Duke; G. Grissom to MB, 12 Jan., 23, 24 Feb.

1912; MB to J. M. Morehead, 10, 17 Feb. 1912; MB to G. Grissom, 23, 26 Feb. 1912; J. M. Morehead to MB, 17 Feb. 1912; MB to M. Parker, 27 Jan. 1912; all in BP.

29. *Caucasian*, 29 Feb., 7 Mar. 1912; *Hickory Times-Mercury*, 6 Mar. 1912; J. J. Marshburn to MB, 2 Apr. 1912; G. Grissom to MB, 18 Mar. 1912; MB to A. Uzzell, 20 Apr. 1912; all in BP; W. A. Hildebrand to T. Roosevelt, 4, 8 Mar. 1912; R. Pearson to T. Roosevelt, 4, 8, 11 Mar. 1912; S. S. McNinch to T. Roosevelt, 6 Mar. 1912; all in Roosevelt Papers, LC; T. Roosevelt to R. Pearson, 8 June 1912, Pearson Papers, SHC; C. D. Hilles to J. M. Morehead, 12 Mar. 1912, Taft Papers, LC; Roller, "Republican Party of North Carolina," 282–84.

30. J. M. Morehead to Dear Sir, Mar. 1912; J. M. Morehead to Dear Sir, Apr. 1912; Announcement, Mar. 1912; all in BP.

31. MB to N. T. Andrews, 18 Mar. 1912; A. S. Mitchell to MB, 21 Mar. 1912; MB to P. C. Jenkins, 25 Mar. 1912; MB to G. Grissom, 22 Mar. 1912; MB to J. M. Morehead, 28 Mar., 5 Apr., 3 May 1912; J. M. Morehead to MB, 25 Mar. 1912; all in BP; *Hickory Times-Mercury*, 17 Apr. 1912; *Clinton News-Dispatch*, 11 Apr. 1912; *Charlotte Daily Observer*, 15 May 1912; *Caucasian*, 11, 18, 25 Apr., 2, 9, 16 May 1912.

32. *News and Observer*, 15, 16 May 1912; *Clinton News-Dispatch*, 4, 11, 25 Apr., 2, 16 May 1912; *Charlotte Daily Observer*, 14, 16 May 1912; MB to J. J. Mott, 23 May 1912, BP; *Union Republican*, 23 May 1912; *Greensboro Daily News*, 16 May 1912; *Charlotte Evening Chronicle*, 14, 15, 16 May 1912; *Caucasian*, 16 May 1912; *Hickory Times-Mercury*, 22 May 1912.

33. MB to J. M. Morehead, 18 May, 11 June 1912; MB to J. J. Mott, 23 May 1912; G. L. Hardison to MB, 20 May 1912; J. M. Morehead to MB, 20 May 1912; MB to F. Butler, June 1912; all in BP; *Caucasian*, 23, 30 May, 6, 13 June 1912; *Union Republican*, 23 May 1912; R. Pearson to T. Roosevelt, 4 May, 5 June 1912; T. Roosevelt to R. Pearson, 7 May 1912; S. S. McNinch to T. Roosevelt, 5 June 1912; W. Loeb to T. Rollins, 11 June 1912; Z. V. Walser to T. Roosevelt, 7, 8 June 1912; J. N. Williamson to T. Roosevelt, 7, 13 June 1912; J. C. Pritchard to T. Roosevelt, 4 June 1912; all in Roosevelt Papers, LC; T. Roosevelt to R. Pearson, 8 June 1912, Pearson Papers, SHC; *Hickory Times-Mercury*, 15 May 1912; *Burlington State Dispatch*, 12, 19 June 1912.

34. Roseboom, *Presidential Elections*, 363–65; *Credentials of Delegates and Alternates*, NCC; *Charlotte Daily Observer*, 19, 20 June 1912; *Union Republican*, 20 June 1912; *Caucasian*, 13, 20 June 1912; *Greensboro Daily News*, 19 June 1912; Mowry, *Theodore Roosevelt and the Progressive Movement*, 220–55.

35. *Clinton News-Dispatch*, 27 June 1912; *Hickory Times-Mercury*, 27 June 1912; *Union Republican*, 27 June, 1 Aug. 1912; *Burlington State Dispatch*, 26 June, 31 July 1912; *Caucasian*, 13, 27 June, 4, 11 July, 1 Aug. 1912; W. H. Taft to E. C. Duncan, 8 July 1912, and J. M. Morehead to W. H. Taft, 7 July 1912, Taft Papers, LC.

36. *Caucasian*, 11, 18 July 1912; Steelman, "Richmond Pearson," 131–32; T. Settle to W. H. Taft, 8 July 1912, Taft Papers, LC; MB to J. M. Dixon, 10 July 1912, BP.

37. MB to T. Roosevelt, 30 July 1912; I. H. Lutterloh to MB, 15 July 1912; O. W. Roosevelt to MB, 5 Aug. 1912; all in BP; Mowry, *Era of Theodore Roosevelt*, 292–95; Cooper, *Warrior and the Priest*, 206–21.

38. Steelman, "Richmond Pearson," 131–32; Roller, "Republican Party of North

Carolina," 293; *Union Republican*, 8 Aug. 1912; *Burlington State Dispatch*, 7, 14 Aug. 1912; *Clinton News-Dispatch*, 8 Aug. 1912.

39. T. Settle to W. H. Taft, 8 July 1912, Taft Papers, LC; J. M. Morehead to MB, 1 Aug. 1912, and MB to I. H. Lutterloh, 3 Aug. 1912, BP; *Greensboro Daily News*, 8 Aug. 1912; *Caucasian*, 15 Aug. 1912.

40. *Hickory Times-Mercury*, 14, 28 Aug. 1912; *Clinton News-Dispatch*, 22, 29 Aug. 1912; *Caucasian*, 15 Aug. 1912; *Greensboro Daily News*, 11 Aug. 1912; W. P. Byrd to R. Pearson, 10 Aug. 1912; J. N. Williamson to R. Pearson, 16, 24 Aug. 1912; E. C. Duncan to R. Pearson, 24 Aug. 1912; J. M. Morehead to R. Pearson, 28 Aug. 1912; R. Pearson to J. M. Dixon, 28 Aug. 1912; R. Pearson to J. N. Williamson, 28 Aug. 1912; MB to R. Pearson, 24 Aug. 1912; all in Pearson Papers, SHC; R. Pearson to My Dear Sir, 19 Aug. 1912, BP; T. Roosevelt to R. Pearson, 20 Aug. 1912, Roosevelt Papers, LC; Steelman, "Richmond Pearson," 133–35; J. M. Morehead to W. G. Brown, 20 Aug. 1912, Brown Papers, Duke; J. J. Mott to W. G. Briggs, 20 Aug. 1912, Briggs Papers, SHC; B. F. Keith to MB, 28 Aug. 1912, BP; *Charlotte Daily Observer*, 2, 4 Sept. 1912; *Union Republican*, 5 Sept. 1912.

41. J. M. Morehead to W. H. Taft, 25 Sept. 1912, and W. H. Taft to E. C. Duncan, 5 Sept. 1912, Taft Papers, LC; *Hickory Times-Mercury*, 11 Sept. 1912; *Caucasian*, 5 Sept. 1912; *Charlotte Evening Chronicle*, 4, 5 Sept. 1912; *Charlotte Daily Observer*, 5 Sept. 1912. The exclusion reminded many Populists of the Democratic tactics of 1892. See *Hickory Times-Mercury*, 11 Sept. 1912.

42. *Charlotte Daily Observer*, 4, 5 Sept. 1912; *Greensboro Daily News*, 4, 5, 6 Sept. 1912; *Burlington State Dispatch*, 4 Sept. 1912; *Caucasian*, 5 Sept. 1912; *Hickory Times-Mercury*, 11 Sept. 1912; *Charlotte Evening Chronicle*, 5 Sept. 1912; Roller, "Republican Party of North Carolina," 301–2; Steelman, "Richmond Pearson," 137.

43. *Caucasian*, 12 Sept. 1912; *Union Republican*, 12 Sept. 1912; *News and Observer*, 11 Sept. 1912; *Greensboro Daily News*, 11, 12 Sept. 1912; *Charlotte Daily Observer*, 11, 12 Sept. 1912; *Charlotte Evening Chronicle*, 11, 12 Sept. 1912.

44. *Caucasian*, 26 Sept. 1912; *Hickory Times-Mercury*, 16, 23 Oct. 1912; *Greensboro Daily News*, 31 Oct. 1912; *Union Republican*, 24 Oct. 1912; *Burlington State Dispatch*, 2, 9, 16 Oct. 1912; Z. V. Walser to MB, 26 Sept. 1912, and J. S. Basnight to MB, 25 Oct. 1912, BP.

45. *Caucasian*, 1, 8 Feb., 1, 22, 29 Aug., 5, 26 Sept., 3, 10, 17, 24, 31 Oct. 1912.

46. Roller, "Republican Party of North Carolina," 303–4; Hicks, *American Nation*, 439; *Caucasian*, 7, 14 Nov. 1912. Although Watson had returned to the Democratic fold, he turned to Roosevelt a few months before the election largely out of revulsion against Woodrow Wilson. Woodward, *Tom Watson*, 416–30.

Chapter 15

1. MB to R. L. Strowd, 22 Nov. 1912; J. W. Dixon to MB, 27 Nov. 1912; MB to J. T. Butler, 6 Dec. 1912; MB to J. F. Click, 8 Feb. 1913; G. Butler to MB, 3 Jan. 1913; Z. V. Walser to MB, 18 Sept. 1913; MB to J. F. Click, 18 Feb. 1913; W. H. Worth to MB, 14 Feb. 1914; all in BP; J. N. Williamson to T. Roosevelt, 30 Apr., 21 May 1913; T. Roosevelt to J. N. Williamson, 24 May 1913; Z. V. Walser to T. Roosevelt, 12 Dec. 1912, 11

June 1913; all in Roosevelt Papers, LC; *Union Republican*, 22 May 1913; *Caucasian*, 19 Dec. 1912.

2. Roller, "Republican Party of North Carolina," 320–23; *Union Republican*, 24 May, 4 June, 13 Aug. 1914; Z. V. Walser to T. Roosevelt, 20 May 1914, and J. N. Williamson to T. Roosevelt, 2 July 1914, Roosevelt Papers, LC; *News and Observer*, 18, 19 Aug. 1914; *Union Republican*, 20, 27 Aug., 8 Oct., 5 Nov. 1914; *Greensboro Daily News*, 18, 19, 21 Aug. 1914; *Charlotte Daily Observer*, 14, 19, 21 Aug. 1914; G. Butler to MB, 13 Nov. 1914; MB to J. Thompson, 20 May 1914; MB to T. Roosevelt, 22 May 1914; MB to G. Butler, 8, 14 Aug. 1914; all in BP; *Clinton News-Dispatch*, 20, 27 Aug. 1914.

3. Note, Jan. 1915; MB to A. G. Bazemore, 10 June 1915; MB to G. Grissom, 8 Oct. 1915; Z. V. Walser to MB, 25 Mar. 1915; W. Loeb to MB, 23 May 1915; MB to *Greensboro Daily News*, 10 Jan. 1916; MB to M. Clapp, 27 Jan. 1916; J. M. Morehead to MB, 28 Jan. 1916; J. M. Morehead to E. C. Duncan, 22 Feb. 1916; all in BP; *Charlotte Daily Observer*, 1 Mar. 1916; *Clinton News-Dispatch*, 26 Feb. 1916; *Union Republican*, 3, 10, 24 Feb. 1916; Roller, "Republican Party of North Carolina," 323–27; *News and Observer*, 2 Mar. 1916.

4. *Greensboro Daily News*, 2, 3 Mar. 1916; *Charlotte Daily Observer*, 2, 3 Mar. 1916; *News and Observer*, 2 Mar. 1916; H. F. Seawell to F. Hitchcock, 2 Mar. 1916, Seawell Sr. Papers, ECU.

5. *North Carolina Republican State Convention*, NCC; *Greensboro Daily News*, 3, 4, 5 Mar. 1916; *Union Republican*, 9, 23 Mar., 2 Nov., 12 Dec. 1916; *Charlotte Daily Observer*, 3, 12 Mar. 1916; E. C. Duncan to H. F. Seawell, 11 Mar. 1916, Seawell Sr. Papers, ECU; Durden, *Reconstruction Bonds*, 253–57; *News and Observer*, 7 Nov. 1916; *Record of Marion Butler*, NCC; *Clinton News-Dispatch*, 12 Mar. 1916; MB to G. W. Perkins, 30 Mar. 1916; T. D. Warren to P. V. Mathews, 19 Aug. 1916; MB to W. S. O'B. Robinson, 20 Mar. 1916; all in BP.

6. J. Vale[?] to J. T. Flanagan, 20 Mar. 1916; MB to G. Perkins, 8 Apr. 1916; MB to W. Loeb, 19, 22, 24, 27 May 1916; all in BP; H. J. Harm to MB, 1 June 1916; T. Roosevelt to MB, 3 May 1916; MB to T. Roosevelt, 6 May, 13 June 1916; all in Roosevelt Papers, LC; Pringle, *Theodore Roosevelt*, 586–87; *Greensboro Daily News*, 5, 6, 7, 10, 11 June 1916.

7. *Clinton News-Dispatch*, 10 Aug., 26 Oct. 1916; *Union Republican*, 5, 26 Oct. 1916; *The Inside of the Political Situation; Progress and Prosperity; The Democrats and Butler*, all in NCC; MB to C. E. Hughes, 21 June, 24 Oct. 1916; J. M. Morehead to MB, 28 Sept. 1916; MB to R. D. Cole, 30 Oct. 1916; all in BP; MB to T. Roosevelt, 5 July 1916, Roosevelt Papers, LC; Roller, "Republican Party of North Carolina," 329–30.

8. MB to H. E. Peterson, 6 Apr. 1917; MB to J. W. Weeks, 26 Mar. 1917; MB to R. M. Ward, 13 Apr. 1917; MB to J. M. Morehead, 17 Apr., 17 May 1917; J. M. Morehead to MB, 13 May, 21 June 1917; MB to G. E. Kestler, 17 Apr. 1917; MB to J. C. Bain, 13 June 1917; MB to Sen. Gallinger, 3 Aug. 1917; all in BP; MB to T. F. Davidson, 27 Sept. 1917, Davidson Papers, SHC; *News and Observer*, 10 Apr. 1918; *Charlotte Daily Observer*, 9 Apr., 18 Oct. 1918; *Greensboro Daily News*, 9 Apr., 18 Oct., 2 Nov. 1918; *Union Republican*, 11 Apr., 17, 24 Oct., 7, 14, 21 Nov. 1918; Broadside, 1918, Nunn Papers, Duke.

9. Z. V. Walser to MB, 16, 29 Apr. 1919; J. F. Wray to MB, 26 Apr. 1919; MB to C. E. Taylor, 28 July 1919; MB to J. J. Jenkins, 18 Aug., 23 Sept., 28 Oct. 1919; MB to C. A.

Reynolds, 19 Sept. 1919; "A Gratuitous Slander at Progressive Republicans," 10 June 1919; all in BP.

10. *Pritchard for President Circular*, NCC; Z. V. Walser to MB, 12 Feb. 1920; MB to L. Lloyd, 15 Mar. 1920; MB to E. C. Duncan, 7 Mar. 1920; A. V. Dockery to MB, 8 Mar. 1920; MB to I. M. Meekins, 22 May 1920; E. C. Duncan to MB, 26 Mar. 1920; W. B. Duncan to MB, 3 May 1920; G. Butler to MB, 15 Mar. 1920; MB to J. J. Parker, 15 Mar. 1920; all in BP; *Union Republican*, 8 Jan., 4 Mar. 1920; *News and Observer*, 2, 3, 4 Mar. 1920; *Charlotte Daily Observer*, 3, 4, 5 Mar. 1920; *Greensboro Daily News*, 4 Mar. 1920.

11. Folder 350, 15–19 Mar. 1920; MB to J. M. Morehead [1920]; MB to F. A. Linney, 16 June 1920; all in BP; *Union Republican*, 27 May 1920; *Greensboro Daily News*, 7, 12, 13 June 1920; Roseboom, *Presidential Elections*, 391–97; *Charlotte Daily Observer*, 9, 13 June 1920; *Union Republican*, 17 June 1920; *Clinton Sampson Democrat*, 17, 24 June 1920; C. D. Hilles to R. Foster, 19 Mar. 1921; J. C. Pritchard to MB, 12 June 1920; MB to H. C. Lodge, 27 June 1920; MB to W. G. Harding, 22, 25, 29 June 1920; all in Harding Papers, OHS.

12. MB to W. G. Harding, 1 July 1920; G. Butler to H. Daugherty, 3 July 1920; MB to H. Daugherty, 10 July 1920; G. B. Christian to MB, 13 July 1920; MB to W. Hays, 17, 22 July, 21 Aug. 1920; R. Herring to MB, 12 July 1920; W. Hays to MB, 27 July 1920; C. Adamson to MB, 23 July 1920; W. G. Harding to MB, 6 July 1920; D. W. Hill to H. Daugherty, 13 July 1920; MB to A. E. Holton, 14 Aug. 1920; J. J. Parker to MB, 4 Nov. 1920; all in BP; MB to W. G. Harding, 19, 20 July, 2 Sept., 22 Oct. 1920; Z. V. Walser to MB, 8 July 1920; J. C. Pritchard to W. G. Harding, 4 July 1920; J. A. K. Hendricks to W. G. Harding, 8 July 1920; G. Butler to W. G. Harding, 9 July 1920; J. J. Parker to W. G. Harding, 10 July 1920; all in Harding Papers, OHS; *Union Republican*, 29 July 1920; *Clinton Sampson Democrat*, 12 Aug., 2, 9, 16, 23, 30 Sept. 1920; *News and Observer*, 1 Nov. 1920.

13. *Clinton Sampson Democrat*, 28 Oct. 1920; *Union Republican*, 22 July, 2 Sept., 21 Oct., 4 Nov., 2 Dec. 1920; J. C. Pritchard to W. G. Harding, 5 July 1920; I. Nedler to G. B. Christian, 6 Apr. 1921; MB to H. Work, 28 Jan. 1922; all in Harding Papers, OHS; Linney, *Circular*, and Hicks, *Think! Think! Think!*, NCC; *News and Observer*, 1 Nov. 1920; MB to W. E. Borah, 15 Dec. 1920, BP; I. M. Meekins to H. F. Seawell, 8 Nov. 1920, Seawell Sr. Papers, ECU.

14. MB to H. Daugherty, 13 Dec. 1920; MB to J. N. Williamson, 5 Dec. 1920; MB to N. M. Palmer, 7 Dec. 1920; all in BP; J. C. Pritchard to W. G. Harding, 18 Dec. 1920; E. A. Alderman to W. G. Harding, 18 Nov. 1920; C. W. Dabney to W. G. Harding, 27 Dec. 1920; W. Clark to W. G. Harding, 10 Nov. 1920; C. Kitchin to W. G. Harding, 12 Nov. 1920; J. J. Parker to W. G. Harding, 20 Nov. 1920; S. S. McNinch to W. G. Harding, 8 Dec. 1920; I. Meares to W. G. Harding, 11 Nov. 1920; J. E. Ransdell to W. G. Harding, 23 Nov. 1920; J. M. Parker to W. G. Harding, 29 Nov. 1920; J. E. Boyd to W. G. Harding, 2 Dec. 1920; all in Harding Papers, OHS.

15. J. H. Quinn to W. G. Harding, 21 Dec. 1920, and A. Adams to Harding's Secretary, 17 Jan. 1921, Harding Papers, OHS; *Union Republican*, 2 Dec. 1920; Clipping, *Wilmington Morning Star*, 20 Nov. 1920, Scrapbook, 1918–28, Hampton Papers, Duke; J. M. Morehead to MB, 31 Jan., 11 Feb. 1921; MB to J. M. Morehead, 5, 14 Feb.

1921; W. G. Briggs to MB, 7 Jan. 1921; MB to R. Herring, 1 Dec. 1920; "Rural Free Delivery and the Official Record," 18 Dec. 1920; all in BP; MB to W. G. Briggs, 18 Feb. 1921, Briggs Papers, SHC.

16. MB to R. F. Pettigrew, 11 Apr. 1921; MB to J. J. Parker, 21 Mar. 1921; MB to G. Butler, 19 Mar. 1921, 23 June, 15 Sept. 1922; MB to W. D. Holland, 25 Jan. 1922; MB to G. Lee, 9 May 1922; MB to W. G. Bramham, 5 July 1922; MB to E. F. Butler, 22 Aug. 1922; MB to W. S. Sessoms, 27 Oct. 1922; all in BP; H. Daugherty to W. G. Harding, 6 May 1921, and H. Work to W. G. Harding, 7 Sept. 1922, Harding Papers, OHS; MB to J. J. Parker, 4 June 1921; G. Butler to W. G. Briggs, 5 Mar. 1921; MB to D. M. Jones, 4 Apr. 1921; MB to S. O. Holmes, 18 Feb. 1921; all in Briggs Papers, SHC; W. B. Duncan to H. F. Seawell, 16 Mar. 1921; MB to H. F. Seawell, 26 Mar. 1921; I. M. Meekins to H. F. Seawell, 9 Oct. 1922; G. Butler to E. L. Gavin, 5 Mar. 1921; all in Seawell Sr. Papers, ECU; *Charlotte Daily Observer*, 11, 13, 14 Apr. 1922; *Union Republican*, 9 Feb., 16 Mar., 13, 20, 27 Apr. 1922; *News and Observer*, 13 Apr. 1922; *Greensboro Daily News*, 13 Apr. 1922; Sumner, "William G. Bramham."

17. J. F. Newell to MB, 16 June 1923; W. S. O'B. Robinson to MB, 25 June 1923; MB to J. Newell, 22 June 1923; C. Morrison to MB, 11 Sept. 1924; MB to C. Morrison, 16 Sept. 1924; all in BP; *Union Republican*, 24 Jan. 1924; W. G. Bramham to G. Butler, 13 Mar. 1924, George Butler Papers, SHC; Tindall, *Emergence of the New South*, 225-27; Magruder, "Governor Cameron Morrison."

18. G. Butler to MB, 26 Feb. 1924, and W. G. Bramham to G. Butler, 28 Feb. 1924, George Butler Papers, SHC; MB to L. E. Dickson, 19 Jan. 1924; MB to My Dear Mr. ————, 24 Feb. 1924; W. G. Bramham to I. M. Meekins, 29 Feb. 1924; I. M. Meekins to MB, 5 Mar. 1924; all in BP.

19. MB to Hawes, 6, 14 Aug. 1923; MB to A. B. Fall, 17 Mar. 1923; I. M. Meekins to MB, 5 Mar. 1924; J. C. Robinson to MB, 14 Mar. 1924; R. F. Pettigrew to MB, 18 July 1923; all in BP.

20. I. M. Meekins to MB, 5, 12 Mar., 5 Apr. 1924; MB to R. F. Pettigrew, 13 Aug., 22 Sept. 1924; MB to W. D. Dorsett, 3 Nov. 1924; MB to E. Butler, 3 Feb. 1925; all in BP; *Union Republican*, 20 Mar. 1924; *Charlotte Observer*, 19, 20, 21 Mar. 1924; *Greensboro Daily News*, 17, 19, 20 Mar. 1924; MB to J. J. Parker, 15 May 1924, Parker Papers, SHC; Roseboom, *Presidential Elections*, 406-11; *Union Republican*, 5 June, 25 Sept., 2, 9, 16 Oct., 27 Nov. 1924; Powell, *North Carolina through Four Centuries*, 479.

21. Folder 432; MB to C. Coolidge, 9 Jan. 1925, BP; C. B. Slemp to H. F. Stone, 3 Dec. 1924, Coolidge Papers, LC; G. Butler to J. J. Parker, 26 Nov. 1924, and G. Flow to MB, 7 Feb., 25 Mar. 1926, Parker Papers, SHC; MB to J. F. Barrett, 22 June, 3, 19 Aug. 1925; MB to R. E. Noble, 15 Sept. 1925; R. Edmonds to R. E. Noble, 16 Sept. 1925; MB to J. E. Cox, 24 Sept. 1925; MB to P. Spivey, 3 Nov. 1925; MB to S. L. Shuford, 29 Dec. 1925; MB to J. H. Quinn, 30 Jan. 1926; Folder 444; MB to O. P. Brower, 13 Jan. 1926; J. Newell to MB, 13 Feb. 1926; C. A. Jonas to MB, 24 Feb. 1926; MB to C. A. Jonas, 26 Feb. 1926; MB to D. T. Moran, 8 Mar. 1926; MB to C. L. Jenkins, 23 Mar. 1926; "The Great Battle of Armageddon Is On," 28 Mar. 1926; "Fallacies of Chairman Bramham Exposed" [1926]; all in BP; *Union Republican*, 7 Jan., 18, 25 Feb., 4, 18 Mar. 1926; *Greensboro Daily News*, 20, 22 Mar., 6, 7 Apr. 1926.

22. *Greensboro Daily News*, 7, 8 Apr. 1926; *Union Republican*, 1, 8, 15, 29 Apr., 13 May,

10, 17 June, 11 Nov. 1926; *News and Observer*, 8, 10 Apr. 1926; *Charlotte Observer*, 6, 8, 10, 11 Apr. 1926; MB to B. Jackson, 18 May 1926; MB to C. B. Goodson, 12 Apr. 1926; B. W. Wilson to MB, 9 Apr. 1926; MB to J. B. Goslin, 8 June 1926; MB to H. F. Seawell, 11 June 1926; MB to S. E. McFadden, 14 June 1926; MB to F. A. Slate, 23 June 1926; B. Jackson to MB, 22 July 1926; MB to J. J. Hayes, 27 Apr., 10 Sept. 1926; MB to J. C. Mathews, 7 Sept. 1926; MB to G. D. Bailey, 18 Sept. 1926; MB to My Dear Mr. ———, 28 May 1926; MB to *Greensboro Daily News* and *Charlotte Observer*, 28 May 1926; all in BP.

23. J. E. Little to MB, 30 Sept. 1927; H. J. Faison to MB, 19 Apr. 1927; MB to H. Morton, 25 Apr. 1927; MB to C. A. Jonas, 3 Oct. 1927; F. F. Butler to C. C. Kirkpatrick, 4 Feb. 1928; C. L. Sniden to MB, 4 Feb. 1928; MB to C. A. Jonas, 23, 27 Feb., 18 June, 26 July 1928; C. A. Jonas to MB, 25 Feb., 2 Mar., 23 Aug. 1928; J. E. Burleson to MB, 6 Mar. 1928; MB to J. B. Long, 9 Oct. 1928; MB to Mrs. W. E. Kennen, 21 July 1928; MB to R. F. Craig, 16 Mar. 1928; MB to W. S. Bogler, 26 Mar. 1928; G. Grissom to MB, 9 Apr. 1928; F. Butler to G. M. Pritchard, 8 Aug. 1928; F. Butler, "Memorandum," 24 Sept. 1928; G. Pritchard to MB, 6 Oct. 1928; all in BP; MB to H. F. Seawell, 28, 30 Mar. 1928; H. F. Seawell to MB, 28 Mar., 2 Apr. 1928; MB Circular, 27 Mar. 1928; all in Seawell Sr. Papers, ECU; *Union Republican*, 19 Jan., 16 Feb., 1 Mar., 12 Apr., 7, 14 June, 6 Sept. 1928; *News and Observer*, 11, 12 Apr. 1928; *Greensboro Daily News*, 12 Apr., 12, 15 June 1928; *Charlotte Observer*, 11, 12 Apr. 1928; F. Butler to Mrs. H. F. Seawell, 19 May 1928; F. Butler to W. G. Mebane, 26 May 1928; G. Mebane to F. Butler, 25 Oct. 1928; F. Butler to B. Jackson, 30 Aug. 1928; F. Butler to C. A. Jonas, 30 Aug. 1928; all in Florence Faison Butler Papers, SHC; *New York Times*, 18 Aug. 1928; Memorandum, Miss Fesler to Mr. Richey, 24 Aug. 1928, Hoover Papers, Hoover Presidential Library, West Branch, Iowa; Hicks, *Republican Ascendancy*, 193-214.

24. MB to H. D. George, 24 Nov. 1928, BP; *Union Republican*, 15 Nov. 1928; Hicks, *American Nation*, 609-10; Powell, *North Carolina through Four Centuries*, 478-79.

25. MB, *An Appeal*, NCC; *Union Republican*, 13, 27 Mar., 3, 10, 17, 24 Apr., 15 May, 5, 12, 19, 26 June, 14 Aug. 1930; *News and Observer*, 4 Mar. 1920, 11 June 1930; *Charlotte Observer*, 11 June 1930; Burris, *John J. Parker*, 33-110; Tindall, *Emergence of the New South*, 541-42; Watson, "Defeat of Judge Parker"; MB to W. Jones, 19 Apr. 1930; MB to H. Allen, 21 Apr. 1930; MB to G. Norris, 12 Apr. 1930; MB to J. Watson, 25 Apr. 1930; T. Howell to MB, 31 May 1930; all in BP; Goings, *NAACP Comes of Age*.

26. G. Butler to MB, 27 Feb. 1932, and MB to G. Butler, 27 Feb. 1932, George Butler Papers, SHC; MB to F. Patton, 29 Mar. 1932; MB to W. B. Rouse, 4 Oct. 1932; I. H. Neihus to MB, 17 Oct. 1932; J. P. Hill to MB, 13 Oct. 1932; Extracts from a Speech by Former Senator Marion Butler at Johnson City, Tennessee, 4 Nov. 1932; Notes for Speech, 1932; MB to J. C. Hambright, 29 Dec. 1932; Interview, folder 521 [Nov. 1932]; Speakers' Information Service, Bulletins dated 12, 13, 22, 31 Oct. 1932; MB to J. Newell, 7 Oct. 1932; S. H. Newberry to MB, 2 Nov. 1932; all in BP; MB to H. Hoover, 24 Feb. 1932, and Memo: To Mr. Newton, 7 Oct. 1932, Hoover Papers, Hoover Presidential Library; *Union Republican*, 18 Feb., 7, 21, 28 Apr., 19 May, 23 June, 27 Oct., 1 Dec. 1932; *News and Observer*, 15, 16 Apr. 1932; *Greensboro Daily News*, 14, 15 Apr. 1932; *Charlotte Observer*, 13, 15 Apr. 1932; W. G. Briggs to I. B. Tucker, 11

Oct. 1932; W. G. Briggs to C. Frazier, 14 Oct. 1932; I. B. Tucker to W. G. Briggs, 4 Oct. 1932; all in Briggs Papers, SHC; Houghton, "North Carolina Republican Party," 58–62.

27. *Union Republican*, 8, 22 Feb., 1, 15 Mar. 1934; *News and Observer*, 3, 5 Apr. 1934; *Greensboro Daily News*, 4 Apr. 1934; *Charlotte Observer*, 3, 4 Apr. 1934; A. Butler to E. Butler, 24 Mar. 1934, Algernon Butler Papers, SHC; *Charlotte Observer*, 5 Apr. 1934; *Greensboro Daily News*, 5 Apr. 1934; MB to A. V. Cole, 25 Apr. 1934, and A. V. Cole to MB, 9 Apr. 1934, BP; Houghton, "North Carolina Republican Party," 64–70.

28. *Union Republican*, 20, 27 Feb., 26 Mar., 16 Apr., 19 Nov. 1936; *Charlotte Observer*, 24, 25 Mar. 1936; *Greensboro Daily News*, 24, 25 Mar. 1936; *News and Observer*, 24, 25 Mar. 1936; M. Ritch to MB, 6 Apr. 1936; G. Grissom to MB, 5 Apr. 1936; E. Butler to MB [1936]; all in BP; MB to A. Butler, 17 Oct. 1936, Algernon Butler Papers, SHC.

29. MB to *Atlantic Monthly*, 11 July 1914; MB to Slayden Lecture Bureau, 4 Feb. 1913; MB to *Charlotte Observer*, 4 Apr. 1913; MB to *Country Gentleman*, 31 Jan. 1914; MB to *Review of Reviews*, 28 Apr. 1915; "The Opposition to Rural Credit Banks—Killing the Goose That Lays the Golden Egg" [1914]; "A Marvelous Superstructure and a Crumbling Foundation" [1914]; "Liberating and Financing the Wealth Producer" [1914]; MB to C. Glass, 7 Dec. 1915; MB to *Progressive Farmer*, 30 Aug. 1915; MB to M. Glynn, 12 Feb. 1914; MB to J. H. Davis, 28 Dec. 1915; H. L. Loucks to MB, 7 Sept. 1915; all in BP.

30. MB to *Atlantic Monthly*, 11 July 1914; MB to *Charlotte Observer*, 4 Apr. 1913; MB to J. Thompson, 26 Mar. 1914; MB, "The Opposition to Rural Credit Banks—Killing the Goose That Lays the Golden Egg"; MB, "Liberating and Financing the Wealth Producer"; MB, "The Ominous Migration of Rural Wealth Producers to the Cities"; all in BP; *Clinton News-Dispatch*, 22 Oct. 1914; *Caucasian*, 15 May 1913.

31. H. L. Boyd to MB, 19 Feb. 1919; S. G. Robinson to MB, 18 Oct. 1919; *Manufacturers' Record* to MB, 29 Apr. 1919; MB to *Metropolitan Magazine*, 16 Feb. 1914; MB, "The Case for Equal Opportunity" [1914]; MB, "Socialism, a Menace or a Promise?" [1914]; all in BP.

32. H. L. Boyd to MB, 19 Feb. 1919; S. G. Robinson to MB, 18 Oct. 1919; MB, "The Case for Equal Opportunity" [1914]; MB, "Socialism, a Menace or a Promise?" [1914]; all in BP.

33. *Clinton News-Dispatch*, 2, 23, 30 Aug. 1917; J. B. Grimes to MB, 18 Aug. 1919; MB to A. C. Townley, 9 Feb. 1917; MB to K. Thompson, 22 Jan. 1917; all in BP.

34. Special to *Union Republican*, 24 July 1915; Interview with *Washington Post* [1916]; MB to M. Clapp, 4 Nov. 1915; MB to A. B. Coltrane, 18 Oct. 1917; MB to *Asheboro Bulletin*, 27 Oct. 1917; MB to H. Johnson, 16 Nov. 1917; MB to R. La Follette, 14 Nov. 1917; MB to R. F. Pettigrew, 26 Nov. 1917; Memo, 25 Mar. 1918; J. Vale to MB, 2 Mar. 1918; R. F. Pettigrew to MB, Apr., 3 Nov. 1917, 29 Mar. 1919; all in BP; *Clinton News-Dispatch*, 24, 31 May, 7, 28 June, 12 July 1917.

35. U.S. Congress, Senate Committee on Indian Affairs, *Hearings on the Equalization of Creek Indian Allotments*, 865–900; U.S. Congress, Select Committee of the House, *Hearings . . . for the Purpose of Investigating Indian Contracts*, 3–8; *Robertson v. Gordon, Butler and Vale*, 226 U.S. 311 (1912); Memo, 10 July 1909; R. F. Pettigrew to MB, 2 Feb. 1909; MB to R. F. Pettigrew, 24 Jan. 1910; M. Grisby to MB, 20 Mar. 1911;

J. D. Clark to Butler and Vale, 23 Nov. 1909; MB to G. Lee, 13 Jan. 1909; J. Vale to H. W. Blakeslee, 18 Oct. 1909; B. Cade to MB, 3 Aug. 1914; J. H. Gallinger to T. Edison, 6 Mar. 1915; MB to J. Street, 11, 12 Nov. 1915; MB to G. T. Withers, 16 June 1913; E. A. Quarles to MB, 14 Oct. 1914; MB to D. H. Hill, 28 Aug. 1915; MB to P. F. Collier and Son, 5 June 1917; MB to Ford Tractor Co., 17 Feb. 1917; F. Butler to MB [1915]; F. Butler to MB, 1 Sept. 1914; all in BP; E. C. Branson to MB, 3 Nov. 1917, Branson Papers, SHC.

36. J. H. Gallinger to MB, 7 Dec. 1909; MB to J. A. Patterson, 11 May 1915; MB to D. Dawson, 15 Mar. 1915; all in BP; U.S. Congress, House Committee on the District of Columbia, *Hearing on . . . the Board of Education of the District of Columbia*; L. P. Roane to F. F. Butler, 10 Oct. 1912, and K. E. Wheatley to F. F. Butler, 11 Dec. 1911, Florence Faison Butler Papers, SHC; Pocahontas Butler Woodson, interview, 20, 27 Sept. 1986.

37. Tindall, *Emergence of the New South*, 113−21; MB to R. P. Kester, 29 Mar. 1922; MB to J. S. Wannamaker, 15 Apr. 1922; MB to W. F. Sessoms, 10 Aug. 1921; MB to W. Clark, 7 May 1923; MB to J. Y. Joyner, 26 Nov. 1921; S. H. Hobbs to Mr. Editor [1920]; B. W. Kilgore to MB, 9 June 1921; Tobacco Cooperative Agreement, 2 Oct. 1920; J. R. Peterson to MB, 1 Aug. 1922; MB to *Greensboro Daily News*, 12 Dec. 1921; B. F. Keith to MB, 15 Dec. 1922; MB to B. F. Keith, 18 Dec. 1922; MB to J. G. McCormick, 21 Oct. 1921; F. E. Smith to MB, 16 Apr., 22 May 1926; all in BP; MB to W. G. Harding, 22 Oct. 1920; W. Christian to H. Hoover, 27 May 1921; J. A. K. Hendricks to W. G. Harding, 8 July 1920; all in Harding Papers, OHS.

38. U.S. Congress, House Committee on Military Affairs, *Muscle Shoals Propositions*, 217−37, 900−935, 989−91; U.S. Congress, Senate Committee on Agriculture and Forestry, *Hearings . . . on S. 3420*; Link and Catton, *American Epoch*, 319−21; *Union Republican*, 12 Jan. 1922; MB to J. Weeks, 28 Dec. 1921, and Folder 388, BP; Hicks, *Republican Ascendancy*, 62−64.

39. U.S. Congress, House Committee on Military Affairs, *Muscle Shoals Propositions*, 217−37, 900−935, 989−91; U.S. Congress, Senate Committee on Agriculture and Forestry, *Hearings . . . on S. 3420*; MB to J. S. Wannamaker, 15 Apr. 1922; MB to R. P. Kester, 29 Mar. 1922; MB to C. Skyes, 18 Feb. 1922; MB to C. Poe, 18 Mar. 1922; Folder 394; G. Goethals to MB, 29 July 1922; MB to F. Engstrum, 2, 6 June 1922; MB to G. Norris, 5 July 1922; all in BP; *New York Times*, 4, 15 Mar. 1922.

40. L. C. Wagner to MB, 20 Mar. 1928; MB to B. C. Reece, 10 Mar. 1931; MB to J. W. Taylor, 30 May 1931; MB to J. C. Stone, 19 Aug. 1931; all in BP; MB to W. H. Newton, 10 June 1931, Hoover Papers, Hoover Presidential Library; "Fine Work by the Federal Farm Board," in MB to A. V. Cole, 6 Feb. 1930, Cole Papers, Duke; *Union Republican*, 16 Jan. 1930, 27 Aug., 27 Sept. 1931; Hicks, *American Nation*, 601−2; Hicks, *Republican Ascendancy*, 193−202, 217−19.

41. MB to W. E. Borah, 23 Nov. 1933, BP.

42. U.S. Congress, Senate Finance Committee, *Hearings . . . on S. 1712 and H.R. 5755, Bills to Encourage National Industrial Recovery*, 357−61; U.S. Congress, House Ways and Means Committee, *Hearings on . . . H.R. 5664, a Bill to Encourage National Industrial Recovery*, 254−57.

43. U.S. Congress, Senate Finance Committee, *Hearings . . . on S. 1712 and H.R.*

5755, Bills to Encourage National Industrial Recovery, 357–61; U.S. Congress, House Ways and Means Committee, *Hearings on . . . H.R. 5664, a Bill to Encourage National Industrial Recovery*, 254–57.

44. MB to C. A. Jonas, 14 Oct. 1937, and MB to E. D. Smith, 24 July 1937, BP.

45. MB to C. A. Jonas, 29 Sept. 1937, BP. Historians have made comparisons between Progressivism and the New Deal, finding both continuity and difference. See, for example, Graham, *Encore for Reform.* The passage of time, however, makes similar work for Populism and the New Deal less possible. Almost no Populist leaders survived into the mid-1930s. The Populists who did survive in North Carolina felt more hostility to the New Deal than support for it, as Butler's activities demonstrate. The opposition is partly explained by the fact that the New Deal derived from the hated Democratic Party, but at least in Butler's case it also relates to the New Deal's failure to put an attack on monopoly at the forefront, its early penchant for government planning over the market, and its ad hoc development. The New Deal, unlike Populism, opposed nationalization of the money supply or the transportation and communication systems. In the 1930s, Butler did not fear the supremacy of national government over monopoly, but he did not believe in high taxes or that government agents in Washington should dictate such things as the details of cotton farming. Moreover, Populism had clearly expressed principles, an independent political organization, and definite legislative goals. In contrast, the New Deal was the creation of a Democratic president after taking office, and its aims varied from year to year. Further, the New Deal was heavily dependent on elite government agencies with enormous legal discretion. Elizabeth Sanders has recently distinguished the "discretionary bureaucracy" of the New Deal from the more agrarian, democratic, and legislatively driven reforms of the Progressive Era. See her *Roots of Reform*, 416–19. Of course, unlike Populism, the New Deal also succeeded for a time, while Butler and a few others provided lonely Populist voices in Congress. Ultimately, Populism and the New Deal shared a number of characteristics, but the differences in purposes, program, and effect outweigh their similarities.

46. C. A. Jonas to MB, 5 Oct. 1937; C. A. Jonas to Associated Press, 28 Aug. 1937; C. A. Jonas to J. W. Arnold, 27 Sept. 1937; all in BP; C. A. Jonas to G. Butler, 6 July 1938, George Butler Papers, SHC.

47. L. R. Wilson to MB, 29 May 1929; F. Butler to J. G. deRoulhac Hamilton, 24 June 1929; A. Butler to MB, 25 Mar. 1926; H. Pope to MB, 13 Apr. 1937; W. D. Sheldon to MB, 9 Feb. 1934; R. J. Barlett to MB, 20 Oct. 1930; W. A. Mabry to MB, 23 July, 21 Aug. 1930; MB to A. Henderson, 10 Apr. 1935; all in BP; MB to F. P. Graham, 4 June 1935, Graham Papers, SHC; S. Robins to J. Morrison, 14 Jan. 1962, Morrison Papers, SHC; "140th Commencement"; Woodward, *Tom Watson*, 288 n. 23. Previously, Butler helped protect his place in history by arranging for a favorable biographical sketch of himself in Samuel A'Court Ashe's *Biographical History.* Friends warned him that Ashe would distort his career. The final product resulted from a joint effort between Butler and James B. Lloyd, the former Tarboro Populist. W. S. Thompson to MB, 5 Oct. 1904; J. B. Lloyd to MB, 21 Jan. 1905; C. Van Noppen to MB, 14 Jan., 1 Feb. 1905; all in BP.

48. MB to O. J. Peterson, 2 Feb. 1933; Notes for a History of the People's

Party [1933]; Reference Books Needed [1933]; Patrons of Husbandry [1932]; all in BP.

49. MB to F. Butler, 14 Apr. 1933; MB to F. M. Moye, 18 July 1935; Mamie to MB, 3 Dec. 1931; M. A. Roberts to MB, 23 June 1931; MB to F. H. Daniel, 14 June 1932; MB to E. F. Butler, 28 Dec. 1932; MB to Mrs. H. Cairns, 3 Mar. 1933; all in BP; *Union Republican*, 26 May, 24 July 1930; *Charlotte Observer*, 4, 5 June 1938; *Greensboro Daily News*, 4, 6 June 1938; *Washington Post*, 4 June 1938; *News and Observer*, 4, 5 June 1938; *New York Times*, 25 May 1938; J. Newell to G. Butler, 25 May 1938, George Butler Papers, SHC.

50. *New York Times*, 4 June 1938; *Washington Post*, 4 June 1938; *Union Republican*, 9 June 1938; *News and Observer*, 4 June 1938; *Charlotte Observer*, 4 June 1938; *Greensboro Daily News*, 4 June 1938.

BIBLIOGRAPHY

Primary Sources

MANUSCRIPT COLLECTIONS

Chapel Hill, North Carolina
North Carolina Collection, Wilson Library, University of North Carolina
Ayer, Hal. *To the Populist Voters of the Eighteenth Senatorial District* (October 1896).
A Bill to Be Entitled an Act for the Relief of the Stockholders of the State Alliance Business Fund (1895).
Butler, Marion. *An Appeal* (1930).
———. *An Open Letter* (1907).
———. *The Republican State Convention at Greensboro* (1908).
Butler in His Own Mirror (1910).
Chapters from the Republican Hand-book (1910).
Credentials of Delegates and Alternates (May 1912).
The Democrats and Butler (1916).
Dr. Thompson's Great Speech (1898).
Guthrie, William A. *Supplemental Address to the People's Party Voters of North Carolina* (30 October 1896).
Hicks, T. T. *Think! Think! Think! That's What the Head Is For* (1920).
The Inside of the Political Situation (1916).
Instructions to Judges of Election (1900).
Is the Democratic Party Honest? (1898).
Linney, Frank A. *Circular* (1920).
Marion Butler's Raleigh Speech, Second Edition (1911).
Marion Butler: Who Is Trying to Capture the Approaching Republican State Convention . . . (1910).
No. 12 — Democrats on the Run (1898).
North Carolina Republican State Convention (1916).
People's Party Handbook of Facts (1898).
Populist Handbook Answered (1898).
Pritchard for President Circular (1920).
Progress and Prosperity (1916).
The Record of Marion Butler (1916).
Vance and Settle: Their Record as Public Men (1876).

Southern Historical Collection, Wilson Library, University of North Carolina
   Eugene C. Branson Papers
   Willis G. Briggs Papers
   Algernon Butler Papers
   Florence Faison Butler Papers
   George Butler Papers
   Marion Butler Papers
   Calvin J. Cowles Papers
   Theodore F. Davidson Papers
   Frank Porter Graham Papers
   J. Bryan Grimes Papers
   Walter A. Montgomery Papers
   Joseph L. Morrison Papers
   John J. Parker Papers
   Richmond Pearson Papers
   William J. Peele Papers
   Leonidas La Fayette Polk Papers
   James G. Ramsey Papers
   Matthew W. Ransom Papers
   Daniel L. Russell Jr. Papers
   Thomas Settle Papers
   John H. Small Papers
   Cyrus Thompson Papers
   Thomas E. Watson Papers
University Archives, Wilson Library, University of North Carolina
   Dialectic Society Minutes, 1881–85
   Dialectic Society Papers, 1881–85
   Dialectic Society Periodical Register, 1881–85
   Library Journal of the Dialectic Society, 1882–86
   Student Reports, 1875–85

Clinton, North Carolina
Sampson County Courthouse
   Marriage Register, 1892–1908
   Will of Wiley Butler, Estates Records Office

Columbus, Ohio
Ohio Historical Society
   Warren G. Harding Papers (microfilm)

Durham, North Carolina
Perkins Library, Manuscript Department, Duke University
   William Garrot Brown Papers
   Thomas Clawson Papers
   Arthur V. Cole Papers

J. Elwood Cox Papers
Cronly Family Papers
John S. Cunningham Papers
Benjamin N. Duke Papers
Frank A. Hampton Papers
William D. Hardin Papers
Hugh W. Johnson Papers
Romulus N. Nunn Papers
Edward A. Oldham Papers
Edward Chambers Smith Papers
Alexander Sprunt Papers
Edward A. Thorne Papers

Greenville, North Carolina
J. Y. Joyner Library, Manuscript Collection, East Carolina University
    Elias Carr Papers
    William B. Rodman Papers
    Herbert F. Seawell Sr. Papers
    Albert R. Smith Papers

Madison, Wisconsin
State Historical Society of Wisconsin
    Luhman H. Weller Papers

St. Paul, Minnesota
Minnesota Historical Society
    Ignatius Donnelly Papers

Raleigh, North Carolina
North Carolina Division of Archives and History, Manuscripts Section
    Private Papers
        Samuel A'Court Ashe Papers
        Henry Bright Papers
        Robert B. Creecy Papers
        James W. Denmark Papers
        Leonidas Polk Denmark Papers
        Marmaduke J. Hawkins Papers
        North Carolina Farmers' State Alliance Papers
        Fred A. Olds Papers
    Unpublished Public Records
        Eighth Census of the United States, 1860: Sampson County, North Carolina,
            Social Statistics, Free Inhabitants, Slave, and Agricultural Schedules
        Fifth Census of the United States, 1830: Sampson County, North Carolina,
            Population Schedule
        First Census of the United States, 1790: Sampson County, North Carolina,
            Population Schedule

Ninth Census of the United States, 1870: Sampson County, North Carolina,
    Agriculture Schedule
Sampson County Deeds, Grantee Index
Sampson County Miscellaneous Records (Elections), 1878–1926
Sampson County Tax List, 1877, 1882, 1887, 1888, 1889
Second Census of the United States, 1800: Sampson County, North Carolina,
    Population Schedule
Seventh Census of the United States, 1850: Sampson County, North Carolina,
    Social Statistics, Free Inhabitants, Slave, and Agricultural Schedules
Sixth Census of the United States, 1840: Sampson County, North Carolina,
    Population Schedule
Tenth Census of the United States, 1880: Sampson County, North Carolina,
    Agriculture and Population Schedules
Third Census of the United States, 1810: Sampson County, North Carolina,
    Population Schedule
Works Progress Administration, Survey of Pre-1914 Cemetery Records

Washington, D.C.
Library of Congress, Manuscript Division
    Calvin Coolidge Papers (microfilm)
    Josephus Daniels Papers
    William McKinley Papers (microfilm)
    Theodore Roosevelt Papers (microfilm)
    William Howard Taft Papers (microfilm)

West Branch, Iowa
Herbert Hoover Presidential Library
    Herbert Hoover Papers (microfilm)

NEWSPAPERS

Asheboro Randolph Bulletin
Asheville Daily Gazette
Burlington State Dispatch
Caucasian (Clinton, Goldsboro, and Raleigh)
Charlotte Daily Observer
Charlotte Evening Chronicle
Charlotte Observer
Charlotte People's Paper
Clinton Independent
Clinton News-Dispatch
Clinton Sampson Democrat
Clinton Sampson Republic
Daily Industrial News (Greensboro)
Daily State Chronicle (Raleigh)
Dallas Southern Mercury

Dunn State's Voice
Durham Daily Globe
Elizabeth City Economist
Elizabeth City Economist-Falcon
Elizabeth City North Carolinian
Fayetteville Observer
Fisherman and Farmer (Edenton and Elizabeth City)
Goldsboro Headlight
Granville County Reformer (Oxford)
Greensboro Daily News
Greenville King's Weekly
Henderson Gold Leaf
Henderson Vance Farmer
Hertford Perquimans Record
Hickory Mercury
Hickory Press
Hickory Times-Mercury
Hillsboro Alliance Weekly
Kings Mountain Progressive Reformer
Marshville Our Home
Moravian Falls Yellow Jacket
Mountain Home Journal (Asheville)
News and Observer (Raleigh)
News-Observer-Chronicle (Raleigh)
New York Times
Patron and Gleaner (Lasker)
People's Party Paper (Atlanta)
Pinnacle Era
Pittsboro Chatham Citizen
Progressive Farmer (Winston and Raleigh)
Raleigh Daily Caucasian
Raleigh Daily Tribune
Raleigh Gazette
Raleigh Hayseeder
Raleigh Home Rule
Raleigh Morning Post
Raleigh North Carolinian
Raleigh Signal
Raleigh Special Informer
Reidsville Webster's Weekly
Rockingham Anglo-Saxon
Salisbury Carolina Watchman
Tarboro Farmers' Advocate
Taylorsville Index
Topeka Farmers' Advocate

Trinity College Country Life
Twice-a-Week Tar Heel (Greensboro)
Union Republican (Winston and Winston-Salem)
Wadesboro Plow Boy
Warren Plains People's Paper
Washington National Economist
Washington Post
Weekly State Chronicle (Raleigh)
Weekly Tar Heel (Greensboro)
Whitakers Rattler
Wilmington Messenger

PUBLISHED MATERIALS

Butler, Marion. "Election in North Carolina." *The Independent*, 16 August 1900,
    1953–55.
———. "The Hour's Need." *University Magazine*, March 1886, 157–61.
———. "The People's Party." *Forum*, February 1900, 658–62.
———. "Trusts—the Causes That Produce Them—the Remedy." *Arena*, March
    1898, 288–89.
———. "Why the South Wants Free Coinage of Silver." *Arena*, April 1896, 625–32.
Catalogue of the Members of the Dialectic Society. Baltimore: Isaac Friedenwald, 1890.
Catalogue of the University of North Carolina at Chapel Hill, 1881–1882. Raleigh:
    Uzzell and Wiley, 1882.
Catalogue of the University of North Carolina at Chapel Hill, 1883–1884. Raleigh: Ed-
    wards, Broughton, and Co., 1884.
Daniels, Josephus. *Editor in Politics*. Chapel Hill: University of North Carolina Press,
    1941.
———. *Tar Heel Editor*. Chapel Hill: University of North Carolina Press, 1939.
Democratic Hand-Book, 1894. Raleigh: E. M. Uzzell, 1894.
N. W. Ayer and Son's Newspaper Annual. Philadelphia: N. W. Ayer and Son's, 1887.
N. W. Ayer and Son's Newspaper Annual. Philadelphia: N. W. Ayer and Son's, 1888.
N. W. Ayer and Son's Newspaper Annual. Philadelphia: N. W. Ayer and Son's, 1891.
"140th Commencement Is a Record Breaker." [UNC] *Alumni Review*, June 1935,
    253–54.
Peffer, William A. *Populism: Its Rise and Fall*. Edited by Peter H. Argersinger.
    Lawrence: University Press of Kansas, 1992.
*Proceedings of the Eighth Annual Session of the North Carolina Farmers' State Alliance,
    1894*. Raleigh: Edwards and Broughton, 1894.
*Proceedings of the Fifth Annual Session of the North Carolina Farmers' State Alliance,
    1891*. Raleigh: Edwards and Broughton, 1891.
*Proceedings of the Fourth Annual Session of the North Carolina Farmers' State Alliance,
    1890*. Raleigh: Edwards and Broughton, 1890.
*Proceedings of the Ninth Annual Session of the North Carolina Farmers' State Alliance,
    1895*. Raleigh: Edwards and Broughton, 1895.

Proceedings of the North Carolina Teachers' Assembly. Raleigh: E. M. Uzzell, 1884.
Proceedings of the North Carolina Teachers' Assembly. Raleigh: E. M. Uzzell, 1887.
Proceedings of the Seventh Annual Session of the North Carolina Farmers' State Alliance, 1893. Raleigh: Edwards and Broughton, 1893.
Proceedings of the Sixth Annual Session of the North Carolina Farmers' State Alliance, 1892. Raleigh: Edwards and Broughton, 1892.
Proceedings of the Third Annual Session of the North Carolina Farmers' State Alliance, 1889. Raleigh: Edwards and Broughton, 1889.
Wiles, Walter E. "Marion Butler." *N.C. Magazine,* March 1921, 23–24.

GOVERNMENT REPORTS

Agriculture of the United States in 1860. Washington: Government Printing Office, 1864.
Code of North Carolina: Enacted March 2, 1883. New York: Banks and Brothers, 1883.
Congressional Directory. Washington: Government Printing Office, 1892.
Congressional Directory. Washington: Government Printing Office, 1893.
Congressional Directory. Washington: Government Printing Office, 1896.
Congressional Record. 54th Cong., 1st sess., 1895–96. Washington: Government Printing Office, 1896.
Congressional Record. 54th Cong., 2d sess., 1896–97. Washington: Government Printing Office, 1897.
Congressional Record. 55th Cong., 1st sess., 1897. Washington: Government Printing Office, 1897.
Congressional Record. 55th Cong., 2d sess., 1897–98. Washington: Government Printing Office, 1898.
Congressional Record. 55th Cong., 3d sess., 1898–99. Washington: Government Printing Office, 1899.
Congressional Record. 56th Cong., 1st sess., 1899–1900. Washington: Government Printing Office, 1900.
Congressional Record. 56th Cong., 2d sess., 1900–1901. Washington: Government Printing Office, 1901.
De Bow, J. D. B. *Statistical View of the United States.* Washington: Beverly Tucker, 1854.
Journal of the Executive Committee of the Senate of the United States, 55th Cong., 3d sess. Washington: Government Printing Office, 1899.
Journal of the Senate of the General Assembly of the State of North Carolina at Its Session of [1891].
Journal of the Senate of the General Assembly of the State of North Carolina at Its Session of [1895].
Laws and Resolutions of the State of North Carolina Passed by the General Assembly at Its Session [1889].
Laws and Resolutions of the State of North Carolina Passed by the General Assembly at Its Session of [1891].
Public Laws and Resolutions of the State of North Carolina Passed by the General Assembly at Its Session of [1895].

Report on the Statistics of Agriculture in the United States. Washington: Government
    Printing Office, 1895.
Robertson v. Gordon, Butler and Vale, 226 U.S. 311 (1912).
State v. Butler, 151 N.C. 672 (1909).
U.S. Census Office. *The Statistics of the Population of the United States . . . from the Origi-
    nal Returns of the Ninth Census (June 1, 1870).* Washington: Government Printing
    Office, 1872.
U.S. Congress. House Committee on Military Affairs. *Muscle Shoals Propositions.*
    67th Cong., 2d sess., 1922. Washington: Government Printing Office, 1922.
U.S. Congress. House Committee on the District of Columbia. *Hearing on . . . H.R.
    7569, to Transfer the Authorities, Duties, Discretion, and Powers of the Board of Educa-
    tion of the District of Columbia to the Commissioners of the District of Columbia.* 64th
    Cong., 1st sess., 1916. Washington: Government Printing Office, 1916.
U.S. Congress. House Ways and Means Committee. *Hearings on . . . H.R. 5664, a
    Bill to Encourage National Industrial Recovery, to Foster Fair Competition, and to Provide
    for the Construction of Certain Useful Public Works, and for Other Purposes.* 73d Cong.,
    1st sess., 1933. Washington: Government Printing Office, 1933.
U.S. Congress. Select Committee of the House. *Hearings . . . for the Purpose of Investi-
    gating Indian Contracts with the Five Civilized Tribes and the Osage Indians in Okla-
    homa.* 61st Cong., 2d sess., 1910. Washington: Government Printing Office, 1911.
U.S. Congress. Senate Committee on Agriculture and Forestry. *Hearings . . . on
    S. 3420, to Provide for the Manufacture of Explosives for the Use of the Army and Navy,
    to Provide for the Manufacture of Fertilizer for Agricultural Purposes, to Incorporate the
    Federal Chemical Corporation, and for Other Purposes, and on the Henry Ford Muscle
    Shoals Offer.* 67th Cong., 2d sess., 1922. Washington: Government Printing
    Office, 1922.
U.S. Congress. Senate Committee on Indian Affairs. *Hearings on the Equalization of
    Creek Indian Allotments.* 62d Cong., 2d sess., 1912. Washington: Government
    Printing Office, 1913.
U.S. Congress. Senate Committee on Post Offices and Post Roads. *Report of Hear-
    ings regarding Postal Telegraphy by the Machine System, Issued as Senate Doc. 54-291.*
    54th Cong., 1st sess., 1896. Washington: Government Printing Office, 1896.
U.S. Congress. Senate Committee on Post Offices and Post Roads. *Senate Minority
    Rep. 1517, pt. 2.* 54th Cong., 2d sess., 1897. Washington: Government Printing
    Office, 1897.
U.S. Congress. Senate Finance Committee. *Hearings . . . on S. 1712 and H.R. 5755,
    Bills to Encourage National Industrial Recovery, to Foster Fair Competition, and to Pro-
    vide for the Construction of Certain Useful Public Works, and for Other Purposes.* 73d
    Cong., 1st sess., 1933. Washington: Government Printing Office, 1933.

INTERVIEWS AND CORRESPONDENCE WITH AUTHOR

Butler, Lester C., Jr. Interview with author. Durham, N.C., 20 July 1987.
Moore, Claude. Interview with author. Turkey, N.C., 16 July 1985.
Woodson, Pocahontas Butler. Telephone interview with author. 20, 27 September
    1986.

Woodson, Thomas D., Jr. Telephone interview with author. 20, 27 September 1986.
Woodward, C. Vann. Letter to the author. 30 March 1991.

Secondary Sources

BOOKS

Alumni History of the University of North Carolina, 1795–1924. Durham: Christian
 and King, 1924.
Anderson, Eric. *Race and Politics in North Carolina, 1872–1901: The Black Second.*
 Baton Rouge: Louisiana State University Press, 1981.
Argersinger, Peter H. *The Limits of Agrarian Radicalism: Western Populism and Ameri-
can Politics.* Lawrence: University Press of Kansas, 1995.
———. *Populism and Politics: William A. Peffer and the People's Party.* Lexington: Uni-
versity Press of Kentucky, 1974.
Ashe, Samuel A., et al., eds. *Biographical History of North Carolina: From Colonial
Times to the Present.* 8 vols. Greensboro: C. L. Van Noppen, 1905–17.
Battle, Kemp P. *History of the University of North Carolina.* 2 vols. Raleigh: Edwards
 and Broughton, 1907, 1912.
Billings, Dwight B., Jr. *Planters and the Making of a "New South": Class, Politics, and De-
velopment in North Carolina, 1865–1900.* Chapel Hill: University of North Car-
olina Press, 1979.
Biographical Directory of the American Congress. Washington, D.C.: Government Print-
ing Office, 1961.
Bizzell, Oscar M., ed. *The Heritage of Sampson County, North Carolina.* Winston-Salem:
 Hunter Publishing, 1983.
Bode, Frederick A. *Protestantism and the New South: North Carolina Baptists and
Methodists in Political Crisis, 1894–1903.* Charlottesville: University Press of Vir-
ginia, 1975.
Brodhead, Michael. *Persevering Populist: The Life of Frank Doster.* Reno: University of
 Nevada Press, 1969.
Burris, William C. *Judge John J. Parker and the Constitution.* Bessemer, Ala.: Colonial
 Press, 1987.
Cantrell, Gregg. *Kenneth and John B. Rayner and the Limits of Southern Dissent.* Ur-
bana: University of Illinois Press, 1993.
Cheney, John L., Jr., ed. *North Carolina Government, 1585–1979: A Narrative and Sta-
tistical History.* Raleigh: North Carolina Department of the Secretary of State, 1981.
Clanton, Gene. *Congressional Populism and the Crisis of the 1890s.* Lawrence: Univer-
sity Press of Kansas, 1998.
Clay, James W., Douglas M. Orr Jr., and Alfred W. Stuart. *North Carolina Atlas.*
 Chapel Hill: University of North Carolina Press, 1975.
Coates, Albert. *A Century of Legal Education.* Chapel Hill: University of North Car-
olina Press, 1949.
Coletta, Paolo E. *The Presidency of William Howard Taft.* Lawrence: University Press
 of Kansas, 1973.

————. *William Jennings Bryan.* 3 vols. Lincoln: University of Nebraska Press, 1964–69.

Cooper, John M., Jr. *The Warrior and the Priest: Woodrow Wilson and Theodore Roosevelt.* Cambridge: Harvard University Press, 1983.

Crow, Jeffrey J., and Robert F. Durden. *Maverick Republican in the Old North State: A Political Biography of Daniel L. Russell.* Baton Rouge: Louisiana State University, 1977.

Crow, Jeffrey J., Paul D. Escott, and Charles L. Flynn Jr., eds. *Race, Class, and Politics in Southern History: Essays in Honor of Robert F. Durden.* Baton Rouge: Louisiana State University Press, 1989.

Degler, Carl. *The Other South: Southern Dissenters in the Nineteenth Century.* New York: Harper and Row, 1974.

Dowd, Clement. *Life of Vance.* Charlotte: Observer Printing, 1897.

Durden, Robert F. *The Climax of Populism: The Election of 1896.* Lexington: University of Kentucky Press, 1965.

————. *Reconstruction Bonds and Twentieth-Century Politics: South Dakota v. North Carolina (1904).* Durham: Duke University Press, 1962.

Edmonds, Helen G. *The Negro and Fusion Politics in North Carolina, 1894–1901.* Chapel Hill: University of North Carolina Press, 1951.

Edwards, Laura F. *Gendered Strife and Confusion: The Political Culture of Reconstruction.* Urbana: University of Illinois Press, 1997.

Escott, Paul D. *Many Excellent People: Power and Privilege in North Carolina, 1850–1900.* Chapel Hill: University of North Carolina Press, 1985.

Fuller, Wayne E. *The American Mail.* Chicago: University of Chicago Press, 1972.

————. *R.F.D.: The Changing Face of Rural America.* Bloomington: Indiana University Press, 1964.

Garraty, John A., and Mark C. Carnes, eds. *American National Biography.* 24 vols. New York: Oxford University Press, 1999.

Gilmore, Glenda Elizabeth. *Gender and Jim Crow: Women and the Politics of White Supremacy in North Carolina, 1896–1920.* Chapel Hill: University of North Carolina Press, 1996.

Ginger, Ray. *The Age of Excess: The United States from 1877 to 1914.* New York: Macmillan, 1965.

Glad, Paul W. *McKinley, Bryan, and the People.* Philadelphia: J. B. Lippincott, 1964.

————. *The Trumpet Soundeth: William Jennings Bryan and His Democracy, 1896–1912.* Lincoln: University of Nebraska Press, 1960.

Goings, Kenneth W. *The NAACP Comes of Age: The Defeat of Judge John J. Parker.* Bloomington: Indiana University Press, 1990.

Goodwyn, Lawrence. *Democratic Promise: The Populist Moment in America.* New York: Oxford University Press, 1976.

Graham, Otis. *An Encore for Reform: The Old Progressives and the New Deal.* New York: Oxford University Press, 1967.

Grantham, Dewey W. *Southern Progressivism: The Reconciliation of Progress and Tradition.* Knoxville: University of Tennessee Press, 1983.

Hahn, Steven. *The Roots of Southern Populism: Yeoman Farmers and the Transformation of the Georgia Upcountry, 1850–1890.* New York: Oxford University Press, 1983.

Haley, John H. *Charles N. Hunter and Race Relations in North Carolina.* Chapel Hill: University of North Carolina Press, 1987.

Hamilton, J. G. deRoulhac. *North Carolina since 1860.* Chicago: Lewis Publishing, 1919.

Hicks, John D. *The American Nation.* Boston: Houghton Mifflin, 1946.

———. *The Populist Revolt.* Minneapolis: University of Minnesota Press, 1931.

———. *Republican Ascendancy, 1921–1933.* New York: Harper and Brothers, 1960.

History of Salemburg Baptist Church, 1842–1952. Salemburg, N.C.: Salemburg Baptist Church, 1952.

Hollingsworth, J. Rogers. *The Whirligig of Politics.* Chicago: University of Chicago Press, 1963.

Hughes, Jonathan, and Louis P. Cain. *American Economic History.* Reading, Mass.: Addison-Wesley, 1998.

Johnson, Allen, et al., eds. *Dictionary of American Biography.* 32 vols. New York: Charles Scribner's Sons, 1928–96.

Jones, Stanley. *The Presidential Election of 1896.* Madison: University of Wisconsin Press, 1964.

Kantor, Shawn E. *Politics and Property Rights: The Closing of the Open Range in the Postbellum South.* Chicago: University of Chicago Press, 1998.

Kantrowitz, Stephen. *Ben Tillman and the Reconstruction of White Supremacy.* Chapel Hill: University of North Carolina Press, 2000.

Kousser, J. Morgan. *The Shaping of Southern Politics: Suffrage Restriction and the Establishment of the One-Party South, 1880–1910.* New Haven: Yale University Press, 1974.

Larson, Robert W. *Populism in the Mountain West.* Albuquerque: University of New Mexico Press, 1986.

Leech, Margaret. *In the Days of McKinley.* New York: Harper and Brothers, 1959.

Lefler, Hugh T., ed. *North Carolina History Told by Contemporaries.* 4th ed. Chapel Hill: University of North Carolina Press, 1965.

Lefler, Hugh T., and Albert R. Newsome. *North Carolina: The History of a Southern State.* Chapel Hill: University of North Carolina Press, 1973.

Leloudis, James L. *Schooling the New South: Pedagogy, Self, and Society in North Carolina, 1880–1920.* Chapel Hill: University of North Carolina Press, 1996.

Link, Arthur S., and William B. Catton. *American Epoch: A History of the United States since 1900.* Vol. 1, *1900–1945.* 5th ed. New York: Alfred A. Knopf, 1980.

Logan, Frenise. *The Negro in North Carolina, 1876–1894.* Chapel Hill: University of North Carolina Press, 1964.

Mabry, William. *The Negro in North Carolina Politics since Reconstruction.* Durham: Duke University Press, 1940.

McMath, Robert C., Jr. *American Populism: A Social History, 1877–1898.* New York: Hill and Wang, 1993.

———. *Populist Vanguard: A History of the Southern Farmers' Alliance.* New York: W. W. Norton, 1975.

Millis, Walter. *Arms and Men: A Study of American Military History.* New Brunswick, N.J.: Rutgers University Press, 1981.

Mitchell, Theodore R. *Political Education in the Southern Farmers' Alliance, 1887–1900*. Madison: University of Wisconsin Press, 1987.

Morrison, Joseph L. *Josephus Daniels Says . . . : An Editor's Odyssey from Bryan to FDR*. Chapel Hill: University of North Carolina Press, 1962.

Mowry, George E. *The Era of Theodore Roosevelt*. New York: Harper and Row, 1958.

———. *Theodore Roosevelt and the Progressive Movement*. Madison: University of Wisconsin Press, 1946.

National Cyclopedia of American Biography. 63 vols. New York: J. T. White, 1898–1984.

Noblin, Stuart. *Leonidas La Fayette Polk: Agrarian Crusader*. Chapel Hill: University of North Carolina Press, 1949.

North Carolina Votes. Chapel Hill: University of North Carolina Press, 1962.

Orr, Oliver H. *Charles Brantley Aycock*. Chapel Hill: University of North Carolina Press, 1965.

Orth, John V. *The Judicial Power of the United States: The Eleventh Amendment and American Constitutional Law*. New York: Oxford University Press, 1986.

Ostler, Jeffrey. *Prairie Populism: The Fate of Agrarian Radicalism in Kansas, Nebraska, and Iowa, 1880–1892*. Lawrence: University Press of Kansas, 1993.

Palmer, Bruce. *"Man Over Money": The Southern Populist Critique of American Capitalism*. Chapel Hill: University of North Carolina Press, 1980.

Pollack, Norman. *The Humane Economy: Populism, Capitalism, and Democracy*. New Brunswick, N.J.: Rutgers University Press, 1990.

———. *The Just Polity: Populism, Law, and Human Welfare*. Urbana: University of Illinois Press, 1987.

Powell, William S. *The North Carolina Gazetteer*. Chapel Hill: University of North Carolina Press, 1968.

———. *North Carolina through Four Centuries*. Chapel Hill: University of North Carolina Press, 1989.

———, ed. *Dictionary of North Carolina Biography*. 6 vols. Chapel Hill: University of North Carolina Press, 1979–96.

Prather, H. Leon. *We Have Taken a City: Wilmington Racial Massacre and Coup of 1898*. Rutherford, N.J.: Fairleigh Dickinson University Press, 1984.

Pringle, Henry F. *Theodore Roosevelt: A Biography*. New York: Harcourt, Brace, 1931.

Ridge, Martin. *Ignatius Donnelly: Portrait of a Politician*. Chicago: University of Chicago Press, 1962.

Rippy, J. Fred, ed. *Furnifold Simmons, Statesman of the New South: Memoirs and Addresses*. Durham: Duke University Press, 1936.

Ritter, Gretchen. *Goldbugs and Greenbacks: The Antimonopoly Tradition and the Politics of Finance in America, 1865–1896*. Cambridge: Cambridge University Press, 1997.

Rogers, William Warren. *The One-Gallused Rebellion: Agrarianism in Alabama, 1865–1896*. Baton Rouge: Louisiana State University Press, 1970.

Roseboom, Eugene H. *A History of Presidential Elections*. New York: Macmillan, 1957.

Roster of the Soldiers from North Carolina in the American Revolution. Durham: Seeman Press, 1931.

Rothman, David J. *Politics and Power: The United States Senate, 1869–1901*. Cambridge: Harvard University Press, 1966.

Sanders, Elizabeth. *Roots of Reform: Farmers, Workers, and the American State, 1877–1917.* Chicago: University of Chicago Press, 1999.

The Sash and the Sabre. Salemburg, N.C.: Pineland College-Edwards Military Institute, 1952–53.

Shaw, Barton C. *The Wool-Hat Boys: Georgia's Populist Party.* Baton Rouge: Louisiana State University Press, 1984.

Shirley, Franklin R. *Zebulon Vance: Tar Heel Spokesman.* Charlotte: McNally and Loftin, 1962.

Steelman, Lala Carr. *The North Carolina Farmers' Alliance: A Political History, 1887–1893.* Greenville, N.C.: East Carolina University Publications, 1985.

Tindall, George B. *The Emergence of the New South, 1913–1945.* Baton Rouge: Louisiana State University Press, 1965.

Tyler, Ron, ed. *The New Handbook of Texas.* 6 vols. Austin: Texas State Historical Association, 1996.

Welch, Richard E. *George Frisbie Hoar and the Half-Breed Republicans.* Cambridge: Harvard University Press, 1971.

Who Was Who in America. Chicago: A. N. Marquis, 1943.

Woodward, C. Vann. *Origins of the New South, 1877–1913.* Baton Rouge: Louisiana State University Press, 1954.

———. *Tom Watson: Agrarian Rebel.* New York: Oxford University Press, 1975.

Wright, James E. *The Politics of Populism: Dissent in Colorado.* New Haven: Yale University Press, 1974.

ARTICLES

Argersinger, Peter H. "'No Rights on This Floor': Third Parties of the Institutionalization of Congress." *Journal of Interdisciplinary History* 22 (Spring 1992): 655–90.

———. "'A Place on the Ballot': Fusion Politics and Antifusion Laws." *American Historical Review* 85 (April 1980): 287–306.

Beeby, James M. "'Equal Rights to All and Special Privileges to None': Grass-Roots Populism in North Carolina." *North Carolina Historical Review* 77 (April 2001): 156–86.

Brabham, Robin. "Defining the American University: The University of North Carolina, 1865–1875." *North Carolina Historical Review* 57 (October 1980): 427–55.

Bromberg, Alan Bruce. "'The Worst Muddle Ever Seen in N.C. Politics': The Farmers' Alliance, the Subtreasury, and Zeb Vance." *North Carolina Historical Review* 56 (January 1979): 19–40.

Clanton, Gene. "'Hayseed Socialism' on the Hill: Congressional Populism, 1891–1895." *Western Historical Quarterly* 15 (April 1984): 139–62.

Coates, Albert. "The Story of the Law School at the University of North Carolina." *North Carolina Law Review* 47 (October 1968): 1–109.

Coletta, Paolo. "Bryan, McKinley, and the Treaty of Paris." *Pacific Historical Review* 26 (May 1957): 131–47.

Crow, Jeffrey J. "Thomas Settle Jr., Reconstruction, and the Memory of the Civil War." *Journal of Southern History* 42 (November 1996): 689–726.

DeLap[p], Simeon A. "The Populist Party in North Carolina." *Trinity College Histori-cal Society Papers* 14 (1922): 40–74.

Faulkner, Ronnie W. "North Carolina Democrats and Silver Fusion Politics, 1892–1896." *North Carolina Historical Review* 59 (July 1982): 234–41.

Fuller, Wayne E. "The Populists and the Post Office." *Agricultural History* 65 (Winter 1991): 1–16.

Gilbert, Edith F., and Jule B. Warren. "The North Carolina Teachers' Assembly." *North Carolina Teacher* 5 (September–November 1928): 7, 34–35, 49, 80, 95, 122.

Hamby, Alonzo L. "Progressivism: A Century of Change and Rebirth." In *Progres-sivism and the New Democracy*, edited by Sidney M. Milkis and Jerome M. Mileur, 40–80. Amherst: University of Massachusetts Press, 1999.

Hicks, John D. "The Farmers' Alliance in North Carolina." *North Carolina Historical Review* 2 (April 1925): 162–87.

Hunt, James L. "Populism, Law, and the Corporation: The 1897 Kansas Supreme Court." *Agricultural History* 66 (Fall 1992): 28–54.

Ingle, H. Larry. "A Southern Democrat at Large: W. H. Kitchin and the Populist Party." *North Carolina Historical Review* 45 (April 1968): 178–94.

Kantrowitz, Stephen. "Ben Tillman and Hendrix McLane, Agrarian Rebels: White Manhood, 'the Farmers,' and the Limits of Southern Populism." *Journal of South-ern History* 66 (August 2000): 497–524.

Miller, Worth Robert. "Building a Progressive Coalition in Texas: The Populist-Reform Democrat Rapprochement, 1900–1907." *Journal of Southern History* 52 (May 1986): 163–82.

Redding, Kent Thomas. "Failed Populism—Movement-Party Disjuncture in North Carolina, 1880–1900." *American Sociological Review* 57 (June 1992): 340–52.

Schlup, Leonard. "Adlai Stevenson and the 1892 Campaign in North Carolina: A Bourbon Response to Southern Populism." *Southern Studies*, n.s. 2 (1991): 131–49.

———. "Charles A. Towne and the Vice-Presidential Question of 1900." *North Dakota History* 44 (Winter 1977): 14–20.

Steelman, Joseph F. "Jonathan Elwood Cox and North Carolina's Gubernatorial Campaign of 1908." *North Carolina Historical Review* 41 (October 1964): 436–47.

———. "Republicanism in North Carolina: John Motley Morehead's Campaign to Revive a Moribund Party, 1908–1910." *North Carolina Historical Review* 42 (April 1965): 153–68.

———. "Republican Party Politics in North Carolina, 1902: Factions, Leaders, and Issues." In *Studies in the History of the South, 1875–1922*. Greenville, N.C.: East Carolina College Department of History, 1966.

———. "Republican Party Strategists and the Issue of Fusion with Populists in North Carolina, 1893–1894." *North Carolina Historical Review* 47 (July 1970): 244–69.

———. "Richmond Pearson, Roosevelt Republicans, and the Campaign of 1912 in North Carolina." *North Carolina Historical Review* 43 (April 1966): 122–39.

———. "The Trials of a Republican State Chairman: John Motley Morehead and

North Carolina Politics, 1910–1912." *North Carolina Historical Review* 43 (Winter 1966): 31–46.

———. "Vicissitudes of Republican Party Politics: The Campaign of 1892 in North Carolina." *North Carolina Historical Review* 43 (Autumn 1966): 430–42.

Sumner, Jim. "William G. Bramham." *Carolina Comments* 37 (July 1989): 116–22.

Tipton, Thomas W. "William V. Allen." In *Proceedings and Collections of the Nebraska State Historical Society*, 2d ser., 4. Lincoln: State Journal, 1902.

Trelease, Allen W. "The Fusion Legislatures of 1895 and 1897: A Roll-Call Analysis of the North Carolina House of Representatives." *North Carolina Historical Review* 57 (July 1980): 280–309.

Turner, James. "Understanding the Populists." *Journal of American History* 67 (September 1980): 354–73.

Voss-Hubbard, Mark. "The 'Third Party Tradition' Reconsidered: Third Parties and American Public Life, 1830–1900." *Journal of American History* 86 (June 1999): 121–50.

Watson, Richard L., Jr. "The Defeat of Judge Parker: A Study in Pressure Groups and Politics." *Mississippi Valley Historical Review* 50 (September 1963): 213–34.

Winston, Robert W. "Chief Justice Shepherd." *North Carolina Law Review* 3 (February 1925): 1–13.

York, Maurice. "The Dialectic and Philanthropic Societies' Contributions to the University of North Carolina, 1886–1906." *North Carolina Historical Review* 49 (October 1982): 327–53.

UNPUBLISHED THESES AND DISSERTATIONS

Beeby, James M. "Revolt of the Tar Heelers: A Socio-Political History of the North Carolina Populist Party, 1892–1901." Ph.D. diss., Bowling Green State University, 1999.

Bromberg, Alan Bruce. "'Pure Democracy and White Supremacy': The Redeemer Period in North Carolina, 1876–1894." Ph.D. diss., University of Virginia, 1977.

Cotten, Jerry W. "Negro Disfranchisement in North Carolina: The Politics of Race in a Southern State." Master's thesis, University of North Carolina at Greensboro, 1973.

Cowden, Frances Kay. "H. S. P. Ashby: A Voice for Reform, 1886–1914." Ph.D. diss., University of Oklahoma, 1996.

Creech, Joseph W., Jr. "Righteous Indignation: Religion and Populism in North Carolina, 1886–1906." Ph.D. diss., University of Notre Dame, 2000.

Faulkner, Ronnie W. "Samuel A'Court Ashe: North Carolina Redeemer and Historian, 1840–1938." Ph.D. diss., University of South Carolina, 1983.

Houghton, Jonathan T. Y. "The North Carolina Republican Party: From Reconstruction to the Radical Right." Ph.D. diss., University of North Carolina, 1993.

Hunt, James L. "Marion Butler and the Populist Ideal, 1863–1938." Ph.D. diss., University of Wisconsin, 1990.

Magruder, Nathaniel F. "The Administration of Governor Cameron Morrison of North Carolina, 1921–1925." Ph.D. diss., University of North Carolina, 1968.

Muller, Philip R. "New South Populism: North Carolina, 1884–1900." Ph.D. diss., University of North Carolina, 1971.

Roller, David C. "The Republican Party of North Carolina, 1900–1916." Ph.D. diss., Duke University, 1965.

Silverman, Max. "A Political and Intellectual History of the Silver Movement in the United States, 1888–1896." Ph.D. diss., New York University, 1986.

Simpson, Evander S. "History of Education in Sampson County, North Carolina." Master's thesis, University of North Carolina, 1943.

Smith, Florence E. "The Populist Movement in North Carolina." Ph.D. diss., University of Chicago, 1929.

Smith, Robert W. "A Rhetorical Analysis of the Populist Movement in North Carolina." Ph.D. diss., University of Wisconsin, 1957.

Steelman, Joseph F. "The Progressive Era in North Carolina, 1884–1917." Ph.D. diss., University of North Carolina, 1955.

Thurtell, Craig M. "The Fusion Insurgency in North Carolina: Origins to Ascendancy, 1876–1896." Ph.D. diss., Columbia University, 1998.

Wooley, Robert W. "Race and Politics: The Evolution of the White Supremacy Campaign of 1898 in North Carolina." Ph.D. diss., University of North Carolina, 1977.

WEBSITES

Miller, Worth Robert. "Worth Robert Miller, Department of History, Southwest Missouri State University." ‹http://history.smsu.edu/wrmiller›. 22 July 2002.

Palmer, Bruce. "Harry Tracy." *The Handbook of Texas Online*, ‹http://www.tsha.utexas.edu/handbook/online›. 22 July 2002.

INDEX